Ruby on Rails® Bible

Ruby on Rails® Bible

Timothy Fisher

WILEY

Wiley Publishing, Inc.

Ruby on Rails® Bible

Published by
Wiley Publishing, Inc.
10475 Crosspoint Boulevard
Indianapolis, IN 46256
www.wiley.com

Copyright © 2008 by Wiley Publishing, Inc., Indianapolis, Indiana

Published simultaneously in Canada

ISBN: 978-0-470-25822-4

Manufactured in the United States of America

10 9 8 7 6 5 4 3 2 1

For general information on our other products and services or to obtain technical support, please contact our Customer Care Department within the U.S. at (800) 762-2974, outside the U.S. at (317) 572-3993 or fax (317) 572-4002.

Library of Congress Control Number: 2008927915

About the Author

Timothy Fisher has over 17 years of experience in the software development industry. He has served in a variety of roles including chief architect, technical team lead, and senior architect and developer. Tim is currently an architect with the Compuware Corporation Professional Services Group in Detroit, Michigan.

Ruby and the Ruby on Rails framework have consumed Tim's interest and have led him to find the Southeastern Michigan Ruby Users Group, as well as owning and maintaining the Michigan Ruby Users Group Web site, `www.rubymi.org`. Tim is currently working on a large Ruby/Rails collaborative project management and planning application to be released as an open source project in 2008.

Tim is an experienced technical writer and author who has contributed to *Java developer's Journal* and *XML Journal* and written the *Java Phrasebook* published by Pearson Ed. in 2006. In addition to his technical skills Tim holds a degree in electrical engineering and a masters degree in education with a specialty in instructional design for online learning. He lives in Flat Rock, Mich., with his wife, Kerry, and two sons, Timmy and Camden.

Credits

Acquisitions Editor
Stephanie McComb

Project Editor
Chris Wolfgang

Technical Editor
Scott Deming

Copy Editor
Marylouise Wiack

Editorial Manager
Robyn Siesky

Business Manager
Amy Knies

Sr. Marketing Manager
Sandy Smith

Vice President and Executive Group Publisher
Richard Swadley

Vice President and Executive Publisher
Bob Ipsen

Vice President and Publisher
Barry Pruett

Project Coordinator
Erin Smith

Graphics and Production Specialists
Melanee Habig
Laura Pence

Quality Control Technician
Caitie Kelly

Proofreading and Indexing
Christine Sabooni
Infodex Indexing Services, Inc.

This book is dedicated to my parents, Thomas and Betty Fisher. Throughout my life, my mom and dad made it possible for me to achieve anything that I set my heart and mind to. Without their love and guidance, an accomplishment such as this book would not be possible. I am thankful to be able to show this accomplishment to my dad, and I know that my mom has been with me as I wrote this book. I am sure she would be proud.

Acknowledgments

It is impossible to write a book of this size without a great deal of help from those around me and some that I've never even met face-to-face. First I'd like to thank Wiley for giving me the opportunity to write this book. Writing a Rails book was something that I had wanted to do as Rails has become a passion of mine the past few years. Specifically, I'd like to thank the people at Wiley whom identified me as a candidate to write this book, and those that made the process smooth and successful. Stephanie McComb is the acquisitions editor that gave me the opportunity to be the author of this book. For that I am thankful. Chris Wolfgang served as my editor for this book. Without her, I am quite certain the content you are about to read would not have been nearly as clear and as readable as I hope it has become.

Ruby on Rails is a large framework that has been the subject of many books, many web sites, and hundreds if not thousands of articles. There has been a great deal of knowledge and expertise baked into the Rails framework. It would be impossible for a single person to write a comprehensive Rails book without assistance others who review and provide feedback of the content. I'd like to acknowledge the contributions of Scott Deming for his work as the Technical Editor of this book. The job of a Technical Editor is at times more difficult than that of the author. It is the technical editor's job to review everything I have written and correct the mistakes and faulty knowledge that may have passed through into the book. Scott's advice and feedback have been invaluable in creating this book.

The next person I'd like to thank also played a very large role in getting this book completed. That person is Noel Rappin. Noel stepped in late in the writing phase and assisted with completing some of the content. Noel contributed significant content to the following chapters: 5, 9, 10, 11, and 12. Noel also wrote both of the appendixes for the book. Noel has his own book published by Wrox, *Professional Ruby on Rails*.

Finally, I must acknowledge those who are closest to me, my family. Any author with a young family appreciates the challenge of maintaining quality family life while writing a book. I have two boys, Timmy and Camden, who like to keep their dad busy whenever they can. The time I put into writing a book is time that has to come away from other tasks that I'd normally have more time for. I thank my wife, Kerry, for her understanding of what it means to me to write this book and her unwavering support and ability to help me find the time and effort to write. You can read more about what interests me and perhaps learn a bit from my blog at `http://blog.timothy fisher.com`. Now that this book is completed, I hope to become a much more active blogger!

Contents at a Glance

Contents

Contents

Part II: Rails In Depth   105

Chapter 3: Using Active Record 107

Contents

Contents

Contents

Contents

Contents

Introduction

In 2006, I wrote a book called the *Java Phrasebook,* something like a cookbook for Java. While I was writing that, my interest and love of Ruby and the Rails framework grew tremendously. Often during my writing, I would think how much nicer it would be to be writing a Ruby- or Rails-related book. Early in 2007, I had to pass up my first opportunity to step into the world of Ruby and Rails writing. The book that I was asked to write at the time, *Professional Ruby on Rails,* has since been written by a very capable writer, Noel Rappin, who also contributed content to this book.

Jump ahead a few months, and the opportunity to write this book, *Ruby on Rails Bible,* came along. I knew it would be a tight fit working on this book along with a full-time job and the holidays coming up, especially having two young children, but I took it! That is how you ended up holding this book now.

Like many who consider themselves users and, more importantly, fans of the Ruby language, I was pulled into the world of Ruby by the Rails framework. Prior to Rails, I had heard of Ruby but had not used it. I first became aware of it through the writing and speaking of Dave Thomas, a tireless advocate of Ruby well before Rails made it a marketable skill. Ruby had been around for quite awhile before Rails but had not been able to grab the attention of the masses here in the United States. Rails has not only brought Ruby to the masses, but it has had a tremendous influence on the entire Web development industry. Rails clones have sprung up in many languages, including Java, Perl, Python, and PHP. Many of the patterns and methods of Rails have influenced other frameworks in other languages as well.

By the time you read this book, you'll have a choice of many books on the subject of Ruby on Rails. I hope that you find this book was worth your energy!

Who the book is for

This book is for any Web developers who are interested in learning how to create Web applications using the Ruby on Rails framework. You do not have to know Ruby to use this book. In part I of the book, you can get an introduction to Ruby and learn enough about it to effectively create basic Rails applications. You should have some experience with common Web development technologies such as HTML, JavaScript, and preferably some server-side language such as Java, .net, Perl, PHP, Ruby, or any other language that you might use to write the server-side of a Web application. Although not required, basic knowledge of DOM and CSS would also prove helpful as you write Rails applications shown in this book.

How the book is organized

This book is organized into five main parts:

- Part I: First Steps with Rails
- Part II: Rails In Depth
- Part III: Developing a Complete Rails Application
- Part IV: Advanced Rails
- Part V: Appendixes

Each of these parts is broken down into several chapters.

Part I

This part of the book will teach you the underpinnings that you need to effectively develop a Ruby on Rails application. You can learn the basics of Ruby and get your first introduction to the Rails framework.

Part II

After you've been exposed to the basics of Ruby and Rails, you can immerse yourself in the details of each of the main components that make up the Rails framework, the Model, Controller, and View layers.

Part III

I hope you'll enjoy reading and following along with this part of the book as much as I enjoyed writing it! In this part, you can follow along with the development of a complete Rails application. You'll go from nothing up to a usable application that you can use within any group or organization to share information about a collection of books.

Part IV

This part of the book covers more advanced Rails topics, such as extending Rails through plugins, generators, and engines. You'll also get an introduction to the Prototype and Scriptaculous JavaScript libraries in this part.

Part V

If you need extra resources on the Ruby language or references for Rails, these appendixes can offer you a quick place to look up facts in a hurry.

How to use this book

This book is organized such that it can be read from cover to cover. If you're a new Rails developer reading it from cover to cover is the best way to learn about Rails. If you are new to Rails but know

Ruby already, you can skip the Ruby introduction and just read the chapters that discuss Rails. As you read through the book, your knowledge of Rails will build with each chapter.

If you know Rails already, you may want to skip ahead to Chapter 6 and read about the development of the Book Shelf Web application. I think you'll find the development of that application will interest even a seasoned Rails developer.

After you've read the book, it is also suitable as a Rails reference that you'll want to keep within reach on your bookshelf. The two appendixes at the end of the book provide a thorough reference to both the Ruby language and the Rails API.

Quick Start

Ruby on Rails
Quick Start

Before you can get started doing Ruby on Rails development, you have to set up the software that you will need to develop, run, and test your applications. There are at least three pieces of software that you will need. They are:

- The Ruby language runtime
- The Rails framework
- A database (such as MySQL, PostgreSQL, SQLite, Oracle, and DB2)

If you install those three components, you will have all that you need on your computer to write, run, and test Ruby on Rails Web applications. If you have past experience writing Web applications, you might be thinking that something is missing from that list, some type of HTTP and/or application server. You would be correct in that every Web application needs a server to run; however, the Rails framework includes a server that works very well for developing your applications. The server bundled with Rails is called WEBrick, and it serves as both an HTTP and an application server. This makes it very easy to set up a local development environment without having to install and configure a potentially large and complex server environment.

Sometimes, it's easier to see how the technologies fit together from a visual perspective. Figure QS.1 shows the technology stack that makes up a Web application built with the Rails framework. Each item in the stack has a dependency on what lies beneath it. The middle three layers of the diagram are the three components that you will install software for Rails, Ruby, and the database.

Actually, to be completely accurate, a database is not required to write a Rails Web application. It is possible to write Web applications with the Rails framework that do not use a database. However, without a database to store data, you are very limited in the types of applications that you can create.

IN THIS CHAPTER

Installing Instant Rails on Windows

Installing Ruby and Rails on Mac OS X and Linux

Setting up a development environment

1

One of Rails' greatest strengths is its ability to make working with a database extremely simple, and so without a database, you are also not taking advantage of one of the best features of the Rails framework.

The Rails Application Stack

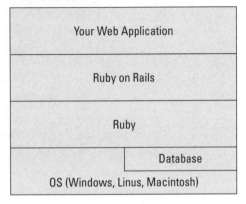

For this book, the database of choice will be MySQL. MySQL is a popular open source database that is available to everyone at no cost, and it is probably the database that most people are familiar with. MySQL is also a database that Rails supports out-of-the-box with no extra software or libraries required. It is probably the most widely used database on the Internet today. It provides a full-featured and robust database for your applications that is easy to set up and use. Commercial support and commercial versions of MySQL are also available through the company MySQL AB, which was recently acquired by Sun Microsystems.

The next three major sections provide instructions for installing the required components on the three most popular operating systems for Rails development, Windows, Linux, and Macintosh. If you already have these components installed, you are welcome to skip these sections.

Installing Instant Rails on Windows

If you are developing on the Windows platform, there is an installer available that installs all three of the components that you need to begin Rails development. Instant Rails provides you with installs of:

- Ruby
- Ruby on Rails
- MySQL database
- Apache Web server

If you are not developing with Windows, you can skip the remainder of this section. It is convenient to have a single installer for these components; however, a potential disadvantage is that these types of installers may not always be up to date with the most current releases of all of the individual components. They will likely install the most recent stable versions of the components, which is what you will want in most cases.

Below are the steps for installing and configuring Instant Rails.

1. **Download Instant Rails.** The first thing you should do is download the Instant Rails installer application, from `http://instantrails.rubyforge.org`. At the time of this writing,
the most recent version of Instant Rails is 2.0, and it is downloaded as InstantRails-2.0-win.zip.

2. **Install Instant Rails.** The file that you downloaded in step 1 is a compressed ZIP file that contains everything you need to run the Instant Rails environment. Installing Instant Rails after you have downloaded the ZIP file is as simple as extracting the contents of the ZIP file into the directory that you want to install into. Make sure that the directory you choose to unzip the file into does not contain any spaces. Spaces cause problems when you try to run the Instant Rails environment.

After you have completed the Instant Rails installation steps above, you should perform the following tasks to verify that you have everything set up correctly.

1. **Run Instant Rails.** After you have extracted Instant Rails into a directory, navigate into that directory and double-click the file InstantRails.exe. Make sure that you are logged onto the Windows computer as an Administrator before you do this.

   The first time you run InstantRails.exe, it detects that it is a fresh installation and prompts you to regenerate its configuration files. You see the dialog box similar to Figure QS.2. Go ahead and click OK.

FIGURE QS.2

The Instant Rails configuration prompt

After the configuration is regenerated for you, you see the Instant Rails Administration screen, shown in Figure QS.3. On that screen, confirm that it says that the Apache and MySQL servers are started, as shown in Figure QS.3.

FIGURE QS.3

The Instant Rails Administration screen

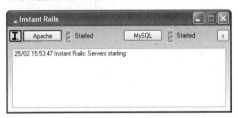

2. **Start a sample application.** Now that you have the Apache and MySQL servers running, the next verification step is to start a Rails application that is included with Instant Rails. Instant Rails includes two sample applications, a cookbook application, and an installation of the Typo blogging system.

    Rails includes an application server that can be used during development for running your Web applications, called WEBrick. This is the application server that I will refer to primarily throughout this book, because it is included with every installation of Rails. The Instant Rails package, however, includes another popular server for running Rails applications, the Mongrel server. Mongrel can be used in place of WEBrick. Mongrel is often preferred because it performs much better and can be easily used in conjunction with Apache as a Web server.

    Verify the installation by starting the cookbook application. Click the "I" that you see on the main Instant Rails Administration screen. This is the left-most icon on the top of the screen. Clicking the "I" gives you a drop-down menu like the one you see in Figure QS.4. From that menu, click the Rails Applications option. You get another submenu from which you should click Manage Rails Applications.

FIGURE QS.4

Selecting the Manage Rails Applications command

BitNami Ruby Stack

A rising contender to Instant Rails comes from a group called BitNami. They provide easy installations for many open source applications and frameworks. One of the pre-packaged stacks that they provide a simple installer for is the Ruby stack which includes everything you need to do Ruby on Rails development, including Ruby, Rails, and MySQL. Unlike Instant Rails which is only available for the Windows platform, the BitNami Ruby Stack is available for Windows, Linux, and Mac platforms. You can read more about the BitNami Ruby Stack and download it from `http://bitnami.org/stack/rubystack`.

This takes you to a screen similar to that shown in Figure QS.5. This is the screen that you use to start and stop your Rails applications. In the list of applications, you should see the two Rails applications that come with Instant Rails, cookbook, and typo-2.6.0. Click the check box next to the cookbook application so that it is selected. Then click the Start with Mongrel button. This starts up the Mongrel server to listen on port 3001.

FIGURE QS.5

The Rails Applications interface

3. **View the cookbook application.** After you have started the cookbook application through the Instant Rails Administration console, you can verify that it is running by navigating to it in your browser. Open up your browser of choice and navigate to `http://localhost:3001/`. You should see the cookbook application screen shown in Figure QS.6.

That completes the Instant Rails installation and verification.

FIGURE QS.6

The cookbook application home screen

Installing Ruby and Rails on Mac OS X and Linux

Both the Mac OS X and Linux systems are also popular choices for Ruby and Rails development. Years ago, very little software development was done on a Mac computer. Things have changed dramatically in the past few years, though. Today, the Mac is the platform of choice for many software developers, especially Ruby and Rails developers. If you go to a conference that features a lot of Ruby and Rails speakers, pay attention to what type of computer they are using. You will likely notice that the vast majority of them use a Mac. Fortunately, for most Mac and Linux users, there is very little work you need to do to begin Rails development.

Installing on Linux

Linux remains a popular operating system for software development. Linux is also fully compatible with Ruby and Rails development. In fact, many version of Linux will come with Ruby and Rails pre-installed. Before you attempt any installation, you'll want to first check to see if your computer already has Ruby and Rails.

You can find detailed information about installing Ruby and Rails on Linux here: `http://users.drew.edu/bburd/RubyOnRails/InstallingRoRinLinux.pdf`.

Installing on Mac OS X

If you have a Mac and are running OS X 10.5 (Leopard) or later, you are in very good shape, because your computer already has both Ruby and Rails installed on it. There is no work for you to install Ruby and Rails on OS X 10.5 or later.

If you have OS X version 10.4 or earlier, you may have Ruby pre-installed, however it is likely a version of Ruby that is not compatible with Rails. In that case you will want to update the Ruby on it to be the latest stable release.

You can find detailed information about setting up Ruby and Rails on a Mac at this Apple site: http://developer.apple.com/tools/rubyonrails.html.

Setting up a Development Environment

Now that you have the essential components installed for developing and running a Rails application, let's look at some other components that, while not strictly required, make for a much better development environment.

- Source code version control
- IDE or Editor

Source code version control

After you have the components installed that you need to run a Rails application, before you write a single line of code, the very next thing you should do is decide upon a source code version-control application and install it.

The two most popular version-control applications are CVS and SVN. CVS stands for Concurrent Versioning System, and SVN stands for Subversion. Most Web hosting accounts offer you the ability to set up either CVS or SVN projects within your hosting account. There are also a few companies that provide you with a free SVN project space. If you are interested in using a free SVN account, check out these providers:

- `http://beanstalkapp.com/`
- `https://opensvn.csie.org/`

While CVS and SVN probably still remain the most used version-control systems, a new kind of version-control system — distributed version control — is rapidly gaining popularity. A distributed version-control system uses a distributed model, whereas version control systems such as SVN and CVS use a centralized version-control system. In a centralized version-control system changes are always pushed only to the central repository (in fact there is only one repository in this type of system). In a distributed version-control system, each developer maintains a complete copy of the code repository on their computer.

Developers update their code with other's changes by getting updates from the central repository. By contrast, in a distributed version-control system, developers are allowed to push their changes to individual developers without pushing to a central repository, since each developer maintains a complete repository on their own computer. The distributed version-control model fits the open source development model particularly well. How well it can work inside of an enterprise remains to be seen.

The most popular distributed version-control system today is GIT. The GIT version-control system is especially popular in the Ruby on Rails community; it is the official repository for the Rails source code as well as many of the Rails plug-ins. More open-source applications are moving to GIT every day. Git Hub is a popular hosted version of GIT that includes social networking features. Git Hub offers both commercial plans and free plans for open source projects. Git Hub is the home for the Rails project.

IDE or Editor?

So now that you have most of the infrastructure in place that you will need to begin writing a Rails application, the next thing to consider is what tool you will use to actually write your code in. If you are coming from a Java or .Net background, you are probably used to using an integrated development environment, or IDE as they are commonly called. If you are coming from a background in Perl, PHP, or another scripting language, you probably did most of your development using a simpler tool, perhaps just a text editor. For Rails development, you have your choice of using either an IDE or a simple text editor.

- TextMate
- E
- Intellij IDEA
- NetBeans
- Eclipse
- Heroku
- Aptana Studio

TextMate

If you are using a Mac to do your development on, the editor of choice is TextMate. In fact, I would venture to guess that at least 90 percent of developers who use the Macintosh for Rails development are using TextMate (see Figure QS.7). TextMate is a powerful source code editor that allows you to write extensions to the base environment. The extensions plug into TextMate to add new features to the base editor. The extensions are called Bundles. You can find a great deal of Bundles online that will let you set up TextMate to suit your preferences.

FIGURE QS.7

The TextMate interface

E

The E text editor is an attempt to port the popular TextMate editor to the Windows platform. It duplicates many of the features of TextMate and even allows you to use your TextMate Bundles. Like TextMate, there is a small cost to purchase it.

IntelliJ IDEA

IntelliJ IDEA is a commercial IDE made by JetBrains (see Figure QS.8). Java developers rave over the features of this IDE. I have used it myself and have to say that it is my Java IDE of choice. Many of the other IDEs have implemented features that were first introduced by JetBrains. Version 7 of IntelliJ IDEA added support for developing Ruby and Rails applications.

NetBeans

NetBeans is an IDE from Sun. In the past, NetBeans has been an IDE for Java development. However with version 7.0, Sun has added Ruby and Rails support into NetBeans.

FIGURE QS.8

The IntelliJ IDEA 7.0 interface

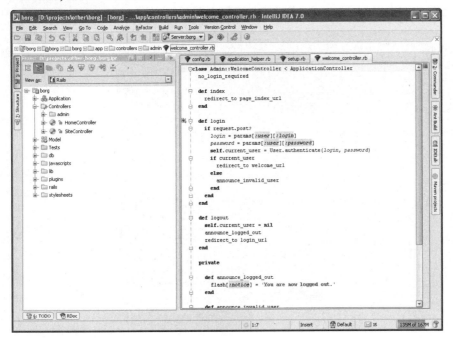

Eclipse

Eclipse is probably the most used IDE today. It is developed by the Eclipse Foundation, an open-source initiative spearheaded by IBM. Much of the Eclipse code base was donated by IBM and was a part of its commercial IDE product. With a plug-in, you can add full Ruby and Rails support to the Eclipse environment. RadRails is a popular Eclipse plug-in that gives you the Ruby and Rails support.

Heroku

Heroku provides a new and unique way of writing Rails applications. Heroku is a completely online solution for developing applications. You do not install any software on your computer to use Heroku, other than a Web browser. At the time of this writing, Heroku works only with the Firefox 2 Web browser. It does not work under Internet Explorer. You can see an example of what the Heroku interface looks like in Figure QS.9.

FIGURE QS.9

The Heroku interface

Aptana Studio

Aptana Studio, a product from the company Aptana, is a very attractive option for Ruby on Rails development. The Aptana Studio product is a stand-alone desktop IDE based on the Eclipse project. If you are familiar with Eclipse, you will have no problem getting used to working with Aptana Studio. It provides excellent support for front-end development, including JavaScript, CSS, and HTML editing. The Ruby and Rails features are packaged as a plug-in to the Aptana Studio environment. The features of Aptana Studio are also available as a plug-in for the generic Eclipse IDE.

Summary

This chapter introduced you to the environment that you will need to begin Ruby and Rails development. At this point, you should have installed the tools that you will need to write Ruby and Rails applications, as well as to write the code that is used in this book.

You also were given an overview of several version-control systems, as well as IDEs and editors that are available for Rails development. These are important tools for any developer, and you should choose the tools that will work best in your environment and with your team. Also, keep in mind that Ruby and Rails development is evolving rapidly and new tools are released frequently. It is likely that by the time you read this, there may very well be additional choices available for editing your Ruby and Rails applications. The Internet is your best source for current information about the latest preferred development tools.

Part I

First Steps with Rails

Chapter 1

Learning Ruby

R uby on Rails is a Web application development framework built using the Ruby programming language. Ruby is a dynamic language that was created in Japan by Yukihiro Matsumoto. You'll often see Matsumoto referred to simply as Matz. While Ruby had been growing and flourishing in Japan and Europe, it took the Rails framework to finally thrust Ruby into the limelight in the United States. Ruby is steadily growing in popularity worldwide as a programming language of choice.

It is often described as an elegant language that allows developers to create concise and very readable code.

If you already consider yourself a Ruby expert, you can probably skip this chapter; otherwise, I highly recommend reading this chapter before getting into the details of using Rails. A solid knowledge of the Ruby programming language makes an excellent foundation for learning and using the Ruby on Rails framework. A solid understanding of Ruby will also help you if you want to explore the internals of Rails. Remember that Rails is an open source project, meaning that all of its source code is available to anyone who wants to look at it. You can learn a great deal about advanced Ruby techniques from reading the Rails source code. The power of Ruby plays a large part in the success of the Rails framework.

The Nature of Ruby

Programming languages tend to have various elements of commonality. I'm not referring to the syntax of a language, but rather higher-level designs that apply to a programming language. These elements are what make up the nature of the language. Here you begin by learning about the nature of Ruby, or what kind of programming language Ruby is. Each of the characteristics you will read about in this section will help you better understand the type of programming language that Ruby is, and how it is different from or the same as other languages that you might have experience with. The elements of Ruby discussed here are dynamic or static typing systems, duck typing, and compiled or scripted language.

Dynamic or static typing

Programming languages can be classified by the type system they use. A *type system* defines how a programming language classifies its data and methods into types. Examples of types used in various languages include int, float, String, and Object. A *type* describes the kind of data used in a particular variable. There are two general classes of type systems that are used by programming languages: dynamic typing and static typing. In a *static typed* language, the compiler enforces type checking before run-time. In a *dynamic typed* language, type checking is deferred until run-time.

In a static typed system, the programmer uses variable declarations to provide type information. For example, in Java, which is a statically typed language, variables must be declared with their type prior to being used. Examples of statically typed languages include Java, C, C++, C#, and Pascal.

NOTE   Other languages, such as OCaml and Haskell, use *type inference*. This is a form of static typing where the type is determined at compile time but without the programmer having to declare it.

In a dynamically typed language, the programmer does not have to declare data types with variable declarations. Data types are not known until run-time, and type checking of variables does not occur until run-time. Examples of dynamically typed languages include Python, JavaScript, Perl, Lisp, and Ruby.

A closely related concept is that of how strictly a type system enforces type rules. A *strongly typed system* enforces type rules strongly, allowing for automatic conversions between types only when information is not lost due to the conversion. A *weakly typed system* does not enforce type rules and allows you to easily convert from one type to another without complaint. Ruby is a weakly typed, dynamic programming language.

Languages that are statically typed are usually recommended for new developers, as they provide more protection from run-time errors than a dynamically typed language provides. In a dynamically typed language, it's easy to make programming errors that are not detected until run-time. However, if you have solid unit-testing practices, this can alleviate that concern. Because of this, unit testing is even more important when you're programming in a dynamically typed language such as Ruby.

Duck typing

You will likely hear someone refer to Ruby as having duck typing. The term *duck typing* refers to the popular quote, "If it looks like a duck and quacks like a duck, it must be a duck." So how does that quote have anything to do with a programming language? Let's figure that out.

In Ruby, object instances are not forced to be of any certain type when they are used. As long as the object being used meets the requirements of the situation in which it is being used, Ruby will not complain. Another way of saying this is that in Ruby, an object's type is determined by what it can do, not by its class. Say you were calling a `calculate_average` method on an object. In Ruby, as long as the object you are calling that method on implements a `calculate_average` method, everything works fine.

Your code doesn't have to require the object you are calling the `calculate_average` method on to be of any certain class. You might have a method that is expecting an object of a certain class, but if you had some code that passed in a different class of object, but implemented all the methods used within that method, the code would execute perfectly fine. This is how programming in Ruby relates back to the quote, "If it looks like a duck and quacks like a duck, it must be a duck." If your objects behave like the type expected at any given place in your code, then as far as Ruby is concerned, they are of that type, regardless of their real class.

This is very different than the way that many other languages work, including Java. In Java, you must declare the class type of all of your method parameters. You cannot pass in an instance of a class that does not match the class type that the method is expecting, even if that instance implements the same methods as the expected class.

Compiled or scripting language

Another way you can classify languages is by whether they require a compile step or not. Depending on whether or not they require compilation, a language can be said to be a compiled language or a scripting language.

Compiled languages

A *compiled language* requires you to perform a compile step before running the application you are writing. The language's run-time executable that runs applications cannot directly understand the source code of a compiled language. The compiler converts your source code into a binary format that can be understood by the run-time executable. After you compile your source code, you end up with files in the compiled format, such as the .class files used by Java. Examples of compiled languages include C, C++, C#, and Java.

Scripted languages

A *scripted language* does not require you to compile your source code into another form. The source code that you write is also the code that the language's run-time executable uses to execute your application. The run-time executable of a scripting language is usually called an *interpreter*. The interpreter interprets the source code at run-time and converts it to a format that the computer can execute. The interpreter is specific to a particular language. Examples of scripted languages include Perl, Python, JavaScript, and Ruby.

Compiled languages are usually faster at run-time because the code is already closer to that of the computer, whereas code from a scripted language has to be interpreted at run-time. However, many people believe that scripted languages make up for the run-time performance deficit by being faster to develop an application in. With a compiled language, every time you make a change, you have to go through a compile phase and an application restart to see the results of that change. In a scripting language, your application can immediately see the results of a source code change, as it is running directly from your source code.

Object Oriented Programming

Object oriented programming (OOP) is a style of programming that uses objects to represent data, and actions that you can perform on that data. OOP allows you to more closely model the real world with your objects than was possible prior to the advent of OOP. Instead of dealing with functions and procedures when designing an application, OOP allows you to model the application in terms of objects that make up the application's domain. For example, if you were creating an application that catalogued books, in an OOP design you would model the application using objects extracted from the domain, such as Books, Titles, Inventory, and Publisher.

In OOP, you'll often hear the terminology of sending messages to objects. Sending a message to an object is the equivalent of asking that object to perform some action for you. The action usually manipulates or provides you with data that the object contains. These actions are called *methods*. For example, with a Book object, you might have a method called `get_page_count` that would return the book's page count.

An object can have both methods and data. An object stores data in fields called *attributes*. Considering the Book object example again, a Book object may have attributes of `title`, `publisher`, and `publication_date`. Methods and attributes are the two components that make up the definition of an object.

The objects in your application will relate to the domain your application serves. For example, if you are writing an accounting application, you might have objects called Account, User, and Bank. Your Account object might contain methods for depositing and withdrawing money from an account. The attributes of the Account object might include an account number, an account name, and an account balance. When you are writing an application using an object-oriented language, your work consists of defining objects and using those objects to perform the logic of your application.

Ruby is a pure object-oriented programming language. In Ruby, everything is an object, including literal strings and numeric types. Objects are at the center of all the code you will write in Ruby. Unlike most other languages, Ruby does not have any native types that are not objects. Even numeric types such as integers and floats are represented as objects in Ruby.

People new to Ruby often don't initially grasp the fact that in Ruby, everything is an object. As an example, look at the following line of code:

```
3.methods
```

This is a valid line of Ruby code that might look a bit strange to you if you're coming to Ruby from an object-oriented language that considers numeric values as native types instead of objects. This line asks for the methods that are available on the 3 object. If you wanted to find out what type of object the number 3 is, you could find that out using this line of code:

```
3.class
```

This will return the class `Fixnum`. In Ruby, integer numbers are instances of the `Fixnum` class. The methods `class` and `methods` are available on any object that you use in Ruby.

The Basics of Ruby

Before you get into the details of working with Ruby objects, this section provides you with some of the basics that you should be familiar with when writing and running Ruby programs. With the knowledge that this section provides you, you should have no problem walking through the examples that are used throughout the remainder of this chapter. You'll also know how to interactively follow along with the examples and run them on your own computer. If you are new to Ruby, an active learning style in which you try out the examples yourself will help you master the language more efficiently than if you choose to only read through all of the examples.

The basics of Ruby that will prepare you to successfully learn the remainder of the language are Ruby's interactive shell, Ruby syntax basics, and Running Ruby programs.

Ruby's interactive shell

Assuming that you already have Ruby installed on your computer, you have access to a powerful, interactive Ruby-programming environment called irb. The *irb* environment is a command-line Ruby interpreter that lets you enter any valid Ruby syntax and instantly see the results of your actions. This is being covered before you even learn Ruby because of its great use as a Ruby learning tool. Throughout this chapter, you will be able to try out the short snippets of Ruby code that are discussed so that you can interactively follow along as you read. That is a much better style of learning than just reading through the code samples.

Use the following steps to start irb:

1. **Start irb in any command-line environment simply by typing** irb. This assumes that the `bin` directory of the Ruby installation is in your executable path, which would be the case if you used an automatic installer like the one-click Ruby installer for Windows.
    ```
    C:\> irb
    ```

2. **After typing irb, you should see a command prompt that looks like this:**
    ```
    irb(main):001:0>
    ```

3. **At the command prompt, go ahead and type the following line of Ruby code:**
    ```
    irb(main):001:0> puts "Hello, World"
    ```
    The `puts` method writes the passed-in string to the console output.

4. **Press Enter.** You should see this:

```
Hello, World
=> nil
Irb(main):002:0>
```

You see the "Hello, World" string printed. You may not have expected the next line: `=> nil`. Anytime you execute a line of code in irb, the return value of the executed method is printed to the console after any values that the method itself may have printed. The `puts` method always returns a `nil` value. The value `nil` is Ruby's equivalent to a null or empty value.

You can even create methods and then execute them within irb. Try this within irb:

```
irb(main):001:0> def add_nums(a,b)
irb(main):001:0> return a+b
irb(main):001:0> end
=> nil
```

You have just created a method named `add_nums` that takes two parameters. The method returns the value of those two parameters added together. You can now try out your new method.

Make sure you are still in the same irb session and type this:

```
irb(main):001:0> add_nums(5,7)
=> 12
```

Here, you called the method that you created and passed the values 5 and 7. The method returned the sum of those two values, 12, and so that value is printed to the console.

The irb tool will become one of your best friends as a Ruby programmer.

> **TIP** As you work through the remainder of this chapter, I strongly suggest that you leave the irb console open and try out the small code snippets as you see them.

Ruby syntax basics

Ruby's syntax borrows some of the best features from languages such as Java and Perl. Before you begin to program in Ruby, there are a few basic syntax elements that you'll learn here. These include adding comments in Ruby, use of parentheses, use of white space, and use of semicolons.

Adding comments

A language's support for comments allows you to add lines to your source code that the interpreter or compiler ignores. Comments can be added to Ruby source code using the hash (or pound) symbol, #. All text that follows a # symbol is considered a comment and ignored by the Ruby interpreter.

```
# This is a comment in a Ruby source code file
puts 'Camden Fisher' # This line outputs a string to the console
```

As you see in the example above, a comment can be a complete line, or it can follow a line of Ruby code.

If you have a large block of text that you want to use as a comment, instead of beginning each line of the comment with a # symbol, you can use Ruby's multi-line comment syntax shown here:

```
=begin
This is a multi-line block of comments in a Ruby source file.
   Added: January 1, 2008
   By: Timothy Fisher
=end
Puts "This is Ruby code"
```

The =begin marks the beginning a multi-line comment, and the =end closes the multi-line comment.

It's a good idea to add comments explaining any code that is not understandable simply by looking at it. If you often find yourself writing complex code that requires comments to explain, you may consider refactoring that code to make it easier to understand and eliminate the need for the comments.

Using parentheses

The use of parentheses in Ruby is most often optional. For example, when you call a method that takes parameters, you could call it like this:

```
movie.set_title("Star Wars")
```

or you could call it like this without the parentheses:

```
movie.set_title "Star Wars"
```

If you are chaining methods together, you may get a warning (depending on the version of Ruby you are using) if you do not use parentheses around your parameters. For example, if you were writing this code:

```
puts movie.set_title "Star Wars"
```

You may see the a warning message similar to this:

```
warning: parenthesize argument(s) for future version
```

You can avoid the warning by using parentheses like this:

```
puts move.set_title("Star Wars")
```

It is a generally accepted convention amongst Ruby developers to use parentheses if they help a reader understand an expression. If the parentheses add no value to the readability of an expression, your code usually looks cleaner without them.

Using white space

White space is not relevant in Ruby source code. You can use indentation, blank lines, and other white space to make your code readable with no effect on its syntax. While white space has no effect on Ruby syntax, it does have a significant effect on the readability of Ruby code. You should therefore pick a consistent style that uses white space to enhance the readability of your code.

Common convention is to indent your class bodies, method bodies, and blocks. Here is an example showing recommended use of white space in a class:

```
class
    def a_method
        puts 'You called a method'
    end

    def b_method
        puts 'You called b method'
    end
end
```

Most text editors that understand Ruby syntax will help you apply appropriate indentation of your methods and code blocks. Many Ruby authors have adopted an informal standard in the Ruby community of indenting with two spaces and no tabs, so this may be the standard applied in much of the code that you find in the open source community. However, I believe that you should choose an indentation size that works best for you and your team.

Using semicolons

Semicolons are a common indicator of a line or statement ending. In Ruby, the use of semicolons to end your lines is not required. The only time using semicolons is required is if you want to use more than one statement on a single line.

Take a look at a method in Ruby:

```
def add_super_power(power)
    @powers.add(power)
end
```

Notice that there are no semicolons in any of this code, and yet this is perfectly valid Ruby code. Not requiring semicolons is part of what gives Ruby its reputation as allowing for very clean and readable code.

Here is an example of Ruby code that would require the use of a semicolon:

```
def add_super_power(power)
    @powers.add(power);puts "added new power"
end
```

In this method, two Ruby statements are being executed in one line of code. The semicolon separates the statements. In most cases, though, this style of coding is not recommended. Unless you have a good reason to do otherwise, you should always give each statement its own line of code. This avoids the use of semicolons and makes the code more readable by other developers.

Running Ruby programs

The Ruby source files that you create become the input to the Ruby interpreter. Unlike with compiled languages, with Ruby there is no build step required prior to running your Ruby programs. Running a Ruby program is as simple as calling the Ruby executable and passing it the name of the file containing your Ruby code. The actual executable program that you use to run your Ruby source code files is named `ruby`. Throughout the book, when you see `ruby` written in lowercase letters in the mono-space code font, you can assume it is referring to the actual Ruby executable program.

CROSS-REF   Before you continue, you should have Ruby installed on your computer. Installation instructions were provided in the Quick Start chapter. If you skipped that, now is a good time to go back and get Ruby installed.

You also need a text editor to create your Ruby source code in. You can use any text editor that you are comfortable with. The Quick Start chapter gave a few recommendations for good text editors to use that feature Ruby code recognition to give you syntax highlighting and some other nice features.

At this time, you should create a directory that you can use to store all of the samples you write in this chapter. Anytime you want to create a Ruby source file, go to that directory and create the file. From that same directory, you can run it with the `ruby` program.

Let's walk through an example of creating and running a simple Ruby program.

1. **In a text editor of your choice, create a file called** `test_app.rb`. Enter the following Ruby source code:

```
class SimpleRubyClass
    def simple_method
        puts 'You have successfully run a Ruby program.'
    end
end

my_class = SimpleRubyClass.new
my_class.simple_method
```

2. **From a command line, use the Ruby interpreter to run your program.**

```
> ruby test_app.rb
```

3. **You should see the output from the method you wrote.**

```
> You have successfully run a Ruby program.
```

In this example, you created a simple Ruby class and two additional statements outside of the Ruby class. When you run a Ruby source file, lines of code that are outside of a class definition are automatically executed. In the file you created, the last two lines are automatically executed when you call `ruby test_app.rb`. The first line executed creates an instance of the `SimpleRubyClass`, and the next line calls the `simple_method` on that instance.

When you create a Ruby source file, you do not have to use any classes. Many useful scripts can be written without using any Ruby classes at all.

Table 1.1 lists some commonly used options that you can use with the ruby interpreter. For example, especially if you have a large program file, you might find it useful to run a syntax check on the source file before you execute it. You can do that with the -c command-line option.

TABLE 1.1

Command-line Options Used with the Ruby Interpreter

Option	Description	Usage
-c	Checks the syntax of a source file without executing it.	`ruby -c test_script.rb`
-e	Executes code provided in quotation marks.	`ruby -e 'puts "Hello World"'`
-l	Prints a new line after every line; also called line mode.	`ruby -l -e 'print "Add a newline"'`
-v	Displays the Ruby version information and executes the program in verbose mode.	`ruby -v`
-w	Provides warnings during program execution.	`ruby -w test_script.rb`
-r	Loads the extension whose name follows the -r option.	`ruby -rprofile`
--version	Displays Ruby version information.	`ruby --version`

Classes, Objects, and Variables

Objects are not tacked on to the Ruby language as an afterthought as they are in some languages, such as Perl or early versions of PHP. Nor are objects optional as they are in C++. As you learned previously, Ruby is a pure object-oriented language. In Ruby, everything is an object. This makes learning about objects in Ruby very important. They are the foundation for all of the code you will write in Ruby, and so that is where you'll now begin to explore the details of the Ruby language.

Using objects in Ruby

Since objects and classes are core to Ruby programming, Ruby provides a rich syntax for using them. In this section, you'll learn how to create objects and classes in Ruby. You'll also learn how to create methods and variables that will be contained by the classes and objects that you create.

Defining objects

Objects provide a way of modeling your application's data and actions. In Ruby, you define the structure of your objects inside of a class. A class is similar to the concept of a type. A class defines a type of data structure. Looking at Figure 1.1, you see a User class that contains two attributes (login, password) and two methods (set_password, set_login). When you use the User class, you create an instance of the class. An *instance* of a class is also called an *object*. In Figure 1.1, the object a_user is an instance of the User class. A class is a way of defining common behavior for all of the objects that are of that class type. In this example, all instances of the User class will have the login and password attributes, and the set_password and set_login methods.

FIGURE 1.1

The User class

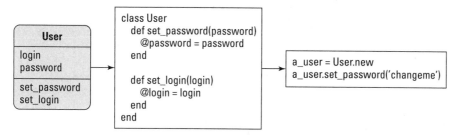

You define a class in your source code using the class keyword. The minimum code you need to define a class is a class statement with your class name, and the end statement to close the class definition. The following code would define a User class:

```
class User
end
```

It is usually good practice to have each of your classes defined in a separate file. The User class would typically be stored in a file called user.rb. If you follow this recommendation, your code becomes better organized, and thus more readable and more maintainable.

Classes are made up of attributes and methods. The remainder of this section will show you the details of how to create each of these elements in the Ruby classes you write.

Writing methods

A class's methods define its behavior. Methods allow Ruby classes to perform useful actions and process data in useful ways. When you are writing a Rails application, your application's business logic will be contained in methods that you add to classes. In Ruby, you define methods within classes using syntax that looks like this:

```
class Notifier
    def print_message
        puts 'Wherever you go, there you are.'
    end
end
```

In this example, the class `Notifier` contains one method, named `print_message`. Take a look at that method definition line-by-line to understand all of its parts. The first line is

```
def print_message
```

Ruby uses the `def` keyword to signify the start of a method definition. The `def` keyword is followed by the name of the method you are defining. The method name is also used when the method is called someplace else in your code. In this example, the method name is `print_message`. Your method names should be concise, yet descriptive of the actions that are performed within the method. While some people don't like long method names, it is better to have longer names than short names that do not accurately convey the purpose of a method.

The next line of the method is the first line of the method body:

```
puts 'Wherever you go, there you are.'
```

This line prints a message to the console. The method `puts` is a built-in Ruby method for writing string output to the console. In this case, the method name, `print_message`, is good because it accurately describes what this method does. If you find yourself wondering what a method does after looking at its name, perhaps you should consider renaming the method.

The method body continues until an end statement is reached. The end statement marks the end of the method. For those coming from Java or Perl, note that you do not surround your method body in curly braces,{ and }, as you do in those languages.

Methods with parameters

You saw an example of a very simple method in the previous section. Methods can also have data passed to them. The data passed to a method can then be used within the body of the method. Data values passed to a method are called *parameters*, or *arguments*, of that method. Here is an example of a method that uses parameters:

```
def add_numbers(number1, number2)
    number1 + number2
end
```

This method, `add_numbers`, takes two parameters, `number1` and `number2`. The parameters are then used within the body of the method. The variables listed between the parentheses are called the *parameter list*. Anytime you use a parameter in the body of your method, you must use the same name for it that is given in the parameter list. Notice that in your parameter list, you do not declare any types for the parameters as you do in Java and other statically typed languages.

You might be wondering if a `return` statement was accidentally left out of the previous method. Perhaps you were expecting to see the method body written like this:

```
return number1 + number2
```

In Ruby, that line is actually equivalent to the line that does not contain the `return` statement. In Ruby, the value of the last statement executed is also returned from the method. Because the statement `number1 + number2` is the last statement in this method body, its value is returned from the method.

Creating instances of a class

A class defines a type of object. To use an object of that type, you must create an instance of that class. Consider a class designed to implement simple math operations. You might start with a class defined like this:

```
class SimpleMath
    def add_numbers
        number1+number2
    end
end
```

This is the definition of a class called `SimpleMath` containing one method called `add_numbers`. To use the `SimpleMath` class as an object, you have to first create an instance of it. Every class has a method called `new` that is used to create instances of that class. The `new` method is called without any parameters, like this:

```
math = SimpleMath.new
```

The variable `math` now contains an instance of the `SimpleMath` class. Now you can call methods on that instance, like this:

```
result = math.add_numbers(3, 5)
```

This is the first example you've seen of how methods are called in Ruby. Ruby uses the dot operator (.) to indicate that what follows is the name of a method that is to be called on the object preceding the dot operator.

NOTE It is common naming practice in Ruby to begin class names with an uppercase letter and capitalize the first letter of each additional word in the class name. Instance names, and all other variables in Ruby, should begin with a lowercase letter and have multiple words joined with an underscore character.

Initializing instances with the initialize() method

Often, you'll want to initialize the state of an object when you create an instance. Many languages include a method that is called when instances are created. Often, this is called an *object constructor*. In Ruby, the concept of a constructor is implemented with the `initialize` method. You can include an `initialize` method in any of your classes, and it will be called when an instance is created using the `new` method. For example, you could have a class defined like this:

```
class PhotoAlbum
    def initialize
        @album_size = 10
    end
end
```

Here, you have a `PhotoAlbum` class containing an `initialize` method that sets the album size to 10 each time an instance of the class is created.

The `initialize` method can also take parameters. Instead of hard-coding an album size, you might prefer an `initialize` method like this:

```
class PhotoAlbum
    def initialize(album_size)
        @album_size = album_size
    end
end
```

In this example, the `initialize` method takes a single parameter, the album size. You pass this parameter to the new method when you create an instance of the `PhotoAlbum` class, like this:

```
my_photo_album = PhotoAlbum.new(20)
```

This creates your new instance, initialized with an album size of 20.

Instance and class methods

There are two types of methods that a class can define: instance methods and class methods. Instance methods allow you to interact with instance objects, and class methods allow you to interact with class objects.

Instance methods

In the previous example, the `add_numbers` method that is declared in the `SimpleMath` class is called an instance method. It can only be called on instances of the `SimpleMath` class. Instance methods manipulate only the instance on which they are called. An object instance must be created in order to use instance methods.

Any method defined in a class using the simple format of the `def` keyword followed by a method name is an instance method. Here is a class that contains three instance methods:

```
class SuperHero
    def add_power
        # method body here...
    end

    def use_power
        # method body here...
    end

    def find_enemy
        # method body here...
    end
end
```

The three methods defined in this class are instance methods. You must create an instance of the SuperHero class using the new method to be able to use any of these methods. Once an instance is created, an instance method is called using the instance variable followed by the dot operator, like this:

```
spiderman = SuperHero.new
spiderman.add_power('super_strength')
spiderman.use_power
```

The majority of the methods you write within your classes will probably be instance methods.

Class methods

There is another type of method that classes can define, called class methods. A class method can only be called on a class and cannot be called from an object instance. You've already seen one example of a class method — the new method that is used to create instances of a class.

Class methods can be defined in a few different ways. You do one of the following to define a class method:

- Prefix a method name with the class name and the dot operator.
- Prefix a method name with the self keyword and the dot operator.
- Use class << self syntax see the following example).

When you call methods or access attributes on a class, you are not using any specific instance of that class. Class methods are called like this:

```
methods = User.methods
```

This line calls the methods class method of the User class. This would return you an array of all the class methods for the User class.

The first way you can define a class method is to write it with a preceding class name, like this:

```
class PhotoAlbum
    def PhotoAlbum.delete(album_id)
        ...
    end
end
```

In this example, the delete method is created as a class method of the PhotoAlbum class. The delete method cannot be called from an instance of this class. Instead, you call the delete method as shown in the following example, passing an integer that represents the ID of an album you want to delete:

```
PhotoAlbum.delete(12)
```

Another way to define a class method is to use the `self` keyword like this:

```
class PhotoAlbum
    def self.delete
        ...
    end
end
```

This creates a `delete` class method for `PhotoAlbum` that behaves identically to the previous version.

The final style you see for defining class methods is useful when you have several class methods that you want to define in one class. You can define a group of class methods using the `class << self` syntax like this:

```
class PhotoAlbum
    class << self
        def delete(album_id)
            ...
        end
        ...
        def move(album_id)
            ...
        end
        ...
        def rename(album_id)
            ...
        end
    end
end
```

In this example, all three of the methods contained within the block surrounded by `class << self` are defined as class methods.

Instance and class variables

Just as there are two types of methods that a class can contain, there are also two types of variables that a class can contain. The two types are the instance variables and the class variables.

Instance variables

It is very common that you'll want to associate data with specific instances of your classes. For example, you might have a `User` class, with each instance representing a different user. Each instance of user would need its own variables to maintain its object state. Variables that are associated with an instance of a class are called *instance variables*. The following is true of all instance variables:

- Instance variable names always begin with @ (the at sign).
- You can access instance variables only through the specific class instance to which they belong. Each instance of a class has its own instance variables.

■ You can define an instance variable anywhere within a class and it will still be visible to all instance methods within the class.

To illustrate these bullet points, consider this example:

```
class House
    def print_value
        puts @value
    end

    def set_value(a_value)
        @value = a_value
    end
end
```

In this example, because of the @ symbol, you should be able to identify @value as an instance variable. Notice that you do not have to define instance variables outside of your methods as you do in some other languages, such as Java. Anytime you use a variable that begins with an @ symbol, that variable becomes an instance variable. The print_value method accesses the same @value variable set by the set_value method. Each instance of the House class maintains its own copy of the @value variable.

Class variables

In addition to instance variables, a class can also define class variables. A *class variable* is a variable that is shared among all instances of a class. Class variables are not referred to in relation to an instance, as instance variables were. You reference a class variable by using the Class name and the dot operator, like this:

```
total_house_value = House.total_value
```

Using the example of the House class again, a house's value was stored as an instance variable. This makes sense because each instance of the House class represents a different house, and each house will have its own value. The total value of all houses is a good example of a field that could be represented as a class variable. Each instance, or house, does not need to maintain its own copy of the total house value. This value is not a data element of any individual house, but rather a data element that describes all of the houses. Therefore, it makes sense to represent this value as a class variable.

Class variable names start with two @ signs, @@. The class definition for the House class, including the total value class variable, would look like this:

```
class House
    @@total_value = 0

    def print_value
        puts @value
    end
```

```
        def set_value(a_value)
            @value = a_value
        end
    end
```

In this code example, the @@total_value class variable is initialized to a value of zero. You must initialize class variables before they are used. To keep track of the total value of all houses, this variable must be updated every time a house value is updated. This requires a slight modification of the set_value method, like this:

```
class House
    @@total_value = 0

    def print_value
        puts @value
    end

    def set_value(a_value)
        @value = a_value
        @@total_value = @@total_value + @value
    end
end
```

Now, every time the value of a house is set, that value is also added to the total value of all houses, which is tracked with the @@total_value class variable. There is actually a potential problem with this code. Did you spot it? If the set_value method is called more than once for a single instance — that is, a single house — rather than updating the total value with the new value being set for that particular house, both values that you've set for that house are added to the total value. This gives a false total value. Having noted that, the code accurately illustrates the use of class and instance variables.

Getters and setters in Ruby objects

If you've done any amount of object-oriented program in a different language, you are probably familiar with the terms *getters* and *setters*. Even if you are not, the concept is relatively simple. As you've learned, an object instance contains data stored in instance variables. Frequent tasks that you will want to perform are setting the value of those variables and getting the value of those variables. The methods that perform those actions of setting and getting the values of instance variables are known as *getters* and *setters*.

 Getters and setters are also sometimes referred to as accessors and mutators in some such as C++.

In many other object-oriented languages, you must explicitly define these getter and setter methods using relatively verbose and repetitive syntax. For example, in Java you might see code that looks like this in many of the classes:

```
Class JavaObject {
```

```
        String stringVal
        int intVal;

        public String getStringVal() {
            return stringVal;
        }

        public void setStringVal(String stringVal) {
            this.stringVal = stringVal;
        }

        public int getIntVal() {
            return intVal;
        }

        public void setIntVal(int intVal) {
            this.intVal = intVal;
        }
    }
```

While these methods are relatively simple, this can be very tedious and perhaps error-prone if you make any typographic mistakes as you write these methods for every instance variable that you want to access outside of a class instance. These methods clutter up your class definitions with many lines of code that do relatively little. You've probably also noticed that the pattern for each instance variable getter and setter is the same. It seems that by writing all of these methods, you are doing a task that is more ideally suited for the computer. Isn't getting the computer to do work for you precisely the reason you are writing a software application in the first place?

Fortunately, Ruby saves you from having to repeat these getter and setter methods in all of your classes by giving you a built-in method that automatically generates the methods for you at run-time. Before you see that, however, it is educational to see how you would implement getters and setters in Ruby.

Getters in Ruby

Getters are relatively simple if you recall that methods in Ruby return the value of the last statement executed, even if you do not include a `return` statement. Therefore, the above Java class could be rewritten in Ruby like this (for the moment, you include only the getter methods, not the setters):

```
class RubyObject
    def string_val
        @string_val
    end

    def int_val
        @int_val
    end
end
```

In this Ruby code, notice that the instance variable names have been changed to reflect the style commonly used in Ruby code: lowercase variable names with words separated by underscores. Also notice that in Ruby, you do not have to declare the instance variables prior to using them.

Setters in Ruby

Let's take a look at how you implement setters in Ruby code. With your growing knowledge of Ruby code, your first attempt at creating a setter might look like this:

```
def set_string_val(new_string_val)
    @string_val = new_string_val
end
```

You would use this method to set the @string_val instance variable like this:

```
my_ruby_obj.set_string_val('a good string')
```

This method is valid Ruby code and will work just fine, but you can do better. Keep reading to see a more elegant way to express this setter method.

Using the equal sign in method names

Ruby allows you to define setter methods for the purpose of a more elegant setter method by using an equal (=) sign at the end of the method name. The following example illustrates how you would do this using an equal sign method:

```
def string_val=(new_string_val)
    @string_val = new_string_val
end
```

It doesn't look like you've saved much in terms of the definition of the setter method. Its size is similar, and some might even think this definition is a bit more complex. But, look at how this method is used:

```
my_ruby_obj.string_val=('a good string')
```

Here you see the new method being called just as the set_string_val method was called; however, by ending the method name with an equal sign, you begin to see how this makes the method call look less like calling a method and more like just setting the attribute value directly. Go a step further and remember that, in Ruby, you do not have to surround your parameters with parentheses. You can now write the setter like this:

```
my_ruby_obj.string_val='a good string'
```

Ruby lets you go even a step further by providing you with a syntax that is special to methods that end with the equal sign. You can write these methods with a space between the method name and the equal sign. For example, you could also write the setter like this:

```
my_ruby_obj.string_val = 'a good string'
```

When the Ruby interpreter sees the `string_val` method followed by the =, it automatically ignores the space and assumes you are calling the `string_val=` method. This line makes for a very readable setter method. This type of special syntax is often referred to by Ruby programmers as syntactic sugar.

The attr_ methods

Earlier, I said that you didn't really have to write your own getter and setter methods in Ruby, and I mentioned that there was a way to have these automatically generated for you at run-time. This is where the `attr_` methods come in. You will find yourself often using these methods.

The attr_reader method

Using the `attr_reader` method, you can avoid having to create getter methods for instance variables that you want to be readable from outside of your class. To use the `attr_reader` method, simply call it with a symbol representing the instance variable that you want a getter method for, like this:

```
class Message
    attr_reader :body

    def initialize(body)
        @body = body
    end
end
```

The @body instance variable is now readable from outside of the class by referencing it through an instance, like this:

```
a_message = Message.new("Dear John")
message_body = a_message.body
```

The `message_body` variable would now contain the value `"Dear John"`, which was the value of the @body instance variable.

The attr_writer method

Ruby also provides a method that will automatically create a setter method for you. The `attr_writer` method creates an accessor method to allow assignment to an attribute that is equivalent to a setter method. Using `attr_writer` is just as easy as `attr_reader` was. Take a look at this example.

```
class Message
    attr_writer :body
end

a_message = Message.new
a_message.body = 'I like school.'
```

In this example, you are able to set the body attribute of the a_message instance because an attr_writer was created for the body attribute. In practice, you will not use the attr_writer method very often. For attributes that you want to have both read and write access to, the attr_accessor method, described next, is a better choice.

The attr_accessor method

If you want to use both getters and setters with instance variables, the attr_accessor method is what you want to use. The attr_accessor method generates both getters and setters for the instance variables you pass to it.

```
class Message
    attr_accessor :body, :recipients
end
```

Now the @body and @recipients instance variables can be read and set from outside of the class. You get or set these instance variables just as if you were directly accessing the variable, like this:

```
a_message = Message.new
a_message.body = ''
a_message.recipients = ['tim@timothyfisher.com','john@doe.com']
```

You can see how easy this makes it to set instance variables without having to write any setter code inside the class.

Inheritance

All object-oriented languages support inheritance. Inheritance is one of the ways in which classes can be related. You may often hear the term class hierarchy, or maybe object hierarchy. A *class hierarchy* is a hierarchical mapping of classes. *Inheritance* is the main building block of a class hierarchy, and specifically models the IS-A relationship. For example, a baseball IS-A ball. A football IS-A ball also.

Consider the example shown in Figure 1.2. You see the Ball class as a parent class of the Baseball and Football classes. The Baseball and Football classes will *inherit* all of the attributes and methods of the Ball class. In Figure 1.2, the Ball class has two attributes, a size and a weight. These attributes will be inherited by both the Baseball and Football classes. So instances of Baseball and Football will have size and weight attributes.

The Baseball and Football classes can also add their own attributes and methods to *specialize* the class to their particular type. Again referring to Figure 1.2, the Baseball class has a hard_or_soft attribute that is unique to the Baseball class. The Football class has an inflation_limit attribute that is unique to the Football class. These attributes specify things about the specific type of ball that the class represents that are not common to balls in general. Methods and attributes that are inherited from a parent class can be used in the child class just as if they were defined inside the child class. The parent class of an inheritance relationship is also commonly called the *base class*.

FIGURE 1.2

A class hierarchy

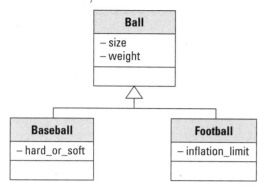

Inheritance is a technique that is very often used by object-oriented programmers. Rails applications rely very heavily on the use of inheritance. The classes that you write in a Rails application gain the power of the Rails framework primarily by inheriting from existing Rails classes. When you create a class that inherits from a parent class, you can also say that your new class *extends* the parent class. Referring back to Figure 1.2, the Baseball and Football classes extend the parent class, Ball.

To implement class inheritance in Ruby, you use the greater-than symbol (<) when you define your class, like this:

```
class Football < Ball
    ...
end
```

This code means that the Football class is extending or inheriting from the Ball class.

Built-in Classes and Modules

Now that you have learned the basic syntax and structure of Ruby programming, it is time to learn about the built-in features of the language. Ruby contains a wealth of built-in capability that saves you from having to write a tremendous amount of low-level code in your applications.

The built-in classes and modules that you'll learn about in this section can be divided into two areas: scalar objects and collections. As you learn about these built-in features, it's a great idea to follow along with an open irb session. You can type all of the code snippets used in this section directly into irb. Lines in the code snippets that begin with => denote output that you will see in irb if you try out the code snippet.

Scalar objects

Scalar objects are objects that represent single values, as opposed to collections of values. In this section, you'll learn about some of the built-in scalar objects that you'll use often in Ruby programs. The scalar objects discussed here include the following:

- Strings
- Numerics
- Symbols
- Times and dates

Strings

Strings are used to represent text, or sequences of characters, in Ruby. You can create string literals in Ruby using single or double quotes, like this:

```
"This is a string in Ruby."
```

or like this:

```
'This is a string in Ruby.'
```

However, there are differences in how strings are interpreted that you should be aware of so that you can use the correct quote style in different situations.

Substitution in strings

Substitution occurs in strings when you type in one or more characters that the Ruby interpreter will change into different characters. A backslash character followed by another character is a common indicator for string substitution. For example, in a single quoted string, you can place a single quote inside of a string by escaping the quote with a backslash character, like this:

```
puts 'I went to Dad\'s house.'
```

This string outputs the string value:

```
I went to Dad's house.
```

The \' is turned into a single quote. This allows you to use single quotes within single-quoted strings. You can also use a backslash character within a single-quoted string by putting two backslashes in the string, like this:

```
puts 'A backslash looks like this: \\'
=> A backslash look like this: \
```

These are the only two substitutions that occur in single-quoted strings. Any other backslash characters remain just as you typed them.

Double-quoted strings, however, allow you to use a richer set of backslash sequences for substitution. For example, the \n sequence turns into a newline character in a double-quoted string.

String interpolation

String interpolation allows you to use Ruby expressions inside of double-quoted strings. Take a look at the following example:

```
subject = 'zombies'
    puts "Timmy likes #{subject}."
=> Timmy likes zombies.
```

The # and { sequences tell Ruby that what's enclosed is a Ruby expression that you would like evaluated, and its result is inserted into the string. In addition to using variables like this, you can also interpolate other expressions, such as this:

```
puts "If you add 2 and 5 you get the value #{2+5}."
=> If you add 2 and 5 you get the value 7.
```

You can skip the braces for instance, class, and global variables. For example, you could use interpolation with an instance variable like this:

```
@subject = 'cooking'
    puts "Camden likes #@subject."
=> Camden likes cooking.
```

String interpolation allows you to write concise code without having to perform a lot of string concatenation that you might do in other languages.

String operations

Ruby provides your strings with a great deal of built-in functionality. Here are some of the more common string methods that you'll use:

- `length`

  This method returns the length of the string that it is called on.

  ```
  short_str = "This is a short string."
  puts short_str.length
  => 22
  ```

- `include?`

  Returns `true` if the string it is called on contains the string passed as a parameter.

  ```
  "Superman can fly".include?('Superman')
  => true
  ```

- `slice`

  This method returns a substring of the string that it is called on. The substring is specified by passing an argument of one of the following types: `fixnum`, `range`, `regular expression`, or `string`. There is also a variant of this method that deletes the specified substring from the string that it is called on and returns the deleted substring. This variant is named `slice!`.

An example taken from the official Ruby documentation site at http://ruby-doc.org illustrates use of this function well:

```
string = "this is a string"
string.slice!(2)        #=> 105
string.slice!(3..6)     #=> " is "
string.slice!(/s.*t/)   #=> "sa st"
string.slice!("r")      #=> "r"
string                  #=> "thing"
```

In the above example, note that the end of the statements include a comment showing what the return value of that method call would be. For example, `string.slice!(2)` would return the ascii character value `105`. The string `#=>` is commonly used to indicate the return value of a statement in Ruby documentation.

The fourth line of the above example containing the expression `string.slice!(/s.*t/)` uses a regular expression as a parameter. In Ruby, regular expressions are created with the / delimiter. Ruby provides strong support for using regular expressions, and though this book does not get into the details of how to use regular expressions, I strongly advise you to become familiar with them. Regular expressions are very useful in any programming language.

- gsub

    This method allows you to specify a portion of a string to be replaced with a different string. Just as with the `slice` method, there is a variant available that will change the string that the method is called on. This variant is named `gsub!`. These methods take two parameters. The first parameter is a regular expression or a string to match on, and the second parameter is a string that you want to replace the matched text with. The following examples show how this method is used:

    ```
    "hello".gsub(/[aeiou]/, '*')         #=> "h*ll*"
    "Superman".gsub("Super", "Bat")      #=> "Batman"
    "hello".gsub(/([aeiou])/, '<\1>')    #=> "h<e>ll<o>"
    ```

    In the last line of the example, the replacement string is `'<\1>'`. In this string, the `\1` sequence will match the result of the `[aeiou]` regular expression. Surrounding the regular expression in parentheses, as in this example, creates a matching group. You could have additional matching groups in the regular expression by including additional regular expressions surrounded by more sets of parentheses. In the replacement string, you can match subsequent matching groups using `\2`, `\3`, and so on. See this line of code for an example of multiple matching groups:

    ```
    "hello".gsub(/(e)(ll)/, '<\1><\2>')       #=> "h<e><ll>o"
    ```

    In the previous line of code, the `\1` sequence matches the regular expression group (`e`) and the `\2` sequence matches the regular expression group (`ll`).

There are many more methods that you can use on String objects. For a complete description of all of the methods available for String objects, you should refer to the official Ruby documentation for Strings at `www.ruby-doc.org/core/classes/String.html`.

Numerics

Ruby has special classes that represent numbers that you use in a Ruby application. These classes include `Float`, `Fixnum`, and `Bignum`. The `Bignum` and `Fixnum` classes represent integers. They both extend the `Integer` class. The classes `Float` and `Integer` extend the `Numeric` class, which provides basic functionality to all numeric objects.

You can find out the class that a particular number uses by calling its `class` method, like this:

```
1980.class
=> Fixnum

3.1459.class
=> Float

10000000000.class
=> Bignum
```

Now, take a look at a few methods that are commonly used with numbers:

- `integer?`

  Returns `true` if the number is an integer value.

  ```
  1980.integer?
  => true
  ```

- `round`

  Rounds the number to the nearest integer.

  ```
  18.3.round    #=> 18
  18.7.round    #=> 19
  ```

- `to_f`

  Converts a `Fixnum` or `Bignum` to a `Float`.

  ```
  15.to_f                  #=> 15.0
  1000000000000.to_f   #=> 1000000000000.0
  ```

- `to_i`

  Converts a `Float` to an `Integer` type (either `Fixnum` or `Bignum` depending on its size). The decimal portion of the number is truncated. There is no rounding performed during the truncation.

  ```
  15.1.to_i    #=> 15
  15.8.to_i    #=> 15
  ```

- `zero?`

  Reruns true if the value has a zero value, otherwise it returns false.

There are many more methods available for the numeric classes. For complete method information, refer to the official Ruby doc Web site.

Symbols

If you are coming to Ruby from a Java or C language background, symbol objects are probably going to be something new to you. You can think of symbols as placeholders for strings. Symbols are easily recognized in Ruby code because they are always prefixed with a colon (:). You can convert any string into a symbol by using the `to_sym` method. The following is an example of creating a symbol using this method:

```
city = "Detroit"
city_sym = city.to_sym
puts city_sym
```

The `to_sym` method converts the string `"Detroit"` into an equivalent symbol object. The symbol, `city_sym`, contains the value `:Detroit`. When you print the symbol to the console using the `puts` method, the console output is:

```
Detroit
```

You might be wondering why the value printed was not `:Detroit`. The reason why you don't see that value printed is because the `puts` method automatically converts the symbol back into a string before printing it. The string equivalent of a symbol is the symbol value without the colon. However, if you look at the class type of the variable `city_sym`, you will see that it is indeed a Symbol object.

```
city_sym.class  #=> Symbol
```

You can convert a symbol back into a string using the `id2name` method. Here, you see how the `:Detroit` symbol is converted back to the original string value:

```
city_string = city_sym.id2name
```

When you get into Rails development, you will use symbols frequently. Although they may seem a bit foreign at first, they are simple to use and often make for cleaner and faster code.

Times and dates

In many applications you write, you will have to work with times and dates and usually perform some manipulation of those values. Ruby provides you with built-in classes to support times and dates in your application. The classes that provide Ruby's support for times and dates are `Date`, `Time`, and `DateTime`. The `Time` class is the only one of those three that is included with the Ruby core. The `Date` and `DateTime` classes are a part of the Ruby standard library which is included with Ruby but they must be explicitly included using a require statement when you want to use them. Below is an example of how you would include the `Date` and `DateTime` classes in your code:

```
require 'date'
```

The date library included using the above require statement will give you both the `Date` and the `DateTime` classes.

The `require` statements should always be placed at the very top of your source files. You can also use these classes within an `irb` session simply by using the same `require` syntax at the command prompt.

Below you'll see some of the methods and features of the date and time classes. There are many more methods available for these classes than what is covered in this book. For complete information, refer to the official Ruby documentation site `www.ruby-doc.org`.

Using the Time class

You can create instances of the Time class using the new method as shown here:

```
time = Time.new
```

When you use the new method of the `Time` class, an instance of the `Time` object representing the current time is created. To get a `Time` instance referring to the current time you can also use the `Time.now` method. If you want to create an instance that is preset to a given time, you the `Time.local` method as shown here:

```
time = Time.local(2008, "jun", 22, 10, 30, 25)
#=>  Sun Jun 10:30:25 -0400 2008
```

In this example, an instance of `Time` is created and set to the date June 22, 2008, and the time 10:30 and 25 seconds. The parameters passed to `Time.local` in this example are in this order year, month, date, hours, minutes, and seconds.

You can also call `Time.local` to create a time instance with these parameters: seconds, minutes, hour, day, month, year, day of the week, day of the year, is it daylight savings time?, and timezone. Here is an example of how you would create the same time using these parameters:

```
time = Time.local(25, 30, 10, 22, "jun", 2008, 0, 174, true,
   "EST")
#=>  Sun Jun 10:30:25 -0400 2008
```

Once you have a Time instance created, you can easily get specific field information from it using instance methods available. Here are some examples:

```
time.day        #=> 22
time.yday       #=> 174
time.wday       #=> 0
time.year       #=> 2008
time.month      #=> 6
time.zone       #=> "Eastern Daylight Time"
time.hour       #=> 10
time.min        #=> 30
time.sec        #=> 25
```

You can also perform addition and subtraction of time instances. To get the difference between two times, subtract them, as shown here:

```
time1 = Time.local(2008, "jun", 22, 10, 30, 25)
time2 = Time.local(2008, "jun", 20, 10, 30, 25)
time1 - time2   #=> 172800.0
```

The value returned from subtracting the two times is the time difference expressed in seconds. Knowing that there are 86,400 seconds in a day (60*60*24), you could convert the result to days by dividing the result by 86,400, to get two days.

You can add seconds to a time using the addition operator, as shown here:

```
time = Time.local(2008, "jun", 22, 10, 30, 25)
time + 60    #=>  Sun Jun 10:31:25 -0400 2008
```

In this example, 60 seconds are added to the time instance.

You can compare time instances using either the `eql?` method or the `<=>` operator. The `eql?` method will return true if the time that it is called on and the time passed to it are both `Time` objects with the same seconds and fractional seconds. The `<=>` operator also compares time objects down to the fractional seconds, however its return value is different. Instead of returning true or false, the `<=>` operator will return 0 if the time instances are equal, -1 if the time instance on the left occurs before the time instance on the right, and +1 if the time instance on the left occurs after the time instance on the right. Here are some comparison examples:

```
time1 = Time.local(2008, "jun", 22, 10, 30, 25)
time2 = Time.local(2008, "aug", 12, 10, 30, 25)
time3 = Time.local(2008, "jun", 22, 10, 30, 25)

time1.eql? time2        #=> false
time1.eql? time3        #=> true

time1 <=> time2         #=> -1
time2 <=> time1         #=> 1
time1 <=> time3         #=> 0
```

Using the Date class

To create a new `Date` instance, you use the new method, as you did with the `Time` class. However, unlike the `Time` class, when you create a date with the new method, you will not get the current date. To get a meaningful date instance you should pass parameters to the new method like this:

```
date = Date.new(2008, 3, 12)
```

This creates a date instance representing March 12, 2008. The `Date` class represents dates only and does not include time information. To see a string representation of the date, use the `to_s` method:

```
date.to_s        #=> "2008-03-12"
```

There are accessor methods provided for getting the year, month, and day components of the date:

```
date.year      #=> 2008
date.month     #=> 3
date.day       #=> 12
```

Another useful method is the `next` method. This method will return the next day, as shown here:

```
date.next.to_s  #=> "2008-03-13"
```

In the above example, the `next` method is chained with the `to_s` method to return the string representation of the next date. Method chaining can be a convenient way of writing concise expressions in Ruby. If you want to get the next month, or perform month addition, you can use the `>>` operator with the date instance. The `>>` operator will advance a date by the given number of months. Similarly, the `<<` operator will subtract the given number of months from the date. Both of these operators will return the modified date but will not change the date instance on which they are called. Here are some examples:

```
(date >> 1).to_s        #=> "2008-04-12"
(date << 1).to_s        #=> "2008-02-12"
date.to_s               #=> "2008-03-12"
```

Just as with `Time` instances, you can test the equality of two dates using the `eql?` method, or the `<=>` operator. The operators behave just as they do for the Time instances, except dates are compared instead of times. Here are some examples:

```
date1 = Date.new(2008, 3, 12)
date2 = Date.new(2008, 7, 15)
date3 = Date.new(2008, 3, 12)

date1.eql? date2        #=> false
date1.eql? date3        #=> true

date1 <=> date2         #=> -1
date2 <=> date1         #=> 1
date1 <=> date3         #=> 0
```

Using the DateTime class

The `DateTime` class is a subclass of the `Date` class and thus inherits its methods and much of its behaviour. The `DateTime` class adds time information to the date information provided by the `Date` class.

You can create a DateTime instance with both date and time values set using the new method and parameters passed in this order (year, month, day, hour, minute, second) as shown here:

```
date_time = DateTime.new(2008, 3, 12, 10, 30, 25)
date_time.to_s   #=> "2008-03-12T10:30:25+00:00"
```

The DateTime class has access to these accessor methods for getting the time information:

```
date_time.hour    #=> 10
date_time.min     #=> 30
date_time.sec     #=> 25
date_time.zone    #=> "+00:00"
```

Formatting times and dates

All three of the time and date related classes, Time, Date, and DateTime, include a to_s method that allows you to get a string representation of the time or date. However, the format provided by the to_s method may not always be what you want. You can create a formatted date string using a format that you define using the strftime method that is available to all of these time and date classes. The strftime method takes a single parameter that is the format string. The format string can contain text and any of the format specifiers listed in Table 1.2 for printing date and time fields.

TABLE 1.2

Date and Time Formatting Codes for Use with strftime

Format Code	Description	Example
%a	The abbreviated weekday name	Sun
%A	The full weekday name	Sunday
%b	The abbreviated month name	Jan
%B	The full month name	January
%c	The preferred local date and time representation	03/12/08
%d	Day of the month	10
%H	Hour of the day, 24-hour clock	21
%I	Hour of the day, 12-hour clock	10
%j	Day of the year	215
%m	Month of the year	11
%M	Minute of the hour	25
%p	Meridian indicator	AM or PM
%S	Second of the minute	55
%U	Week number of the current year, starting with the first Sunday as the first day of the first week	5
%W	Week number of the current year, starting with the first Monday as the first day of the first week	4
%w	Day of the week (Sunday is 0)	2
%y	Year without a century	95
%Y	Year with century	1995
%Z	Time zone name	EST

Here are some examples of dates and times formatted using the `strftime` method:

```
date = Date.new(2008, 10, 18)
date.strftime("The day is %A, %B %d %Y")
#=> "The day is Saturday, October 18 2008

time = Time.local(2008, "jun", 22, 10, 30, 25)
time.strftime("Date: %a %b %d %Y, Time: %I:%M:%S")
#=> "Date: Sun Jun 22 2008, Time: 10:30:25"
```

Collections

All program languages support some method of representing groups of objects or other data elements. The objects that store collections of other objects are called the *collection objects*. These objects are defined by the collection classes, which are some of the most often used classes in any programming language. In almost any application you write, you will find times when you have to work with multiple items, and that is where collection classes help you.

Ruby provides you with built-in support for collections using the following collection classes, which you'll learn about in this section:

- Arrays
- Hashes
- Ranges

Arrays

The array is the most common collection class and is also one of the most often used classes in Ruby. An *array* stores an ordered list of indexed values, with the index starting at 0. Ruby implements arrays using the `Array` class. Here is an example of how arrays are used in Ruby:

```
great_lakes = ["Michigan","Erie","Superior","Ontario","Huron"]
puts great_lakes[0]
puts great_lakes[4]
```

This code creates an array containing the names of the Great Lakes, and stores it in the `great_lakes` variable. The second and third lines print the names of the first and fifth elements of the array. The output would be:

```
> Michigan
> Huron
```

Arrays do not have to be populated when they are created. You can also create an array object using the `Array.new` method, like this:

```
sports = Array.new
```

You can also create a new empty array using this style of declaration:

```
sports = []
```

The `Array` class also gives you plenty of built-in functionality. Here are some commonly used methods that you'll use when working with arrays:

- `empty?`

  Returns `true` if the array is empty.

  ```
  sports = Array.new
  puts sports.empty?
  => true
  ```

- `delete`

  Deletes the named element from the array and returns it.

  ```
  sports = ['Baseball','Football','Soccer']
  sports.delete('Soccer')
  sports
  => ['Baseball','Football']
  ```

- `first`

  Returns the first element of the array.

  ```
  names = ['Tim','John','Mike']
  puts names.first
  => Tim
  ```

- `last`

  Returns the last element of the array.

  ```
  names = ['Tim','John','Mike']
  puts names.last
  => Mike
  ```

- `push`

  Adds a new element to the array.

  ```
  sports = ['Baseball','Football','Soccer']
  sports.push('Tennis')
  => ['Baseball','Football','Soccer','Tennis']
  ```

- `size`

  Returns the number of elements contained in the array.

  ```
  sports = ['Baseball','Football','Soccer']
  puts sports.size
  => 3
  ```

Hashes

Like arrays, *hashes* store a list of values. However, if you use a hash instead of integer indexing, a hash lets you specify a unique index for each element that you store in the hash.

```
leagues = {"AL"=>"American League", "NL"=>"National League"}
puts leagues["AL"]
```

Once you have a hash, you can retrieve the value for an element in the hash by referencing its key value, as you see being done in the second line above. Notice that when you create a hash, you use the curly braces to enclose the hash, but when you refer to an element of the hash, you use the straight brackets. If you attempted to use the curly braces when referring to an element of the hash, you would get a syntax error.

You will also often hear the contents of a hash described as *key-value pairs*. The terms *index* and *key* are used interchangeably with respect to hashes.

Just as with arrays, the Hash class gives you plenty of built-in functionality. Here are some commonly used methods that you'll use when working with hashes:

- empty?

  Returns `true` if the hash is empty.

  ```
  leagues = {"AL"=>"American League", "NL"=>"National League"}
  puts leagues.empty?
  => false
  ```

- keys

  Returns an array of the hash's keys.

  ```
  leagues = {"AL"=>"American League", "NL"=>"National League"}
  leagues.keys
  => ['AL','NL']
  ```

- values

  Returns an array of the hash's values.

  ```
  leagues = {"AL"=>"American League", "NL"=>"National League"}
  leagues.values
  => ['American League','National League']
  ```

- size

  Returns the number of key or value pairs contained in the hash.

  ```
  leagues = {"AL"=>"American League", "NL"=>"National League"}
  leagues.size
  => 2
  ```

Ranges

Ruby provides another type of collection that you are probably not familiar with if you are new to Ruby: the Range class. You can use ranges to represent a sequence that has a defined start point, a defined end point, and a well-defined procession of elements. You create a range in Ruby using a start point, two dots, and an end point, like this:

```
(0..6)
```

This would create a range containing all the integer numbers from zero to six. You can verify that you have indeed created a `Range` object by looking at its class, using the following code:

```
(0..6).class
=> Range
```

A good way to verify what are all of the elements contained within a range is to convert the range into an array. You can convert the range into an array using the `to_a` method of the range, like this:

```
(0..6).to_a
=> [0,1,2,3,4,5,6]
```

You can use ranges not only for representing sequences of numbers, but also for representing any elements that have a well-defined sequence. Here is an example that expresses a sequence of letters as a range:

```
('a'..'e').to_a
=> ['a','b','c','d','e']
```

As with the other collection types in Ruby, you get plenty of built-in functionality with the `Range` class. Here are some common methods you can use with ranges:

- `first`

  Returns the first element of a range.

  ```
  (1..6).first   #=> 1
  ```

- `last`

  Returns the last element of a range.

  ```
  (1..6).last    #=> 6
  (1...6).last   #=> 6
  ```

  Notice that the last the last element specified in the Range declaration is returned as the last element of the range, even if that element is not included in the range, such as when you use the triple period range notation.

- `include?`

  Checks to see if the passed parameter value is included within the range.

  ```
  ('a'..'f').include? 'k'     #=> false
  ('a'..'f').include? 'd'     #=> true
  ```

  There is also a method available named `member?` that has the same behavior as `include?`.

- `each`

  This method allows you to iterate through each of the elements of a range and pass them to a block specified as a parameter. Blocks are covered later in this chapter, so if this doesn't make sense to you now, feel free to have another look after you've read about blocks.

```
(1..4).each do |number|
    puts number
end
```

Each element of the range 1, 2, 3, 4 will be printed to the screen on a separate line using the `puts` method.

- step

  Like the `each` method, the `step` method is also an iterator method. Using the `step` method, you can iterate through a range using a stepping size specified by the parameter passed.

  ```
  (1..6).step(2) do |number|
      puts number
  end
  ```

  This example will print out the numbers 1, 3, and 5 each on a separate line.

Control Flow

The control flow features of a programming language specify how the programming language allows you to control the path of execution through the code that you write. For example, there may be a group of statements that you only want to be executed under certain conditions, or there may be a group of statements that you want to repeat until a specified condition becomes true. These are the types of things that you will use control flow techniques to accomplish. Every programming language has control flow features built into it, and Ruby is no exception. Ruby's primary control flow mechanisms are:

- Conditionals
- Loops
- Blocks
- Iterators

Each of these mechanisms provides a different style of controlling the flow of your application. As you write more Ruby programs, you will find scenarios in which each of these mechanisms becomes valuable.

Conditionals

Conditionals allow you to specify a block of code that is executed conditionally, based on the result of some expression. Ruby supports three types of conditional statements:

- `if` statement
- `unless` statement
- `case` statement

The if statement

The `if` statement tests whether an expression is true or false. The expression being tested immediately follows the keyword `if` in a line of code. If the expression evaluates to true, the block of code following the `if` statement is executed. If the expression evaluates to false, the contained block of code is skipped.

In this example, the variable `value_a` is compared with the variable `value_b`. The statement `value_a is bigger` is only executed if the statement `value_a > value_b` is true.

```
if value_a > value_b
    puts 'value_a is bigger'
end
```

You can also specify a second block that is executed if the `if` expression evaluates to false. This is called the `else` block and is preceded by an `else` statement, like this:

```
if value_a > value_b
    puts 'value_a is bigger'
else
    puts 'value_b is bigger'
end
```

In this example, the correct statement is printed, depending on the values of the two variables.

There is one more statement that you can use with an `if` statement. That is the `elsif` statement. The `elsif` statement allows you to specify a block that is executed conditionally if the previous `if` or `elsif` statement did not evaluate to true. Here is an example:

```
if color == 'red'
    puts 'The color is red'
elsif color == 'blue'
    puts 'The color is blue'
else
    puts 'Could not determine color'
end
```

The unless statement

Another conditional supported by Ruby is the `unless` statement. The `unless` statement works opposite to how the `if` statement works. The block of code contained by the `unless` statement is executed only if the expression passed to the `unless` statement evaluates to false. Take a look at the following example:

```
unless value_a > value_b
    puts 'Value B is the larger number'
end
```

This code would print the message `'Value B is the larger number'` only if the value stored in `value_b` is larger than the value stored in `value_a`.

The case statement

The case statement allows you to compare a variable to a number of different possible values and execute a group of methods based on which of the values it matches. This construct can replace a series of if..else statements. Consider the following block of if..else statements:

```
if   color == 'red'
     puts 'The color is red'
elsif color == 'blue'
     puts 'The color is blue'
elsif color == 'green'
     puts 'The color is green'
else
     puts 'Unrecognized color name.'
end
```

In this series of if..else statements, the color variable is compared against a series of different values to find one that matches. If it does not find a match, there is an ending else to print a default message. This example illustrates how you could implement the very same logic using a case statement:

```
case color
    when 'red'
        puts 'The color is red'
    when 'blue'
        puts 'The color is blue'
    when 'green'
        puts 'The color is green'
    else
        puts 'Unrecognized color name.'
end
```

As you see here, after the case statement, you specify the variable that you want to match. Each when statement is the equivalent of an elseif in the previous implementation. When a matching condition is found, the statement or statements following that when statement (up until the next when statement) are executed. After executing those statements, the control flow passes to the line after the case statement's closing end statement.

 You can also specify groups of valid values, as in the following example:

```
when 'red','purple'
```

Loops, blocks, and iterators

Loops, blocks, and iterators allow you to define sections of code that you want to execute repeatedly, often until a given condition is satisfied. The constructs you'll learn about here include:

- for loops
- while and until loops
- code blocks

If you have experience with other programming languages, you are probably familiar with the concept of for, while, and until loops. However, code blocks may be very new to you. They are a feature that gives Ruby a great deal of its unique power and capability for writing clean, elegant, and concise code.

for loops

The Ruby for loop allows you to execute a given block of code an amount of times specified by an expression preceding the block. If you are used to using the for loops in Java, JavaScript, C, C++, or a language similar to one of those, pay particular attention here, as the Ruby for loops are different than the for loops in those languages. Here is an example of a Ruby for loop:

```
cities = ['Southgate','Flat Rock','Wyandotte','Woodhaven']
for city in cities
    puts city
end
```

Executing this loop would result in each of the city names contained in the cities array being printed to the console. Here is another example of a for loop that iterates over a hash variable, using both the key and value elements as variables within the block.

```
hash = {:r=>'red', :b=>'blue, :y=>'yellow'}
for key,value in hash
    puts "#{key} => #{value}"
end
```

Executing this loop will result in the following output:

```
y => yellow
b => blue
r => red
```

while and until loops

In addition to the for loop, Ruby supports other looping constructs that are also common in many other programming languages: the while loop and the until loop. The while and until loops execute a block of code while a certain condition is true, or until the condition becomes true. Here are some examples:

```
num = 10
while num >= 0 do
    puts num
    num = num - 1
end

num = 0
until num > 10 do
    puts num
    num = num + 1
end
```

Blocks

In several of the previous examples that used iterators, such as the `each` or `step` method of a Range object, you have seen Ruby blocks in use. *Blocks* are groups of statements that can be passed into a method as a parameter. They are commonly used with iterators. The `each` method, which is available on any class that is enumerable in Ruby, is probably the place you will use blocks most often. Here is an example of a block used with the `each` statement:

```
colors = ['red','blue','yellow','green']
colors.each do |color|
    puts color
    color_count = color_count + 1
end
```

In this example, the block is enclosed by the `do` and `end` statements. The block is passed a single parameter which is enclosed in the pipes. The block is passed as a parameter to the `each` method. Blocks can also be enclosed by curly brackets. The example below is equivalent to the previous one:

```
colors = ['red','blue','yellow','green']
colors.each { |color|
    puts color
    color_count = color_count + 1
}
```

Although not a syntax rule, common usage is to use the curly brackets around blocks when you have a short block that will fit on the same line as the method invocation to which the block is passed, such as this example:

```
colors.each { |color| puts color}
```

If your block spans multiple lines, the `do`/`end` syntax is preferred.

Blocks are a construct that is new to many programmers, especially those coming from Java or C language backgrounds. They are frequently used in Ruby code so you should become very familiar with them. I have just touched on what you can do with blocks. There is a great deal more to learn about them. You can learn more with many good online references; just do a Google search on Ruby Blocks.

The yield statement

You can create your own methods that accept blocks as a parameter and be able to pass parameters into those blocks using the `yield` statement. Take a look at an example of a method that can accept a block as a parameter:

```
class TimsBooks
    def initialize
        @books = ['Ruby on Rails Bible', 'Java Phrasebook']
    end

    def each
        @books.each {|book| yield book }
```

```
        end
    end

    books = TimsBooks.new
    books.each do |book|
        puts book
    end
```

In this example, the `TimsBooks` class contains an instance variable that is an array of books. The `@books` variable is initialized at object creation time. The `each` method is implement to iterate through the `@books` array and yield each book value to the block that is passed to the `each` method. Toward the bottom of the example, you see how the `each` method can be used with an instance of `TimsBooks` to print the name of each book. Using this technique you could write your own `each` methods for any classes that you write that contain some data that can be iterated upon.

The `yield` statement calls the passed in block, passing any parameters that are passed to it along to the block. So in the above example, each time `yield` is called, the block containing the `puts book` statement is called passing the name of a book from the `@books` array. The resulting output will be a list of the books in the `@books` array.

Iterators

An *iterator* is a method that allows you to step through a group of values in a systematic way. Iterators are featured in many programming languages, and Ruby has rich support for them. You have seen some of the iterator methods already. Some of the iterator methods supported by Ruby described here.

- `each`

  The `each` method is the most common iterator. You can use the `each` method to step through any element that is enumerable such as an array or hash.

  ```
  students = ['Tim','Camden','Kerry','Timmy']
  students.each do |student|
      puts student.name
  end
  ```

- `times`

  The `times` method is an iterator used on integer values. It is used to repeatedly execute a block of code.

  ```
  3.times {puts 'Ruby rules'}
  ```

  This will print the line `'Ruby Rules'` three times.

- `map`

  The map method is commonly used with `Array` objects. It calls the passed block once for each element of the array on which it is called. Its return value is a new array containing each of the values returned by the subsequent calls to the block.

  ```
  [1,2,3].map {|x| x * x}
  #=> [1,4,9]
  ```

This example returns an array that contains the squares of each of the elements contained in the original array.

- upto

  The upto method is an iterator used with elements that have some form of ordering associated with them. Common examples of where you can use this method include integers and alphabetic characters as shown below:

  ```
  4.upto(7) {|x| puts x}
  ```

  ```
  'a'.upto('c') {|char| puts char}
  ```

  In the first example above, the values 4, 5, 6, and 7 are printed. In the second example, the characters a, b, and c are printed.

Exception handling

Every good developer should be familiar with error handling techniques and know how to handle errors that occur in a program. No matter how well you have written and tested your program, there will always be error conditions that occur in your program. These error conditions are not always the fault of the developer, but could be triggered by a number of things, including bad input from an external component , unavailable external resources, or incorrect usage by the end user

Before OOP became popular, error handling was mostly accomplished using return values and error codes. All of your functions would return a value that would indicate whether the function succeeded or failed. On failure, the return value would contain an error code or perhaps an error message. Unfortunately, this style of programming tends to require error-handling code around all of your functions and within the functions. Often, the purpose of a particular function is lost in so much error-handling code.

Object-oriented languages introduced a new style of error handling with a more object-oriented approach. This style uses *exception* objects that can be *thrown* and *caught* by your code and handled where appropriate. This style of error handling is usually referred to as *exception handling*. The exception handling features of Ruby allow you to handle unexpected conditions that occur while your code is running.

Exceptions in Ruby

In Ruby when an exceptional condition occurs, you can raise an exception using either the raise statement or the throw statement. When you raise an exception, control flow is diverted away from the current context to exception handling code. Exceptions that are raised can be caught with a rescue block. Rescue blocks are created with the rescue statement. Exceptions are represented as Exception objects. Exception objects are instances of the Exception class or a subclass of the Exception class. Ruby includes a hierarchy of built-in exception classes. There are seven classes that are direct subclasses of Exception. These are the following:

- NoMemoryError
- ScriptError

- `SecurityError`
- `SignalException`
- `SystemExit`
- `SystemStackError`
- `StandardError`

The `StandardError` exception class represents exceptions that are considered normal and that you should attempt to handle in your application code. The other exception classes represent lower-level and more serious errors that you most likely will not be able to recover from. Most programs do not attempt to handle these exception classes. There are many built-in subclasses of `StandardError`, and you are free to also create your own subclasses to define custom exceptions for your application.

The `Exception` class defines two methods that will help you get more information about the problem that occurred. These two methods should be implemented by all of its subclasses. The two methods are `message` and `backtrace`. The `message` method returns a string that gives human-readable information about the cause of the exception. The `backtrace` method returns an array of strings that represent the call stack at the point the exception was raised.

Using begin, raise, and rescue

The three statements that are used most often to perform exception handling in Ruby are the `raise`, `begin`, and `rescue` statements. The `raise` statement is used to create, or throw, and exception. You can call `raise` with zero, one, two, or three arguments. If you use `raise` with no arguments, a `RuntimeError` object is raised. If you use one argument with raise, one of the following conditions will apply:

- If the single argument is an `Exception` argument, that exception is raised.
- If the argument is a string, a `RuntimeError` is raised and the string is set as its message.
- If the argument is an object that has an `exception` method, that method should return an `Exception` class. The `Exception` class returned will be raised.

If you use raise with two arguments, the second argument should be a string that will get set as the message of the exception defined by the first argument. Finally, you can call raise with three arguments also. In that case, the first argument will define an exception class, the second argument will define a string to be set as the exception's message, and the third argument will contain an array of strings which will be set as the backtrace for the exception object.

Here is an example of how you might raise a `RuntimeError` exception with a specified message:

```
raise RuntimeError, "Bad value used."
```

The `begin` statement designates the start of a block of code for which you want to apply exception handling. The `rescue` statement specifies the start of a block of code that is executed if an exceptional condition occurs within the block of code that began with the `begin` statement. To illustrate the uses of exception handling in Ruby, you'll see how exception handling is commonly used along with Ruby's built-in file support to catch errors that might occur when you are trying to open a file.

```ruby
def read_file(file_name)
    begin
        afile = File.open(file_name, "r")
        buffer = afile.read(512)
    end

    rescue SystemCallError
        # handle error
    end

    rescue StandardError
        # handle error
    end

    rescue
        # default exception handler
    end
end
```

This method attempts to open a file with the name you pass into the method, and to read the first 512 bytes from it. An exception can be raised from within either the `File.open` or the `afile.read` methods. If an exception is raised within either of those methods, the control flow of the code will jump out of the `begin` block. The block that begins with the code `rescue SystemCallError` will be executed if a `SystemCallError` exception is raised. If the exception raised is a `StandardError` exception, the block that rescues `StandardError` will be executed. If the exception thrown is neither of those two types, the default exception handling block will be executed (this is the `rescue` block that does not specify a parameter).

As you saw in the previous example, a `rescue` block can specify a specific type of exception to handle, or not specify an exception type at all. If no exception type is specified, the block will handle any exception type that has not been handled by a previous `rescue` block. You can specify more than one exception type for a `rescue` block to handle also. For example, if you wanted to handle `SystemCallError` and `StandardError` the same way, you might write an exception handler like this:

```ruby
rescue SystemCallError, StandardError
    # handle error
end
```

In many cases, you will want to get information about the exception that occurred in the rescue block that handles it. You can access the exception object by defining a rescue block like this:

```ruby
rescue => ex
    puts "#{ex.class}: #{ex.message}"
end
```

In the above example, the exception object is stored in the ex variable. You can access any of the exception's methods through the ex variable. If your rescue clause is for a specific type of exception, the syntax to get the exception object would look like this:

```
rescue ArgumentError => ex
    puts "#{ex.class}: #{ex.message}"
end
```

More exception handling using ensure, retry, and else

Now that you have the basics of Ruby exception handling down, let's look at three additional statements that are part of Ruby's exception handling support. These are the ensure, retry, and else statements.

The retry statement

If you put a retry statement inside of a rescue block, the block of code that the rescue block is attached to will be run again. This is a good option for errors that are likely to resolve themselves. For example, if the load on a server was too high when you called it the first time, if you wait a bit and attempt the call again, it may succeed. The following code illustrates that scenario:

```
network_access_attempts = 0
begin
    network_access_attempts += 1
    open('http://www.timothyfisher.com/resource') do |f|
        puts f.readlines
    end
rescue OpenURI::HTTPError => ex
    if (network_access_attempts < 4)
        sleep(100)
        retry
    else
        # handle error condition
    end
end
```

In the begin block of this code, it attempts to open a network resource. If an exception is thrown while attempting to open that resource, the rescue block will be executed. Within the rescue block, we check to see if we have attempted to access the resource less than four times. If so, the code sleeps for 100 mS and then uses the retry statement to retry the begin block. If the same exception occurs four times, we give up and attempt to handle the error.

The else statement

A begin-rescue code block may also include an else block. The else block will be executed if the code in the begin block completes without raising any exceptions. Below is an example of how you might use an else block:

```
begin
    network_access_attempts += 1
```

```
    open('http://www.timothyfisher.com/resource') do |f|
        puts f.readlines
    end
rescue => ex
    puts 'Error reading file'
    puts "#{ex.class}: #{ex.message}"
else
    puts 'Successfully read the entire remote file'
end
```

If any exceptions are raised in the else block, they are not caught by any of the rescue statements attached to the begin block.

The ensure statement

The ensure statement is used to start a block that will always be executed, no matter what happens in the preceding begin block. The ensure block will be run after the begin block completes, or after a rescue statement completes if the begin block resulted in an exception. If the code also contains an else block, the else block will be run before the ensure block. The ensure block will always be the last block run. If control is transferred away from the begin block before it completes, perhaps by using a return statement, the ensure block will still be run, however the else block would not be run in that case. An else block is only run if the begin block runs to completion. An ensure block is always run no matter what happens in the begin block. Here is an example of exception handling code that uses an ensure block:

```
begin
    file = open("/some_file", "w")
    # write to the file
rescue => ex
    puts 'Error writing file'
    puts "#{ex.class}: #{ex.message}"
else
    puts 'Successfully updated file'
ensure
    file.close
end
```

In this example, the code opens a file and would then attempt to write to that file. If an exception occurs, the exception is printed to the screen. If the write completes successfully, a success message is printed to the screen using the else block. In either case, the ensure block runs to make sure that the file gets closed.

The normal use of an ensure block is to ensure that your code performs necessary housekeeping tasks, such as closing files, close database connections, or completing database transactions. Unless an ensure block contains an explicit return statement, it will not affect the return value of your method. For example, in the following code, the value returned will be hello and not goodbye. If you're wondering why hello is used as a return value, recall that the last value of a method is also the value that gets returned. The ensure block will not overwrite that return value.

```
begin
    'hello'
ensure
    'goodbye'
end
```

Organizing Code with Modules

One of the most commonly touted benefits of object oriented programming is that it can result in more reusable code. You can use reusable code in multiple applications, and it saves developers time and money. Organizing your code into classes and separating your classes into different files is one way of creating reusable chunks of code. Often, though, you may have a situation where you have a bunch of methods that don't naturally fall into a specific class, and yet they are methods that you find yourself using again and again, perhaps in many of your classes. This is where Ruby's concept of a module can help you out.

A *module* in Ruby provides a namespace that allows you to group methods and constants together, similar to the way a class groups methods and attributes. A Ruby module definition looks like this:

```
module Messaging
    def send_email
        ..
    end

    def send_im
        ...
    end

    def send_text_message
        ...
    end
end
```

This creates a `Messaging` module that bundles together methods related to sending a message over various protocols, e-mail, instant messaging, or text messaging. Any place where you wanted to use these methods, you could include this module as a mixin.

In addition to providing a convenient namespace and place to put methods and constants that do not fall naturally into a class definition, modules also give you the ability to use mixins. The Ruby concept of a *mixin* is a way of including methods and constants defined in a module into another module or class. Previously you saw how to define a Messaging module. Now if you have a `Notifier` class that you want to use these methods in, you would simply include this module like this:

```
require 'messaging'

class Notifier
```

```
        include Messaging
        …
    end
```

The `Notifier` class uses a `require` statement to import the file containing the `Messaging` module. This example assumes that the module is stored in a file contained in the same directory as the `Notifier` class, with a filename `messaging.rb`. The `include` statement imports all of the methods contained in the `Messaging` module into the `Notifier` class.

Perhaps the most common examples of mixins are the `Enumerable` and `Comparable` modules that are included with Ruby. These modules are mixed into quite a few classes by default, and you can easily mix them into your own classes as well. The `Enumerable` module defines useful iterators for any class that defines an `each` method. It is important to remember that the `Enumerable` module does not define the `each` method. You must define the `each` method in any class that you include the `Enumerable` module into. `Enumerable` defines methods such as `all?`, `any?`, `collect`, `find`, `find_all`, `include?`, `inject`, `map`, and `sort`. See the Ruby documentation Web site for a complete description of the methods of the `Enumerable` module `www.ruby-doc.org/core/classes/Enumerable.html`.

The `Comparable` module defines general comparison methods for any class that defines the `<=>` method. You can include the `Comparable` module into any class for which you have defined the `<=>` method. The `Comparable` module defines methods that look like operators such as: `<`, `<=`, `==`, `>`, and `>=`.

Advanced Ruby Techniques

In this section, you'll learn some additional techniques that will be useful to you when you are writing and studying Rails programs. The techniques described in this section are also used internally by Rails.

Variable length argument lists

All of the method examples that you've seen so far in this chapter have used fixed argument lists. Ruby also supports variable length argument lists. A method that allows a variable length argument list lets you call it with different numbers of methods in different situations. Take a look at the following example:

```ruby
def print_strings(*strings)
    strings.each { |str| puts str }
end
```

This is a method that will accept a variable number of arguments. The `strings` variable contains an array holding all of the arguments that are passed to this method. In the body of a method, the `each` iterator is used to step through each of the strings passed in and to print its value.

Dynamic programming with method_missing

The method_missing method is a feature of Ruby that you will find very useful in certain situations. Before you get into the details of that, though, let's talk about what is meant by the term *dynamic programming*. Dynamic programming is a style of programming in which you create code or change the nature of your program's code at run-time.

If you attempt to call a method that does not exist for the object you are using it on, you normally get an undefined method error. For example, try typing this code in irb:

```
class EmptyClass
end

obj = EmptyClass.new
obj.say_hello
```

In this code, you are attempting to call the method say_hello on an instance of the EmptyClass. Because this method does not exist, you will see an error message like the following printed to the console:

```
NoMethodError: undefined method 'say_hello' for
    #<EmptyClass:0x28f7d64>
      from (irb):31
      from :0
```

Here, irb is telling you that it cannot find this method in your class. Go ahead and exit that irb session to clear its memory and restart irb. Recreate the EmptyClass, slightly modified, as shown here:

```
class EmptyClass
    def method_missing(method, *args)
        puts 'Sorry, I could not find the method you are
    calling.'
        Puts "The method you called is #{method}."
    end
end

obj = EmptyClass.new
obj.say_hello
```

Now when you call the say_hello method in irb, you see this output:

```
Sorry, I could not find the method you are calling.
The method you called is say_hello.
```

As you can see, because the method you called could not be found in the EmptyClass, the method_missing method was called. The method_missing method is called by Ruby anytime you try to call a method that does not exist. The name of the method, and any arguments that you passed to the method you were trying to call, are also passed to the method_missing method.

Reopening classes

In Ruby, no class definition is ever final. You can reopen the definition of any Ruby class, including classes that you previously defined, even classes that are built into Ruby, and modify those class definitions to change the behavior of those classes.

Let's look at an example where you will reopen a commonly used built-in Ruby class, the `String` class. Try this out by typing the following code into an `irb` session:

```
class String
   def reverse_and_capitalize
      self.reverse.capitalize
   end
end
```

You've added a new instance method named `reverse_and_capitalize` to the `String` class. This method combines the features of the built-in `reverse` and `capitalize` methods. The `reverse_and_capitalize` method is now available on any string that you create. Try it out:

```
str = "say hello"
str.reverse_and_capitalize
=> "Olleh yas"
```

You created a string object the normal way and called the new method that you added. Your method is now a part of the `String` class, just like any other method that you use with the `String` class. In addition to adding methods, you could also redefine a method by reopening the class.

You can use this technique to extend external libraries that you use, as well as the built-in Ruby classes.

CAUTION Developers have expectations from commonly used methods, and if you change the behavior of those methods, you must make sure that it is well documented and everyone who uses your modification is aware of those changes.

Summary

This chapter has provided you with a basic overview of the Ruby programming language. While what it provided is far from a complete overview of Ruby, it should be more than enough to get you started writing Rails applications, which is the ultimate goal of this book.

As you begin writing Rails applications and as you gain more experience with both Ruby and Rails, your Ruby skills will increase, and I am certain you will seek out additional resources to further enhance your Ruby programming skills. *Programming Ruby: The Pragmatic Programmers' Guide* is often referred to as the Ruby Bible (also commonly called the pickaxe book because of the image of a pickaxe depicted on its cover) and is probably a book that you will want to own at some point. This book is written by a Ruby pioneer, Dave Thomas, and was one of the first Ruby language books published in the United States. It remains the most referenced and most used Ruby language book.

Chapter 2

Getting Started with Rails

In the summer of 2003, David Heinemeier Hansson was building the Basecamp Web application for a small company called 37signals. In the process of developing Basecamp, he created a core of functionality that he wanted to reuse on other applications he was developing. He extracted it and turned it into an open-source project that became Ruby on Rails.

Rails was first released to the public in the summer of 2004 as version 0.5. Hansson presented Ruby on Rails at the 2004 International Ruby Conference. Since its release, Rails has grown in popularity at an incredible pace. Version 1.0 of Rails was released on December 13, 2005. At the time of this writing, Rails is at version 1.2.

Rails' growth is not limited to the existing community of Ruby developers. It has pulled in converts from languages such as Java, PHP, and Perl, among others. By the time you read this, there will be more books available about Ruby on Rails than any other framework from any language. The Ruby on Rails framework has served as a catalyst for incredible growth of awareness and use of the Ruby programming language. The creator of the Ruby programming language, Yukihiro Matsumoto (known online as Matz), has referred to Rails as Ruby's Killer App.

> **TIP** To take a look at some existing applications created using Rails, check out the list of real-world Rails applications maintained on the official Ruby on Rails wiki site at http://wiki.rubyon rails.org/rails/pages/RealWorldUsage. You can find a list of the top 100 Rails sites, as ranked by Alexa.com, at http://rails100. pbwiki.com. Finally, the site www.happycodr.com provides a showcase for applications built with Rails.

IN THIS CHAPTER

What is Ruby on Rails?

Rails architecture

Rails scripts

Your first Rails application

More to get you started

What is Ruby on Rails?

Ruby on Rails is an application framework composed of several libraries; together, these libraries supply a complete framework for building Web applications. You can use Rails to build any kind of Web application. Common examples of applications built using Rails include blogs, wikis (sites that can be edited by anyone with access to them), project tracking applications, photo gallery applications, social networking applications, and online shopping sites. Any database-backed Web application is a good candidate for Rails development.

So what has made Rails such a popular framework over such a short span of time? A simple response is that Rails lets you build powerful Web applications quickly and easily by doing a majority of the work common to most Web applications. What makes Rails different from the many other existing Web application frameworks, such as Apache Struts, Apache Cocoon, and Perl's Maypole, is that Rails makes development fun and easy for the developer. Rails accomplishes this through many innovations that have not been seen before in any other framework.

The boost in productivity that can be gained by building a Web application with the Rails framework is well documented and has been one of its strongest selling points. More than one case study has shown that Web application development can be sped up by a factor of as much as ten by using the Rails framework and the Ruby language instead of more traditional Java or .Net architectures.

Rails provides a *full-stack framework*. This means that Rails provides all the pieces needed to build a complete Web application in one package. You don't need to cobble together several different frameworks to get the functionality that is common to most Web applications. Using the analogy of building a house, Rails supplies the complete plumbing, electrical, and framework already built. You just have to add the functionality and features specific to your application. The basic functions provided by Rails are:

- HTML templating
- Database storage and retrieval
- Handling of Web request and response
- HTML form handling

If you've done a significant amount of Web development in the past, with or without a framework, you've probably gotten used to having to know several different languages. It is common to have to switch back and forth between languages from task to task in typical Web application development. For example, your database setup and access is coded in SQL, your front end may be coded in some specific templating language, and your business logic may be in Java, .Net, or some other programming language.

When you write a Web application using Rails, almost all of the development you do is in Ruby. You can define your database in Ruby, access your database in Ruby, use Embedded Ruby (ERb) in your templates, and code your business logic in Ruby. This frees your mind to focus on one language to learn and know well.

Both within the Rails source code and externally, Rails espouses several design paradigms that you will run into again and again as you develop with Ruby on Rails. The following sections describe these paradigms.

DRY

Don't Repeat Yourself (DRY) is a philosophy that can be seen throughout the Rails framework. What this philosophy means is that you should not have to repeat yourself in code, configuration, or in many cases even documentation, within a single Web application. For example, in a Rails application, you define your database structure in one place and one place only.

You do not have your database structure defined in SQL files, configuration files, or model object files. This saves you work and prevents errors, as well. When something in your application changes, you only need to make the change in one place. You generally do not need to hunt through a mess of files in a Rails application to make a change to your application.

Convention over configuration

Rails relies on accepted convention over configuration. A common characteristic of many application frameworks is that you have to configure them using lengthy and complex XML files. Rails does what you might think it should do in most cases without having to specify any configuration. You are also able to override the default behavior of Rails in most areas when you need to do something that may be unconventional.

A good example of this philosophy in use within Rails is in the standard Rails routing mechanism. Without having to type a single line of configuration, Rails figures out which classes and methods handle every page request, simply by inspecting the URL. Rails has a standard or conventional format for specifying the URLs your application uses. The name of a controller class, an action method, and a primary key identifying a record being worked with are specified in the URL.

Opinionated software

The development team behind Rails is not shy about admitting that Rails contains built-in opinions of how Web applications should be developed and designed. Some developers might tell you that an application framework should be completely free of opinions, and designed to be as flexible as possible, accommodating any design decisions that application developers might want to use. Rejecting that view, the developers of Rails have staked out a vision and have taken a definite side on how applications should be developed.

The creator of Rails, David Heinemeier Hansson, has said that the *opinionated software* aspect of Ruby on Rails has been a large contributor to its ease of use and its overall success. By not trying to be all things to all people, Rails focuses on doing what it does exceptionally well, and in most cases it succeeds with flying colors. By sacrificing some flexibility at the infrastructure layer provided by Rails, you gain tremendous flexibility at the application layer, where you will be more productive and better able to implement your application the way you want it sooner and better.

Throughout the remainder of this book, David Heinemeier Hansson is referred to by his initials DHH. This practice is common throughout Rails literature, probably due to the length of his name. Anytime you see a reference to DHH, you now know that it refers to the Rails creator.

The paradigm *convention over configuration* is a characteristic of opinionated software. By following the opinions set forth by the designers of Rails, you gain tremendous productivity by avoiding having to deal with configuration files. Rails also has an opinion of how your database should be designed, including details such as table-naming conventions. If you adhere to those opinions, you gain tremendous productivity by giving Rails the ability to automatically generate the vast majority of your database access code.

Rails Architecture

When developers are talking about *architecture*, they are speaking about the way an application's code and other components are assembled together into a whole that makes up the application. A good software architecture can make an application easier to develop, maintain, understand, and extend. A good software architecture also improves the quality of an application.

The architecture of the Rails framework is one of its many strengths. It provides a solid foundation upon which you can build your own applications.

MVC

The *Model-View-Controller,* or MVC, design pattern, has long been accepted as a better way to architect software applications. MVC is accepted as a better way because it makes applications easier to develop, understand, and maintain. MVC simplifies the implementation of an application by dividing it into several layers, each with a given role and responsibilities.

The layers that make up an MVC application are the Model, the View, and the Controller layers. The model layer is responsible for maintaining the state of an application. It encapsulates an application's data and business logic for manipulating the data. The view layer provides the user interface of an application. The controller layer is responsible for figuring out what to do with user and other external input. The controller layer interprets user input and responds to user requests by communicating with the model layer, and rendering views using the view layer.

You can think of the controller as the conductor of the application. It determines which views to show, based on the input received.

MVC was originally created with desktop GUI applications in mind. When developers first started writing Web applications, they took a step backward and seemed to have forgotten the benefits of MVC. Many of the early Web applications mixed business logic, presentation, data access, and event handling all in giant, complex script files written in languages such as PHP, Perl, and Java's JSP. As Web applications became larger and grew in complexity, developers and Web architects realized they would need a better architecture to support these large applications. Web development frameworks such as Struts and WebObjects began to emerge, which brought the MVC design pattern back to Web applications.

The MVC design pattern, as applied to a Web application, is shown graphically in Figure 2.1. In the context of a Web application, the view layer represents the Web pages that make up the user interface of a Web application. The controller layer handles the HTTP requests and communicates with the model layer. The model layer communicates with a database and performs necessary business logic required to manipulate the data.

FIGURE 2.1

MVC architecture of a Web application

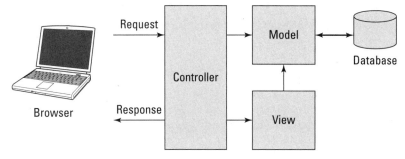

Rails and MVC

The MVC design pattern is at the core of the Rails framework. By using Ruby on Rails, your Web application will also use the MVC design pattern. The implementation of Rails is divided into libraries based around each layer of the MVC pattern. Model, view, and controller layer separation is very visible to Rails application developers. Most classes that you will write while building a Rails application will be one of these three types and, as discussed later in this chapter, they are even organized into model, view, and controller directories.

The ActiveRecord library provides the foundation of the model layer. ActiveRecord, and the model classes that you build on top of ActiveRecord, provide the model layer of your application. This layer provides *object relational mapping* (ORM) between Rails classes and the database you use, such as MySQL, Oracle, or some other database. An ORM maps relational database structures to an object hierarchy. It is possible to build a Rails application that does not use a database, but that is not common. If you were not using a database, your model layer might use some other form of persistent storage, or perhaps just provide business logic if your application does not provide any persistent storage.

NOTE ActiveRecord is based on a design pattern by Martin Fowler. You can read more about the ActiveRecord design pattern at www.martinfowler.com/eaaCatalog/ activeRecord.html.

The view layer of a Rails application is implemented in ERB template files. These files contain a mixture of HTML and embedded Ruby code (ERb), and are similar to JSP, ASP, or PHP files. There are two other built-in template file types that Rails supports. One file type is RXML files, which give you an easy way to create XML files using Ruby code.

The other file type is RJS files, which allow you to create JavaScript fragments using Ruby code. RJS stands for Ruby JavaScript. The JavaScript fragments are executed in the client browser just as JavaScript embedded in an HTML file is. The use of RJS is a common technique used for creating AJAX features. The Rails code that implements this feature comes from a library called Action Pack.

CROSS-REF For more information on using RJS to create AJAX features, see Chapter 5.

The Rails controller implementation, also part of the Action Pack library, insulates developers from having to deal with CGI and related request and response data, including form data. Controllers handle incoming browser requests, call appropriate functions on model objects, and render your view templates into pure HTML, which the Web server then returns to the browser.

Rails provides you with very simple methods for getting data sent from a Web page, and simple methods for returning data for presentation in Web pages. In the course of developing a Rails application, you will write many controller classes. Controller classes are written in pure Ruby and contain methods referred to as *actions*. Generally, a single controller corresponds to a single Web page, and each action corresponds to an action that you can perform on that Web page.

Figure 2.2 shows how a Rails application implements the MVC design pattern, and how requests are routed from a browser through the application.

FIGURE 2.2

Ruby on Rails MVC implementation

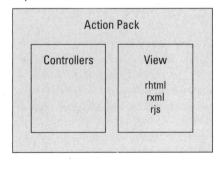

All Rails applications are laid out in an identical style in terms of directory structure and locations of files. Following is an overview of the standard directory structure of a Rails application. Later in this chapter, when you create your first Rails application, you can see how easy it is to automatically generate this entire directory tree. Each directory and its contents are described here:

- **app:** Where all the application's MVC code goes
- **config:** Application configuration files
- **db:** Database schema and migration files
- **doc:** Documentation for your application
- **lib:** Application-specific custom code that isn't part of your MVC code
- **log:** The application log files automatically created by Rails
- **public:** JavaScript, CSS, images, and other static files
- **script:** Rails scripts for code generation, debugging, and performance utilities
- **test:** Unit-test related code and related files
- **tmp:** Cache, session information, and socket files used by the Web server
- **vendor:** Where Rails plug-ins are installed

Rails Scripts

In addition to providing an application development framework that you use to write your Web application, Rails also provides some excellent tools that assist you in the process of developing your application. These tools are packaged as scripts that you run from the command-line of whatever operating system you develop on.

The most important scripts to become familiar with and use regularly in your development are:

- Rails Console
- WEBrick Web server
- Generators
- Migrations

Each of these script types is described in the next section.

Rails Console

The Rails Console is a command-line utility that lets you run a Rails application in a full Rails environment right from the command-line. This is an invaluable tool for debugging during the development process. You may recall that the last chapter introduced the Interactive Ruby console (irb). The Rails Console is an extension of irb, offering all the features of irb along with the ability to auto-load your complete Rails application environment, including all its classes and components. Using the Rails Console, you can walk through your application step-by-step and look at its state at any point of execution.

WEBrick

WEBrick is a Web server included with the Rails framework, and is ideal for local developer testing. The WEBrick server is written in pure Ruby and runs on any platform that you develop on, including Windows, Mac, or Unix. Rails is configured to automatically make use of the WEBrick server. Alternatively, if you have the Mongrel or lighttpd sever installed on your system, Rails uses either of those servers.

A really great feature about WEBrick, Mongrel, and lighttpd is that they all feature automatic reloading of code. This means that when you change your source code, you do not have to restart the server to have it take effect. You can immediately reload a Web page to see any of your changes take effect.

Generators

Rails includes code generation scripts, which are used to automatically generate model and controller classes for your application. Code generation is an important part of Rails that can increase your productivity when developing Web applications. By running a simple command-line script, you can generate skeleton files for all of your model and controller classes.

The code generation script also generates database migration files for each model it generates, as well as unit tests and associated fixtures. With more experience, you can even write your own generators to automatically generate pieces of your application that you find yourself using frequently.

CROSS-REF For more information about writing your own generators, check out Chapter 11.

Migrations

Migrations are a very cool feature of Rails that can make your life simpler and easier. They bring the principle of DRY to life. *Migrations* are pure Ruby code that define the structure of a database. When you use migrations, you no longer have to write SQL to create your database. Over the course of a project, it is very common for your database schema to evolve as you learn more about your problem domain.

Migrations are written such that each change you make to your database schema is isolated in a separate migration file, which has a method to implement or reverse the change. This makes it an easy process to roll forward or backward across revisions of your project's schema. Migration files are run with a special Rails script.

Your First Rails Application

At this point, although this chapter has barely scratched the surface of Rails and has not yet gone into any detail on any of the components that make up Rails, you can write your first Rails application. This section shows you how easy it is to write a simple Rails application, and how quickly you can get up and running with a basic application skeleton. The application you create in this section even includes a database.

As you work through this application, you are very much encouraged to follow along on your computer and build the application as you read this section. Reading coupled with practice is a much more efficient way of learning than through reading alone. However, for those who just want to download the completed application, you can find it on this book's Web site, `rubyonrails bible.com`. Even if you download the completed application, you should still read through this section, as it presents many general Rails development concepts in the context of developing the application.

If you've been reading this book from the start, you should already have a working installation of Rails and MySQL on your computer. If you do not yet have Rails or MySQL installed and need help getting them installed, see this book's Quick Start chapter for complete installation instructions.

Each of the following five steps is described in the sections that follow.

1. **Create the project using the `rails` command.**
2. **Set up the database.**
3. **Create the model.**
4. **Create the controller and views.**
5. **Style the application.**

Create the project

The first step in creating a Rails application is to use the `rails` command-line program to generate the directory structure for your application. For your first Rails application, this section walks you through steps to create a very simplified version of a contact list manager.

This application implements a reasonable amount of real-world functionality, while remaining simple enough to not make your learning curve too steep. First create a directory called `rails_projects` that will serve as the root of the Rails projects that you can build throughout this book. After you've created the `rails_projects` directory, navigate into that directory and run the `rails` project generation script, as shown here:

```
cd rails_projects
rails contactlist
  create
  create app/controllers
  create app/helpers
  create app/models
  create app/views/layouts
  create config/environments
  create config/initializers
  create db
  create doc
  create lib
  ...
  create log/production.log
  create log/development.log
  create log/test.log
```

This script creates a directory called `contactlist` inside your `rails_projects` directory. Inside the `contactlist` directory, you can see that the `rails` command created the complete Rails standard directory structure that is common to all Rails applications. Standard versions of many files required by Rails were also created and put in their appropriate directories.

For example, the last three files created are the Rails log files. A separate log file is created for each environment used in the standard development process: development, test, and production. This simple command has done a tremendous amount of work for you. It also provides the benefit of creating a standard directory structure that is common across all Rails applications.

If you work on several Rails applications, you can always rely on files being located in the same places, no matter what the application is. Although it is easy to take this for granted, few other frameworks prior to Rails enforced such a practice. If you've spent a lot of time developing Java applications, you never know where you are going to find a given file or what the directory structure might look like as you transition across Java projects.

As mentioned earlier, Rails is compatible with many different Web servers. For your first application, stay with the Web server that is distributed with Rails, WEBrick. This allows you to launch the Web server to test out your application at any time without going through the trouble of installing another Web server. Now that you've generated the skeleton of your first application, start WEBrick and see what you've achieved with a single command.

```
ruby script/server Webrick
    Booting WEBrick
    Rails application started on http://0.0.0.0:3000
    Ctrl-C to shutdown server; call with --help for options
    ..
```

The `script/server` command tells Rails to start up the server specified as a parameter, in this case WEBrick. In UNIX environments, you normally would not have to precede the command with `ruby`, so you could just type `./script/server Webrick`. Also, the server name parameter is not required if WEBrick is the only server you have configured for your Rails application. As a result, this command would also start the WEBrick server: `ruby script/server`.

By default, WEBrick always binds to port 3000. If you want to change the default port assignment, you can do that in the `environment.rb` file, which is covered later in this book. You can also specify a different port from the command-line when you start up the server using the `-p` option as shown here:

```
ruby script/server -p 80
```

This command would start the server bound to port 80.

Now open your browser of choice and navigate to `http://localhost:3000` to see the screen shown in Figure 2.3. You can see that by simply running the Rails generation script, you have the skeleton of a working Web application with no additional work yet on your part. Of course, a skeleton is all the application is in its current form. Now comes the more interesting task of actually making your application do something useful, or at least useful in the context of saying you wrote your first Rails application.

If you look back at the console window where you started the server, you can see that some log messages have printed. As your Rails application runs, it continuously outputs messages to this window, which allows you to trace your application and figure out what it is doing.

Note that the default Rails Web page shown in Figure 2.3 also lists the typical steps involved in getting your application built. Follow the steps shown in this figure for the remainder of this section.

> **NOTE** Throughout the rest of this chapter, the root directory, `rails_projects/contactlist`, will not be specified. When you see a directory mentioned, such as `app/models`, you should assume that it is located in the `rails_projects/contactlist` directory unless otherwise specified.

FIGURE 2.3

The default Rails application start page

Set up the database

Begin by creating a simple database using MySQL with one table that will hold a list of contacts. In this database, titled `contactlist_development`, create one table with the name contacts. This table will hold contact information for your application. Use the command-line interface of MySQL to do this:

```
mysql -u root -p
Enter password:
Welcome to the MySQL monitor. Commands end with ; or \g.
Your MySQL connection id is 2
Server version: 5.0.45-community-nt MySQL Community Edition (GPL)

Type 'help;' or '\h' for help. Type '\c' to clear the buffer.

mysql> create database contactlist_development;
Query OK, 1 row affected (0.29 sec)

mysql> use contactlist_development;
Database changed
mysql> create table contacts (
        -> id          int           not null auto_increment,
        -> first_name varchar(100)  not null,
        -> last_name  varchar(100)  not null,
        -> address    varchar(255)  not null,
        -> city       varchar(100)  not null,
        -> state      varchar(2)    not null,
        -> country    varchar(100)  not null,
        -> phone      varchar(15)   not null,
        -> email      varchar(100),
        -> primary key(id) );
Query OK, 0 rows affected (0.40 sec)
```

You can verify that you created the database and table correctly using the Show and Describe commands, as shown here:

```
mysql> show tables;
+----------------------------------+
| Tables_in_contactlist_development |
+----------------------------------+
| contacts |
+----------------------------------+
1 row in set (0.00 sec)

mysql> describe contacts;
+------------+--------------+------+-----+---------+-------------
   ---+
| Field | Type | Null | Key | Default | Extra |
+------------+--------------+------+-----+---------+-------------
   ---+
| id | int(11) | NO | PRI | NULL | auto_increment |
| first_name | varchar(100) | NO | | | |
| last_name | varchar(100) | NO | | | |
| address | varchar(255) | NO | | | |
| city | varchar(100) | NO | | | |
| state | varchar(2) | NO | | | |
```

```
| country | varchar(100) | NO | | | |
| phone | varchar(15) | NO | | | |
| email | varchar(100) | NO | | NULL | |
+-----------+--------------+------+-----+---------+-------------
    ---+
9 rows in set (0.02 sec)
```

You should now have your database completely set up and ready to use. The database is strategically named `contactlist_development`, which is the same name you gave to your project, with the addition of the `development` suffix. This allows you to take advantage of more Rails automation, or convention-over-configuration, magic.

Rails automatically looks for databases that have the same name as the project, plus the environment suffixes (`_development`, `_test`, `_production`). Of course, if you want to use a different name for your database, you are able to do that by specifying the name of your database in the `config/database.yml` file.

CROSS-REF In Chapter 3 you will learn an easier way to create your database without having to use the `mysql` command-line application at all. Instead you will use a simple rake task to create the database.

Create the model

Now that you have a working database, the next step in creating your Rails application is to create your model classes. In case you forgot, the model classes are responsible for managing an application's data and business logic. If you were to look at a description of the business problem your application is trying to solve, the model classes will usually correspond to the nouns that show up in that description.

For a contact list application, the most obvious noun that would show up would be the noun, contact. Rails gives you a generate script which allows you to automatically generate class files for models, views, and controllers.

The generate script is located in the script directory at the root of your Rails application. The first generate script parameter is the name of the object type you want to generate, in this case a model object. The second parameter is the name you want to give the model that is generated. Use the name Contact for your model class. This parameter is case-insensitive, and so you could specify it as either `Contact` or `contact`.

Using the generate script, go ahead and create the `Contact` model.

```
ruby script/generate model Contact
exists app/models/
exists test/unit/
exists test/fixtures/
create app/models/contact.rb
create test/unit/contact_test.rb
create test/fixtures/contacts.yml
create db/migrate
create db/migrate/001_create_contacts.rb
```

Notice that the choice of the name Contact for the model class is the same name given to the name of the table minus the plural. This is not an accident. By giving the model the same name as your table name, Rails provides you with a wealth of functionality for this model object, without having to write any code yourself. Again, you see an example of convention over configuration here. By sticking with the Rails conventions for naming database tables and model classes, you will gain a great deal of functionality with no configuration required.

Notice that by running this generate script, Rails created four files. The first file created, `contact.rb`, is your model object. This was created in the `app/models` directory. The `app` directory is the home for all of an application's model, view, and controller classes.

The second file created is the `contact_test.rb` file. This file contains the skeleton for a unit test that you can use to write unit tests in for the `Contact` object. This was created in the `test/unit` directory. Rails places all test-related files into the project's `test` directory. The subdirectory of `test`, called `unit`, contains unit test files. The third file created is another test-related file, `contacts.yml`. This file is called a *fixture file*, which is used to set up test data for your unit tests. Fixtures are covered in more detail later in this book.

CROSS-REF Developer testing in a Rails application is covered in detail in chapter 9. Developer testing includes unit, functional, and integration testing. Rails provides built-in support for each of these types of tests.

The fourth file created is a migration class, `001_create_contacts.rb`. This contains an empty migration class that you could use to create a migration for creating the contacts table in the database. Because you already did that using MySQL, you don't need to worry about the migration file in this chapter.

CROSS-REF For more information about cover migrations, check out the details of the model layer, as discussed in Chapter 3.

Take a look at the contents of the `app/models/contact.rb` file. Your file should look like this:

```
class Contact < ActiveRecord::Base
end
```

Were you expecting to see more? This is an empty class definition of a class called `Contact` that extends from the `ActiveRecord::Base` class. While this doesn't look like it provides much functionality, your class has gained quite a bit of functionality just by extending from the `ActiveRecord::Base` class. Thanks to magic provided by ActiveRecord, your `Contact` class now fully understands the contacts table that you created in the database earlier. You can use this class to create Contact objects, read contact records from the database, and store contact data to the database. All this without writing a single line of model code.

You probably want to see this for yourself, so start the Rails Console and play around with your new `Contact` class a little.

1. **Start the Rails Console.** From the root directory of your contactlist project, type this:

```
ruby script/console
Loading development environment
>>
```

This starts up the Rails Console and loads your application's environment.

2. **Create a new Contact model object.** At the >> prompt, you can now type any valid Ruby syntax. Try this:

```
>> my_contact = Contact.new
=> #<Contact:0x476d488 @attributes={"city"=>"", "country"=>"",
   "first_name"=>"", "address"=>"", "last_name"=>"",
   "email"=>nil, "state"=>""}, @new_record=true>
>>
```

After you type the first line, the second line shown above is the response you get. Throughout this book and while you're in the Rails Console, you can differentiate input that you type from output by the prompt preceding the line. The >> prompt is the input line prompt. The => prompt begins lines that contain the Console output.

The Rails Console always prints the final return value of whatever method was executed by the statement you typed. In this example, what you see is the notation for a Contact object instance. The `Contact.new` statement caused a new instance of Contact to be created and returned. This instance contains an attribute for each field that you created in the contacts database table. This is the first proof you have that the Contact object really has been tied to the contacts database table, through no code of your own. The hexadecimal number near the beginning of the return value following `#<Contact:` is probably a different value on your computer. This is the address that is assigned to the object that was created. You usually don't have to pay much attention to that number.

3. **Continue by assigning some values to the object's attributes.** As you type each of the lines below, you will see the attribute value printed as output:

```
>> my_contact.first_name = 'Timothy'
>> my_contact.last_name = 'Fisher'
>> my_contact.address = '25296 Hunter Lane'
>> my_contact.city = 'Flat Rock'
>> my_contact.state = 'MI'
>> my_contact.country = 'USA'
>> my_contact.phone = '555-555-5555'
>> my_contact.email = 'tim@timothyfisher.com'
```

4. **Save the contact object.** Run the object's `save` method to have this data saved to the database. The `save` method is inherited from the `ActiveRecord::Base` class.

```
>> my_contact.save
=> true
```

You have now created a new contact using the `Contact` model object. By calling it `save` method, a new record has been created in your `contactlist_development` database. Now you can use the `Contact` object to find and retrieve from the database the record that you just created. To do this, use a class method of Contact called `find`.

1. **Load your contact object from the database.** Make sure you are still in the Rails Console, and then try this:

```
>> result = Contact.find(:first)
=> #<Contact:0x474c864 @attributes={"city"=>"Flat Rock",
   "country"=>"USA", "id"=>"1", "phone"=>"555-555-5555",
   "first_name"=>"Timothy", "address"=>"25296 Hunter Lane",
   "last_name"=>"Fisher", "email"=>"tim@timothyfisher.com",
   "state"=>"MI"}>
>>
```

An instance of the `Contact` class representing the data record found in the database is returned and printed to the console after executing the `find` method. The single argument you passed to the `find` method is `:first`. This is a Ruby symbol that the `find` method interprets to mean 'find the first row in the contacts table.'

2. **Print an attribute.** Try printing the `first_name` attribute of the `result` object to verify that it contains the data you expect:

```
>> puts result.first_name
Timothy
=> nil
>>
```

As you can see, the value `Timothy` is printed to the screen by the `puts` command. The return value of `puts` is always `nil`. That is why you also see `nil` printed following the `first_name` value.

Now you've created your `Contact` model object and convinced yourself that it is connected to the contacts table through some Rails code contained in the `ActiveRecord::Base` class.

Create the controller and views

You have a database and you have a model class. Now you need a way to talk to the model class from a Web application. This is where you use the controller and view layers of the MVC architecture. The controller you create will allow you to perform three of the four standard create, read, update, and delete (CRUD) operations on your contact list data. You will implement create, read, and update. Because this controller provides functionality related to the Contact model, call the controller the `ContactController`.

If you look at sample Rails code, you'll find that some developers would name the controller `ContactsController` instead of `ContactController`. Note the difference in plurality. Later in this chapter, you will see an example of Rails scaffolding which automatically creates controllers for your model objects. When you generate scaffolding, a pluralized controller is created. Pluralizing the controller name would seem to make sense as it is a controller that allows you to work with your contacts. I believe it is easy to justify either name, so my suggestion is to use the naming style you prefer and stick with it.

Just as you used the generate script to create your model class, use the generate script to create the controller and view classes. You simply have to change the first parameter to the generate script to the word `controller`, and Rails will generate the controller class given the name you pass as the second parameter. When you specify your controller name to the generator, you do not append the word Controller. For example, for the `ContactController`, you would just use the word Contact. Go ahead and generate your controller now:

```
ruby script/generate controller Contact
exists  app/controllers/
exists  app/helpers/
create  app/views/contact
exists  test/functional
create  app/controllers/contact_controller.rb
create  test/functional/contact_controller_test.rb
create  app/helpers/contact_helper.rb
```

From the output you see after generating your controller, notice that Rails has generated more than just your controller object; Rails has also created a directory to hold views, a helper file, and a functional test file. These are objects that you generally always need to use in conjunction with a controller, and so the developers of Rails have simplified your life by just creating them all at once —you don't have to do any extra work. The `app/views/contact` folder will hold the `html.erb` view files associated with this controller.

The controller object is in the `app/controllers/contact_controller.rb` file. Take a look at that file. You should see this:

```
class ContactController < ApplicationController
end
```

After having seen the model file, perhaps you're not surprised to see such a short file. The `ContactController` class extends the `ApplicationController` class. You can find the `ApplicationController` class in the `app/controllers` directory with the filename `application.rb`. The `ApplicationController` class is where you place functionality that you want to be available to all of your application's controllers. If you were to look at the `ApplicationController` class, you would see that it inherits from another Rails class, `ActionController::Base`. `ActionController::Base` is a Rails class that provides all controllers with methods for performing common Web programming tasks, such as accessing form and session data.

To implement the required functionality for the contact list application, you will be adding the following methods to the controller class: `index`, `show`, `new`, `create`, and `update`. In many Rails applications it is common convention to use a method named index as the method that displays a list of all the objects of a given type. So for your application, the `index` method will display a list of all available contacts. The functionality of the other methods should be self-explanatory based on their name.

Open the `contact_controller.rb` file and add these methods, as shown here:

```
class ContactController < ApplicationController
      def index
      end

      def show
      end

      def new
      end
      def create
      end

      def update
      end
end
```

Each of these methods will handle a different type of request from the browser. There will also be a view template associated with the index, show, and new methods. The create and update methods to not need view templates because they simply process the forms displayed by new and show respectively and then redirect the user to the index method to show all contacts again.

By default, Rails looks for a view template that contains the same name as the controller method and renders that template after running the controller method. As a result, the index method would render a template located in app/views/contact with the name index.html.erb. Methods in a controller class that handle Web requests are called *actions* in Rails nomenclature.

You have created actions for index, show, new, create, and update in the ContactController. As you complete the remainder of the Contacts application in this chapter, you'll implement these actions to perform the following functions:

- index: This action is called to display a list of all contacts stored in the database.

- show: This action is called to display the details of a selected contact. The details are displayed on an editable form that the user can also use to make updates to the contact.

- new: This action is used to display a form that will be used by the user to create a new contact. Do not confuse this instance method with the class method named new that is common to all classes.

- create: This action is called to process the request to create a new contact.

- update: This action is called to process the request to update an existing contact.

From these descriptions, note that show and update form a related pair of actions, as do new and create. The show action will always be called before the update action is called, and the new action will always be called before the create action is called. In both of these instances, one action displays a form, and the other action processes the form submit.

Implementing the index action

First, focus on the `index` method. The `index` method prints a list of all the contacts stored in the database.

Create the index action. Open up the `app/controllers/contact_controller.rb` class and create the index method as shown here:

```
def index
    @contacts = Contact.find(:all)
end
```

The single line you've added to the `index` method is enough for your application to be able to retrieve all of the contact records contained in the database. This is done using the `find` class method on the `Contact` class. The parameter `:all` tells the `find` method that you want it to return all of the contacts that it finds. The contacts are returned as an array of `Contact` objects and stored in the `@contacts` instance variable.

Recall that in Ruby, the `@` symbol preceding a variable name makes that variable an instance variable. It is very important that you store the results of `Contact.find(:all)` into an instance variable because instance variables are also accessible from the view templates. This bit of controller code has made the list of contacts available to your index view template, which you will implement next.

You need to create a view template to display the contacts, but before you do that, you've now reached a good point in your application to discuss how Rails routes to a specific controller and method based on a URL. The routing mechanism that Rails uses is another example of the framework's use of convention over configuration. By default, Rails uses the following pattern to decide where to route URLs:

```
www.someapp.com/controller/method/id
```

The first path element in the above example URL `controller` is the name of the controller to use. The second path element `method` is the specific method contained in the controller to call. A method in a controller class that handles requests and can be routed to directly is also often referred to in Rails as an action.

Finally, the `id` is the id of an element that is passed to the method as a parameter called id. Not all of the controller methods require the id to be passed, and so that element is optional. The method `index` is a default action in Rails and can be omitted if you want to call that action. As a result, if you pass only a controller name in your URL, your request is routed to the default action name `index`.

Try starting the server again, and view the application to this point in the browser to see what kind of results you've achieved. This is also a good check to make sure you've done everything right up to this point. Start the server with this command:

```
ruby script/server
```

Once you see the response messages telling you that the server has successfully started, open a browser and navigate to this address: `http://localhost:3000/contact/index`.

Based on what was discussed about how Rails routes URLs, you should be able to realize that this URL will route to the `index` method of the Contact controller. You should see the message shown in Figure 2.4. This screen tells you that Rails is trying to render a template located in `app/views/contact/index.html.erb`.

Because you have not yet created that template, you get the `Template is missing` error display. Since `index` is the default method for a controller, you could also have navigated to it without specifying the action, like this: `http://localhost:3000/contact`.

FIGURE 2.4

The Missing Template page

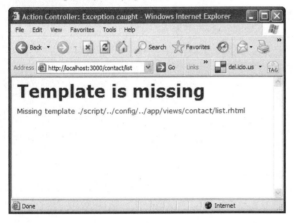

Create the index template. In order to display the list of records on a Web page, you now need to create an `index.html.erb` template in the `app/views/contact` directory.

Create a file called `index.html.erb` in the `app/views/contact` directory. Type the following line into it and then save it:

```
My Contacts
```

Now go back to your browser, still pointing at `http://localhost:3000/contact/index`, and refresh the page. You should see the contents of the `index.html.erb` file displayed.

You've now reached an important milestone in your development. You have successfully routed a URL to a method in a controller that you wrote, and a view template that you wrote. You still can't see the list of contacts that you are after, though, and so you need to go back into `index.html.erb` and do the real work of displaying the contact list. Type this code into `index.html.erb`:

```
<h1>My Contact List</h1>
<% if @contacts.blank? %>
 <p>No contacts to display.</p>
<% else %>
  <ul id="contacts">
    <% @contacts.each do |c| %>
      <li>
        <%= link_to c.first_name+' '+c.last_name,
                  {:action => 'show', :id => c.id} -%>
      </li>
    <% end %>
  </ul>
<% end %>
<p><%= link_to "New Contact", {:action => 'new' } %></p>
```

Now if you refresh the browser, you should see the screen shown in Figure 2.5. If you have been following along with this example, the contact list should contain the single record that you created in the database earlier when you were testing the `Contact` model class using the Rails Console. The contact should be a link, and you should also see a *New Contact* link. Let me walk you through the code that you typed in to get this screen.

First, I'll explain some embedded Ruby (ERb) syntax. Notice that several lines in the above code are surrounded by `<% %>` and `<%= %>`. These symbols let Rails know that what's enclosed is Ruby code, which should be interpreted prior to returning the page. The `<% %>` syntax surrounds Ruby statements that do not return strings to be displayed. The `<%= %>` syntax surrounds Ruby statements that result in a string that is inserted into the HTML at the location of the statements.

Look at lines 2 and 3:

```
<% if @contacts.blank? %>
  <p>No contacts to display.</p>
```

The ContactList list view

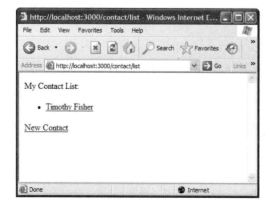

87

Check to see if the `@contacts` array is blank or empty. The `blank?` method returns true if the array is empty; otherwise, it returns false. If the array is empty, the message `"No contacts to display"` appears on the screen.

The next portion of the code, lines 5 to 11, is reached if the `@contacts` array contains one or more items:

```
<ul id="contacts">
  <% @contacts.each do |c| %>
    <li>
      <%= link_to c.first_name+' '+c.last_name,
                  {:action => 'show', :id => c.id} -%>
    </li>
  <% end %>
</ul>
```

This block of code creates an unordered list that contains a list item for each of the contacts in the `@contacts` array. The `each` method is an iterator that steps through each of the items contained in the `@contacts` array. For each item in the array, the block of code surrounded by the `do` and `end` statements is executed. Immediately following the `do` statement is the syntax `|c|`. This means that each item in the `@contacts` array is placed in the `c` variable.

For each item, the Rails `link_to` helper method is used, which creates an HTML link. The first parameter passed to `link_to` is the text that is placed between the `<a>` and `</a>` tags. The second parameter specifies the action that is called when the link is clicked. For example, this code:

```
<%= link_to 'Timothy Fisher', {:action => 'show', :id => 1} -%>
```

ends up on the resulting Web page as:

```
<a href="contact/show/1">Timothy Fisher</a>
```

For each of the contacts, then, a link is created containing the contact's first and last name joined together. The `href` of the link will consist of `contact/show/` followed by the `id` of the contact being displayed.

In the last line of the template:

```
<p><%= link_to "New Contact", {:action => 'new' } %></p>
```

you again use the `link_to` method to create a link for adding a new contact. This link displays the text `New Contact` and calls the action `new` when clicked.

You now have a completed list view. No matter how many contacts you have in the database, this simple view displays a list of all the contacts. When you click any contact, you are routed to the `show` action. That action should cause the Web application to display a page that can be used to view and edit the details of a contact. Next you'll implement the `new` action and its associated view template so that you will be able to add additional entries into your contacts database.

Implementing the new action

With what you have implemented so far, you can start the contact list application and view a list of all of your contacts. Now let's go ahead and create the controller method and view template that will allow you to display a form from which a user can create a new contact.

1. **Create the new action.** Open up the `contact_controller.rb` file and modify the new method to look like this:

```
def new
    @contact = Contact.new
end
```

The single line in the new method creates a new `Contact` object that will be used to hold the new contact information you create. Next, you'll create a view template to display the new contact form in the browser.

2. **Create the new template.** In the `app/views/contact` directory, create a new file named `new.html.erb`. This will be the template for creating a new contact. Type the following code into this file:

```
<h1>Create New Contact</h1>
<% form_for :contact, :url => {action=>'create'} do |f|
 <p><label for="contact_first_name">First Name:</label>
 <%= f.text_field 'contact', 'first_name' %></p>

 <p><label for="contact_last_name">Last Name:</label>
 <%= f.text_field 'contact', 'last_name' %></p>

 <p><label for="contact_address">Address:</label>
 <%= f.text_field 'contact', 'address' %></p>

 <p><label for="contact_city">City:</label>
 <%= f.text_field 'contact', 'city' %></p>

 <p><label for="contact_state">State:</label>
 <%= f.text_field 'contact', 'state' %></p>

 <p><label for="contact_country">Country:</label>
 <%= text_field 'contact', 'country' %></p>

 <p><label for="contact_phone">Phone:</label>
 <%= f.text_field 'contact', 'phone' %></p>

 <p><label for="contact_email">Email:</label>
 <%= f.text_field 'contact', 'email' %></p>

 <%= f.submit "Create" %>
<% end %>

<p><%= link_to 'Back', {:action => 'index'} %></p>
```

Now let's walk through the code you created in the `new.html.erb` template. There are really only a few interesting things going on in this template. First, look at the second line of the template:

```
<% form_for :contact, :url => :action=>'create' do |f| %>
```

In this line, you use a Rails helper method `form_for`. This method creates the opening tag for an HTML form. You pass three parameters to the `form_for` tag. The first parameter specifies the object type for which the form is being created. In this case that is a contact object. The second parameter specifies where the form should be submitted. In this case, the form is submitted to the `create` action.

Since a controller is not specified it will default to the current controller, which is the contact controller. The last parameter that is passed to the `form_for` tag is the code block that begins with the `do |f|` statement. Inside the block is where you will specify the body of the form.

Now look at the contents of the form that you are creating. Within the form body, you see several repetitions of the following lines, one for each field in the contacts table:

```
<p><label for="contact_first_name">First Name:</label>
 <%= f.text_field 'first_name' %></p>
```

These lines create an HTML label tag and an HTML text input field. The input field is created using another Rails method called `text_field` which is called on the `form_builder` which was passed into the block as the `f` variable. The `text_field` method takes a single parameter. The parameter is the name of the attribute that this text field will contain. The output of the `text_field` method will be HTML code like the following:

```
<input id="contact_first_name" name="contact[first_name]"
   size="30" type="text" value="" />
```

After all of the labels and text fields, the last three lines of the new template contain this code:

```
 <%= f.submit "Create" %>
<% end %>
<p><%= link_to 'Back', {:action => 'index'} %></p>
```

Here you see another Rails helper method. The `submit` method creates a form submit button. The button will use the parameter to the `submit` method as its label. The `end` statement ends the contents of the form block. Finally, the last line of the template uses the Rails helper method `link_to` to create a link back to the `index` view.

When a user clicks the Create button on this form, the data will be submitted to the `create` action of the `Contact` controller. The `create` action will handle the record creation for creating a new contact. In the next section you'll create the `create` action.

Make sure your WEBrick server is still running and go back to the contact list page. Now click the `New Contact` link, and you should see the new contact screen shown in Figure 2.6.

FIGURE 2.6

The ContactList new contact view

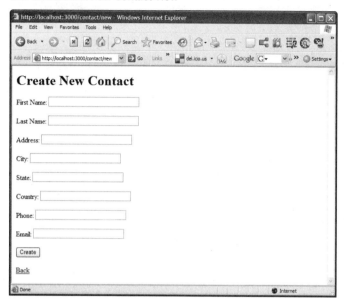

You should see the new contact form with a blank edit field for all of the attributes of the new contact. Don't click the Create button just yet. You need to create the create action next so that your application correctly handles the creation of a new contact.

Implementing the Create action

In the previous section you created the new action and a view template that allows you to display an empty form that the user can use to create new contact records. The form you created will get submit to the create action of the contact_controller. That is a method you have not written yet, so that will be the next action method that you will create.

Create the create action. Open up the contact_controller.rb file and add a create method using the code below:

```
def create
    @contact = Contact.new(params[:contact])
    if @contact.save!
        redirect_to :action => "index"
    else
        render :action => "new"
    end
end
```

In this `create` method, you create a new instance of a `Contact` object passing the parameters from the new form into the `Contact.new` method. After creating the new `Contact` instance and setting it to the `@contact` instance variable, you attempt to save that using the `save!` instance method.

If the `save!` method returns successfully the `redirect_to` method is used to redirect the user back to the `index` method which will show the list page. The list should now contain the new contact that was created. If the `save!` method does not return successfully, the new form is re-rendered.

Create a few new contacts using the new contact page and make sure that everything works as expected. After you create a new contact, you should see the new contact listed along with your other contacts on the contacts list page. If you see any errors reported, or if the contacts are not being created as expected, read back through the previous sections, and make sure that you've done everything correctly up to this point.

Implementing the show action

At this point, your application is able to display a list of contacts, and you are able to create new contacts using a new contact form. You do not yet have a way to view and edit existing contacts. In this section, you'll take the first step towards creating the view and edit functionality by creating the `show` action. The `show` action will display a form containing an existing record's attributes. From the show form you can update the contact and then submit those changes to the `update` method that you'll implement in the next section.

1. **Create the `show` action.** Go back to the `contact_controller.rb` file. Create the show method so that it now looks like this:

    ```
    def show
        @contact = Contact.find(params[:id])
    end
    ```

    The show method uses the `Contact.find(params[:id])` statement to find the contact whose `id` matches the `id` passed on the URL. If found, the contact is loaded into the `@contact` instance variable. The `find` method accepting the contact id is another method provided to all model classes that extend `ActiveRecord::Base`. Because you know that instance variables are also accessible from the view templates, you now have what you need to proceed with creating the view template to display the contact's details.

2. **Create the show template.** As you create the view, remember that it also has to support editing of the contact data, not just a static display. In the `app/views/contact` directory, create a file called `show.html.erb` with the following content:

    ```
    <h1>View/Edit Contact</h1>
    <% form_for :contact, @contact, :url => {:action=>'update',
       :id=>@contact.id} do |f| %>
     <p><label for="contact_first_name">First Name:</label>
     <%= f.text_field 'contact', 'first_name' %></p>
    ```

```
<p><label for="contact_last_name">Last Name:</label>
<%= f.text_field 'contact', 'last_name' %></p>

<p><label for="contact_address">Address:</label>
<%= f.text_field 'contact', 'address' %></p>

<p><label for="contact_city">City:</label>
<%= f.text_field 'contact', 'city' %></p>

<p><label for="contact_state">State:</label>
<%= f.text_field 'contact', 'state' %></p>

<p><label for="contact_country">Country:</label>
<%= f.text_field 'contact', 'country' %></p>

<p><label for="contact_phone">Phone:</label>
<%= f.text_field 'contact', 'phone' %></p>

<p><label for="contact_email">Email:</label>
<%= f.text_field 'contact', 'email' %></p>

    <%= f.submit "Update" %>
<% end %>

<p><%= link_to 'Back', {:action => 'index'} %></p>
```

Assuming your server is still running, go back to the contact list screen from Figure 2.5 and click the contact, Timothy Fisher. Clicking the contact takes you to the show action, and you should now see the view shown in Figure 2.7. On this screen, you see a label and edit field for each of the contact's attributes. There is also an Update button, and a link back to the contact list screen.

Now take a closer look at the code in the show view template. Notice that this code is almost identical to the code you used in the new template. The only differences are a different page title in the first line, `<h1>View/Edit Contact</h1>`, different parameters for the `form_for` method, and a different label on the Submit button, `Update`. Let's take a look at the `form_for` line that is used in this template:

```
<% form_for: contact, @contact, :url => {:action=>'update', :id=>@
    contact.id} do |f| %>
```

Here you are passing four parameters to the `form_for` tag. This is one more than what was passed for the new template. The first parameter specifies the object type for which the form is being created. In this case that is a contact object.

The second parameter specifies a specific object instance that will be used to populate the form elements in the form that is created. Remember that in the `show` action, you set an `@contact` instance variable to contain the contact instance that the user clicked on. That object instance is used to populate the contact form.

FIGURE 2.7

The ContactList View/Edit contact view

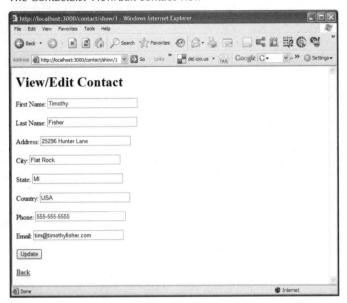

The third parameter specifies where the form should be submitted. In this case, the form is submitted to the `update` action, and an `id` is also specified so that the `update` action will be able to retrieve the correct contact to update it. Since a controller is not specified it will default to the current controller, which is the contact controller.

The last parameter that is passed to the `form_for` tag is the code block that begins with the `do |f|` statement. Inside the block is where you will specify the body of the form.

With the exception of a different label on the form submit button, the contents of the form code block is identical to what you saw for the new form. However, since you passed an instance variable that holds a valid contact object, each of the form input fields will be pre-populated with the values of that contact instance.

If you remember that one of the core philosophies that drive Rails development is *Don't Repeat Yourself*, or DRY, you might be thinking at this point that there is an awful lot of duplication between the `show.html.erb` and `new.html.erb` templates. In Chapter 5, you will learn about another Rails technology called *partials* that will allow you to eliminate all of the duplication for cases such as this one where you have duplicated code between two or more views.

Implementing the update action

In the previous section you implemented the `show` action. This action allowed you to click on an existing contact and be taken to a form where you can view and change the details of an existing contact. Now you will implement the update action which will handle the submission of the form displayed by the show action to make changes to a contact.

Create the update action. Open up the contact_controller.rb file and add an update method using the code below:

```
def update
    @contact = Contact.find(params[:id])
    @contact.attributes = params[:contact]
    @contact.save!
    redirect_to :action => "index"
end
```

In this method, you first find the correct Contact object to update using the Contact.find method with the id of the contact that was edited. Remember that you specified the id of the contact being edited along with the update action in the form_for tag of the show template. After you have the correct contact instance, you update its attributes using the attributes= method of the contact instance.

You specify the new attributes by grabbing them from the request parameters using the syntax params[:contact]. The attributes= method is provided by ActiveRecord::Base to all of your model classes. Using this method is a quick way to update all of a model object's attributes with a single line of code. With the contact's attributes updated, you'll then call the save! method to save the new attributes to the database. Finally, the user is redirected back to the main contact list using the redirect_to method with the :action=>"index" parameter.

This completes the implementation of the show and edit functionality. Now you can try out the new functionality by clicking a contact from the contact list view. You should be taken to the contact display/edit view. From that view, go ahead and edit a few of the contact's fields and then click the update button. If you changed the contact's name, you should see that reflected in the display of the contat list. You can verify changes to other attributes by viewing the contact's details again by clicking on that contact again.

Assuming all went well for you, you have now completed the functionality that you originally set out to implement, that is the ability to create, view, and update contacts in your contact list application. If all did not go well and your show-and-edit functionality does not seem to work as advertised, I'd suggest that you double-check all of your code and make sure you did not skip any steps in the previous sections. In most cases, the error screens that Rails presents when something does go wrong are informative enough to be able to quickly diagnose a problem.

What you have accomplished

Let's recap what you have been able to accomplish so far. From absolutely nothing, you have created a new Rails application, and a MySQL database to serve as a Contact List application. With the Contact List application, you can show a list of contacts stored in the database, view and edit an existing contact, and create a new contact. If you've been creating the application as you read this, you were probably able to create everything in less than one hour. Not bad for your first experience with writing a Rails application. Now to finish off this first application, add a bit of style so that it looks better. You'll do that in the next section.

Style the application

You have a complete application that meets the requirements set forth when you started developing it, but most people would find it lacking in appeal. The look and feel of an application is often an important part of whether or not it is successful.

A Rails application is typically styled using CSS style sheets. When you created the project, the `public/stylesheets` directory was created. This is the directory where you will place any style sheets that you create.

You want to be able to include a style sheet in every page without having to modify every view template file to link the style sheet. Rails gives you the answer you need through another file type called *layouts*.

You can put boilerplate HTML in a layout file and have that included in all of your view templates. The layout file can include content that goes both before and after the content of your view templates. The content in a layout file wraps the view templates with which it is associated. If you create a layout file with the same name as your controller, it is used automatically with all of the views associated with that controller. If you want to give the layout file a different name, you can specify the name of a layout file in any controller class.

If you want a layout file to apply to all of your view templates, regardless of the controller, you can use a layout file named `application.html.erb` in the `application/views/layouts` directory. This layout will be applied to all of your views that do not have a more specific layout file specified. If you have an application layout file and a controller specific layout file, the controller specific layout file will be used for views rendered from that controller.

To style the contact list application, you will create an `application.html.erb` layout file that will be used for each of your view templates.

CROSS-REF   Specifying the name of a layout file in any controller class is covered in Chapter 4, along with details about the controllers.

Create a layout template. In the `app/views/layouts` directory, create a file called `application.html.erb`. Type the following content into the file:

```
<!DOCTYPE HTML PUBLIC "-//W3C//DTD XHTML 1.0 Strict//EN"
  "http://www.w3.org/TR/xhtml1/DTD/xhtml1-strict.dtd">
<html>
  <head>
    <title>Contact List Manager</title>
    <%= stylesheet_link_tag 'styles' %>
  </head>
  <body>
```

```
      <%= yield %>
    </body>
  </html>
```

This provides the standard template for an HTML Web page. Now, all of your views rendered by the contact controller will be wrapped with this code and be a little more standards-compliant. The content of a view template is inserted where the `<%= yield %>` statement is also.

In the HTML HEAD section, a title is provided in the layout so that the title bar in the browser will show your application name as Contact List Manager. Finally, the layout includes a style sheet using a Rails helper method, `stylesheet_link_tag`.

The `stylesheet_link_tag` helper method allows you to easily link to a CSS style sheet without having to remember the standard HTML method of doing so. The parameter passed to this method specifies the name of your style sheet without the `.css` extension. Rails looks for style sheets in the `public/stylesheets` directory of your project. So with the link you've added to your layout template, Rails will look for a file named `styles.css` in the `public/stylesheets` directory.

NOTE Within layout templates in older Rails application code, you might see the line `<%= @content_for_layout %>` instead of `<%= yield %>`. In new applications, the preferred method for indicating where content is inserted in a layout is to use `<%= yield %>` instead of `<%= @content_for_layout %>`. The `<%= yield %>` method is more indicative of the fact that Ruby blocks are involved in how the content insertion happens, because the yield keyword is associated with Ruby blocks.

Create a stylesheet. Create the `styles.css` file in `public/stylesheets` and begin adding some style to the application. Use the following content:

```
body {
    font-family: "Trebuchet MS";
}

h1 {
    font-weight: bold;
    text-align:center;
}

ul {
    font-size: 1.2em;
    line-height: 1.5em;
}

label {
    float: left;
    width: 125px;
    font-weight: bold;
}
```

```
input {
    float: left;
    width: 170px;
}

a, a:visited {
    color: blue;
    font-weight: bold;
}

form {
    float:left;
    margin-bottom: 20px;
}

p {
    clear:both;
    float: left;
    margin-top: 0px;
    margin-bottom: 10px;
}

#contact_submit {
    clear: both;
    float: left;
    width: 75px;
    margin-top: 15px;
    margin-left: 220px;
}
```

It is not a goal of this book to teach CSS skills, so I will not walk through the details of the CSS style sheet. However, CSS is an important skill for any Web developer to have. The style sheet shown above is fairly basic and should not be confusing to a Web developer. If you are not familiar with any of the styles used in this style sheet, it would be a very good idea for you to pick up a book about CSS and polish up on that skill. Whether it is your job to develop front-end code or not, you will find it helpful to understand basic CSS styling.

Now if you reload the application, you should see a nicer looking index view and much nicer looking form views also. On the form views, each of your text input boxes should be aligned on the left. With a bit of CSS styling you can turn any Web page into something that is nicer to look at.

WebScaffolding

Now that you've completed your first basic Rails application, here's another bit of Rails magic. You could have generated the model, controller, and view classes that you needed using a single Rails generator script called *scaffolding*. Scaffolding is an excellent resource for quickly prototyping an application or to get something up and running in the early stages of application development.

Let's walk through a quick example of how you might start an application using the Rails scaffolding generator. From a command-line, use the `rails` command to create a new Rails project:

```
> rails scaffold_test
```

That will create the skeleton for a new Rails project for you. For this example, let's assume you were creating an interface to manage a list of users. Use the scaffold generator to create complete scaffolding for a User model:

```
> ruby script/generate scaffold User name:string email:string
  birthdate:date
    exists app/models/
    exists app/controllers/
    exists app/helpers/
    create app/views/users
    exists app/views/layouts/
    exists test/functional/
    exists test/unit/
    create app/views/users/index.html.erb
    create app/views/users/show.html.erb
    create app/views/users/new.html.erb
    create app/views/users/edit.html.erb
    create app/views/layouts/users.html.erb
    create public/stylesheets/scaffold.css
  dependency model
    exists app/models/
    exists test/unit/
    exists test/fixtures/
    create app/models/user.rb
    create test/unit/user_test.rb
    create test/fixtures/users.yml
    create db/migrate
    create db/migrate/001_create_users.rb
    create app/controllers/users_controller.rb
    create test/functional/users_controller_test.rb
    create app/helpers/users_helper.rb
     route map.resources :users
```

As you see by the output of this command, the scaffold generator creates quite a few files for you with no additional work. You get everything that you need to support a users model including a controller, a helper, the model class, views, and tests.

Now take a look at a few of the files that were generated for you. First, open up the `User` model from `app/models/user.rb`. Your file should be similar to this:

```
class User < ActiveRecord::Base
end
```

There is nothing too interesting here. This looks just like a model class that is generated with the regular model generator. Now, open up the UsersController from app/controllers/ users_controller.rb. You should see the code shown in Listing 2.1.

LISTING 2.1

app/controllers/users_controller.rb

```ruby
class UsersController < ApplicationController
  # GET /users
  # GET /users.xml
  def index
    @users = User.find(:all)

    respond_to do |format|
      format.html # index.html.erb
      format.xml  { render :xml => @users }
    end
  end

  # GET /users/1
  # GET /users/1.xml
  def show
    @user = User.find(params[:id])

    respond_to do |format|
      format.html # show.html.erb
      format.xml  { render :xml => @user }
    end
  end

  # GET /users/new
  # GET /users/new.xml
  def new
    @user = User.new

    respond_to do |format|
      format.html # new.html.erb
      format.xml  { render :xml => @user }
    end
  end

  # GET /users/1/edit
  def edit
    @user = User.find(params[:id])
  end

  # POST /users
  # POST /users.xml
  def create
```

```
      @user = User.new(params[:user])

   respond_to do |format|
     if @user.save
       flash[:notice] = 'User was successfully created.'
       format.html { redirect_to(@user) }

  format.xml  { render :xml => @user, :status => :created, :location =>
  @user }
     else
       format.html { render :action => "new" }

  format.xml  { render :xml => @user.errors, :status => :unprocessable_
  entity }
     end
   end
 end

 # PUT /users/1
 # PUT /users/1.xml
 def update
   @user = User.find(params[:id])

   respond_to do |format|
     if @user.update_attributes(params[:user])
       flash[:notice] = 'User was successfully updated.'
       format.html { redirect_to(@user) }
       format.xml  { head :ok }
     else
       format.html { render :action => "edit" }

  format.xml  { render :xml => @user.errors, :status => :unprocessable_
  entity }
     end
   end
 end

 # DELETE /users/1
 # DELETE /users/1.xml
 def destroy
   @user = User.find(params[:id])
   @user.destroy

   respond_to do |format|
     format.html { redirect_to(users_url) }
     format.xml  { head :ok }
   end
 end
end
```

Now you see the real power of the scaffold generator. The users controller contains a complete implementation of all of the CRUD methods for users. The methods implemented for you include: `index`, `show`, `new`, `edit`, `create`, `update`, and `destroy`. The implementation of these methods uses the RESTful architecture style which is covered in detail in Chapter 12.

In addition to a controller that implements all of the CRUD methods, the scaffold generator also creates view templates for you that correspond to all of the CRUD methods. Within the app/views directory, you should see the following subdirectories and files:

```
-- layouts
------ users.html.erb
-- users
------ edit.html.erb
------ index.html.erb
------ new.html.erb
------ show.html.erb
```

With the controller methods and the view templates created by the scaffold generator, you have a complete implementation of the CRUD functionality for a given model. Many developers like to start their projects by generating scaffolding for all of their model objects. This gives them a head start on development and an excellent code base to build upon.

CROSS-REF In Chapter 11, you can read about some additional scaffolding implementations that are available as Rails plugins. These external scaffolding plugins generally will generate richer user interfaces in the view templates.

More to Get You Started

On the Web, you can find many excellent learning resources to get you started with Rails development. The Official Ruby on Rails Web site (`www.rubyonrails.org`) is the first place to look. A sampling of the learning resources you can find on this site includes the following:

- **Creating a Weblog in 15 minutes:** This shows you how to create a simple Web log application from scratch in less than 15 minutes. The Web log you create includes a comments feature and an administration interface.

- **Putting Flickr on Rails:** In this, you'll create a photo search application that makes use of the public API to the popular photo-sharing site, Flickr.com.

- **Evolving your database schema without a sweat:** This 20-minute tutorial provides a great overview of the features available for managing your database schema using Rails migrations.

There are several very good Rails presentations on the Ruby on Rails site, and many excellent Rails resources are also available on other Web sites. If you do a Google search on Rails and tutorials you can find many excellent Rails tutorials, some emphasizing a certain feature, and others more general in nature. An excellent site with many online forums dedicated to Rails is the Rails Forum, available at `www.railsforum.com`.

You may also be interested in the Ruby on Rails mailing list. You can find more information about this at `www.rubyonrails.org/community`. Be warned, though, that the mailing list tends to generate a tremendous amount of traffic, so you may want to set up a filter to automatically sort these messages into a folder of their own or just subscribe to the weekly digest.

If you like to chat with live peers, you can also find the official Rails IRC channel on the `irc.freenode.net` server, with the channel name #rubyonrails. There are also many good Rails forums on various sites. Just doing a Rails search on Google should be enough to get you started with exploring what is available.

Summary

This chapter provides an overview of Ruby on Rails, a little bit of its history, and an introduction to what it provides and how it is architected. You were also shown how to write your very first Rails application. The steps you used to create the simple Rails application built in this chapter are the same steps that you will usually follow to begin development of any Rails application that you write. The steps to follow are:

1. Use the Rails command to create the project directory structure and default files.
2. Create the database for your project.
3. Create one or more model objects.
4. Create one or more controller objects.
5. Create and style your views.

With the relatively small number of lines of code that you have to actually write, you can create a Web application that allows users to view a list of contacts, add new contacts to a database, view a contact's details, and edit a contact.

Part II

Rails In Depth

Chapter 3

Using
Active Record

Rails applications implement the model-view-controller (MVC) design pattern. The model layer of an MVC application implements the application's business logic and encapsulates the application's data. This is often the most significant part of an application. It is this layer that should contain the core of your functionality. The view and controller layers could be replaced to re-implement your application in another environment, such as when converting a desktop application to a Web application; however, the model layer can ideally remain intact across these different operating environments.

Rails implements the model layer primarily using a component called Active Record. Active Record provides a powerful abstraction layer and is often referred to as elegant because of its use of the following techniques:

- **Convention over configuration:** If you follow Active Record's conventions, you'll save yourself from having to write many lines of configuration code. Active Record is able to automatically discover the details of your database schema and provide you with simple functionality for accessing and managing your data.

- **Metaprogramming:** Using metaprogramming, Active Record dynamically adds features to your model classes, saving you from having to write common code over and over again. For example, Active Record adds attributes to your model objects for every column in your database tables.

- **Domain-specific language:** Rails implements a domain-specific language (DSL) for managing your data. Rails extends Ruby to implement a DSL, making actions such as adding validations and relationships to your objects seem like part of the language.

The model layer is also usually a good place to start your application development.

What is Active Record?

In object-oriented programming, data structures are represented by a hierarchy of classes. In a database, data is most often stored in a set of relational database tables. There is an inherent mismatch between your program's object view and the database's relational view of data. Over the years, there have been many attempts to reconcile this mismatch, including attempts to create object databases. For the most part, object databases never took off. A primary reason for this was the already established base of relational databases and tools supporting them. Another solution to this mismatch problem is through the use of Object-relational-mapping tools. *Object relational mapping* (ORM) is the mapping of relational database tables to object-oriented classes.

A good ORM hides the details of your database's relational data behind your object hierarchy. This is precisely what you get in a Rails application. One of the most important components of Rails is the Active Record library. Active Record implements an ORM for Rails applications.

As you can see in Figure 3.1, an ORM provides the mapping layer between how a database works with its data and how an object-oriented application works with its data. An ORM maps database tables to classes, database table rows to objects, and database table columns to object attributes. This is precisely the mapping that Active Record carries out for you. By using Active Record, your application does not have to deal with database constructs such as tables, rows, or columns at all. Your application only deals with classes, objects, and attributes. Active Record maps these to their database equivalents for you.

FIGURE 3.1

Object relational mapping

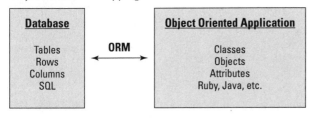

The pattern upon which the Active Record library is based is not unique to Rails; Active Record is based on a design pattern created by Martin Fowler that also goes by the name Active Record. It is from this design pattern that the Active Record library got its name.

There are many ORM implementations available in different languages. What makes Active Record special is its ease of use and the power you get from it with very few lines of code. Unlike most other ORM implementations, you don't have to write lines upon lines of configuration code to set up Active Record. In fact, Active Record will work in your application with absolutely no configuration at all, if you follow recommended naming schemes in your database and classes.

Another feature of Active Record that makes it easier for you to work with is its implementation of a *domain-specific language (DSL)* for working with your application's data. A DSL is a programming language intended for use in a specific problem domain. In general, Ruby's syntax makes it easy to create DSLs. The DSL nature of Active Record means that you can use dynamically generated methods, such as `find_by_first_name('tim')`, to retrieve a record by a column name. You can also perform tasks such as modeling an association between tables with the method `has_one` or `has_many` followed by the name of another model class. Many of the things you will do with Active Record methods will feel like they are a part of the language you are using. This is a side effect of the nature of a DSL.

Active Record Basics

In this section, you can learn some of the basics of Active Record prior to employing them in the sections that follow. Some basics I cover here are classes, objects, and naming conventions.

Active Record Classes and Objects

Active Record is implemented in Rails as a set of base classes from which your model objects extend. Each table in your database is generally represented by a class that extends an Active Record base class. Simply by extending the Active Record base classes, your model objects inherit a wealth of functionality. In fact, your model objects may be as simple as this:

```
class Book < ActiveRecord::Base
end
```

This empty class definition is enough to give your `Book` class quite a bit of functionality merely by extending the `ActiveRecord::Base` class. By using `ActiveRecord::Base`, Rails knows that this class wraps a database table named `books`. Active Record will dynamically add metadata to this class for all of the table columns that are in the `books` table. This includes data such as column names, types, and lengths. Active Record also adds attributes to your class for each of the columns in the database.

Active Record manages database connections for your application. You don't have to write any code to set up database connections or to manage those in your Rails application. Basically, all of the details related to working with a database are hidden from you, the developer, by Active Record. As a developer, you work with objects and do not have to deal with things like database connections, tables, columns, and SQL statements.

Active Record naming conventions

Active Record makes heavy use of the convention-over-configuration principle. If you follow a few simple naming conventions, you can take advantage of many dynamic features of Active Record with no configuration required.

Class and table names

Your database tables should be named with the plural form of the names of your model classes. For example, if you want a model class named `Book`, you would create a corresponding table named `books`. By using this convention, Rails is able to automatically find the table that corresponds to your model class without having to write any configuration code. Rails even supports many irregular plural nouns, such as 'people' being the plural of 'person.'

NOTE   **Rails does not know about all irregular pluralizations, but for the cases when Rails doesn't know the plural form of a model you want to use, you can tell Rails about your custom pluralizations. To define your own pluralizations, you add code to the `config/environment.rb` file, like this:**

```
Inflector.inflections do |inflect|
    inflect.irregular 'sheep', 'sheeps'
end
```

In this example, you are telling Rails to use the word 'sheeps' as the plural form of the word 'sheep'. You can add as many singular/plural definitions as you want within a single `Inflector.inflections` block.

You should name your database tables with all lowercase table names and underscore-separated words. The corresponding model classes use camel-casing. *Camel-casing* is a style of joining words where underscores are removed, and multiple words are joined together with the first letter of each word capitalized. For example, a database table named `comic_books`, would correspond to a model named `ComicBook`.

In some cases, such as when you are working with a legacy database, you may not have the freedom of naming the database tables yourself. In that case, you can override the default table name that Rails expects for a particular model by using the `set_table_name` method. The following code specifies that the `Shape` class should use the `shape_items` table.

```
class Shape < ActiveRecord::Base
    set_table_name 'shape_items'
end
```

TIP   **If you don't like giving your database tables plural names, you can configure Rails to work with singular-named database tables by adding this line to `config/environment.rb`:**

```
ActiveRecord::Base.pluralize_table_names = false
```

Table keys

There are two types of database keys for which naming is important in Rails: primary keys and foreign keys.

Primary keys

The primary key is what uniquely identifies each row in a database table. Your tables should have a primary key with the column name id. The id column should be an integer type and should be auto-incrementing. Rails will automatically use this column as a unique identifier. Rails migrations, which are discussed later in this chapter, automatically create a primary key column named id for each table that is created. If you want to use a different field as the primary key for a table, Rails allows that, but with some restrictions. See the sidebar "Using Alternate Primary Keys with Rails" for more information.

Using Alternate Primary Keys with Rails

By default, Rails uses a field called id as the primary key for all of your database tables. Rails migrations generate this field automatically so you do not have to specify it in your table creation migrations. While this field is suitable for most purposes, there may be times when you have to work with a legacy database for which you do not get to choose the primary key fields. As with many other things in Rails, you can override the default Rails primary key field name and specify any field for a particular model. You do this using the set_primary_key method in the model class definition that wraps the table for which you want an alternate primary key.

For example, say you had a table named images that contained a primary key field named image_id. In the Image model class, you would use this code:

```
class Image < ActiveRecord::Base
    set_primary_key "image_id"
end
```

The most notable restriction on using alternate primary keys in Rails is that you cannot use composite keys as primary keys. Composite keys are keys that use more than one database column. For example, a key that used the image_id field and the created_at field in combination would not be allowed as a primary key in a Rails application. This is a restriction that is often criticized by both Rails enthusiasts and antagonists. It is a restriction that is not likely to change in the near future, though, so if you're writing a Rails application, you will need to deal with it or have a strategy to overcome it. (There is a Rails plugin available that extends the database layer of Rails to support composite primary keys. If you are interested in this plugin, you can find out more about it at http://compositekeys.rubyforge.org. In Chapter 11 you will learn more about using plugins with Rails.)

Your application can use a composite key as long as it is not the primary key. As a result, if you need a composite key, perhaps you have the flexibility to add a new field to serve as your primary key.

If you do override the primary key column name, you also become responsible for creating unique primary key values. Rails will not automatically generate a primary key value for any table that contains a non-default primary key name.

When you work with a non-default primary key field name, you still refer to the primary key attribute as id when you set the primary key value for an object. However, any other time you refer to the primary key attribute, you use the name that you assigned that field in the set_primary_key method.

Foreign keys

Foreign keys are used in a table to identify a row in another table that is related to the row containing the foreign key. For example, in Figure 3.2, the `book_id` column in the `pages` table is a foreign key that relates a row in the `pages` table to a row in the `books` table. Foreign keys in a Rails application should be named with the singular name of the referenced table followed by `id`, just as `book_id` is named in Figure 3.2.

FIGURE 3.2

Primary and foreign keys

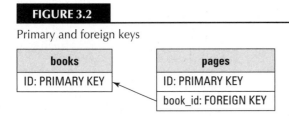

Setting up a Model

If you followed along with the development of your first Rails application in Chapter 2, you saw a simple example of generating a model using the Rails `script/generate` script. Here you will use the Rails `script/generate` script again to create a model class used throughout this chapter to explore the details of a Rails model layer and how Active Record helps you.

Generate a Rails project and model

Begin by using a command-line and creating a Rails project, model, and database. The command-line feedback that you receive when you run the various commands throughout this chapter is not always specifically shown in this book; if you see feedback that is not shown in this book as you run the commands, don't be surprised. You should expect Rails to generate feedback from its commands, similar to what you saw in Chapter 2.

1. **Create a new Rails project that you will use for the examples in this chapter.** This creates the skeleton of a new Rails application, along with the correct Rails application directory structure.

   ```
   rails -d mysql chapter3
   ```

   The `-d` option you used in the command above lets Rails know that you will be using a MySQL database. Valid values for the database type are `mysql`, `oracle`, `postgresql`, `sqlite2`, and `sqlite3`. If you do not use the `-d` option, the default database type is `sqlite3`. This database type is used by Rails to configure a sample database configuration file that you can use to specify your database server. You will see how to use that file, `database.yml`, do that a bit later in this chapter.

2. **Navigate into the new** `chapter3` **directory and generate a model called**
   `ComicBook`. Use the `script/generate` script to do this, as shown below. This creates the `ComicBook` model class, a migration for creating the `comic_books` table, and some related unit test files.

   ```
   cd chapter3
   ruby script/generate model ComicBook
   ```

3. **Create a database for use with this chapter's examples.** Now use the MySQL command-line to create a `comic_books_development` database. You could also use a MySQL GUI if you have one installed that you are comfortable with.

   ```
   mysql -u root -p
   Enter password: << your password >>
   mysql> create database comic_books_development;
   ```

You should now have the basic elements you need to follow along with the examples in this chapter: a Rails project named chapter3, a model within that chapter named ComicBook, and a MySQL database named comic_books_development.

Configure Active Record

You may have noticed that you gave your database a different name from the name you gave the Rails project. When the database is named the same as the project, with the addition of environment suffixes (_development, _test, or _production), and you are using MySQL as your database, you do not have to create any database configuration. For example, had you named your database `chapter3_development`, you could have skipped this configuration step. However, it is not always realistic that you can give your database the same name as the Rails project name you choose. Often you may have to follow a company standard for naming your databases.

Because your database name is completely different than the application name, a small amount of database configuration is required. The code that configures the databases you will use with your Rails application is stored in a configuration file called `database.yml`.

In your `chapter3` project directory, open the file `config/database.yml` and look for the section that contains this code:

```
development:
    adapter: mysql
    encoding: utf8
    database: chapter3_development
    username: root
    password:
    host: localhost
```

This is the default database configuration that Rails created when you generated the `chapter3` application. Notice the default database name of `chapter3_development`. The default configuration also assumes that a `root` username is available with a blank password. The database is assumed to be running on the same computer that you are developing on, `localhost`.

You created a database named `comic_books_development`, so change this line:

```
database: chapter3_development
```

to use the name of your database:

```
database: comic_books_development
```

Also, if you used a username and password other than `root`, be sure to change those lines in the configuration.

You may be wondering about the different database environments that have been referred to. Rails supports the use of three separate environments for running your application in: the development, test, and production environments. The following section has a description of the three environments supported by Rails.

Rails Development Environments

It is a good development practice to use different infrastructure environments when developing a Web application. Each environment should contain a unique database, Web server, and other external components that your application may require. Rails has built-in support for running your applications in three different environments. The environments supported by Rails are called development, test, and production. Each of these environments is described below:

- **Development:** This is the environment used when developing your application. You also perform most of your debugging in this environment. In this environment, Rails reloads classes each time you call a new action. This picks up any changes that you make to the class files dynamically, which makes this environment ideal for debugging your code as you write it.

- **Test:** This is the environment in which you test your application. Rails uses this environment when running unit, functional, and integration tests. Each time your tests are run, the test database is completely replaced; therefore, you should be careful not to specify the same database name for your test environment as you use for your development or production environments.

- **Production:** The production environment is used by your application in production. This must be the most robust and fault-tolerant of your environments. It should be adequately scalable and be able to handle expected load. In this environment, Rails loads your classes only once. If you make changes to your classes, they will not be picked up unless you restart your Rails application. While not ideal for developing in, this feature improves the performance of this environment, making it more suitable for use by end users.

You can specify the environment that you want your application to run in by editing the `config/environment.rb file`. The following line contained in that file specifies the environment that Rails will use:

```
# ENV['RAILS_ENV'] ||= 'production'
```

This line is commented out when you first create a Rails application. If you want to use this line to specify your environment, make sure you uncomment the line.

The databases for each environment are configured in the `config/database.yml` directory of your Rails application. You can also include environment specific configuration for your application by adding the appropriate configuration to the files contained in your application's `config/environments` directory. This directory contains a configuration file specific to each environment; `development.rb`, `test.rb`, and `production.rb`.

Most of the code that you will write in this book targets the development environment. However, when you get to Chapter 9, where testing is covered in detail, you'll see how the test environment is used.

Using Migrations

Rails migrations are an excellent example of the DRY philosophy applied to Rails. Remember that DRY means Don't Repeat Yourself. With the power of migrations, you are able to define and manage the evolution of your database in a single place. You do not need SQL script files, XML configuration files, or any other files to manage the evolution of your application's database. Migrations also make your database definition independent of the specific database that you decide to use. The same migration file that you create for a MySQL database will also work with an Oracle or PostgreSQL database.

Rails migrations are simple Ruby classes that contain instructions that create or modify your database schema. You will create a new migration file for each change that you want to make to your database schema. When you generated your model, you may have noticed that a migration file was also created. Anytime you create a model using the Rails generator, a migration file is also created for you. Writing a migration file is often one of the first things you will do when you begin writing the model layer of your application.

Take a look at the migration file that was created for your `ComicBook` model. You'll find the file `001_create_comic_books.rb` in the `db/migrate` directory of your `chapter3` project.

```
class CreateComicBooks < ActiveRecord::Migration
    def self.up
        create_table :comic_books do |t|
            t.timestamps
        end
    end

    def self.down
        drop_table :comic_books
    end
end
```

The first thing you should notice is that this is a Ruby class that extends another Active Record class, `ActiveRecord::Migration`. The class contains two class methods:

- `self.up`

  Called when a migration is applied, and used to set up your database schema elements.

- `self.down`

  Called when a migration is reversed. This method should undo the actions of the `self.up` method.

In the auto-generated migration, the `self.up` method creates the `comic_books` table using the `create_table` method. A code block is passed to this method that you will use to setup the columns of the table. So far the only columns being setup are created with this line:

```
t.timestamps
```

This will automatically create two columns for the table, one named `created_at` and one named `updated_at`. These columns will hold timestamps for row creation and update. The `self.down` method drops the table.

It is always a good practice to design your data model before you create your migrations. The data model design can be as simple as a table listing all of the columns and their data types for each of your tables. Table 3.1 shows a data model design for the `comic_books` table that you will implement.

TABLE 3.1

Comic Book Table Definition

Field Name	Field Type	Description
id	Integer	The primary key
title	String	The title of the comic book
writer	String	The writer of the comic book
artist	String	The artist of the comic book
issue	Integer	Issue number of the comic book
publisher	String	The publisher of the comic book
created_at	Datetime	Date and time that the record was created
updated_at	Datetime	Date and time that the record was updated

Using the table definition provided in Table 3.1, you can now create a migration that creates the database schema for this table.

1. **Edit the file** `001_create_comic_books.rb` so that it looks like this:

```ruby
class CreateComicBooks < ActiveRecord::Migration
    def self.up
        create_table :comic_books do |t|
            t.string :title
            t.string :writer
            t.string :artist
            t.integer :issue
            t.string :publisher
            t.timestamps
        end
    end

    def self.down
        drop_table :comic_books
    end
end
```

2. **Run the migration by typing the following from a command-line.** This should be run from your `chapter3` project directory.

```
rake db:migrate
```

When you run the migration above, you should see output similar to this:

```
== CreateComicBooks: migrating =====================================
-- create_table(:comic_books)
   -> 0.025s
== CreateComicBooks: migrated (0.257s)
   ==========================
```

You can now take a look at the `comic_books` database using a GUI front-end tool or the MySQL command-line. You can see that the `comic_books` table has been created with the columns you specified in the migration.

Notice that the migration code does not specify a column for the `id` field. That is because the `id` field is the default primary key field for all tables and is created automatically unless you specify that it should not be created. Take a closer look at the block that you passed into the `create_table` method:

```ruby
t.string :title
t.string :writer
t.string :artist
t.integer :issue
t.string :publisher
t.timestamps
```

Each of the lines in this block creates a new column in the table. For example in the first line, a column named `title` is created with a `string` type. Ruby will translate this into an appropriate database field type. In the case of MySQL this would become a `varchar` field. The valid field types that you can use in migrations are: `string`, `text`, `integer`, `float`, `datetime`, `time-stamp`, `time`, `date`, `binary`, and `boolean`. Each of these Ruby types will result in an appropriate database field type. Notice that the name of the field is passed as a symbol object. If you look at the last line in the above code you will see something slightly different. The line contains the code `t.timestamps` and no field names. The `t.timestamps` method creates the `created_at` and `updated_at` columns.

You used the Rake tool to run the database migration. *Rake* is a tool written in Ruby that is used to perform a variety of build-related development tasks. If you are familiar with the UNIX make utility, or the Java Ant utility, Rake is similar to those tools. Scripts that are run using Rake are called Rake files. Rake files are written in pure Ruby code. Rails uses a Rake file to implement a bunch of useful tasks. You can see more of the Rake tasks available for your Rails application by typing this:

```
rake --tasks
```

You will use a variety of rake tasks throughout this book. In addition to the `db:migrate` task which you already used in this chapter, two additional rake tasks are useful to know about now.

- `rake db:create:all`

  This task will automatically create the databases that you have specified in your `config/database.yml` file. This makes it easy for you to specify your database information in a single place, the `database.yml` file and then you can use `rake` to create your database anytime that you need to create it. You do not have to rely on using any external tool, such as the MySQL command line tool.

- `rake db:drop:all`

  This task drops all of the databases that you have specified in your `config/database.yml` file. This is useful if you feel that your database has been corrupted or somehow put into a bad state.

The above commands create or drop all of your databases. You can also use similar commands to create or drop a database specific to a single environment. You specify a single environment like this:

```
rake db:create RAILS_ENV=development
rake db:drop RAILS_ENV=development
```

Schema versions

The first time you run a migration, a new table that you may not recognize is also created in your schema. This table is called `schema_info`, and it keeps track of the current version of the database schema. The *database schema* is the current structure of the database, including the tables and columns that make up the database.

Each migration file that is run creates a new database schema version. The migration you ran is contained in the file `001_create_comic_books.rb`. The 001 at the beginning of the filename is the migration number that corresponds to the database version number that will be created after this migration is run. Each migration that either you create or that is generated for you must have a unique three-digit number as the first three characters of the migration filename.

Migrations that are used to create database tables commonly contain the name of the table prepended with the word 'Create' following the three digit migration number, such as you see in the file name `001_create_comic_books.rb`.

Using the `rake` command that you used to run the migration, you can also specify a specific schema version number to migrate up to or back to. When migrating to a version number that is lower than the current schema version number, each of the migrations past the version that you are migrating to will have their `self.down` methods executed.

The following `rake` command will migrate your database to a specific schema version number:

```
rake db:migrate VERSION=3
```

If your database had been at schema version 5, the `self.down` methods would be run on migrations 004 and 005. If your schema version was 1, the `self.up` methods would be run on migrations 002 and 003. When migrating down, such as from version 5 to version 3, the migration `self.down` methods are run in reverse order. For example, the 005 migration `self.down` method would run first, followed by the 004 `self.down` method. When migrating up, the `self.up` methods are run in numerical order.

Migration methods

There are a large number of built-in migration methods available within your migration files that you inherit from extending the `ActiveRecord::Migration` class. The most common methods that you will use to manipulate tables, columns, and indexes are summarized here. For a complete reference of available migration methods, go to `http://api.rubyonrails.com/classes/ActiveRecord/Migration.html`.

Tables

Migration methods are available to create, drop, and rename a table. These methods are summarized here:

```
create_table(table_name, options)
drop_table(table_name)
rename_table(old_name, new_name)
```

Each of these methods takes one or two table names as parameters. The `create_table` method also takes a second parameter, called `options`, which is a hash containing SQL options that you might want to use when creating your table. An example of using `create_table` with the `options` hash is shown here:

```
create_table('tables', {'DEFAULT CHAR SET'=>'UTF-8'})
```

This would create a table called `players` and set the SQL parameter `DEFAULT CHAR SET` to be `UTF-8`.

Columns

You can also add, rename, or remove columns from a database table using migration methods. The migration methods to perform these tasks are as follows:

```
add_column(table_name, column_name, column_type, options)
rename_column(table_name, old_column_name, new_column_name)
remove_column(table_name, column_name)
```

When you create a column using the `add_column` method, the `column_type` can be any of the following types: `:string`, `:text`, `:integer`, `:float`, `:decimal`, `:datetime`, `:time-stamp`, `:time`, `:date`, `:binary`, `:boolean`.

The `add_column` method also takes an `options` hash that contains parameters related to the table you are creating. For example, you can specify a default value for a column by passing an `options` hash like this:

```
{:default => 10}
```

Other common option parameters are `:limit` and `:null`. These can be used to set a field size limit and to specify whether or not a field can be set to null, respectively.

Indexes

You can add and remove database indexes using the migration methods listed here:

```
add_index(table_name, column_name, options)
remove_index(table_name, options)
```

The options parameter for both of these methods is a hash that can be used to specify the index type and index name, such as in this example:

```
add_index(:comic_books, :writer, :unique=>true, :name=>'writer_
    idx')
```

or like below to remove an index:

```
remove_index(:comic_books, :name=>'writer_index')
```

Inserting data with migrations

In addition to modifying your database schema, you can also insert data into your database in a migration file. This makes it convenient to insert default data that your application might need to run. In this section, you can create a new migration and use it to add some default data into your `comic_books` database.

1. **Create a new migration for inserting data.** From the command-line, create the migration by running the generate migration scripts, as follows:

   ```
   ruby script/generate migration AddDefaultData
   ```

   This creates a new migration file in db/migrations called 002_add_default_data.rb. Recall that the first migration you ran was created automatically for you when you generated the ComicBook model. You can use as many migrations as you want by supplementing the migrations that are generated with your model classes with migrations that you manually generate, such as the one you generated here.

2. **Edit the migration script to add data insertion.** Now you should open the migration file that you just generated in db/migrations/002_add_default_data.rb and edit it so that it looks like this:

   ```
   class AddDefaultData < ActiveRecord::Migration
       def self.up
           ComicBook.create :title=>"Spectacular Spiderman",
                            :writer=>"Roger Stern",
                            :artist=>"Marie Severin",
                            :publisher=>"Marvel",
                            :issue=>"54"
       end

       def self.down
           ComicBook.delete_all
       end
   end
   ```

3. **Run the new migration to add your default data.** From the command-line, run this migration using Rake, as follows:

   ```
   rake db:migrate
   ```

4. **Verify that the default data is now in your database.** Using either the MySQL command-line or a GUI interface, verify that the comic_books table contains the record added in your migration.

After going through the steps above, you could also migrate your database down by using the command:

```
rake db:migrate VERSION=1
```

This command would run the self.down method of your migration defined in 002_add_default_data.rb. You could then verify that the default data has been removed from your database.

Using a migration, you were able to create default data in your database. This is a common way of setting up default data for a Rails application. Remember that in a migration, you have full access to all of the code, including your models. Using the power of Ruby and your model layer, you can perform complex manipulations of your database using migrations.

Create, Read, Update, and Delete

You may have heard the term CRUD used before when referring to database operations. *CRUD* is an acronym that stands for the general categories of operations that you can perform on data stored in a database. These categories are as follows:

- **Create:** Create records in the database.
- **Read:** Read one or more records from the database.
- **Update:** Update a record in the database.
- **Delete:** Delete a record in the database.

Rails makes it easy to perform each of these operations on your data using built-in Active Record methods. In general, each of your model classes wraps a table in your database. For example, the ComicBook model class that you created with the script/generate script wraps the comic_books database table. You will use the ComicBook class and instances of that class to access data in the comic_books table and to create new records for that table.

Each column in a database table becomes an attribute in the class that wraps that table. Your ComicBook class will contain the following attributes: id, title, writer, artist, publisher, issue, created_at, and updated_at.

The following subsections step through each of these operation categories, exploring the details of each.

Creating records

There are several ways of creating new records using your Rails model classes. Each way uses a slightly different syntax, which you can see in this section.

One of the ways in which you can create new records in Rails is by instantiating a new object, setting its attributes, and then performing a save operation. The database operations necessary to insert a record into the database are completely encapsulated behind Active Record. Within your code, you simply deal with Ruby code and Ruby objects. This is in keeping with a good ORM implementation.

Here is an example of creating a record in the comic_books table that you created earlier in this chapter:

```
my_comic_book = ComicBook.new
my_comic_book.title = 'Captain America'
my_comic_book.issue = 20
my_comic_book.writer = 'Ed Brubaker'
my_comic_book.artist = 'Mike Perkins'
my_comic_book.publisher = 'Marvel'
my_comic_book.save
```

This `save` method writes this record to the `comic_books` database table. The `new` method can also accept a hash attribute for setting the attributes of the object instance you are creating. Let's add another record to the database using this style:

```
my_comic_book = ComicBook.new(
    :title => 'Captain America',
    :issue => 10,
    :writer => 'Ed Brubaker',
    :artist => 'Lee Weeks',
    :publisher => 'Marvel')
my_comic_book.save
```

Yet another way of using the new method is to pass it a block. Shown here, this technique is used to add another comic book to your database:

```
ComicBook.new do |book|
    book.title = 'Batman'
    book.issue = 18
    book.writer = 'Bill Finger'
    book.artist = 'Bob Kane'
    book.publisher = 'DC'
    book.save
end
```

Add one more comic book to your database using this technique, which creates a model and database record all in one line:

```
my_comic_book = ComicBook.create(
    :title => 'Superman & Batman',
    :issue => 2,
    :writer => 'John Byrne',
    :artist => 'John Byrne',
    :publisher => 'DC')
```

You may recall that this is the style you used to create a default database record in the second migration you wrote. The create method both instantiates the `ComicBook` instance and saves the record to the database. You can pass an array of hashes to the create method to create multiple objects and database records with one method call. An array of object instances will be returned from that call.

In all of these methods for creating a new object and record, Active Record automatically creates a new unique value and sets that as the `id` attribute while saving the record. After performing a save, you can then access the primary key as an attribute of the object, like this:

```
new_id = my_comic_book.id
```

Using created_at and updated_at Fields

By adding fields with the names `created_at` and `updated_at` to your database tables, you gain a bit of free functionality from Rails. Rails automatically updates these fields every time your records are created or updated. It is easy to add these fields from a migration using the `t.timestamps` method as you used in the examples in this chapter.

You can also choose to use fields with the names `created_on` and `updated_on`. The difference is that these fields are set with a date value, and the `created_at` and `updated_at` fields are set with a date and time value.

Reading data

Rails uses a combination of database introspection and metaprogramming to simplify your life as a developer when it comes to using your model classes and objects to read data from the database.

This section details how Rails helps you read the data that is stored in the database using your Rails model classes and built-in Rails methods. You can learn how to use column metadata, object attributes, and Rails `find` methods in the following subsections:

- Column metadata
- Accessing attributes
- Using the `find` method
- Dynamic finders
- Find using SQL

Column metadata

When a model class such as `ComicBook` is first loaded, Rails is able to infer the database table name to which it corresponds from the name of the class. Rails then gathers information about that database table by querying the database system tables. Detailed information about each column of your database table is placed into the `@@columns` class variable, which makes `@@columns` an array of `Column` objects. Each of the `Column` objects contains the following attributes:

- `name:` The name of the database column.
- `null:` Boolean value that is true if this column attribute can be set to null.
- `primary:` Boolean value that is true if this column is the Rails unique identifier.
- `scale:` Specifies the scale for a decimal column.
- `sql_type:` The type of the attribute this column holds.
- `precision:` Specifies the precision for a decimal column.
- `default:` The default value specified in the table definition for the column.

- `type`: The Ruby type that the column is represented as.
- `limit`: The maximum size of the attribute for this column.

Using the `ComicBook` model class example, the following code would print out each of these metadata attributes, for each attribute of the `ComicBook` model:

```
ComicBook.columns.each { |column|
    puts column.name
    puts column.null
    puts column.primary
    puts column.scale
    puts column.sql_type
    puts column.precision
    puts column.default
    puts column.type
    puts column.limit
}
```

You may never need to use this column metadata, but it is good to know that it is available. A common use of it is to build dynamic user interfaces. This is how Rails scaffolding is built. Scaffolding is a built-in feature of Rails that dynamically creates a basic Web interface for your Web application.

CROSS-REF For more information regarding scaffolding, go to Chapter 11.

Accessing attributes

Attribute accessors for your Rails model classes are implemented using a Ruby metaprogramming technique that allows Rails to dynamically attach accessors to your classes. Rails overrides the `method_missing` method to implement the accessors. The `method_missing` method is called anytime you call a method that does not exist for the object you are calling it on. This allows you to access the attributes of any of your classes like this:

```
the_title = comic_book.title
```

This may look like you are just accessing an attribute of the `comic_book` object without going through a method at all. If you are a Java programmer this may seem like the common way that you access public attributes. However, keep in mind that in Ruby, you cannot access any attributes from outside of their class unless you have explicitly created attribute accessors. From this perspective, you can think of attributes in Ruby classes as always being equivalent to private attributes in Java classes. So in the above code, `title` is actually an accessor method that you are using to access the `title` attribute. Because of the way the accessors are implemented, the accessor methods actually do not exist in your objects until they are called. This means that if you were to try this:

```
comic_book.methods.include? 'title'
```

a value of false would be returned, because the `title` accessor method does not yet exist. Rails uses the same technique to implement dynamic finder methods for your objects.

Using the find method

Active Record provides a powerful `find` method that you can use to find data rows in your tables. The easiest way of finding a record in your database is to pass a primary key value to the `find` method. All of your model classes include a `find` method that takes one or more primary key values as a parameter and returns one or more records as objects. Multiple primary keys can be passed as an array, and an array of matching objects will be returned.

When attempting to find a record by primary key, a `RecordNotFound` exception is thrown if Active Record is not able to find a row with the primary key you are searching for.

The following code either returns an object that has an `id` value of 5, or prints `"Record Not Found"` to the console:

```
begin
    my_comic_book = ComicBook.find(5)
rescue
    puts "Record Not Found"
end
```

Finding with conditions

You can also use the `find` method with a first parameter of `:first` or `:all`, followed by a `:conditions` parameter that specifies criteria for finding records, similar to a SQL where clause. You could use the following code to retrieve all comic books with the 'Captain America' title:

```
ComicBook.find(:all, :conditions=>"title = 'Captain America'")
```

This call returns an array of `ComicBook` objects with the title of 'Captain America'. If no rows can be found that match the criteria, an empty array is returned. If you wanted to find only the first record matching the criteria, you would use the `find` method with the `:first` parameter, like this:

```
ComicBook.find(:first, :conditions=>"title = 'Captain America'")
```

When using the `:first` attribute, a single record's object is returned instead of an array. So the above line would return an instance of `ComicBook`, if a comic book with the title 'Captain America' was found. If a record can not be found meeting the conditions specified, a `nil` value is returned.

The `:conditions` parameter can also use placeholders when specifying attribute values. For example, suppose you wanted to execute the following search:

```
ComicBook.find(:first,
               :conditions=>"title='Spiderman' and writer='Stan
    Lee'")
```

Using attribute placeholders, you could write this as follows:

```
title = 'Spiderman'
```

```
writer = 'Stan Lee'
ComicBook.find(:first,
                 :conditions=>["title=? and writer=?", title,
    writer])
```

Using this style, the :conditions parameter is an array. The where clause is the first element in the array, and the attribute values are the next elements in the array.

Rails automatically quotes and escapes the attribute values when you use this style. You should always use this style when you are using attribute values that have come directly from a Web page. If you did not use the ? placeholders and instead simply inserted the variables containing values that a user typed, you would be opening your application up to adverse attacks.

A malicious user could gain control over your database and execute any SQL statement they desired by submitting parameter values which themselves contained SQL commands. You may have heard this type of attack referred to as a SQL Injection Attack. When you use the placeholder style, Rails prevents this type of attack by quoting and escaping the attribute variables.

You can also pass the :order parameter to the find method to sort the returned objects. Here you find all of the database rows and sort them by the issue attribute in descending order:

```
ComicBook.find(:all, :order => 'issue DESC')
```

There is also a find_all method that returns all of the rows in your database. You can call this method with no parameters and all of your database rows will be returned as an array of objects. Be wary of using this method if your database contains many rows, as this uses a lot of memory to hold all of the objects that are created.

Dynamic finders

In addition to the basic find method, Rails creates additional finder methods dynamically that correspond to each of the columns in your database. For example, in your ComicBook class, you can easily find all of the comic books written by Stan Lee using this code:

```
results = ComicBook.find_by_writer('Stan Lee')
```

You can use find_by method for every column in the table. These methods are dynamically created using the method_missing technique that was also used to create attribute accessors explained earlier in this chapter.

Now what if you want to find all of the comic books written by Stan Lee and drawn by your favorite artist? Rails can help you out there, too. In addition to the single-column find_by methods, Rails will also dynamically generate multiple-column find_by methods. You could answer your question with the following code:

```
results = ComicBook.find_by_writer_and_artist('Stan Lee','Steve
    Ditko')
```

In fact, Rails provides you with `find_by` methods using any number of your column names. Each column name is separated from the preceding by `and`, as in the above two-column example. Going a step further, you could execute the following `find` method, as well:

```
results = ComicBook.find_by_writer_and_artist_and_title('Stan
    Lee','Steve Ditko','Spiderman');
```

Find using SQL

If the `find` methods that Active Record provides for you do not meet your requirements, you can resort to using raw SQL to find the records that you want. You do this by using the `find_by_sql` method. This method takes a SQL statement as a parameter and executes that SQL statement. The records retrieved by the SQL statement you passed are returned in an array from the `find_by_sql` method.

Here's an example that uses the `find_by_sql` method:

```
results = ComicBook.find_by_sql("SELECT * from comic_books WHERE
    issue>25")
```

In this example, the SQL statement `"SELECT * from comic_books WHERE issue>25"` is passed to the database, and the records retrieved are turned into ComicBook objects and returned in an array.

Creating and finding data with the Rails Console

If you've been reading along in this chapter up to this point, you've learned a lot of new techniques for creating and reading data into your application. Let's take a break from the Rails detailed coverage and try out some of what you've learned using the Rails Console.

1. **At a command-line, start up the Rails Console for your chapter3 project.** At the root of the chapter3 project, type this:

    ```
    ruby script/console
    ```

    This starts the Rails Console. Recall that the Rails Console is an interactive environment in which you have full access to your Rails classes and the full power of Ruby.

2. **Find a record stored in the database.** Earlier in this chapter, you ran a migration that added a row to the `comic_books` table. Now use the `find` method to retrieve this record, as shown here:

    ```
    comic_book = ComicBook.find(:first)
    puts comic_book.title
    => Captain America
    ```

    The first line should have found the comic book entry you created earlier, and the second line prints the comic book's title. You should see the comic book's title, `'Captain America'`, printed on the console.

3. **Create a new instance of your** `ComicBook` **class.** Now, create an instance of the `ComicBook` class and set its attributes, like this:

```
comic_book = ComicBook.new
comic_book.title = 'Spiderman'
comic_book.issue = 1
comic_book.writer = 'Stan Lee'
comic_book.artist = 'Steve Ditko'
comic_book.publisher = 'Marvel'
```

4. **Create a new row in the database by saving the** `ComicBook` **instance.**

```
comic_book.save
```

   By executing the `save` method, you have saved the new comic book to the database. Your database should now contain two records. Verify that in the next step.

5. **Retrieve all database rows.** Use the `find_all` method to get all of the rows in the database as an array of ComicBook objects. Use the `Array#length` method to get a count of objects in the database.

```
all_rows = ComicBook.find_all
puts all_rows.length
=> 2
```

   This should print a value of `'2'` to the console, because the `comic_books` table should now contain two records. If you created the comic book records that were shown in the "Creating Records" section, you probably are up to six comic books in the database instead of two.

6. **Retrieve a database row by its primary key.** Use the `find` method and the `id` from the comic book you saved in Step 3 to retrieve that item from the database.

```
id = comic_book.id
new_comic_book = ComicBook.find(id)
puts new_comic_book.writer
=> Stan Lee
```

   This should have found the comic book that you created in Step 1 and printed its writer to the console.

7. **Retrieve a database row using a dynamic finder method.** Use one of the dynamic finder methods, such as `find_by_title` shown here, to retrieve the new record by its title.

```
a_comic = ComicBook.find_by_title('Spiderman')
puts a_comic.issue
=> 1
```

   This should have found the comic book that you created in Step 1 and printed its issue number to the console.

By now, you've learned how to create and retrieve records from your database the Rails way. Next, you'll learn how to update and delete records.

Updating records

After you've made changes to a model, you usually want to save those changes back to the database. With Rails, you update your database records just by working with your model classes. You do not have to write any SQL code to perform database updates.

Before you can update a record, you first need to retrieve it. Here you retrieve the first record in the database and change the issue number:

```
comic = ComicBook.find(:first)
comic.issue = 100
comic.save
```

This code is very simple. You retrieve the desired record from the database, update one or more attributes on the returned object, and then perform a save.

You can simplify the above code even further by using the `update_attribute` method, as shown here:

```
comic = ComicBook.find(:first)
comic.update_attribute :issue, 100
```

The `update_attribute` method allows you to set the value of an attribute and save the changed value back to the database in one step.

Deleting records

Rails has two methods for deleting objects from your database. These methods are slightly different in their behavior, and are as follows:

- `delete`: Aborts on minor errors.
- `destroy`: Does not abort unless there is a critical database error.

You can call either of these methods on any of your model object instances, such as your comic book instance:

```
comic.destroy
```

After calling the method, the record associated with the object is deleted from the database immediately.

Using development log files

Rails insulates you, the developer, from having to write SQL statements to access your database. However, there are times when you're debugging an application and you'd like to know what SQL Rails is using internally. For this purpose, the place to look is the development log file.

Open up the `development.log` file in the `chapter3/log` directory. You should see something similar to Figure 3.3.

The `development.log` file

The `development.log` file contains every SQL statement that is sent to the database server, including the details of how long it took to execute each SQL statement.

This level of logging would impact the performance of your production environment. You'd also end up with a very large log file that you'd somehow have to manage. For these reasons, you only get the SQL statement logging when you are in the development environment.

Defining Relationships

Modeling data relationships in your classes is an important part of mapping data that is stored in a relational database. The word *relational* implies that there are relations among the database tables that contain your data. Active Record provides powerful yet very easy-to-use syntax for representing data relationships in your model classes.

You define relationships in your data models using the data modeling domain-specific language (DSL) that is built into Active Record. Throughout this section, you can see examples of how Active Record's DSL makes data modeling easy for you, the developer.

The relationships that you'll define are of the following types:

- One-to-one
- Many-to-one
- Many-to-many

To implement these relationship types, Rails uses the following methods, which make up the Rails association DSL:

- belongs_to
- has_one
- has_many
- has_and_belongs_to_many
- acts_as_list
- acts_as_tree

You use these methods within your model classes to create associations. As you use these methods, their use may seem more like a natural part of the language, as opposed to the fact that you are explicitly calling methods. This is the hallmark of a well-designed DSL. Each of the methods is used with the form shown here:

```
<relationship> <relationship_target> <named parameters>
```

For example, a typical use of the has_many method would look like this:

```
has_many :chapters :order=>position
```

In this example, the relationship is has_many, the relationship target is :chapters and :order=>position is a named parameter that specifies how the associated chapters should be ordered. The following sections cover in more detail how these methods are used for each of the relationship types.

One-to-one relationships

The *one-to-one relationship* is the simplest relationship, and can be modeled as shown in Figure 3.4. This type of relationship implies that there is a one-to-one correspondence between objects of one type and objects of another type. A one-to-zero-or-one relationship is actually modeled in the same way. In a one-to-zero-or-one relationship, one side of the relation can be empty.

The example used in Figure 3.4 considers books and their cover images. Assuming that the same image is never used on two different book covers, there is always a one-to-one relationship between books and cover images. Another way of saying this is that a book has one cover image, and a cover image belongs to one book.

Modeling this type of relationship in a Rails application requires a foreign key in one of the database tables and the use of some Rails DSL magic in your model classes. The foreign key should be used in the table that represents the zero-or-one side of the relationship. If it is a strict one-to-one relationship, one of the objects will usually seem to be naturally more dominant. The foreign key goes with the table of the less dominant object.

In the example of Figure 3.4, the cover_images table contains a foreign key book_id associating a cover_image with a specific book.

FIGURE 3.4

One-to-one relationship

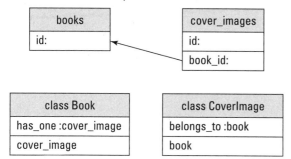

The Book class uses the `has_one` method to create the relationship with a `CoverImage` object:

```
class Book < ActiveRecord::Base
    has_one :cover_image
end
```

Methods added by has_one

The `has_one` method causes the following methods to be automatically added to the `Book` class:

- `cover_image`

  Returns the associated `CoverImage` object, or `nil` if no object is associated.

- `cover_image=`

  Assigns the `CoverImage` associate object, extracts the primary key, sets it as the foreign key, and saves the `Book` object.

- `cover_image.nil?`

  Returns true if there is no associated `CoverImage` object.

- `build_cover_image(attributes={})`

  Returns a new `CoverImage` object that has been instantiated with `attributes` and linked to this `Book` object through a foreign key, but has not yet been saved. This will only work if the association already exists. It will not work if the association is `nil`.

- `create_cover_image`

  Returns a new `CoverImage` object that has been instantiated with `attributes`, linked to this `Book` object through a foreign key, and that has already been saved. Notice how this is different from the `build_cover_image` method, in that this method saves the associated `CoverImage` instance that is returned.

These methods are all related to the associated class, which is the `CoverImage` class. For general purposes, replace the text `cover_image` in the methods above with the singular form of the associated class for whatever classes you are associating with the `has_one` relationship to get the methods added.

133

The `CoverImage` class also requires some special Rails code. For this side of the relationship, you use the `belongs_to` method, like this:

```
class CoverImage < ActiveRecord::Base
    belongs_to :book
end
```

Methods added by belongs_to

The `belongs_to` method causes the following methods to be automatically added to the `CoverImage` class:

- `book`

  Returns the associated `Book` object, or `nil` if no object is associated.

- `book=`

  Assigns the `Book` associate object, extracts the primary key, sets it as the foreign key.

- `book.nil?`

  Returns true if there is no associated `Book` object.

- `build_book(attributes={})`

  Returns a new `Book` object that has been instantiated with `attributes` and linked to this `Book` object through a foreign key, but has not yet been saved.

- `create_book`

  Returns a new `Book` object that has been instantiated with `attributes`, linked to this `CoverImage` object through a foreign key, and that has already been saved. Notice how this is different from the `build_book` method, in that this method saves the associated `Book` instance that is returned.

These methods are all related to the associated class, which is the `Book` class. For general purposes, replace the text `book` in the methods above with the singular form of the associated class for whatever classes you are associating with the `belongs_to` relationship to get the methods added.

Many-to-one relationships

The *many-to-one relationship* is the most common type of data relationship. The simplest way of explaining a many-to-one relationship is with a picture. Figure 3.5 shows a many-to-one relationship that exists between books and chapters. A book represents the 'one' side of the relationship, and the chapters are the 'many' side of the relationship; one book contains many chapters.

Both chapters and books are models in your Rails application. In your database, each of the models is represented in a separate table. Databases use a concept called foreign keys to create a relationship between two tables. A *foreign key* is a column in one table that points to a row in a different table. In a Rails application, the foreign keys must be named with the singular form name of the table they are pointing to, followed by `_id`. For example, the foreign key column in the chapter's table would be named `book_id`. This column specifies the book that a chapter is contained within.

FIGURE 3.5

Many-to-one relationship

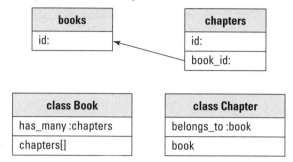

In addition to setting up your database schema in the correct way to model a many-to-one relationship, you also add special code to your model classes in a Rails application. Using the books and chapters example, your Book class would look like this:

```
class Book < ActiveRecord::Base
    has_many :chapters
end
```

The has_many method indicates that a book has many chapters.

Methods added by has_many

By using the has_many method, the following methods are added to your Book class:

- collection

  Returns an array of all the associated objects. An empty array is returned if none are found.

- collection<<(object,..)

  Adds one or more objects to the collection by setting their foreign keys to the collection's primary key.

- collection.delete(object,..)

  Removes one or more objects from the collection by setting their foreign keys to NULL. This will also destroy the objects if they are declared as belongs_to and dependent on this model.

- collection=objects

  Replaces the collection's content by deleting and adding objects as appropriate.

- collection.singular_ids

  Returns an array of the associated objects' ids.

- collection.singular_ids=ids

  Replace the collection with the objects identified by the primary keys in ids.

- `collection.clear`

  Remove every object from the collection. This associated objects are destroyed if they are associated with `:dependent => :destroy`, or deleted from the database if associated with `:dependent => :delete_all`, otherwise their foreign keys are set to NULL.

- `collection.empty?`

  Returns true if there are no associated objects.

- `collection.size`

  Returns the number of associated objects.

- `collection.find`

  Finds an associated object using the same rules as when you use the `find` method from one of your Active Record models directly.

- `collection.build(attributes = {})`

  Returns one or more new objects of the collection type that have been instantiated with `attributes` and linked to this object through a foreign key, but have not yet been saved. This will only work if the associated object already exists and is not `nil`.

- `collection.create(attributes = {})`

  Returns a new object of the collection type that has been instantiated with attributes, linked to this object through a foreign key, and that has already been saved. This will only work if the associated object already exists and is not `nil`.

Where the `collection` is referenced, in the case of the Book class this would be `chapters`. For example to determine how many chapters are associated with a given book, you could use this method:

```
chapter_count = book.chapters.size
```

You also add code to the Chapter model, which would look like this:

```
class Chapter < ActiveRecord::Base
    belongs_to :book
end
```

Here you used the `belongs_to` method, which is the other side of a `has_many` relationship.

Methods added by belongs_to

You have already seen the methods that are added by the `belongs_to` relationship previously when we discussed the `has_one` and `belongs_to` relationships.

Many-to-many relationships

In a *many-to-many relationship*, each side of the relationship can point to more than one related object. Again, the best way to illustrate this kind of relationship is through a picture. Let's look at the many-to-many relationship in Figure 3.6. This example uses a Book and a Store model. A store contains many books, and thus it's easy to understand this 'many' side of the relationship. Looking at the relationship from the other direction, a book is usually sold in many different stores. Because both objects can be related to many of the other objects, you have a many-to-many relationship.

In a many-to-one relationship, a foreign key was used to model the relationship in the database. A many-to-many relationship must be modeled in the database using a slightly more complex technique. You use a relationship join table to model the many-to-many relationship. In Figure 3.6 this join table is shown as `books_stores`. In order for Rails to recognize the table and correctly build the association, this join table should be named with the names of the two related tables in alphabetical order and separated by an underscore. Thus in this case, you end up with the table named `books_stores`. You would create this table using a migration, just as you create regular model object tables. However, you do not need to generate a model class to represent this table.

FIGURE 3.6

Many-to-many relationship

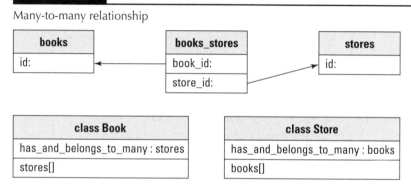

As with the other Rails recognized relationships, you also have to add some code to each of the related models. The method call that you will add to each model is the same in this case. It is the `has_and_belongs_to_many` method. You will often see this shortened as HABTM in discussions online. So following through with the example shown in Figure 3.6, you would add this method to each of the `Book` and `Store` classes.

```
class Book < ActiveRecord::Base
    has_and_belongs_to_many :stores
end

class Store < ActiveRecord::Base
    has_and_belongs_to_many :books
end
```

Methods added by has_and_belongs_to_many

By using the `has_and_belongs_to_many` method, the following methods are added to your `Book` and `Store` classes:

- `collection`

  Returns an array of all the associated objects. An empty array is returned if none are found.

- `collection<<(object,..)`

  Adds one or more objects to the collection by creating associations in the join table (`collection.push` and `collection.concat` are aliases to this method).

- `collection.delete(object,..)`

  Removes one or more objects from the collection by removing their associations from the join table. This does not destroy the objects.

- `collection=objects`

  Replaces the collection's content by deleting and adding objects as appropriate.

- `collection.singular_ids`

  Returns an array of the associated objects' ids.

- `collection.singular_ids=ids`

  Replace the collection with the objects identified by the primary keys in `ids`.

- `collection.clear`

  Remove every object from the collection. This does not destroy the objects.

- `collection.empty?`

  Returns true if there are no associated objects.

- `collection.size`

  Returns the number of associated objects.

- `collection.find(id)`

  Finds an associated object responding to the `id` and that meets the condition that it has to be associated with this object.

- `collection.build(attributes = {})`

  Returns a new object of the collection type that has been instantiated with `attributes` and linked to this object through the join table, but has not yet been saved.

- `collection.create(attributes = {})`

  Returns a new object of the collection type that has been instantiated with `attributes`, linked to this object through the join table, and that has already been saved.

Where the `collection` is referenced, in the case of the `Book` class this would be `stores`, and in the case of the `Store` class, this would be `books`. For example to determine how many stores are associated with a given book, you could use this method:

```
store_count = book.stores.size
```

and to find the number of books in a given store, you could use this method:

```
book_count = store.books.size
```

Implementing Validations

Validations allow you to define valid states for each of your Active Record model classes. Rails makes it easy to add validations to your model classes. As you saw with modeling relationships in Rails, you make use of more of Active Record's domain-specific language to model validations in your Rails application. You can do several kinds of validations using the built-in validation DSL.

When an attribute in one of your Active Record model classes fails a validation, that is considered an error. Each of your Active Record model classes maintains a collection of errors in an attribute called `errors`. This makes it easy for you to display appropriate error information to the users of your application when validation errors occur.

Now let's look at some examples of how you might use validations in your code. Remember the example of comic books that you worked with in previous sections of this chapter? Add a validation to ensure that a comic book always contains a title. Open the `app/models/comic_book.rb` file and edit it as follows:

```
class ComicBook < ActiveRecord::Base
    validates_presence_of :title
end
```

The `validates_presence_of` method adds a validation to the `ComicBook` class that will make sure every comic book has a title. If you attempt to save a `ComicBook` instance that does not contain a title, you will get an error preventing the record from being saved. There is a method available to you named `valid?` that you can use to test the validity of your attributes at any time. The `valid?` method will run the validations and return true or false indicating whether the validations passed for the model instance on which it was called. In the example below, you would get a return value of false when you call the `valid?` method.

```
comic = ComicBook.new
comic.valid? #=> false
```

You could then look at the errors collection to see what the validation problems are.

```
comic.errors.each_full do |message|
    puts message
end
```

Since you have only defined one validation for the `ComicBook` class, this would print the following message:

```
Title can't be blank
```

If you had defined additional validations, you would see an error message for each validation that was unsuccessful. This is very useful to use when displaying errors to the user of a Web application.

There are also methods available on the errors collection that are useful for obtaining additional information about your validation errors. The method `invalid?` allows you to pass it a specific attribute name and it will return true or false to tell you whether that specific attribute is valid or not. Using the comic book example, you could use this method like this:

```
comic = ComicBook.new
comic.valid?
comic.errors.invalid?(title) #=> true
```

Calling `invalid?` on the title attribute returns true since that attribute does not pass the `validates_presence_of` validation. If you want to get the error message associated with a specific attribute, you can use the on method as shown here:

```
comic = ComicBook.new
comic.valid?
comic.errors.on(:title) #=> can't be blank
```

This returns the string `"can't be blank"`. Notice that the word `"Title"` is not a part of the string that is returned.

Note that you can only call these methods on the `errors` collection after you have performed a validation, such as by using the `valid?` method.

The next validation method we'll look at is the `validates_format_of` method. This method is useful for ensuring that an attribute conforms to a specific format. One of the places this is used most often is to `validate the format of` an email address. Below is an example of how you might use the `validates_format_of` method within a `User` class to validate an `email` attribute.

```
class User < ActiveRecord::Base
    validates_format_of :email
end
```

Rails includes many more built-in validation methods. These are briefly described in Table 3.2. For complete details of how these methods work and the options that you can use with these, you should refer to the Rails documentation on validations available online at the following URL:

http://api.rubyonrails.org/classes/ActiveRecord/Validations/ClassMethods.html

If you want to save an object despite any validation errors that you might have you can call the save method with an argument of false. The line below will force the object to be saved even with validation errors:

```
comic = ComicBook.new
comic.save(false)
```

TABLE 3.2	

Rails Built-in Validation Methods

Method	Description
validates_ acceptance_of	This validation is best described using an example. You could use this validation to validate that the user has accepted a terms of service agreement by checking a check box.
validates_associated	Validates whether associated objects are all valid themselves. Works with any kind of association.
validates_ confirmation_of	Allows you to validate that the user has confirmed fields such as a password or email address in a second entry field.
validates_each	Validates each attribute against a block.
validates_ exclusion_of	Validates that an attribute is not in a particular enumerable object.
validates_format_of	Validates the value of an attribute using a regular expression to insure it is of the correct format.
validates_inclusion_ of	Validates whether the value of an attribute is available in a particular enumerable object.
validates_length_of	Validates that the length of an attribute matches length restrictions specified.
validates_ numericality_of	Validates whether an attribute is numeric.
validates_presence_ of	Validates that the attribute is not blank.
validates_size_of	This is an alias for validates_length_of
validates_ uniqueness_of	Validates that an attribute is unique in the database.

Custom Validations

If you find that the built-in validation methods do not meet your needs, you can create custom validations that still allow you to use Rails errors collection and validations mechanics. You do this by defining a `validate` method for the Active Record class that you want the custom validations on. In this `validate` method you can check the state of multiple attributes and manipulate the errors collection as needed.

This might be very useful for cases when you want to determine the validity of your object based on the values of multiple attributes. For example, suppose you want to be sure that a user has either entered a login name, or an email address when registering. You could do this with the following custom validation:

```
Class User < ActiveRecord::Base
    def validate
        if login.blank? && email.blank?

    errors.add_to_base("You must enter either a login or an email
    address")
        end
    end
end
```

If both the `login` and the `email` are blank, an error message is added to the `errors` collection. This is done using the `add_to_base` method of the `errors` collection. This method allows you to add an error message that is not associated with a specific attribute, but instead it is associated with the object as a whole.

If you wanted to add your own error message specific to an attribute, you can do that using the `add` method of the `errors` collection. This method takes the name of an attribute and the error message you want to associate with that attribute as parameters. Below is an example of how you might use this method:

```
comic_book.errors.add('login', 'You must enter a login name')
```

There is one more method that you'll find handy when using the errors collection. That is the `clear` method. The `clear` method will clear the `errors` collection of all errors. To repopulate it, you must validate the object again through either built-in or custom validations, or simply add error messages to it manually using the above add methods.

```
comic_book.errors.clear
```

Advanced Active Record

You can create many very powerful Web applications using only the techniques and methods that were covered in the previous sections of this chapter. However, there are times when you may want to implement more advanced data related code. This section walks you through several more advanced things that you can do with Active Record. You'll learn how to implement single table inheritance, how to use composition, and how to implement transactions using Active Record and Rails.

Single table inheritance

Active Record uses a database technique called single table inheritance to support inheritance in your model classes. With *single table inheritance*, a class and all of its descendents use the same database table. For example, the `ComicBook` model that you've been working with in this chapter could have extended a model class called `Book`, because a comic book is a type of book. Your application might also work with other types of books, such as text books. You might have a `TextBook` model which also extends the `Book` model. With single table inheritance, books, comic books, and text books would be stored in the same table. See Figure 3.7 for an example of how the classes and database should be laid out.

FIGURE 3.7

Single table inheritance

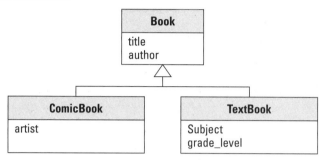

Notice that the common table is given the plural name of the base class. In this case, the table is named `books`. The `books` table contains a column named `type`, which specifies for a particular record whether that record is a text book or a comic book. Active Record automatically manages the `type` column.

Your model classes would be defined like this:

```
class ComicBook < Book
end

class TextBook < Book
end

class Book < ActiveRecord::Base
end
```

If you perform a query using the `Book` class, it returns both text books and comic books. A query using the `ComicBook` class returns only comic books and a query using the `TextBook` class returns only text books, as expected.

If you ever need to see the type field, you cannot access it using `book.type` because the type field is a class attribute. However, you can access it from your objects like this:

```
book[:type]
```

The above line would return the type of the object, either `ComicBook` or `TextBook`.

Composition

Composition is a design pattern in which you have one class composed of several other classes. Note that this is not the same as inheritance, in which a subclass extends a base class. With composition, you have a main class and one or more component classes. This design pattern is also referred to as *aggregation*.

Rails implements the composition pattern using one table that is mapped to multiple classes. Consider the example of a Book that is composed of a Publisher. Figure 3.8 shows how the classes and database table would be laid out. As you can see, the books table contains columns for attributes that exist in both the Book and Publisher classes. You would implement the composition in your Book model class like this:

```
class Book < ActiveRecord::Base
    composed_of :publisher, :class_name => "Publisher",
                :mapping => [[:publisher_name, :name],
                             [:publisher_country, :country]]
End
```

FIGURE 3.8

Rails implementation of the Composition Pattern

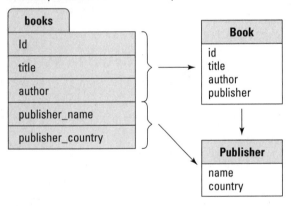

The first parameter to composed_of is the name that the component class is referred to by the main class. In this example, because the first parameter to composed_of and the component class name are the same, you could have eliminated the :class_name parameter. By default, Rails looks for a class that contains the same name as the first parameter to composed_of.

The :class_name parameter allows you to override the Rails default and use a different name from that of the class as the first parameter. For example, you could have used this line:

```
composed_of :publisher_info, :class_name => "Publisher",
```

The second parameter to `composed_of` specifies the attribute mappings. The `:mapping` array associates columns in the books database with attributes in the `Publisher` class. For the mapping in this example, the `publisher_name` column in the books table is mapped to the `name` attribute of the `Publisher` class, and the `publisher_country` column is mapped to the `country` attribute of the `Publisher` class.

You also have to add some code to your component class, `Publisher`. `Publisher` would look like this:

```
class Publisher
    def initialize(name, country)
        @ name = name
        @ country = country
    end

    attr_reader : name,: country
end
```

You must create an `initialize` method that contains a parameter for each attribute that the component represents. Within the `initialize` method, you have to create instance attributes for each of the component attributes.

Rails adds accessors to the main class for the component class and each of its attributes. You could access the `Publisher` object from an instance of the `Book` class using: `book.publisher`. You can also set the publisher of a book using this code:

```
book.publisher = Publisher.new('', '', '')
```

You access each of the attributes in the component class through the parent class attribute of the main class. From an instance of the `Book` class, you would access the `Publisher` attributes like this:

```
pub_name = book.publisher. name
pub_country = abook.publisher. country
```

Composition is often used when you have a class that you want to use across many models. An often-cited example is the case of a `Person` and `Address` class. A `Person` is composed of an `Address`. In this example, you might want to also use the `Address` class across other models. The `Business` and `Museum` classes might also be composed of an `Address`. Employing composition in this example would save you from having to repeat the attributes and behavior contained in the `Address` model in all of the models that are composed with it.

Transactions

Many applications that you write will require the use of database transactions. Transactions are a way of grouping database actions together, such that they either all execute as expected, or none of them execute in the case of an error.

Rails supports transactions using a transaction class method that is available on all model classes that extend `ActiveRecord::Base`. A typical example of when transactions are required is when you are working with bank accounts. When you transfer money from one account to another, that process can be broken down into the following actions:

1. Subtract the transfer amount from the account that you are transferring from.
2. Add the transfer amount to the account that you are transferring to.

If the first action, subtracting the money from the 'from' account succeeded, but the second action of adding the money to the 'to' account failed, you would have many unhappy customers if your application did not make use of transactions. If both of these actions were wrapped in a transaction, a failure in the second action would cause the first action to be undone, or rolled back. A *roll back* is a database term for undoing an action that was performed on the database.

Using this example, in your Rails application, you would likely have a class named Account. The Account class would have a transfer method implemented as follows:

```
def transfer(from, to, amount)
    Account.transaction do
        from.withdraw(amount)
        to.deposit(amount)
    end
end
```

Now if any failures occur in either of the method calls contained in the block that begins with the `Account.transaction` do line, all of the database actions will be rolled back. Therefore, either both the withdrawal and deposit actions succeed, or they are both rolled back. This is exactly the behavior that you were seeking.

Summary

This chapter explored the details of Active Record and how you can use its features to create the model layer of your Web application. You were shown how to use Active Record to perform the following tasks:

- Create models for your application using the Rails `script/generate` script
- Use Rails migrations to create and modify your database
- Find records in your database using a variety of ActiveRecord methods
- Update and delete rows in your database
- Model your database relations using ActiveRecord methods
- Add data validations to your model classes

You also learned how to use some advanced features of Rails, including Single Table Inheritance, Composition, and Transactions. Active Record allows you to create the model layer of your Web applications with ease and simplicity.

Chapter 4

Controller: In Depth

I n this chapter, you will learn about the controller layer of the MVC framework implemented in Rails applications. The controller layer of an MVC application is responsible for figuring out what to do with external input. The controller layer interprets user input and responds to user requests by communicating with the model layer, and rendering views using the view layer. You can think of the controller as the conductor of the application; it determines which views to show based on the input received.

The controller layer should be the only layer of your application that knows the client is actually a Web browser. All interaction with the Web server and knowledge of such interaction should be confined to methods in your controller classes. This layer should not contain a great deal of your business logic; the business logic should be contained within your model layer. Theoretically, you could rewrite the controller layer to adapt the application to a different platform, such as a non-browser environment.

Rails implements the controller layer primarily using a component called *ActionController*. ActionController is joined with ActionView to make up the Action Pack component of Rails. Action Pack provides the functionality for processing incoming requests from the browser and for generating responses to the browser.

What is ActionController?

In Rails, your application's controller and view layers use the Action Pack components of Rails. Controllers are implemented using the

ActionController component of Action Pack. The ActionController component provides you with an easy-to-use functionality related to the following areas:

- Routing
- Interfacing with the Web server
- Using sessions
- Cache management
- Rendering view templates

Throughout this chapter, you can learn how ActionController helps you with each of these tasks.

In a typical Rails application, you might have many controller classes. Each of your application's model classes will typically have a controller class for working with that model. For example, you might have defined a user model or a book model. You would probably also want to create a `UserController` class and a `BookController` class. These controller classes would handle requests to show, create, update, and delete these types of model objects. Each controller class you write will inherit from the Rails class, `ActionController::Base`. This is how your controller classes gain the power of Rails.

All About Routing

A Web application receives requests from a browser, takes action to process those requests, and returns a response that is directed back to the browser. Sitting in between the browser and the Web application is usually a Web server. The Web server passes the browser requests to your Rails Web application, but once they are passed into your application, where do they go from there? The ActionController component uses a routing subsystem to route the Web requests to the appropriate method in your Rails application. The routing subsystem routes requests to methods that are called *action methods*. The action methods are contained in controller classes.

The action methods in your application's controller classes receive the incoming requests and invoke methods contained in other layers of the application, such as the model layer; using the view layer, a response is generated and returned to the requesting browser.

The Rails routing mechanism is very flexible and can be adapted to meet any special requirements that you might have. However, you can get basic routing functionality immediately without having to write a single line of configuration code. The basic routing functionality is useful for many complete Web applications that you may write.

Let's start by looking at an example request from the browser to this URL:

```
www.bookstore.com/book/show/1234
```

This request is received by the Web server and passed to the routing subsystem of Rails. The routing subsystem interprets this as a request to invoke the show method of the BookController class and pass an id parameter of 1234. The flow of events that occur when this request is received looks like this:

1. The Web server passes the request to the Rails routing subsystem.

2. The routing subsystem parses the request, identifying the requested controller and action.

3. A new instance of the requested controller is created.

4. The process method of the controller is called and is passed request and response details.

5. The controller calls the specified action method.

CROSS-REF **For more information on templates, see Chapter 5.**

Observe the pattern here in relation to how the request was routed:

```
http://server_url/controller name/action name/optional id
```

This is the default routing mechanism that is built into Rails. The first path element following the server URL is the name of a controller to invoke. The second path element is an action contained within that controller, and the last path element is the id of a data item. Not all of your actions will require a parameter, and so the id path element is optional. For example, a request to list all of the books contained in the store might look like this:

```
http://www.bookstore.com/book/list
```

Defining custom routes

You do not have to use the default routing mechanism if it does not meet your needs. Let's look at an example of where you might want to define a custom routing mechanism. You might have a Web application that lets users view articles posted on previous days. Perhaps you want to be able to accept URLs that look like this sample:

```
http://myarticles.com/article/2008/1/20
```

You would like this to be interpreted as a request for articles that were created on the date 1/20/2008, and so the general routing pattern would look like this:

```
http://myarticles.com/article/year/month/day
```

So how do you tell Rails about that routing pattern? The answer is through a file that was generated when you generated the Rails skeleton for your application using the rails command. This file is the routes.rb file found in the config subdirectory of your Web application directory. Open up config/routes.rb and take a look at the default routes. You should see these routes already defined:

```
map.connect ':controller/:action/:id.:format'
map.connect ':controller/:action/:id'
```

Each of the `map.connect` statements defines a route that connects URLs to controllers and actions. The string passed to the `map.connect` method specifies a pattern to match the URL against. The routes you see defined look for three path elements. The path elements are mapped to the fields named in this string and placed into a parameters hash. For example, the path `book/show/1234` produces the following parameters hash:

```
@params = { :controller => 'book'
  :action => 'show'
  :id => 1234 }
```

The routing subsystem then invokes the `show` method of the `store` controller and passes a parameter of `:id` with a value of `1234`.

Now that you understand how the default route is implemented, let's figure out how you would define a route to map the URL containing year, month, and date path elements. Remember that, as in the case of the default route, you must pass a route pattern string to the `map.connect` method. The pattern string matching the desired URLs would look like this:

```
"article/:year/:month/:day"
```

This pattern matches the path elements of the URLs that you want to use. If you create a route using this string passed to the `map.connect` method, does that define a complete route? If you think it does, let me ask this: What action method would these requests be routed to? This route pattern does not include an action name. Therefore, you know the route is not complete as is. The pattern string is complete, though. It contains enough information to match the desired URL format. You need to pass an additional parameter to `map.connect` to specify an action. This would give you a route that looks like this:

```
map.connect "article/:year/:month/:day",
  :controller => "article",
  :action => "show_date"
```

This route works as long as the URL always contains a year, a month, and a date. Suppose you want to also allow users to enter only a year, or only a year and month, and see the articles corresponding to those timeframes. To make that work, you can tell the route that the `:day` and `:month` elements do not have to be there, or in Ruby code, you can say that these elements can have a `nil` value. You would now modify the route to look like this:

```
map.connect "article/:year/:month/:day",
  :controller => "article",
  :action => "show_date",
  :day => nil,
  :month => nil
```

Now things are beginning to look pretty good, but what if someone tried to use a URL that looked like this:

```
http://myarticles.com/article/8
```

This URL doesn't look like it is meant for the route you just defined. However, remember when you said that the `:day` and `:month` elements are not required, and the route was modified to allow those elements to not be present? Given that, this URL can match the route you defined. It would interpret the value 8 as the `:year` parameter. This is probably not what you want, though. The route would be better if it restricted the date fields to be valid date values. Let's add that validation by modifying the route to look like this:

```
map.connect " article/:year/:month/:day",
 :controller => " article",
 :action => "show_date",
 :requirements => { :year => /(19|20)\d\d/,
 :month => /[01]?\d/,
 :day => /[0-3]?\d/ },
 :day => nil,
 :month => nil
```

Now, a `:requirements` parameter is added that specifies requirements for the `:year`, `:month`, and `:day` fields. Regular expressions are used to make sure that each of the date fields contains a valid value. Now you have a well-defined route for accepting requests like the one you originally specified:

```
http://myarticles.com/article/2008/1/20
```

Defining a custom default route

Now you understand a bit about how requests are routed to your controllers and actions in a Rails application. Routing is accomplished by parsing path elements of a URL to map a request to a controller and action method. This convention is okay for most of your Web application, but what about your application's home page? Typically, you want the home page to be routable just by going to your application's server URL without specifying any path elements. For example, the home page for `myarticles.com` should be reachable by using this simple URL:

```
http://www.myarticles.com
```

Further suppose that your home page featured some dynamic functionality that required processing by your code. How would Rails know what controller and method to route the home page request to? The answer is to define a route that matches a URL with no path elements, like this:

```
map.connect "",
 :controller => "home",
 :action => "index"
```

By specifying an empty pattern string, this pattern matches against any URL that it sees, including the home page request with no path elements. It tells the routing subsystem to send this request to the index method of the home controller.

> **CAUTION** You must also delete public/index.html in order for the default route to work. This is because Rails will bypass the routing mechanism for any html files that it finds directly in the public directory.

Be careful where you place this in the routes.rb file, though. If a URL matches multiple routes defined in routes.rb, the first one matched will be the route used. This is important to keep in mind. If you placed this route as the first route listed in your routes.rb file, this would catch every request, and every request would end up getting routed to the index method of the home controller. You would want to list this route at the end of all your routes.

Using named routes

The routes that you've seen so far are called *anonymous routes*. There is also a way of creating a named route. A named route will allow you to simplify the URLs that you use in your code.

Named routes are very simple to create. Instead of using the method map.connect in your routes.rb file, you replace the word connect with the name you want to give to that route. For example, you could create a named route for the year/month/date articles route that was created previously by renaming it like this:

```
map.dates " article/:year/:month/:day",
  :controller => " article",
  :action => "show_date",
  :requirements => { :year => /(19|20)\d\d/,
  :month => /[01]?\d/,
  :day => /[0-3]?\d/ },
  :day => nil,
  :month => nil
```

You should also rename your home page route to home, like this:

```
map.home "",
  :controller => "home",
  :action => "index"
```

This creates a name route called home that will use the home controller and the index action. Next, you'll see how useful named routes can be.

Within the code that you write, either in classes or view templates, you'll often need to specify links. Especially for situations where there is a link that you find yourself using over and over again, such as a link to an action that is accessible from every page, it is useful to have a way of specifying that link without having to hardcode the full URL into every page template. Named routes give you the ability to specify a link URL using a convenient name.

Without taking advantage of a named route, you might have a link specified like this repeated in many of your template files:

```
<%= link_to 'Home', :controller => 'home', :action => 'index' %>
```

However, if you take advantage of the named route you created above using map.home in the routes.rb file, this link can be specified like this:

```
<%= link_to 'Home', home_url %>
```

By using home_url, Rails knows that you are referring to the route named home and will automatically use the controller and method specified in that route. Not only does this reduce the amount of code that you have to type, but it also abstracts the home page link into a single place—the named route. If you decided to change the name of the controller or action method used to display the home page, you will not have to change all of your view templates that use that link. You only have to change the named route.

You can use named routes to generate URLs in your controller code by using the name of the route followed by _url. For example, in the previous link, you used the home_url method to create a link to the home page of the application.

You can also pass parameters to the URL generation methods as a hash to specify details of the URL. For example, here is how you could create a URL to request all articles for the year 2007 using the dates route that you created earlier:

```
@articles_2007 = dates_url(:year => 2007)
```

The parameter :year maps to the :year parameter that you defined in the dates route definition. You can also pass in parameters that are not defined in the route and they will be appended to the query string as additional parameters. For example, consider the following code:

```
@articles_2007 = dates_url(:year => 2007, :group_by => 'weekday')
```

This would result in having an additional parameter named group_by passed into your action method. You could then use this additional parameter to construct an appropriate query.

Constructing URLs with url_for

Rails provides a method named url_for that allows you another way of constructing URLs within your code. Recall the route that is defined for you when you first generate a new Rails application:

```
map.connect ':controller/:action/:id'
```

Assume that somewhere in your code, you want to create a URL that would map to the action and controller specified in that route. The url_for method constructs a URL given a set of options that you pass to it.

```
@link = url_for(:controller=>"article", :action=>"show",
    :id=>123)
```

This would create a link in the @link variable with a value similar to this:

```
http://www.myapp.com/article/show/123
```

The url_for method takes the parameters passed to it and creates a URL that maps those parameters to a pattern specified in one of your routes. This abstracts the details of how your URLs are specified out of your code. The details of your URLs have to exist in one place only, your routes.rb file.

In addition to specifying the controller and action when you call the url_for method, there are a number of additional parameters that url_for supports that allow you to customize the URLs that it generates. These options are listed in Table 4.1.

TABLE 4.1

url_for Supported Parameters

Option	Data Type	Description
:anchor	String	Adds an anchor name to the generated URL.
:host	String	Sets the host and port name used in the generated URL.
:only_path	Boolean	Specifices that only the path should be generated. The protocol, host name, and port are left out of the generated URL.
:protocol	String	Sets the protocol used in the Generated URL, that is, 'https.'
:user	String	Used for inline HTTP authentication. (used only if :password is also present)
:password	String	Used for inline HTTP authentication. (used only if :user is also present)
:escape	Boolean	Determines whether the returned URL will be HTML escaped or not. (true by default)
:trailing_slash	Boolean	Appends a slash to the generated URL.

CROSS-REF With the release of Rails 2.0 a new style of routing become popular. That style is called RESTful routes. This is a way of constructing routes that correspond to a RESTful architecture. RESTful architecture and routes are covered in Chapter 12.

Creating and Using Controllers

Now that you understand routes, you should know how requests end up in the action methods of your controller classes. Now let's see what your controller methods do with those requests.

Generating controllers

Controller classes can be automatically generated for you using the Rails `script/generate` script. You pass the controller parameter and the name of the controller you want to generate to the script like this:

```
ruby script/generate controller User
```

You would run the previous command from the root of your Rails application directory. If you run this command, you will see output similar to this:

```
exists  app/controllers/
exists  app/helpers/
create  app/views/user
exists  test/functional/
create  app/controllers/user_controller.rb
create  test/functional/user_controller_test.rb
create  app/helpers/user_helper.rb
```

Three files are created by running the script: the controller class file, a functional test file for the controller, and a helper file. The controller file is what you want to look at now, so open up the `app/controllers/user_controller.rb` file. The file should look like this:

```
class UserController < ApplicationController
end
```

The only thing you see in this file is that it is a class that extends the `ApplicationController` class. The `ApplicationController` class was automatically generated by Rails when you created the application skeleton using the `rails` command. Take a look at that file, which you can find in `app/controllers/application.rb`:

```
# Filters added to this controller apply to all controllers in
  the application.
# Likewise, all the methods added will be available for all
  controllers.

class ApplicationController < ActionController::Base
    helper :all # include all helpers, all the time

    # See ActionController::RequestForgeryProtection for details
    # Uncomment the :secret if you're not using the cookie session
  store
    protect_from_forgery # :secret =>
    '7dbe320f76e9f0135ab2eb16457a5b20'
end
```

The `ApplicationController` extends a Rails internal class called `ActionController::Base`. Extending this class is what gives your controllers all of the built-in functionality that they have, which you'll learn about in this chapter. In the `ApplicationController`, you see a method named `protect_from_forgery` being called. This method adds protection from malicious attacks against your application.

A common type of attack that is carried out against Web applications is called a cross-site request forgery (CSRF). This type of attack is prevented by adding a token based on the current session to all forms and Ajax requests. This allows your controllers to accept only the requests that contain this forgery protection token.

There is a parameter named `:secret` that is commented out by default. The `:secret` parameter can be used to specify a salt value which is used to generate the forgery protection token. The salt value assists in making the token more secure. If you do a Google search on CSRF you can learn more about this kind of attack.

In the `ApplicationController`, you also see a call to the method `helper` with a parameter of `:all` being passed. This makes all of the helper classes available to all of your controllers.

Take a look at the helper file that was created by the generator. Open up `app/helpers/user_helper.rb`.

```
module UserHelper
end
```

This is an empty Ruby module. Helper modules are where you will place methods that you want to share across your view templates. Often, you'll need a method that is used by all of the view templates associated with the controller. All of the methods that you put into the helper modules are automatically made available to all of the view templates associated with that controller.

CROSS-REF You can start defining methods for the helper files in Chapter 5 when views are covered.

If you know the names of some of the action methods that you want to include in your controller class, you can also specify those to the `script/generate` script and have stubs for those methods created, as well. For example, run this `generate` command:

```
ruby script/generate controller Book list show new
```

This creates a `Book` controller class for you with method stubs for each of the method names you passed: `list`, `show`, and `new`. Your generated controller class will look like this:

```
class BookController < ApplicationController
 def list
 end

 def show
 end
```

```
   def new
   end
 end
```

You might have also noticed that a few additional files were created corresponding to each of the action methods:

```
app/views/book/list.html.erb
app/views/book/show.html.erb
app/views/book/new.html.erb
```

These are Rails view templates, which you will use to describe the pages rendered as a result of each of those actions. You'll learn more about the view templates in Chapter 5 when views are covered in depth. For the remainder of this chapter, it's safe to ignore those files.

That's all you need to get started with creating a controller class. In the remainder of this chapter, you'll see how you can build up the empty controller class to handle all of your browser requests.

Action methods

Methods contained in your controllers that have requests routed to them are called *action methods*. Note that not all methods in your controllers are necessarily action methods. You may have some helper methods used by your action methods that are never routed to.

As you saw in the previous section, you can have the `script/generate` script create stubs for your action methods, or you can hand-code any action methods that you want to add. Action methods are defined just like any standard instance method. What makes action methods different is that they are able to use functionality provided to your class by Rails to access the Web request and response information.

Naming Your Controllers and Actions

You may come across many different opinions of how you should name your controllers and actions in a Rails application. I believe that your naming style is important to the readability and maintainability of your application, and thus worth discussing.

Controller classes should be named with nouns, while action methods should be named with verbs. If you find yourself needing to use a verb-noun combination as the name of your actions, this is often characteristic of needing a new controller. For example, consider a controller, properly named using a noun as `User`. Also assume that you have a page that shows a user's profile and a different page that shows a user's address information. You might have methods in your `User` controller to display these pages named `show` and `show_address`. The second method, `show_address`, is an example of a verb-noun combination that might indicate the need for a new controller. Rather than have both of these methods in the User controller, it is probably a good idea to use two controllers — one named `User` and the other named `Address`. Now each of these controllers can have a `show` method without requiring the verb-noun action name.

Rails provides built-in functionality to allow you to easily perform the following functions in the action methods of your controllers:

- Use request parameters submitted by the browser.
- Render a template in response to a request.
- Send a redirect to the requesting browser.
- Send short feedback messages to the browser.

Using request parameters

Many of the requests that your action methods will receive will contain request parameters submitted by the browser, which you will need to process the requested action. This includes parameters submitted in a URL using an HTTP GET request, and parameters contained in the HTTP header of a POST request. As an example, assume the following URL is passed to your Rails application:

```
http://www.myapp.com/user/show/123
```

Using the default route, Rails will route this request to the show method of your UserController class. A user id is also passed to the show method. The show method should look up the user identified by that user id and display details about that user. Let's start creating a show method to perform those actions:

```
class UserController < ApplicationController
    def show
    end
end
```

The first thing you need to do is get the user id that is passed to the show method. Rails makes all of the request parameters available through a params hash. Obtain the user id from the params hash in your show method:

```
class UserController < ApplicationController
    def show
        user_id = params[:id]
    end
end
```

Recall from the earlier discussion of Rails routing mechanisms that the id parameter passed in the URL path is made available as the :id parameter. You could then use a model class to retrieve the user corresponding to that id:

```
class UserController < ApplicationController
    def show
        user_id = params[:id]
        @user = User.find(user_id)
    end
end
```

Assuming, you have a `User` model, calling its `find` method and passing the user id will retrieve the `User` object for the desired user. Notice that an instance variable, `@user`, receives the returned `User` object. Any instance variables are automatically available to your view templates. By setting the `User` object as an instance variable, your view template will be able to use that object to display information about the user.

Rendering templates

Rails *templates* define the views of your Rails application. At the end of your action, you typically will render a template to return a new Web page to the user. Continuing with the example request to display information about a particular user through the `show` method, add a render call to display a user view template:

```
class UserController < ApplicationController
    def show
        user_id = params[:id]
        @user = User.find(user_id)
        render :template => "show"
    end
end
```

Here the render method is called with an options hash containing a single value, the name of a template to render. In this case, the show template is specified. This would cause the view template stored in `app/views/user/show.html.erb` to be rendered. While this correctly illustrates how to render a template, if the template you want to render is named the same as the action method, the render call is not necessary. By default, an action method that does not perform any renders or redirects will render a template containing the same name as the action method, if such a template exists. With that in mind, modify the method to only call the render method if the user being looked up is not found:

```
class UserController < ApplicationController
    def show
        if !@user = User.find(params[:id])
            render :template => "user_not_found"
        end
    end
end
```

Now if the user is found, no explicit render is called, so the default `show.html.erb` template will be rendered, which is what you want. However, if the user is not found, a template named `user_not_found.html.erb` will be rendered. This template could contain an error message for the user. One other change was made here. Instead of using a temporary `user_id` local variable to hold the user id value, the `params[:id]` value is now passed directly to the `User.find` method, saving you a line of code.

CROSS-REF Where views are covered in Chapter 5, you can see many more ways to use the render method to create other responses.

Redirects

In addition to rendering a template, Rails also has built-in functionality that allows you to easily send a redirect to the browser. Let's look at an example of where you might want to use a redirect:

```
def create
    @book = Book.new(params[:book])
    if @book.save
        redirect_to :action=>'show', :id=>@book.id
    else
        redirect_to :action=>'new'
    end
end
```

In this example, a new Book object is created and saved. If the save operation is successful, the user is redirected to the show page to show the details of the new book. If the save is not successful, the user is redirected back to the new book page so that the user can try again. Like the ren-der method, the redirect_to method takes an options hash to determine where it should redirect the browser to. In this first use of redirect_to above, an :action and an :id value are passed. This instructs the browser to redirect to the action method specified. Because a controller is not specified, the same controller that contains this create method is assumed. You could have also passed a :controller value to redirect to a method in a different controller.

The :id parameter passed to redirect_to is also passed on to the show method. There is also a shortcut you can use to specify the book's id. You could write the redirect_to method like this:

```
redirect_to :action=>'show', :id=>@book
```

Just by passing the @book object as the :id value, Rails extracts the id value from the @book object and uses that as the value for the :id parameter.

Sending feedback with flash

The flash feature of Rails is a way of passing simple feedback messages from your application back to the browser. Do not confuse this use of the word flash, with the name of the Flash Web development technology from Adobe. They are not related. In this case, *flash* is the name for an internal storage container used by Rails to store temporary display data. The flash area is implemented as a special kind of hash, and you work with it much like you work with a regular hash in Ruby.

Data that is stored into the flash is kept for the duration of one action, and then it is removed. The flash is a convenient place to store short status messages that need to be communicated from one action to the next. Examples of where flash is commonly used include displaying results of a login attempt, results of a file upload, or results of a form submission.

You populate the flash in a controller method by using a symbol key value passed to flash, like this:

```
flash[:login_result] = 'Successful Login'
```

Take a look at a controller method that uses the flash:

```
def login
    if login_user
        flash[:notice] = 'Successful Login'
        redirect_to :action=>'home'
    else
        flash[:notice] = 'Your login attempt was unsuccessful'
        redirect_to :action=>'create'
    end
end
```

Here, the result of a login attempt is stored in a flash :notice parameter. The flash parameters you use can be any name you choose, but it is common practice to use :notice, :warning, and :error to denote common types of status messages.

The data you store in flash is then used within your view templates. Although view templates are covered in detail in Chapter 5, let's preview a portion of a view template that uses the flash:

```
<div>
    <h1>The Book Store</h1>
    <% unless flash[:notice].blank? %>
        <div id="notification"><%= flash[:notice] %></div>
    <% end %>
</div>
```

This small template snippet displays the flash[:notice] string unless it is blank. This snippet could be put into your layout templates so that the notice would be displayed on any of your views that included a notice. This also gives a reason for using standard names for your flash messages, such as the recommended :notice, :warning, and :error. If the flash names were page-specific, you wouldn't be able to use this snippet in a common layout file.

Using flash.now and flash.keep

Normally any data that you store into the flash area is cleared after one request. If you would like to extend the life of data stored in the flash, you can do that using the flash.keep method. The flash.keep method will extend the life of the flash for one additional request.

In the previous examples where flash was used, after storing a string into flash, the next page was displayed by using a redirect. Remember that when storing data in the flash, it is kept for the life of one action (that is, one request). If, in the controller where you set the flash, you rendered a template instead of doing a redirect, the flash would still be kept until the next page request, which is probably not what you wanted. If you are rendering a template instead of redirecting when you set flash, you should use the flash.now method. The flash.now method changes the behavior of the flash so that the data is kept for only the current request.

Sending other types of data to the browser

You've seen how to render templates and send redirects to the browser. Both of these actions normally result in a new HTML page being displayed. However, Rails also assists you if you want to send non-HTML data to the browser from an action method.

Returning text

If you want to return text to the browser from one of your action methods, you use the `render` method with the `:text` hash key, like this:

```
render :text => "hello, world"
```

This will send the specified text to the browser without being wrapped in any template or layout. This can be useful for testing purposes.

Returning JSON data

If you are using Ajax in your Web application, you may often want to render JSON data from your action methods. This can be done using the `:json` parameter with the `render` method as shown here:

```
render :json => {:name => "Timothy"}
```

This will return the specified hash as a JSON encoded string. This also sets the content type for the HTTP response as `application/json`.

Rendering a specific file

If you want to render a template that is not located in the normal place that Rails looks for view templates, or you want to render some other type of file, you can use the `render` method with the `:file` parameter.

```
# Renders the template located at the absolute path specified
render :file => "c:/path/to/some/template.erb"
```

The call to `render` above will render the Erb template stored in the non-standard location specified.

Returning XML

Returning XML content to the browser is no more difficult than returning text or JSON data was. You use the `render` method with the `:xml` parameter like this:

```
render :xml => book.to_xml
```

This returns the XML string generated by the `book.to_xml` method to the browser. The correct HTTP content type for XML data, `text/xml`, is also set for you.

Using Filters

Filters are methods that are run before or after a controller's action methods are executed. Filters are very useful when you want to ensure that a given block of code is run, no matter what action method is called. Rails supports three types of filter methods:

- Before filters
- After filters
- Around filters

Before filters

Before filters are executed *before* the code in the controller action is executed. Filters are defined at the top of a controller class that calls them. To set up a before filter, you call the `before_filter` method and pass it a symbol that represents the method to be executed before action methods. Here is an example of how you would use a before filter:

```
class UserController < ApplicationController
    before_filter :verify_logged_in
    def verify_logged_in
        ...
    end
end
```

In this example, the method `verify_logged_in` is applied as a before filter. Before any of the action methods are called, the `verify_logged_in` method is called.

Instead of passing a symbol to the `before_filter` method, you could pass a snippet of Ruby code that would be executed as the before filter.

You may not want a filter to apply to all of the action methods in a controller. For example, if the `UserController` class had an action method named `login`, which handled the logging in of a user, you obviously would not want to apply the `verify_logged_in` filter before calling that action. You can exclude methods from a filter by passing the `:except` parameter, like this:

```
before_filter :verify_logged_in, :except => :login
```

Now the filter is called before all of the controller's action methods, except for the `login` method. You can also pass a comma-separated list of methods to exclude:

```
before_filter :verify_logged_in, :except => :login, :list
```

If you find the list of exclusions growing to the point that you want more methods without the filter than you have the filter being applied to, you can use the `:only` parameter, which has the opposite effect. When you pass the `:only` parameter, all action methods will be excluded from the filter, except for those specified in the `:only` parameter:

```
before_filter :verify_logged_in, :only => :show, :edit
```

In this example, the `verify_logged_in` filter method is called only before the `show` and `edit` methods. It is not called before any other action methods in the controller.

After filters

After filters are executed after the code in the controller action is executed. As with before filters, you define after filters at the top of the controller class in which they are called. You use the `after_filter` method to set up an after filter, like this:

```
class PhotoController < ApplicationController
    after_filter :resize_photo
    def resize_photo
        ...
    end
end
```

The setup is identical to the way you set up before filters. The method represented by the symbol passed to `after_filter` is executed after your controller action methods. Like with the `before_filter` method, you could pass a snippet of Ruby code instead of a symbol to the `after_filter` method.

You can also use the `:except` and `:only` parameters with after filters, just as they are used with before filters.

Around filters

Around filters contain code that is executed both before and after the controller's code is executed. Around filters are useful when you would otherwise want to use both a before and an after filter. The way you implement an around filter is different and a bit more complex than how before and after filters are implemented. A common way to implement an around filter is to define a special class that contains `before` and `after` methods. Let's walk through the implementation of a common example of where around filters are used to provide logging for your controllers.

First, create a logging class that contains a before and after method:

```
class ActionLogger
    def before(controller)
        @start_time = Time.new
    end

    def after(controller)
        @end_time = Time.now
        @elapsed_time = @end_time.to_f - @start_time.to_f
        @action = controller.action_name
```

```
            # next save this logging detail to a file or database
      table
        end
   end
```

In this `ActionLogger` class, the `before` method captures the time an action is started, and the `after` method captures the time an action completes, the elapsed time, and the name of the action that is being executed. You could then write this data to a log file, or perhaps use a log model that you would create an instance of here and save it with this data.

Now, look at how you use the `ActionLogger` class as an around filter. In your controller class, simply add the `around_filter` method and pass an instance of the `ActionLogger` as a parameter, like this:

```
class PhotoController < ApplicationController
    around_filter ActionLogger.new
end
```

The `ActionLogger` will now be called before and after all of the action methods that you add to the `PhotoController` class.

You can also pass method references and blocks to the `around_filter` method. If you pass a method reference, the reference must point to a method that has a call to the `yield` method to call the action being called. The example below is borrowed from the Rails API documentation. This shows how you might use an around filter to catch exceptions from your action methods.

```
around_filter :catch_exceptions

private
def catch_exceptions
    yield
rescue => exception
    logger.debug "Caught exception! #{exception}"
    raise
end
```

This provides simple exception handling for all of your action methods.

The final way of using an around filter is by passing a block to the `around_filter` method. When you pass a code block to the `around_filter` method, the block explicitly calls the action using `action.call` instead of using the `yield` method. Below is an example that logs a before and after message around each action method call.

```
around_filter do |controller, action|
    logger.debug "before #{controller.action_name}"
    action.call
    logger.debug "after #{controller.action_name}"
end
```

Protecting filter methods

Something that I haven't talked about yet is the fact that you can potentially route to any method (that you put into a controller class) from a browser. For example, assume that you have the default route defined:

```
map.connect ':controller/:action/:id'
```

You could type the following address in your browser to make a direct call to the after filter method that was defined in the previous section:

```
www.myapp.com/photo/resize_photo
```

However, when you defined the `resize_photo` filter method, you probably did not intend this method to be routable from a browser call. In this case, how can you prevent this method from being routable?

The answer goes back to something that is common in most object-oriented programming languages: the ability to protect methods within a class. All methods contained in Ruby classes have one of these protection levels:

- **Public:** These methods are accessible by any external class or method that uses the class in which they are defined.
- **Protected:** These methods are accessible only within the class in which they are defined, and in classes that inherit from the class in which they are defined.
- **Private:** These methods are only accessible within the class in which they are defined. No external class or method can call these methods.

By default, methods are always public, meaning that any external class or method can access them. You can declare methods as protected or private by putting a `protected` or `private` keyword before the methods that you want to protect. This example contains protected and private methods:

```
class SuperHero
    def say_hello
        ...
    end

    protected
    def use_power
        ...
    end

    private
    def get_real_identity
        ...
    end
```

```
        def assign_sidekick
            ...
        end
    end
```

This class has one protected method and two private methods. In the `SuperHero` class, because you don't want just anyone to know a hero's true identity, the `get_real_identity` method is made a private method. Only other methods within the `SuperHero` class can call it. The `use_power` method can be called only by methods within the `SuperHero` class or methods in classes that inherit from the `SuperHero` class.

 **Protected and private methods are not routable from the browser.**

Getting back to the discussion of filter methods, anytime you define a filter method, you should make it a protected or private method, as you normally do not want your filter methods to be routable from the browser.

Working with Sessions

Sessions are a common technique in Web applications to remember data that you want to preserve across multiple requests. Remember that the underlying protocol of the Web, HTTP, is a stateless protocol, meaning that each request to the server is like calling a new invocation of your application. Inherently, there is no memory or state preserved across requests. This was fine when the Web was used mostly as a home for static informational pages without a lot of dynamic content.

However, as the Web became more dynamic and Web applications became more popular, the need to maintain state across multiple browser requests became pressing. This is where the session comes in handy. The session is a container that allows you to store information that you want to use across multiple requests. The session data is stored either in the server's file system, the server's memory, or in a database.

Sessions are commonly used to store information about a user's browsing session. For example, when a user logs into your application, information about that user is saved to the session so that the user can navigate around within the Web application without having to log in for each new page request. Without sessions, your Web application would not be able to remember the user as they browsed through various pages of the Web application. Sessions are also commonly used to store shopping cart information on a shopping site, as well as user preferences.

Each session stored on the server, either in the database or in the file system, is identified by a unique id. The unique id is stored in a session cookie that is sent to the browser. The browser returns this session cookie with each page request so that the server can look up the session and preserve state across requests.

Rails has built-in support that makes using a session simple in a Rails application. Rails automatically creates a session for each user of your application. You store information into the session by using the `session` hash. The `session` hash is used just like any regular Ruby hash. For example, you can store a user's id into the session like this:

```
session[:user_id] = @user.id
```

As a result of storing this to the `session` hash, the user id is saved to the session store and is available to future requests. Retrieving information from the session is just as easy, using standard hash access techniques like this:

```
user_id = session[:user_id]
```

You may have noticed a directory called `tmp` in your Rails application directory tree. This is the directory in which the session data is stored. There are actually three choices for where Rails stores session data. The available options are as follows:

- File system
- Database
- In memory

The file system is used by default and requires no additional configuration. This is sufficient for development, testing, and many small-scale Web applications. You run into problems with storing the session on the file system if you have a Web application that is load balanced and served off of multiple servers, as is commonly done for performance reasons. In this situation, not all requests are routed to the same physical server. Your application exists on multiple physical servers, and a load-balancing router will route Web requests across the different instances of your application.

If your session is stored on the file system and a user is routed to a different physical server during a browsing session, the application will not be able to find the session associated with that user. This makes storing the session in the database a popular alternative for Rails production environments. Rails also allows you to store session information in memory. This option performs very well because reading and writing from memory is a very fast operation, compared to reading and writing to disk.

Using the ActiveRecord session storage

As its name implies, the ActiveRecord session storage uses ActiveRecord to store the session data into a table in your database. By having the session stored in the database, it becomes accessible from multiple computers and thus works well in an environment where you have load-balanced servers.

Let's look at how you set up a Rails application to use ActiveRecord session storage. There are a few simple steps to follow, which are described here:

1. **Create a migration to set up session storage in your database.** Just as you use migrations to set up the database tables that hold your application's data, you can also use a migration to create the session data table. In fact, you can create this migration automatically using this `rake` command:

   ```
   rake db:sessions:create RAILS_ENV=production
   ```

2. **Apply the session setup migration.** Now you can run the `rake migrate` command to apply the new migration, like this:

   ```
   rake db:migrate RAILS_ENV=production
   ```

3. **Configure Rails to use ActiveRecord session storage.** Next, you have to tell Rails that you are using ActiveRecord session storage. You do this by editing the `config/environment.rb` file. Simply remove the comment from the following line:

   ```
   Config.action_controller.session_store = :active_record_store
   ```

4. **Restart the application.** This is the last thing you need to do. After the application is restarted, sessions will be stored in the database. How you restart the server depends on the server that you are using. To restart a Rails application that is using the WEBrick server, stop the existing server by pressing Ctrl+C in the console window in which you started the server and restart it with the following:

   ```
   ruby script/server
   ```

Using MemCached session storage

MemCached is used to provide the in-memory session storage option. MemCached is based on software that was originally developed by Danga Interactive for the LiveJournal blog-hosting Web site. When using MemCached, sessions are stored in your server's memory and are never written to disk. Because this option does not require any hard disk I/O, it is much faster than the other options. For more information about using Memcached see the Ruby on Rails wiki site, and the Memcached home page:

```
http://wiki.rubyonrails.org/rails/pages/MemCached
```

```
www.danga.com/memcached/
```

Caching

Caching is an important technique that you can use to increase the performance of any Web application. Caching speeds up Web applications by storing the result of calculations, renderings, and database calls for subsequent requests. The Action Controller component of Rails includes built-in support for caching in your Rails applications.

Rails support for caching is available at these three levels of granularity:

- Page
- Action
- Fragment

Page caching

Page caching is a caching technique where the entire output of an action is stored as an HTML file that the Web server can serve without having to go through Rails to call the action again. Using this technique can improve performance by as much as 100 times over having to always dynamically generate the content. Unfortunately, this technique is only useful for stateless pages that do not differentiate between application users. Applications in which a user logs in and is given unique views of data are not a candidate for this technique. Applications that do not require a user logon to view data, such as wikis and blogs, may benefit from this technique.

You can turn on page caching for any methods in your controller classes by using the `caches_page` method call. You pass the actions that you want to cache as parameters to `caches_page`. You do not have to include all of your controller's actions. Here is an example:

```
class BlogController < ActionController::Base
    caches_page :show, :new

    def show
        ...
    end

    def new
        ...
    end
end
```

This causes the results of the show and new methods to be cached. The first time the actions are run, the HTML result is cached. This HTML cache file will be returned on subsequent calls to these methods without having to call the actions again.

You can expire cached pages by deleting the cached file. When a cached file is deleted, it is regenerated on the next call to the action to which it applies. To delete a cached page, you use the `expire_page` method. A common time to delete a cached page is when you perform an update to the page that is cached. In your update action method, you would also delete the cached page like this:

```
class BlogController < ActionController::Base
    def update
        ...
        expire_page :action => "show", :id => params[:id]
        redirect_to :action => "show", :id => params[:id]
    end
end
```

The action and id for which the page has been cached are passed to the expire_page method to delete the cached page. You can then perform a redirect to regenerate the newly updated page and thus create a new cached page.

Action caching

As with page caching, action caching saves the entire output of an action response. The difference is that with action caching, the action calls are still routed to the controller so that any filters can still be applied. This is useful when you have a filter setup to provide a restriction on who can view the cached action.

```
class BookController < ApplicationController
    before_filter :authenticate
    caches_action :show, :list
end
```

In this example, the methods show and list require that the user is authenticated before the methods are called. This is accomplished with the authenticate before filter. If, the show and list actions were cached using page caching, the before filter would never be called once the page was cached. Therefore, to preserve the authentication requirement, these pages must be cached using the action caching technique.

Fragment caching

Fragment caching is used to cache blocks within templates rather than caching the entire output of an action method. This technique is useful when certain parts of an action change frequently and would be difficult to cache, and other parts remain relatively static and thus can be cached. Fragment caching is done in view templates instead of the controller classes as the other forms of caching were.

A fragment cache is designated with a cache_do block. The lines inside the block enclosed in the cache_do statement will be cached. Here is an example of code that you might use in a view template:

```
<b>Welcome <%= @user.name %></b>
<% cache do %>
    Please choose a topic:
    <%= render :partial => "topic", :collection => @topics %>
<% end %>
```

In this example, the first line displays a user's name. Because the name is different for every user that logs in, this is not a good candidate for caching. Following the user's name, a list of topics is displayed. Because the list of topics remains relatively static, this is a good candidate for caching, and thus the lines that display the topic lists are wrapped with the cache_do statement.

Summary

In this chapter, you learned how Rails helps you to implement the controller layer in an MVC Web application. The ActionController component of Rails is what allows you to easily create controllers for your applications.

Some of the topics that are related to the controller layer of a Web application that you learned about in this chapter are: routing, creating and using controllers in a Rails application, using filters, sessions, and content caching. These are all topics that you will find yourself making use of over and over again as you develop real world Rails applications.

You have now learned about how Rails helps you create the model and controller layers of your Web application. In the next chapter, you will learn how Rails helps you with the final layer of your MVC Web application, the view layer. The view layer is closely related to the controller layer and it is a good idea to have the knowledge you gained in this chapter fresh in your mind as you read that chapter.

Chapter 5

View:
In Depth

So far you've read about the model and controller layers of a Rails application. There is one layer remaining to discuss in an MVC (Model-View-Controller) application. That is the view layer. The view layer is the layer that presents your application to the end users. Although this layer shouldn't handle any of your application's business or processing logic, it is at least as important to the success of an application as the model and controller layers. You may have the greatest technology in the world, but if you can't present it in a way that is easy to use and appealing, ultimately your technology will go unused.

Rails offers you a number of tools that will assist you in creating a well-designed, maintainable and rich view layer.

IN THIS CHAPTER

ActionView

Embedded Ruby

Layouts

Partials

Helpers

JavaScript, Ajax, and RJS

ActionView

The Rails component that manages the view layer of your application is called ActionView. ActionView is what provides you with most of the technologies that you will read about in the remainder of this chapter. These technologies include the following:

- Embedded Ruby (ERb)
- Layout templates
- Partial templates
- Helper methods

In a Rails application, your view templates are placed into a directory under the app directory called views. Within the views directory, each controller has its own subdirectory for views relating to actions in that controller. In addition, there is a special controller called *layouts* which contains the common layouts used throughout the application. You can create your own subdirectories for other shared view files. In an application that has a BooksController, a UsersController, and an ImagesController, your view directory would look like this:

```
app
 |-- views
        |-- book
        |-- image
        |-- user
        |-- layout
        |-- shared
```

The `book`, `image`, and `user` directories hold views that are rendered by their corresponding controllers. The `layout` directory holds layout files, which you'll learn more about later in this chapter. The `shared` directory is not created automatically, but you'll end up using it in many of the applications that you write. The `shared` directory holds partial views — another Rails view technology that you'll learn about in this chapter — that are used by views from multiple directories.

Getting to the view

Recall from Chapter 4 that views are rendered by actions contained in controller classes. If the view to be rendered is not explicitly declared by an action, Rails looks for a view with the same base name as the action method contained in the view directory corresponding to the controller name. In Chapter 4, you saw the following controller code:

```
class UsersController < ApplicationController
 def show
   user_id = params[:id]
   @user = User.find(user_id)
   render :action => "show"
 end
end
```

In this example, the `render` statement is not actually required because it is reiterating the default by telling Rails to render a template with the name `show`. Since this is the same name as the action method, Rails will look for this template by default even if the `render` line were omitted. Because this is the UserController, Rails will look for the `show` template in `app/views/users/show.html.erb`.

An individual controller method can only call `render` or `redirect_to` one time during any particular call to the method. This applies only to render calls in the controller that render a full file — the view code can render as many partial views as needed. Performing a second render or redirect in the controller will result in an exception. However, calling render or redirect does not automatically stop execution of the method. The recommended idiom for ensuring exit from a method after a render looks like this:

```
def conditional
  if params[:id].blank?
    render :action => "nothing" and return
  end
  render :action => "conditional"
end
```

The and return at the end of the first render line ensures that the method will be exited. Again, the last line is a repetition of the default action and is included here for clarity.

Rendering options

The render method has more than one trick up its sleeve. There are a several different options you can use in your controllers and views to specify different kinds of output. The render method takes an option hash as its arguments (some types also take a block argument). Although the order of the hash is unimportant, by convention the type of the render is the first argument.

As alluded to earlier, the default type of render is :action, where the value is the name of the action file to render. The following call:

```
render :action => "show"
```

will cause Rails to render the file app/views/<controller_name>/show.html.erb (but see the next section for how the format of the output can be changed.). By default, the layout of the current controller is used, however the optional argument :layout allows you to specify the string name of a layout to use instead. It's fairly unusual for this to be used explicitly, normally code that chooses to render the view from another action will just redirect to that action.

There are two other ways to specify an entire template file as the target of the rendering. The first is render :template => "controller/template". The :template option is identical to :action, except that it requires you to specify the entire path to the template from within the views directory (minus the .erb extension). This allows you to specify a template in a different directory.

The layout from the current controller is applied. The other method is render :file. The value for file is the absolute filename of a file somewhere that you want to use as the template. Passing the second argument :use_full_path => true causes file to search relative to the views directory and add the correct extension — in other words, behaving just like render :template. By default no layout is used, the argument :layout => true causes the current controller layout to be used. The :file and :template versions of render are used very rarely — I don't think I've ever seen a legitimate usage in production code. Redirects and partial rendering are the preferred methods.

Any template system needs a way to allow common parts of templates to be extracted and inserted into the full template. The most commonly used method within Rails to manage this is the *partial template*. A partial template is just like any other ERb file in your views directory, except that the names of partial templates are required to begin with an underscore character (_).

There are two common use cases for partial templates. Within an ERb view file, partial templates are invoked to allow sharing of a piece of view code used multiple times. Within a controller, calling a partial template most often means that the partial page view is being sent back to the browser as the result of an Ajax call.

The syntax in both cases is the same:

```
render :partial => "partial_name"
```

You do not include the leading underscore in the partial name when you invoke a partial; Rails will add that for you.

There are two less frequently used methods for rendering a piece of text. The call `render :text => string` will place the value of the string in the output stream. The string can be a double-quoted Ruby string with interpolation. This is generally used for short Ajax or error messages.

A similar argument `render :inline => "<%= hello %>`, takes an inline ERb string, processes it, and returns the result to the output stream. If there is a second argument `:type => :builder` than the string is evaluated by Ruby's Builder module instead of ERb. In both the text and inline case, it is assumed that the layout is not to be added unless explicitly specified as in a partial render.

Two types of standard render output different formats than the standard HTML: `:xml` and `:json`. In both cases, the value of the argument is an object to be converted to the specified format. You do not need to explicitly perform the conversion; Rails will do it for you.

Finally, `:render :update` triggers Ruby JavaScript (RJS) processing, which will be discussed in detail later in this chapter.

All render methods, by default, return an HTTP status code of 200 if successful. This can be overridden in all render methods by explicitly passing a `:status` option with the code you want returned. Also, the method `render_to_string` takes all the same arguments as the ordinary `render`, but returns the value as a string without outputting the value to the response object.

Responding to different formats

Prior to Rails version 2.0, view templates were named with the extension `.rhtml`. So in this example, the show template would have been in a file named `show.rhtml`. Rails 2.0 changed the naming of view templates to use the `.html.erb` extension. This extension gives a better indication of the templating technology being used, which is embedded Ruby or ERb.

Now although .html.erb is the most common extension for a Rails view file, the general form is `.<format>.<mechanism>`, where the format usually represents the MIME type of the file being created, and the mechanism is the template engine used to create the file. So, a `.html.erb` file is an ERb file that renders into an HTML file, while a `.js.erb` file renders to JavaScript and `rss.erb` renders to an RSS file. Standard Rails comes with a second mechanism option, the Builder module, which is most often used to create XML files. You can specify a builder file with the extension `.builder`. Other template engines, such as Markaby or Haml, are available as plugins that register their own extensions.

A file whose name ends in `.erb` without a format will match any requested format. This is useful if you have an file that is rendered in response to both a regular controller call (which is an HTML request looking for `html.erb`) and an Ajax call (which is a JavaScript request looking for `js.erb`). A file that is just plain `.erb` will be found by both requests.

You'll notices that this naming is another example of Rails using convention over configuration. The name of your view file specifies both the kind of request it responds to and the method used to render it. That's a nice shortcut, and it allows an elegant way to have the same controller action emit multiple formats from the same data. The controller method `respond_to` allows the same controller to easily serve separate output depending on the incoming request.

The most basic `respond_to` looks like this:

```
def index
  @users = User.find(:all)
  respond_to do |format|
    format.html
    format.xml { render :xml => @users }
  end
end
```

Conceptually, what's going on here is very similar to a case expression on the format of the incoming request. Each expression inside the block represents a format that the method can handle. When a request comes in, the matching expression is fired — if the expression has a block, as the `.xml` expression does in this example, then the block is invoked.

If the expression does not have a block, like the `.html` expression in this example, then default behavior is invoked. This means that Rails will search for a file in the `app/views/<controller>` directory for a file that matches the controller method name and the format — in this case `index.html.erb` or `index.html.builder` — and the file will be rendered. If the format requested does not have a matching expression inside the `respond_to` block, then Rails will respond with an error.

The exact implementation isn't quite identical to a case statement. The block passed to the `respond_to` method is invoked with an object of the Rails core type `Responder`. Inside the block, the `Responder` object can be called with methods matching known MIME types. For each method called, the `Responder` object determines what it's response would be — either the passed block or the default behavior.

After the block is invoked, the `respond_to` method invokes the response matching the actual user request type. The relevant point is that, although the `respond_to` call looks and acts something like a case statement, the internal mechanism is quite different — the `respond_to` call will not short-circuit. If you have any other code inside the `respond_to` block, that code will always be called, even if it is after a format call that matches the current user request.

In normal usage, the requested format is inferred from the extension of the URL in the browser request, so `users/index.html` returns the HTML version, while `users/index.xml` returns the XML version. By default, Rails recognizes eight format extensions (see Table 5.1). It is the responsibility of your application to ensure that your response is a valid example of the requested format.

TABLE 5.1

Format Extensions

MIME Type	Format
atom	Syndication feed in Atom format.
html	Regular HTML. The default for normal requests if no other format is specified.
ics	iCalendar standard format for calendar data.
js	JavaScript. The default for Ajax requests if no other format is specified.
rss	RSS syndication feed.
text	Plain text, assumed not to be parsed by the browser for output
xml	An XML file that isn't an Atom or RSS feed.
yaml	A YAML file.

Although the format is usually inferred from the file extension of the URL, it can also be passed in the query string portion of the URL like any other parameter, as in `user/index?format=html`. The format can also be set or changed programmatically in your Rails controller code by setting the attribute `request.format`.

You can also add additional formats on your own to augment the eight that Rails provides. The file `config/initializers/mime_types.rb` is the place to put any MIME customization that you are looking for. (In older versions of Rails, this code is placed in `config/environment.b.`)

There are two different commands. If you are creating a file extension for a MIME type not covered in the original list, you use something like the following:

```
Mime::Type.register "image/png", :png
```

The first argument is the MIME type, and the second argument is the file extension that you are registering. After this line of code, the `format` object inside a `respond_to` block will add the `format.png` method, which works exactly like the existing eight methods.

Sometimes, you need to create a new file extension that represents a new context for an existing MIME type — the way that, for example, `atom` and `rss` are new contexts for `xml` documents. Here's the canonical example:

```
Mime::Type.register_alias "text/html", :iphone
```

You want to be able to serve specialized content an iPhone using the same `respond_to` structure, but the output to the iPhone is just another kind of HTML. No problem, just tell Rails that your new pseudo-MIME type is an alias of an existing type, and everything will work out just fine. This example is also a use case for changing the response type programmatically — when you detect the iPhone browser, you can change the format to `iphone` and serve the specialized content.

Embedded Ruby

ActionView uses the Embedded Ruby (ERb) library to provide you with a complete templating system for creating the Web pages that will make up the presentation layer of your application. The Embedded Ruby library allows you to mix Ruby code along with HTML inside of your view templates. If you are familiar with Java, the Rails template mechanism with embedded Ruby is similar to what you get in Java with JSPs and their use of embedded Java.

> **NOTE** Embedded Ruby predates the Rails framework. It is implemented as a stand-alone Ruby library that can just as easily be used outside of a Rails application. The embedded Ruby library makes a powerful templating mechanism for any type of templating engine that you want to create.

Take a look at how you embed Ruby code inside of a Rails view template.

```
Users
<ul>
<% users.each do |user| %>
<li><%= user.name %></li>
<% end %>
</ul>
```

The template mixes regular HTML code along with Ruby code embedded in <% and %> delimiters. If you look closely at the code, you'll actually notice that in line 4, the Ruby code block begins with the <%= delimiter instead of just <%. If the Ruby code begins with the <%= delimiter, the return value of the code will be included in the HTML page. So in this example, the result of calling user. name is included in the HTML page. Assume that the users array contains three users with the names, Tim Fisher, Scott Deming, and Tom Fisher. The HTML code generated by the above template code would be as follows (allowing for some white space cleanup):

```
Users
<ul>
<li>Tim Fisher</li>
<li>Scott Deming</li>
<li>Tom Fisher</li>
</ul>
```

The return value of ERb segments that begin with the <% delimiter is discarded and does not become a part of the generated HTML code. However, variables declared or set in those segments are available to later parts of the ERb template.

Within a Rails ERb template, you have access to any instance variable of the controller that invoked the template — typically, these instance variables are set in the controller method before the view is invoked. The controller object itself is available as the variable `controller`. Several of the controller objects are accessible as variables as well, including `params`, `session`, `logger`, `request`, and `response`. If the ERb template is called as a partial, then further local variables can be made available to the template when it is invoked.

You can place any valid Ruby code in a view template between the `<%` or `<%=` delimiters, there are no technical limitations on the code. However, do not consider that as encouragement to put as much Ruby code as you can in your templates. Rails best practice is to avoid putting extensive amounts of code in your actual ERb template (this is consistent with best practice in other web application engines).

You should limit the Ruby code that you use in your view templates to code that creates your view only. Even complex view code should probably be moved to a helper module, which will be discussed in more detail later in this chapter. You should be careful not to include any business logic inside of your view templates. Business logic should be confined to the actual model objects.

Mixing business logic in your view code is almost always a bad idea and will usually cause headaches down the road for the following reasons:

- Ruby code inside of view templates is harder to test.
- The resulting code, with multiple layers of Ruby and HTML indentation, quickly becomes nearly impossible to read.
- You are breaking the MVC architecture by putting business logic into the view layer, making it hard to find any of your business logic should you ever have to change it in any way.
- Business code embedded in view logic is nearly impossible to refactor into cleaner structures. You will become trapped by early decisions that you can't undo without breaking code.
- With business logic in your view layer, there is now a tighter coupling between your view and model layers. Remember that the ideal situation is low coupling between the MVC layers of your application. Tight coupling makes it difficult to modify the view code as well. Remember the iPhone example earlier? It's much easier to add support for a new view context if the view code is nice and separate from the rest of the world.

Even though you've been warned against overusing embedded Ruby, it is nice to know that you have the full power of the Ruby language in your templates for when you need it.

Using the <%- and -%> delimiters

Often you will have lines in your templates that contain Ruby statements that do not result in anything being printed to the HTML output, such as this one:

```
<% users.each do |user| %>
```

In those instances, a blank line is inserted into the generated HTML output where the lines occur. For the template segment that I've been discussing, the actual generated HTML output, including blank lines, would look like this:

```
Users
<ul>

<li>Tim Fisher</li>
<li>Scott Deming</li>
<li>Tom Fisher</li>

</ul>
```

Notice that there is a blank line in the HTML code where the two lines that are surrounded by the <% and %> delimiters are. If you are using a lot of embedded Ruby lines, this can bloat your HTML output and make the source view harder to read. If you have enough of them, this can even increase the amount of time it takes to serve your page.

Note, however, that these blank lines are not displayed on the page since empty lines in an HTML file are not printed to the browser screen. Even so, it's often useful to be able to clean up the white space a bit.

ERb provides a way to prevent these blank lines from being inserted into the generated HTML output: Instead of using the <% and %> delimiters, use <% and -%> as delimiters — adding the minus sign to the end delimiter. This prevents a newline character from being inserted into the generated HTML output where an ERb template would otherwise emit a blank line. Proper use of these delimiters can allow you to create better-formatted HTML code for your view templates.

Commenting out embedded Ruby

If you want to disable a line of embedded Ruby code, you can use the standard Ruby comment symbol, #. This prevents the following embedded Ruby segment from having any effect. This works on both outputting and non-outputting code segments, that is, segments that begin with either <%= or <%. Take a look at the following example:

```
<%# if name == 'Tim' %>
I am <%=# name %>
<%# end %>
```

The generated HTML output of this code block would be the following:

```
I am
```

The first line, the *conditional statement*, has no effect on whether the second line is displayed because it is commented out. The name variable is also not printed because that segment is also commented out.

Layouts

In a Web application, it is considered good practice to reuse a common template across multiple pages of your site, such that the common features are in one shared file. Quite often, the entire site will have a common template applied. The common template contains the basic layout of your Web site. For example, each page may include a header section at the top displaying your company logo and some navigation, a footer section at the bottom displaying copyright information, and a sidebar area on the left or right displaying navigation and other links.

The HTML skeleton code that defines the overall structure of your Web pages is often known as the *layout*. Using a layout, you can define your site's common structures in a single place and have that template used by all of your pages to avoid having to duplicate code in each of your view templates. Like many things that are done often, and involve consolidating common code, using layouts is very easy in Rails.

Inside the `app/views` directory is a standard directory named `layouts`. You will put your layout templates into the `layouts` directory.

Listing 5.1 shows an example of a typical `application.html.erb` file. This is a layout file that you will create yourself in Chapters 6 through 8 as you write a complete Rails application. This layout contains elements that are common to many layout templates that you will create. These common elements include the following:

- An HTTP `doctype` declaration at the top of the file
- The standard `html`, `head`, and `body` tags
- Standard `head` elements, including page title, JavaScript include tags, and Stylesheet include tags
- Layout of the body content. In this template, the body is divided into three main sections, a header, a sidebar, and a content section. In many applications, you might also want a footer section.

The header section displays a logo and then either a sign in or sign out link, depending on whether or not a user is currently logged in (the `logged_in?` method would most likely be defined in the `ApplicationHelper` class. You don't see the contents of the sidebar, as that is rendered as a partial. The content section starts with a display of flash notices and error messages, if any have been specified by the controller action. The most important line in this template is the one that specifies the location of the body content of the page looks like this:

```
<%= yield %>
```

This line instructs Rails to insert the content of the template being requested at this location, in exactly the same way that a regular Ruby method yields control to a block argument. In this case, the ERb layout template acts as a method and the bock being invoked is the output as specified by the controller action. Most often it's another ERb template, but any Rails render activity could be included there.

LISTING 5.1

application.html.erb Layout Template

```
<!DOCTYPE html PUBLIC "-//W3C//DTD XHTML 1.0 Transitional//EN" "http://
   www.w3.org/TR/xhtml1/DTD/xhtml1-transitional.dtd">
<html xmlns="http://www.w3.org/1999/xhtml">

<head>
  <title><%= @title %></title>
  <%= stylesheet_link_tag "style" %>
  <%= javascript_include_tag :defaults %>
</head>

<body>
  <div id="header">
    <div id="logo_image">
      <%= link_to image_tag('main_logo.png'),
          {:controller=>'home', :action=>'index'} %>
    </div>
    <% if !logged_in? %>
      <%= render :partial=>"user/signin" %>
    <% else %>
      <div id="user_menu">
        <%= link_to 'Logout', :controller=>'user',
              :action=>'logout' %>
      </div>
    <% end %>
    <div style="clear: both; height: 0px;"></div>
  </div>

    <%= render :partial=>"shared/sidebar" %>

  <div id="Content">
    <% if flash[:notice] -%>
      <div id="notice"><%= flash[:notice] %></div>
    <% end -%>
    <% if flash[:error] -%>
      <div id="error"><%= flash[:error] %></div>
    <% end -%>
    <%= yield %>
  </div>
</body>
</html>
```

Take a look toward the top of the sample file and notice the one instance variable referenced in the layout file — @title. Normally, you try to minimize the usage of instance variables in layouts. Each instance variable used is a dependence requiring each and every controller action that uses this layout to define the variable. The variable must be declared either in the controller action or in the view that is the main part of the action. In other words, each view file could start with the line <% @title = "something" %>, and that variable reference would be available in the layout.

A common practice is to specify the instance variable in a before filter, which itself might redirect to another method that is overridden in each specific controller. Another option is to call a helper method in the layout instead of using an instance variable directly.

The layout file includes required JavaScript and CSS files by using the Rails helper methods javascript_include_tag and stylesheet_include_tag, both of which work similarly. Each method takes a list of source files. If an absolute path is not specified, then the appropriate public directory of your Rails application is assumed. If a file extension is not specified, then the normal extension for that file type is assumed.

The JavaScript include method takes a special argument :defaults, which causes the standard Prototype and Scriptaculous libraries (prototype.js and effects.js) to be included. In addition, if the file public/application.js exists, it is included in the defaults. In both the JavaScript and CSS methods, passing the argument :all will automatically include all files in the Rails public directory. For JavaScript files, the default files are guaranteed to be included first, so it is safe to use when other files have dependencies on Prototype or Scriptaculous. As with many other tag helpers, an optional hash argument at the end will be passed on as attributes of the HTML tag being created.

Both the JavaScript and CSS helpers take an optional argument :cache => true. If this argument is present, and if the global property ActionController::Base.perform_caching is also true, then Rails will roll all the files being included into one single file. This reduces the number of HTTP connections required to get the content, and can also reduce the total amount of data sent if your web server compresses response data. The default name of the resulting file is all.js or all.css. If you want to use an alternate name for the file, use that name instead of true as the value of the cache argument.

Another header tag that you might include in a layout is auto_discovery_link_tag, which returns an HTML link tag, suitable for browser auto detection of an RSS or Atom feed. The method takes three arguments. The first is the type of link, which can by :rss or :atom. The second argument is a URL, and takes any of the normal mechanisms for specifying a URL. The final argument is a hash allowing you to specify one of three options, :rel specifies the rel attribute in the tag and defaults to alternate, :title allows you to specify the title of the feed as it shows up in the browser pulldown — the default is the same as the the link type. Finally, :type allows you to specify a MIME type, if the default is unsuitable for some reason.

Under normal circumstances, the layout associated with a given controller action is the layout for that controller, app/views/layout/<controller>.<format>.erb. If there isn't a layout for the given controller, then Rails will look for a file named application.<format>.erb. If no layout is specified and the default file is also not specified, then no layout will be rendered. The format is significant here, you can have different layouts for the same controller but with different formats.

The layout can be specified in two places. Controllers have a class method called `layout` which allows you to specify either the string name of the layout you wish to use or the symbol name of a method which dynamically returns the name of the layout to use. The latter method allows you to dynamically switch layouts based on runtime criteria. The layout method also takes the common conditional options `:except` and `:only`. The value of each option is a symbol or list of symbols corresponding to actions in the controller. The `:only` option specifies that the layout is for only those symbols, while the `:except` option specifies that the layout is for all symbols except those specified.

A layout can also be specified in any `render` call with the optional argument `:layout`, the value of which is the name of the layout to be used. The value `:layout => false` indicates that no layout should be used.

Partials

Partials, which have already been mentioned earlier in the chapter, are sub templates that allow you to organize your view template code in much the same way that classes and methods allow you to organize your Ruby code. If you have a common part of your view that is used on multiple pages, it is a good idea to put the block of template code that created that view component into a partial. Also, if you have a very large template, you can usually break it into more readable and maintainable chunks by using partials.

Partials can be invoked from anywhere inside a view, where you'd normally use them in conjunction with ERb's output delimiter.

```
<%= render :partial => "some_partial" %>
```

This command causes Rails to go off and render the file `_some_partial` in the same directory as the view making the call. The leading underscore in the file name is what makes it a partial — you don't add the underscore to the name when you reference it in a render call.

If no directory is specified, the view directory of the current controller is assumed, however you can specify other directories relative to the view directory, such as `shared/partial_name`. Again, the leading underscore is not included.

By default, any instance variable already declared in the controller action or view is visible from the partial and local variables declared in the controller or view are not available in the partial. However, it's usually considered poor practice to require the partial to depend on the instance variables of the external action, and better practice to explicitly pass any needed objects to the partial.

The optional argument `:object => obj` places `obj` into the partial with the same variable name as the partial itself. For example:

```
render :partial => "task", :object => @most_recent_task
```

The object `@most_recent_task` will be available in the partial using the local variable name `task`. This is reasonably elegant, but I often find that my partial files have longer names that don't really work as variable names. Also, you'll often want to pass more than one argument to a partial. The `:locals` option allows you to specify a hash of objects and their new local names within the partial:

```
render :partial => "display_task",
    :locals => {:task => @task, :user => @user}
```

The keys in the locals hash are symbols denoting the names the variables will be available as within the partial — it's not unusual for the names to be identical to the instance variable names, as in this example. The advantage of specifying the variables explicitly in the partial call is that it keeps the partial from being dependent on the instance variables of the calling controller and allows it to be used more flexibly.

A partial can automatically be called multiple times by using the `:collection` argument, which automatically iterates and runs the partial once for each element in the collection. The following line:

```
render :partial => "task", :collection => @all_tasks
```

is equivalent to:

```
@all_tasks.each do |obj|
  render :partial => "task", :object => obj
end
```

The optional argument `:spacer_template` specifies another partial template to to be inserted between each object — generally these are on the order of a horizontal line, and don't need any arguments.

Normally, a partial render doesn't include the layout — the assumption is that the layout has already been taken care of someplace else. However, if you must, you can specify the layout with the `:layout` option. As with other cases, a value of `true` indicates the current controller.

Helpers

Rails provides a very wide variety of methods designed to encapsulate and simplify common view-layer tasks. Collectively these methods are called `helpers` and are available in any view template. (They are not, however, available from inside the controller, at least not without some possibly awkward hacking.) In addition, Rails generates an `ApplicationHelper` module and another helper module for each controller. As you've probably guessed, those modules are all the files in the `app/helpers` directory.

In Rails, all of your helpers in all of your `app/helper` files are available to all your template files at all times. This behavior is controlled by the following line, placed in your `app/controllers/application.rb` file by Rails when the project is generated.

```
helper :all # include all helpers, all the time
```

And yes, the comment is also generated by Rails. If this line did not exist (or if you removed it), you would get the older behavior, which is that each template would have access to methods defined in `ApplicationHelper`, and all methods defined in the helper corresponding to the controller responding to the request.

You can augment the basic behavior with additional calls to `helper`, which can be placed in the `application.rb` file or in any individual controller. The argument to `helper` can be any or all of the following (you can pass in more than one argument at a time):

- A block. Any methods defined inside the block will be available for all templates in that controller. This looks like so:

```
helper do
  def header
    "<h1>Applicaton Header</h1>"
  end
end
```

- A constant, representing a module that has already been loaded via `require`. The module is included for all templates.

- A string, such as `widgets/fred`. In this case, Rails will look for the file relative to the `app/helper` directory, and will assume the associated module to be included is namespaced, such as `Widgets::FredHelper`.

- A symbol, such as `:my`. In this case, Rails will require the file `app/helper/my_helper.rb` and include the associated module, assumed to be `MyHelper`.

- The special symbol `:all`, which causes the behavior described earlier.

The signature for the helper method is `helper(*args, &block)`, so while you are limited to a single block, the remaining arguments can be included in any combination you want. You can have more than one `helper` method in a controller.

Predefined Rails Helpers

To get a sense of what kind of features are placed in helpers, here's a list of the ones that Rails defines for you, at least as of this writing, along with the most commonly used or useful methods in each helper module. Each of these helper modules is automatically included and available from any template or from any of the standard helper modules. Many of them are most useful when creating your own helper methods. It's occasionally useful to include a specific helper module in an unusual location — it's often necessary to do so in order to test helper methods, for example. Every now and then, a helper will be useful within a model and you'll include a helper module there, but that's something to do sparingly.

HTML Creation Helpers

The following helper modules all assist in the creation of HTML output. As such, they are most often used in your own helper methods, rather than in an ERb file.

AssetTagHelper

The helpers in this module generally create HTML tags pointed at a specific resource. The most commonly used are `javascript_include_tag` and `stylesheet_link_tag`, both of which were discussed in the section on layouts. Another useful methods in this module is `auto_discover_link`, which creates a `link` tag in an HTML header. Suitable for browser discovery of RSS feeds, it takes an argument for the type of feed `:rss` or `:atom`, an argument for the URL of the feed and an argument for any other tag options.

The module also contains the `image_tag` method, which creates HTML `img` tags, given a URL source, and optional keys for `:alt` text, `:size` as a string of the form `(width x height)`, and `:mouseover`, which specifies an alternate image for when the mouse pointer is over the image.

RecordIdentificationHelper

The most useful method in this module is `dom_id` (also available in controllers), which takes an object and an optional prefix, as in `dom_id(@user, :row)`, and converts it to an id of the form `row_user_45`, using the class of the object — if the object is new and doesn't have an ID number then the string is `row_new_user`. This would be used inside a HTML tag in ERb or in your own helpers:

```
<div id="<%= dom_id(@user, :div) %>">
```

or

```
content_tag(:div, :id => dom_id(@user, :div))
```

A similar method, `dom_class`, does the same thing without the ID.

RecordTagHelper

This module contains two helpers that are shortcuts for using both `dom_id` and `dom_class` for the same tag. The general one is `content_tag_for(tag_name, record, *args, &block)`. This method is roughly equivalent to the HTML:

```
<tag_name id="dom_id(record)" class="dom_class">block contents</
    tag>
```

Where the tag name is the first argument to the method. The block contents are evaluated and placed inside the tag. A DOM prefix can be the third argument; there can also be the usual key/value pairs that get put in the tag.

A sample usage might be:

```
content_tag_for(:span, @person, :name) { @person.name }
```

This would evaluate to something like the following depending on the actual contents of the variable:

```
<span class="name_person" id="name_person_43">Hollis Mason</span>
```

The module also contains the method `div_for`, which is a simplified version that always returns `div` tags.

TagHelper

The most commonly used method in this module is `content_tag`, often used in your helpers to build HTML output. It can be used in two forms. The first takes content as a string:

```
content_tag(:td, "Banana", :class => "food")
```

The first argument is the tag, the second is the content, and then the usual key/value pairs. This call would result in:

```
<td class="food"
```

The second form puts the content in a block. Within your helper module, the block form would look like this:

```
content_tag(:td, :class => "food") do
  "Banana"
end
```

See the later section on block helpers to show how this style can be used in an ERb context, rather than a Ruby context.

A simpler method in this module, `tag`, works for HTML tags that have no content. Another method `cdata_section` takes an argument and wraps it in an XML CDATA tag sequence.

UrlHelper

The star of this module is `url_for`, which converts a hash of options to a URL in ways that you've already seen a few times. Remember that in a RESTful universe, the argument to `url_for` can be an ActiveRecord object, the URL and controller action are defined by the HTTP method chose.

Other related methods in this module include calls to `url_for` as part of their functionality. Obviously the most commonly used is `link_to`, which takes a string and a `url_for` argument set and creates an HTML link, the `button_to` method is similar but outputs a button.

The `link_to_if` and `link_to_unless`, and `link_to_unless_current` methods allow you to specify alternate text if a condition is true, the latter method sets the condition to whether the page you are on is or is not the page being linked to — commonly used in a menu or navigation structure to put a special style on the current page. And `mail_to` creates an email link.

Form Creation Helpers

The following modules all contain methods specifically used to create HTML forms or form parts.

ActiveRecordHelper

These are a few relatively little-used methods. The methods `error_message_on` and `error_messages_for` convert ActiveRecord validation errors into useful string, this is used for those error messages displayed when a user inputs invalid information into a form. Use `error_message_on` with strings for an instance variable name and method (similar to form helpers), and `error_message_for` with a string or list of strings. The methods `form` and `input` are rarely used form generation tags.

FormHelper

This module contains the bulk of form creation helpers that work with `form_for` and an ActiveRecord module. Most of these methods take as arguments a symbol representing the object and the method being mapped to the form element, however, if these methods are called inside a `form_for` block, then the object is implicitly set to the object of the `form_for`. So:

```
<%= text_field(:user, :name) %>
```

But:

```
<% form_for(:user) do |f| %>
  <%= f.text_field(:name) %>
<% end %>
```

In the second version, the user sent to the `form_for` method is also associated with any helper called via the form object inside the block.

The typical method in this module takes the object, method and an options hash to be added to the eventual tag. These methods are:

- `check_box`

  Also takes additional parameters for the checked and unchecked value of the field. Rails adds a hidden variable for unchecked checkboxes to ensure that a value is posted for them.

- `file_field`

  File upload element. The form must be declared as multipart for this to work.

- `hidden_field`

  A hidden input tag.

- `label`

  A label tag, often associated with another input field. Takes an argument before the options hash for the text of the label if it's not the same as the method name.

- password_field

  Text field with masked entry for passwords.

- radio_button

  Takes an extra argument before the options hash for the value of the button. All radio buttons with the same object and method are linked, the one whose value matches the value of the object will be selected.

- select

  Takes an argument for the caption of the select button.

- text_area

  A multi-line text entry field

- text_field

  A single-line text entry field.

The form_for method takes a series of arguments, the first of which is typically the object being mapped to the form, if the RESTful URL for that argument is not where you want the form post to be directed, a :url option lets you specify the destination as a hash, string, or routing method. As just shown, the tag takes a block inside of which the fields of the form are entered.

Often, you'll want a part of the form to be attached to another object, most typically if you want a user to be able to enter a main object and a child object from another model at the same time. The fields_for method allows you to wrap those fields and associate them with a separate object. It takes the same argument structure as form_for, except without a URL.

```
<% form_for @user do |f|%>
  <%= f.text_field :name %>
  <% fields_for @user.address do |a| %>
    <%= a.text_field :city %>
  <% end %>
<% end %>
```

Note that the form elements that belong to the inner fields_for block are called on the inner form builder object, in this case a, instead of f.

FormOptionsHelper

Methods that create various flavors of option tags to get placed inside select tags, as well as the select helper method itself, which creates an HTML select. It is similar to the other form builder method, but takes an extra argument before the options containing the list of option tags. The basic form of that argument is a two-dimensional array where each element is [display, value]. If you just want the option HTML tags from a two-dimensional array, the method options_for_select takes a collection and an optional selected value and returns the string of tags.

```
f.select(:state, [["California", "CA"], ["Oregon", "OR"]])
```

All select tags take an option, `:include_blank`, which is a prompt string or true, and always is the first element of the list, and thus what displays if there is no selected value. A similar method, `:prompt`, only includes the extra element if there is no selected value.

There are a few more specialized tag methods in this module

- `collection_select`

  Takes an arbitrary collection of Ruby objects and converts them into a select and option tags. The arguments are the same object and value as for any form element tag, followed by the collection to be used, followed by a method used on those objects for the value of each option and a method used for the text of each option, then the normal key/value pairs:

  `f.collection_select(:state, US_STATES, :mail_abbr, :name)`

- `country_select`

  Returns a select tag with options for selecting many, many countries. An associated method, `country_options_for_select`, returns just the option tags.

- `time_zone_select`

  Returns a select tag of all time zone from the time zone database and has an associated `time_zone_options_for_select` method.

FormTagHelper

This module contains all the form helpers that are used in the older, `form_tag` style of form creation. The primary advantage of this set of helpers as that they are not required to be attached to an ActiveRecord object, making them more flexible. Most of these take a name, value, and options, and are otherwise analogous to the `FormHelper` methods. These methods include `check_box_tag`, `file_field_tag`, `hidden_field_tag`, `image_submit_tag`, `password_field_tag`, `radio_button_tag`, `select_tag`, `submit_tag`, `text_area_tag`, and `text_field_tag`.

The `form_tag` method is used to create the entire form, and `field_set_tag` creates an HTML fieldset. For the form, the argument is the URL being posted to.

JavaScript Creation Helpers

These helper modules are used for JavaScript and Web service support.

AtomFeedHelper

This has one method, `atom_feed`, and a sub module `AtomFeedHelper::AtomFeedBuilder`. An instance including that module is passed the block argument of this method. You would use this to create an Atom feed. Almost all of the action takes place in the block. The builder object works just like the Ruby XML builder, so any unknown method call on it will result in an XML tag. The `feed.title` in the following example:

```
atom_feed do |builder|
  feed.title("Feed For Thought")
end
```

Results in the XML `<title>Feed For Thought</title>`. The feed helpers manage the requirements for the header and whatnot of the feed, you need to pass it the contents. Each entry in the feed needs to call the `entry` method of the builder, and then add at least a title and content to the entry.

```
atom_feed do |builder|
  feed.title("Feed For Thought")
  @posts.each do |post|
    feed.entry(post) do |entry|
      entry.title(post.title)
      entry.content(post.content)
    end
  end
end
```

The Atom specification discusses all the possible fields in an Atom feed.

JavaScriptHelper

In this module, you'll find a number of utilities for escaping JavaScript and otherwise dealing with JavaScript strings inside your Rails program.

The most useful function here is probably `javascript_tag`, which takes JavaScript as either a string or block argument and encloses it in a fully escaped `script` tag.

```
javascript_tag do
  alert("Hey!")
end
```

This module also contains `link_to_function` and `button_to_function`, the first argument to either method is the text for the resulting link or button. The function to be called is either passed as the next string argument, or as a block, which is evaluated as RJS (see the next section for details). Finally, the `escape_javascript` function takes as string and escapes things like HTML tags and quotation marks so the string can be passed to a JavaScript string.

PrototypeHelper

This contains a number of helpers for making Ajax and RJS calls and will be fully discussed in the next section.

ScriptaculousHelper

This contains a number of helpers for making Ajax and RJS calls and will be fully discussed in the next section.

Data Processing Helpers

These helper modules are used for data processing.

CaptureHelper

The big method here is `capture`, which takes a block argument and returns it as a string. This is extremely useful in writing your own block helpers and will be discussed in a bit more detail in just a moment. A related method, `content_for`, takes a symbol and a block and associates them for the life of the request, allowing you to evaluate the block later on:

```
content_for(:banana) { "Yum" }
```

And then later on:

```
yield :banana
```

DateHelper

The DateHelper module has a series of methods for evaluating dates. First, is a method that converts a time range to text. The method `distance_of_time_in_words` — takes three arguments, the start time, the end time (which defaults to now), and a boolean as to whether seconds should be included. It returns a fuzzy time string representing the distance between the two timestamps along the lines of "about a day" or "over 4 years" — the kind of thing you frequently see timestamping blog posts or comments. If you are comparing the time to now, then the shortcut method `time_ago_in_words` will also work.

Next up is a series of methods for picking dates in forms via a series of select tags. These elements come in a `form_for` version and a `form_tag` version, which are slightly different.

The ActiveRecord versions are called `date_select`, `time_select`, and `date_time_select`. The methods take the normal object name and method arguments. They can be specialized by using the `:discard` family of options to drop the year, month, date, hour, minute, or second options, so `:discard_year => true`. The `:order` option takes a list of the sub fields to use, such as `:order => [:day, :year]`. In this version, parts not included in an order list are not included in the generated form. The `:default` option sets the date and time for the initial value of the fields if the supplied ActiveRecord doesn't have a value. All of these methods place their selects into the field in such a way that ActiveRecord will automatically parse them into the date fields correctly.

The non-ActiveRecord versions are called `select_date`, `select_time`, and `select_date_time`. In this version, you can still set an `:order` option to change the order of the fields, but fields not included in the list are still appended to the end of the generated form.

If you want to have a form with a subset of the fields, you must build it yourself from the helper methods `select_year`, `select_month`, `select_day`, `select_hour`, `select_minute`, and `select_second`. All of these methods take a date or time value as their first argument, to set the field or fields. The second argument is an options hash. These helpers generate fields with names that match the type of field, year, month, and so on. To change the default, pass a value to the `:field_name` option.

NumberHelper

A few helpful methods for converting numbers to different formats.

- `number_to_currency`

  Takes the number and an options hash and returns a currency string. The options override the defaults, `:precision => 2, :unit => '$', :separator => ".",` `:delimiter => ",".`

- `number_to_human_size`

  Converts a file size in bytes to a human readable version, like 10GB, or 1.5 MB. The optional second argument is the number of decimal places of precision.

- `number_to_percentage`

  Converts the number to a percentage string, does not multiply it by 100 — `number_to_percentage(100)` returns `100.000%`. There are two optional arguments, with the defaults `:precision => 3, :separator => ",".`

- `number_to_phone`

  Converts an integer to a phone number string, by default in the common American format of 123-456-7890. Options include `:area_code => true`, which puts the area code in parentheses; `:delimiter`, which defaults to -; `:extension`, which adds an extension; and `:country_code`, which adds one of those, too.

- `number_with_delimiter`

  Writes the number using the delimiter to separate thousands, and a separator to separate decimals. The delimiter is the second argument, the separator the third, the default values are the American format of comma and decimal point.

- `number_with_precision`

  Displays the number to an arbitrary number of decimal points, the default is 3.

SanitizeHelper

The methods in this helper are designed to strip HTML or JavaScript entities from a string, you should always use one of these methods to qualify any text being displayed directly from user data entry to prevent cross-site scripting attacks.

The primary method here is `sanitize`, which takes text as an argument and removes anything that looks like an HTML tag, except for a few tags that are on a whitelist. If a `:tags` argument is passed, then only the tags in that list are allowed, if an `:attributes` argument is passed then only those attributes within the allowed HTML tags are allowed. The global white list is specified in the attributes `ActionView::Base.sanitize_allowed_tags` and `ActionView::Base.sanitize_allowed_attributes`. You can set custom lists in the `config.rb` file.

More aggressively, the method `strip_tags` removes all HTML tags from the text, and `strip_links` removes all HTML anchor tags.

TextHelper

This module has kind of a pot-luck set of methods for manipulating text:

- `auto_link`

  Takes incoming text and converts anything that looks like a URL or email address to a link. An optional second argument can be `:all`, `:email_addressses`, or `:urls`, and controls what kind of links are generated. An optional third argument is a hash added to each link.

- `concat`

  Adds text to the ERb output stream, given text and a block biding. See the section on block helpers later in this chapter for why this is useful.

- `cycle`

  Takes one or more text values, and returns an object. When that object is called, it returns the strings one by one in a loop. An optional argument `:name` allows the cycle to be reset with `reset_cycle(name)`. This is often used to alternate colors in a table:

  ```
  <% @books.each do |book| %>
    <tr class="<%= cycle("even", "odd") %>">
    </tr>
  <% end %>
  ```

- `excerpt`

  Takes some text and a phrase and returns a subset of the text centered on the phrase. The optional third argument specifies how long the excerpt should be on each side of the phrase, defaulting to 100 characters.

- `highlight`

  Takes text and a phrase and highlights all instances of the phrase, as in the display of search results. An optional third argument can change the highlighting, which defaults to HTML `strong`.

- `markdown`

  If the BlueCloth gem is installed, parses the given text as Markdown.

- `pluralize`

  Takes a number, then a singular noun. If the number is 1, then the singular is returned, otherwise the plural form of the noun is returned. An optional third argument allows you to specify your own plural form.

- `simple_format`

  Converts the given text to HTML, converting a single newline to a `br` tag and a double newline to a `p` tag.

- `textilize`

  If the RedCloth gem is installed, converts the given text as Textile.

Debugging Helpers

The helpers in this section assist in debugging or performance improvement.

BenchmarkHelper

The sole method in this module is `benchmark`, which takes a block and a text message, and logs the amount of time it takes to run the block of code to the appropriate log file. An optional second argument specifies the log level.

CacheHelper

The sole method in this module is `cache`, which allows you to cache an arbitrary fragment of a view. The method takes an optional argument, which is a URL-style hash allowing you to uniquely identify the fragment (it doesn't have to be a real URL, just a unique identifier) and a block. The result of the block is cached and inserted the next time the fragment is called without having to evaluated the block again.

DebugHelper

The sole method in this helper is `debug`, which takes an object and returns a YAML-compatible inspection of the object wrapped in a `pre` tag so it can be placed in your HTML output for testing.

Creating Your Own Block Helpers

Within your own helpers, you are free to write any valid Ruby you want, and use any other helpers that might assist. There is one technique that you should know about, which is the ability to write a helper that surrounds arbitrary ERb. For the purposes of an example, let's say you want a helper that creates a table row with two cells, the first has a caption, and the second has arbitrary ERb, so:

```
<% captioned_row "Location" do %>
  <%= f.text_field :city %>
  <%= f.text_field :city %>
  <%= f.text_field :zip %>
<% end %>
```

In the code snippet, the helper call is enclosed in a ERb evaluate tag not an ERb evaluate and print tag. This means that the helper method will need to explicitly place the output text into the ERb stream (doing an evaluate and print for blocks doesn't work). However, the text field calls inside the block are entered as evaluate and print, those will be dealt with as string.

The helper to process this code looks like this:

```
def captioned_row(caption, &block)
  caption_cell = content_tag(:td, caption)
  data_cell = content_tag(:td, capture(&block))
  row = content_tag(:tr, caption_cell + data_cell)
  concat(row, block.binding)
end
```

This method uses several helpers that you have already seen. The `content_tag` method builds up the HTML tags for the table cells and row. The `capture` method evaluates the block and returns its result as a string — conveniently, you do not need to specify that the block should be evaluated as ERb; it will be automatically be parsed and processed by the ERb engine. It will not, however, be included in the page output until you call `concat`, which takes the text that you want to place in the output, and the binding for the block. A block binding is something like a frozen set of variable states, and the `concat` helper uses the block binding to get at the ERb output stream.

JavaScript, Ajax, and RJS

One of Rails' earliest advantages over competing frameworks was it's embrace of Ajax as a mechanism for interaction between the browser and the Web application. In an Ajax interaction, the browser makes a behind-the-scenes call to the server, and uses the result to update part of the page on the fly. Rails makes adding Ajax effects to you Web application as easy as adding regular links and actions. This section will cover Rails support for Ajax interaction through helper methods that generate Prototype and `script.aculo.us` code. Chapter 10 contains more information on the Prototype and `script.aculo.us` libraries themselves, including information on the `script.aculo.us` helpers that manage drag and drops.

Ruby JavaScript (RJS) is a later addition to Rails toolkit to support more complex JavaScript interaction by providing Ruby helpers that create JavaScript code.

Prototype Helpers

The helper methods in the `PrototypeHelper` module are all designed to support Ajax interaction by generating a Prototype object that makes a remote call and evaluates the response. The basic mechanism for most of these methods is to take a URL and a DOM ID. The URL is called when the interaction is triggered, and the result replaces the text in the specified DOM element. Although some of these methods have additional options for more complex interactions, the preferred mechanism for more complex Javascript is an RJS template call.

The Ajax helper methods take many common options. Unless otherwise specified, all of these methods have an options argument at the end that takes a `:url` option to specify the server target of the Ajax action, and an `:update` option to take the DOM ID to be updated — if no update is specified, it's assumed that further instructions will come from the JavaScript returned by the server. If you want the text to be an insertion rather than a replacement, specify the `:position` option to be `:after`, `:before`, `:bottom`, or `:top`.

Several further options allow you to specify additional JavaScript code to be executed under various conditions. Again, RJS has largely, but not completely, rendered these obsolete. A JavaScript snippet passed to the `:condition` option can halt the execution of the request before the server is contacted by returning false. The `:confirm` option, if specified, is the text of a confirmation box that must be okayed before the request proceeds. JavaScript, to be executed before the Ajax call is made, should be passed to the :before option. JavaScript can be executed during processing by specifying the :loading, :loaded, or :interactive options. Once those are complete, any JavaScript code passed to :after option is executed.

Additional callbacks can be based on the result of the call by passing the script to the :success or :failure options. In either case, the code passed to the :complete option is executed after that. In place of the success or failure options, any integer corresponding to a specific HTTP response code can be used as an option key. Finally, two non-callback options: the :submit options specifies the parent DOM element for any form element in the Ajax call if for some reason the currently active form isn't the parent; and the :with option is a JavaScript snippet that must return a string suitable to be appended to the query string of the request.

And here are the helpers themselves, along with any further options or quirks specific to that method;

- form_remote_tag

  The Ajax version of form_tag for non-ActiveRecord forms. Its only arguments are the option tag, and the block that will contain the form elements. The :html option specifies an alternate URL for browsers without JavaScript.

- link_to_remote

  The Ajax version of link_to, creates a clickable link with Ajax consequences. By default the HTTP method of this connection is POST. The first argument is the text of the link, the second argument is the options hash. The :html option adds additional attributes to the anchor tag. The :href option provides an alternate target if JavaScript is not enabled.

- observe_field

  The first argument to this method is the DOM ID of a form element the second argument is an options hash. When the form element changes — anything that would trigger a JavaScript changed event — the URL is called and the response is evaluated. Instead of a :url, you can specify :function, which is JavaScript code that will become the body of a function called when the field changes.

  You may assume that the generated function will have the arguments element and value. An additional option, :frequency, specifies the amount of time in seconds between checks of the field. A property called :on purports to allow you to change the event being tracked, but as of this writing, a Prototype bug prevents it from working. Also, when specifying the :with option, you may use the JavaScript variable value, which has the new value of the field element.

- observer_form

  Like observe_field, but the DOM ID is of an entire form, and the URL or function is triggered if any element in the form is changed. The only difference in the options from observe_field is that the value parameter for the :with option contains the entire form.

- `periodically_call_remote`

  Takes just the options hash as an argument. Uses the `:frequency` option to determine how often, in seconds, it should make its remote call. The default is ten seconds.

- `remote_form_for`

  The Ajax version of `form_for` (also can be called as `form_for_remote`). The first arguments specify the ActiveRecord, followed by the options hash, and the form block.

- `remote_function`

  Given the option hash, returns just the JavaScript for making the remote Ajax call, suitable for insertion in some other kind of user or JavaScript event.

- `submit_to_remote`

  Can be used to create a remote submission inside a form.

RJS helpers

RJS allows you to create a wide variety of common JavaScript Ajax functionality by writing Ruby. RJS code can be triggered in many ways. The `render :update` method takes an optional block that is evaluated as RJS:

```
render :update do |page|
  page.replace_html "header", "Clicked!"
end
```

The page variable is the variable that can respond to the RJS generator methods and is automatically created by `render :update`. The helper method doesn't need to have the page in its arguments, but can use page as a local variable.

If the default controller action for a JavaScript request finds a file with the extension `.rjs`, then that file is evaluated as if it was inside a `render :update` block, complete with a `page` variable created for your use inside the template. Finally, the Prototype helper `update_page`, takes a block in exactly the same way as `render :update` and returns the created JavaScript code.

Within an RJS template the `page` variable has about two dozen Ruby methods that create JavaScript. The most commonly used are probably the three that affect HTML for a given DOM id:

- `insert_html`

  Takes three options, a position as in the options for the Prototype helpers in the last section, and a DOM ID to be affected. The third option is either a string to be inserted directly or a key/value hash which is interpreted as though it was a call to render, so typically something like `:partial => 'partial_view'`. The resulting text is placed in the DOM element as specified by the position.

- `replace`

  The first argument is a DOM ID, the second is the text to render in the same way as in `insert_html`. The text completely replaces the DOM element, including its tags, or what JavaScript calls the outer HTML of the element.

- `replace_html`

  As `replace`, but does not effect the tag of the element. In other words, it replaces the JavaScript inner HTML of the element.

Any RJS method that takes a DOM ID as its first element can also be accessed via an alternate method, like so:

```
page.replace_html "header", "new text"
```

This is equivalent to:

```
page["header"].replace_html, "new text"
```

and:

```
page.select("header").first.replace_html, "new text"
```

The last version is the most flexible; the option to the `select` method can be any CSS-style selector. The result is an enumeration of all matching elements. You can then deal with that enumeration using Prototype's iteration methods, which are very similar to Ruby's.

The select form is often used to bulk hide or show a set of DOM elements using the RJS methods `hide`, `show`, and `toggle`, which change the visibility of the DOM element passed to them. The method `remove` takes the element completely out of the DOM tree. All four of these methods can take multiple DOM IDs as arguments at one time.

The `draggable`, `drop_receiving`, and `sortable` methods all take a DOM ID and create a `script.aculo.us` object for that DOM ID

CROSS-REF For more details on creating a `script.aculo.us` object, see Chapter 10.

The `visual_effects` method gives access to the entire range of `script.aculo.us` visual effects. The first argument to this method is the name of the effect, the DOM ID being affected is the second argument, the third argument is an option hash. The exact list of visual effects is dynamically determined by what `script.aculo.us` offers, but commonly used ones include `:highlight`, `:fade`, `:appear`, and `:puff`. The `script.aculo.us` documentation has a complete list.

A few methods let you include arbitrary JavaScript outside of what is provided:

- `>>`

  Inserts its argument as JavaScript directly to the page, as in `page << "1 + 1"`.

- `alert`

  Sends a JavaScript alert call with the given text argument.

- `assign`

  The arguments are a variable name and a value and the generated JavaScript assigns that value to that variable on the client-side.

- `call`

  Takes a JavaScript function and a list of arguments and inserts a call to that function into the RJS JavaScript.

- `delay`

  Takes a numerical argument and a block. Waits that number of seconds on the client and then evaluates the block

- `literal`

  Creates a JSON object from the given text.

- `redirect_to`

  Takes a Rails URL format and redirects the entire client-side browser page to that URL.

Summary

In this chapter, you learned about the view layer of a Rails application. Just as with the other layers of your application, Rails provides significant help to you, the developer, in creating the views for your application.

In Chapter 10, you'll learn about the Prototype and Scriptaculous JavaScript toolkits, which are distributed with Rails. These toolkits provide even more power to you as you develop the views for your Web application.

Part III

Developing a Complete Rails Application

Chapter 6

Developing Book Shelf: The Basic Framework

This chapter marks the beginning of step-by-step development of a complete and useful Rails application. If you are familiar with the Web development market, you know that most of the hottest applications being developed today feature some sort of social aspect. The option for users to provide content and interact with other users is a key component of what is usually referred to as a Web 2.0 application. The application you can write by following along in this chapter fits in nicely with the Web 2.0 paradigm.

This application will allow groups to create an online catalog of books. Using the application, users can add books, share book reviews, share book ratings, and organize the books using tags. Book Shelf, as I've named this application, could be used by a user group, a community group, a school, a local library, a workplace, or just about any group of people that have some interest in books.

You will develop Book Shelf using an iterative process in which you will design a feature and then code that feature. This process is repeated until all of the required features of the application have been implemented. In this chapter, you will put in place the basic framework of the application and implement a user model with authentication so that a user is able to log in to and out of the application. The development continues in the next two chapters.

I strongly encourage you to follow along with the development of the application and to write the code on your computer as you read about it. However, I do recognize that this is not the best learning style for everyone who will read this book. Therefore, if you'd like to see the complete source code for the application, you can download it from www.rubyonrailsbible.com.

Application Overview

Previous chapters have covered the various features that make up Rails; in this chapter you can learn through the experience of writing what I feel is an interesting application.

Your Book Shelf application will include the following features:

- User registration, login, and account management
- Ability to add and remove books to and from user-specific shelves
- Automatic population of book information for added books
- Ability to search the Amazon catalog to find books that a user wants to add
- Links to purchase books online
- Support for book reviews
- Tagging of books
- Rating of books

One of the best ways of communicating the goals for an application upfront is through pictures. To give you a good idea of what is to be developed, I'll cheat a bit here by showing you how the application looks when it's complete. Figures 6.1 to 6.4 show four of the Book Shelf application's main screens, which are described here:

- **Book Shelf Home Page:** The screen shown in Figure 6.1 is what users will see when they first navigate to the Book Shelf application. This is the starting point for all users and visitors.
- **User Home Page:** The page shown in Figure 6.2 is a home page for users who have logged into the application.
- **Add Book Page:** The page shown in Figure 6.3 is where users can view results of searches against the Amazon catalog and find books that they want to add to their book shelf.
- **Book Detail Page:** The page shown in Figure 6.4 is where users view details about a particular book that is on someone's shelf. This is also the page where users are able to read and submit book reviews.

FIGURE 6.1

The Book Shelf Home page

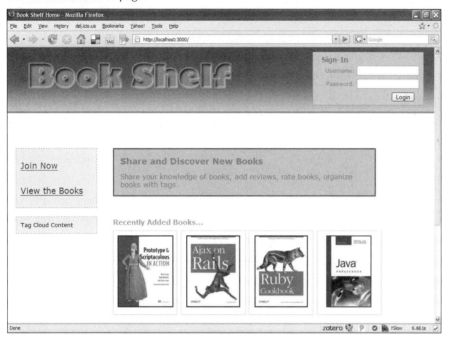

FIGURE 6.2

The User Home page

FIGURE 6.3

The Add Book page

FIGURE 6.4

The Book Detail page

If you follow the development of the Book Shelf application through the next two chapters, I hope you find something missing from the chapters. I am referring to unit tests, something that should normally be a part of your development process. In any real application development cycle, I very strongly recommend that you write your unit tests shortly after you implement a particular feature.

You can also practice test-driven development, in which you actually write your unit tests before you write the code that implement the tests. Either of these development styles will produce higher-quality code that is a great deal more maintainable. For this book, I have chosen to centralize the writing of tests into a chapter of its own so that the reader who wants to look up how to write tests for a Rails application has a dedicated chapter to go to.

CROSS-REF   Chapter 9 includes tests for the Book Shelf application.

Creating a Skeleton for the Application

This section leads you through creating a skeleton for the Book Shelf application. The skeleton will set up the application's directory structure and provide a home for the code you will write throughout the remainder of the chapter. You will also create application databases for three different environments: test, development, and production.

CROSS-REF This chapter assumes that you have already installed Ruby and Rails on your development computer. If you have not, see the Quick Start chapter for help with installing those components.

Begin the Book Shelf project

The project is named Book Shelf, but it is common Rails convention to give the Rails project a name that is lowercase with underscore word separation. You can use `book_shelf` as the name of the Rails project. From your project directory, open a console window and use the `rails` command to generate the directory structure for the Book Shelf application:

```
rails -d mysql book_shelf
```

Prior to version 2.0.2 of Rails, MySQL was the default database for a Rails application. However as of Rails 2.0.2, SQLite is now the default database for a Rails application. If you run the `rails` command above without the `-d` option, your database configuration file will contain setup for a SQLite database. The `-d mysql` option tells Rails that you want it to setup a database configuration file for use with MySQL.

Running this command will output the list of directories and files that are being created for you. The directory structure that is created is common to all Rails applications. Inside of the directory in which you ran the `rails` command you should now see a directory named `book_shelf`. If you look at the drectories inside of the `book_shelf` directory you should see the directory structure shown in Figure 6.5.

From within the `book_shelf` directory, start the WEBrick server using the `script/server` command:

```
ruby script/server
=> Booting WEBrick
=> Rails application started on http://127.0.0.1:3000
=> Ctrl-C to shutdown server; call with --help for options
...
```

FIGURE 6.5

The Rails directory structure

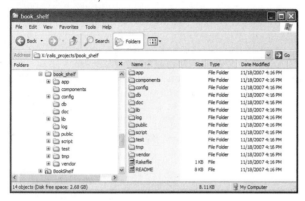

When you see feedback indicating that the WEBrick server has been successfully started on port 3000, open a browser and navigate to `http://localhost:3000`. You should see a screen similar to the one in Figure 6.6.

FIGURE 6.6

The Rails Welcome page

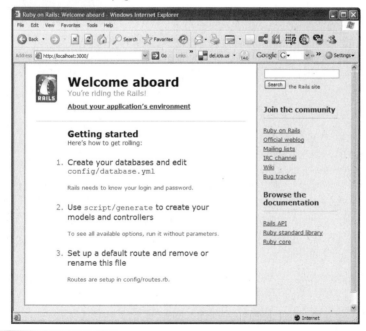

You have now successfully created the Book Shelf project directory and a skeletal framework where all of the code you write will go. You'll continue development by setting up the application's databases.

Setting up the databases

For any database-backed application, Rails supports three distinct environments; production, development, and test. Each of these environments should have their own database associated with it. In a real application, these databases may not all be on the same server. In fact it is very likely that your development and test databases will not exist on the same server that holds your production database. For this application, you will create all three databases on your local development machine.

Create the databases

Prior to Rails 2.0 you would have had to create the databases yourself using either the MySQL command-line tool, or some other tool. However, as of version 2.0 of Rails, you can easily create the databases using a simple Rake command. The first thing you must do is make sure the databases that you want created are configured in your application's `database.yml` file. This is a database configuration file contained in the `book_shelf/config` directory. If you open that up, you should see something similar to Listing 6.1.

The important things to notice in the configuration are the following:

- The adapter is set to `mysql`. This means you will be using MySQL as your database application.

- The database names are a concatenation of the name of the application `book_shelf` with an environment name, such as `book_shelf_development`.

- The username and password fields should contain the username and password of a valid MySQL user. When you first install MySQL the root user is created with no password. If you have changed that, make sure you update this file appropriately.

- The host for each database is set to be localhost, meaning that you will be hosting all of the databases on your local computer.

After you've made any necessary changes to your database configuration file, you can use Rake to create the databases. From a command prompt use the following Rake command:

```
rake db:create:all
```

This will create each of the three databases that were specified in the database.yml file. If for some reason, you made a mistake and need to start over, you can remove all of the databases using a similar command, rake db:drop:all will remove all of the databases specified in database.yml.

Now that you have the application skeleton generated and the databases created, it's time to begin building the application.

LISTING 6.1

Book_shelf/config directory

```
development:
  adapter: mysql
  encoding: utf8
  database: book_shelf_development
  username: root
  password:

  host: localhost

# Warning: The database defined as 'test' will be erased and
# re-generated from your development database when you run 'rake'.
# Do not set this db to the same as development or production.
test:
  adapter: mysql
  encoding: utf8
  database: book_shelf_test
  username: root
  password:
  host: localhost

production:
  adapter: mysql
  encoding: utf8
  database: book_shelf_production
  username: root
  password:
  host: localhost
```

Create a Home Page

In the previous section, you saw that if you run the application right now, you get the Rails Welcome default page. You will now create a home page for the Book Shelf application that the user starts from. The end result of what you'll create in this section is shown in Figure 6.7. It's not yet the final home page that you saw at the beginning of this chapter, but it is a place to start from.

The Book Shelf home page

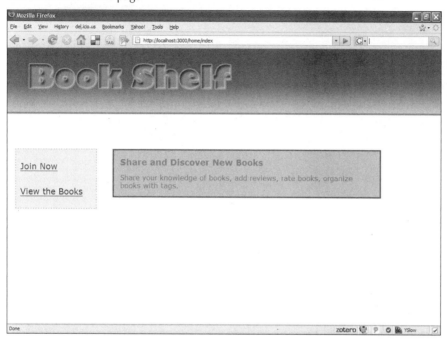

Now that you know what the goal is for this section, let's talk about what you need to do to get there. How do you display a page in a Rails application? You need to create a controller to handle the page request coming from the browser. The controller will contain a method corresponding to the particular action that the browser is requesting. The action method of the controller will render a view template file that defines the page you want to display. There are three steps you need to follow:

1. **Create a controller to handle the home page request.**
2. **Create a method in the home controller to handle the home page request.**
3. **Create a view template to define the page to be rendered.**

Let's get started with a home controller.

Create the Home controller

It is a good practice to create controller classes that correspond to your model classes. For example, if you have a user model, you would also have a user controller that would provide action methods related to working with users. However, for the home page, there is really not a specific model class that you want to work with yet. You can simply call the controller that renders the home page, 'HomeController.'

In a command window, go to the `book_shelf` directory and use the Rails generate script to create the `HomeController` class:

```
> ruby script/generate controller Home
 exists app/controllers/
 exists app/helpers/
 create app/views/home
 exists test/functional/
 create app/controllers/home_controller.rb
 create test/functional/home_controller_test.rb
 create app/helpers/home_helper.rb
```

This creates a stub for your Home controller, a functional test for the controller, a helper for the controller, and a `views/home` directory where you can put view templates that will be rendered by the Home controller.

Open up the `app/controllers/home_controller.rb` file, and you see a currently empty controller class like this:

```
class HomeController < ApplicationController
end
```

You need to add a method that will handle the rendering of the Book Shelf home page. It is a standard practice to name any Web site's start page as index. If you specify a URL containing only a controller name with no action, Rails will, by default, route to an `index` action. You can name the action method to display the home page, `index`. Edit the `HomeController` to add the `index` method:

```
class HomeController < ApplicationController
    def index
    end
end
```

Notice that you did not specify any template to render. By default, a view template with the same name as the action method will be rendered. In this case, when the `index` method is called, it will try to render a template stored in `app/views/home/index.html.erb`.

Now that you have a controller and an action method in place, let's move onto creating the home page view template.

Create a layout and view

You could put all of the HTML necessary to create the home page view into a Rails view template. However, some of the HTML is probably reusable across many of the other views that will also be created. If you look back at the four screen shots that were shown at the beginning of this chapter, you will notice that all four of those views had the same general layout. Rails has great support for common layouts, so it makes sense to start with a Rails layout template.

Rails layouts let you put HTML and embedded Ruby content into an `html.erb` file that can be used with multiple views. Layout files are just like other Rails view template files. Rails will look in the `app/views/layouts` directory for a layout template that contains the same name as the controller that is being requested. If a layout exists with the same name as the controller, Rails uses that layout file. If Rails cannot find a layout template that matches a controller name, it uses the layout file named `application.html.erb`. The `application.html.erb` template is a global template within which you can put your default page layout. Unless you override this by creating controller-specific layouts, Rails will always use the `application.html.erb` template.

You can also override the layout which will be used for any given controller by specifying a layout inside of a controller file. For example, if you wanted to use a layout file named `home.html.erb` with the methods in your home controller, you could modify the home controller adding the layout specification like this:

```
class HomeController < ApplicationController
    layout 'home'

    def index
    end
end
```

For this application, the home controller will use the default `application.html.erb` layout file.

Create the `app/views/layouts/application.html.erb` file now and enter the code shown in Listing 6.2.

This will set up the general layout across all of the application's pages. The following sections break down the various pieces of this layout template.

The HTML head

The HTML head defined in the layout looks like this:

```
<head>
 <title><%= @title %></title>
 <%= stylesheet_link_tag "style" %>

 <%= javascript_include_tag :defaults %>
</head>
```

The page title is set using an instance variable set by the action methods of your controllers. This allows each page to have a unique title while still using the same layout template. The second line of the head section links a style sheet named `style.css` from the `public/stylesheets` directory. Notice that you do not have to specify the `.css` extension. Just specifying the name of the file without the extension is enough for Rails to find the CSS file, assuming that you used the `.css` extension to name the file.

LISTING 6.2

The Application Layout Template in app/views/layouts/application.html.erb

```
<!DOCTYPE html PUBLIC "-//W3C//DTD XHTML 1.0 Transitional//EN" "http://
    www.w3.org/TR/xhtml1/DTD/xhtml1-transitional.dtd">
<html xmlns="http://www.w3.org/1999/xhtml">

<head>
 <title><%= @title %></title>
 <%= stylesheet_link_tag "style" %>

 <%= javascript_include_tag :defaults %>

</head>

<body>
 <div id="header">
 <div id="logo_image">
 <%= link_to image_tag('main_logo.png'),
 {:controller=>'home', :action=>'index'} %>
 </div>
       <div style="clear: both; height: 0px;"></div>
 </div>

 <%= render :partial=>"shared/sidebar" %>

 <div id="Content">
 <% if flash[:notice] -%>
 <div id="notice"><%= flash[:notice] %></div>
 <% end -%>
 <% if flash[:error] -%>
 <div id="error"><%= flash[:error] %></div>
 <% end -%>
 <%= yield %>
 </div>
</body>
</html>
```

The last line of the head section includes default JavaScript files. Rails defines a standard set of JavaScript files that are included with the framework as its defaults. The default JavaScript files that will be included are as follows:

- **application.js:** This is where you write any custom JavaScript that you want to include.
- **controls.js:** This is a part of the Scriptaculous library.
- **dragdrop.js:** This is a part of the Scriptaculous library.
- **effects.js:** This is a part of the Scriptaculous library.
- **prototype.js:** This contains the Prototype library.

Prototype and Scriptaculous are powerful JavaScript libraries that make it easy for you to create cool effects, create rich interactive features, and write well-structured JavaScript.

CROSS-REF For more about the Prototype and Scriptaculous libraries, see chapter 10 of this book.

The body header section

The HTML body section of the layout includes the `main_logo.png` image that links to the home page if the user clicks it.

```
<div id="header">
    <div id="logo_image">
        <%= link_to image_tag('main_logo.png'),
            {:controller=>'home', :action=>'index'} %>
    </div>
    <div style="clear: both; height: 0px;"></div>
</div>
```

NOTE You can download the `main_logo.png` and other image files used by this project from the book's Web site at www.rubyonrailsbible.com.

The link to the home page is created using the `link_to` helper. The `index` action of the home controller is specified as the link's target. The last `div` in the header section is only for layout purposes. This helps to achieve the correct layout. If you are familiar with laying out pages using floating elements, you are probably also familiar with the technique of using a clearing div. For those of you not familiar with this, I'd suggest a good CSS reference book.

The body sidebar section

The sidebar defines the left menu that you see in each of the application screens. This will be rendered as a partial.

```
<%= render :partial=>"shared/sidebar" %>
```

You can create the sidebar partial now. In the `app/views` directory, create a subdirectory named `shared`. The `shared` directory is where you will put view partials that will be used by view templates associated with more than one controller. In the `app/views/shared` directory, create a file named `_sidebar.html.erb`. Edit the file to look the code in Listing 6.3.

LISTING 6.3

_sidebar.rhtml partial

```
<div id="sidebar">
    <div id="Menu">
        <ul id="home_menu">
            <li><%= link_to 'Join Now',
                    :controller=>'user',
                :action=>'signup' %>
        </li>
            <li><%= link_to 'View the Books',
                    :controller=>'book',
                    :action=>'list' %>
        </li>
        </ul>
    </div>
    <div style="clear:both;"> </div>
</div>
```

This creates a menu with a Join Now link and a View the Books link. Notice that the Join Now link is pointed to the `signup` method of the user controller. The View the Books link is pointed to the `list` method of the books controller. These controllers and methods do not exist yet, but you can anticipate their creation. Here again you see the use of the `link_to` helper to create the links.

The body content section

The final section of the layout template defines the main content of the pages. This section is pretty simple. If there are any flash notice or error messages to be displayed, those display at the top of the content section. After those messages are printed, a `yield` method renders content defined in your page view templates.

```
<div id="Content">
    <% if flash[:notice] -%>
        <div id="notice"><%= flash[:notice] %></div>
    <% end -%>
    <% if flash[:error] -%>
        <div id="error"><%= flash[:error] %></div>
    <% end -%>
    <%= yield %>
</div>
```

Remember that the flash hash is a special collection that is built-in to Rails for the purposes of passing simple messages from the controller to the views. The messages stored in flash will be automatically removed after a single request/response cycle. The flash is not a place to store persistent messages that you want to remember for long periods of time.

Firefox versus Internet Explorer

Most Web developers tend to prefer the Firefox Web browser over Internet Explorer. Firefox is generally considered more standards compliant. There is also a powerful development tool available for Firefox called Firebug which will be very useful to you as you develop Web applications. Firefox is the browser that was used during the development of Book Shelf. Although I have tried to make sure everything works equally well in Internet Explorer, some of the layout and style of the application may appear slightly different from what you see in the diagrams if you are viewing the pages using Internet Explorer.

Creating the index view template

With the layout in place, the last task left to perform before you can view the home page is to create an index view template in the `app/views/home` directory. The view template is named `index.html.erb` so that it matches the name of the controller action method. Create that file now and edit it to contain the following code:

```
<div class="home_quote">
    <span class="quote_title">Share and Discover New Books</span>
    Share your knowledge of books, add reviews, rate books,
    organize books with tags.
</div>
```

Testing the home page

You should have all the elements necessary to get the basic home page to come up in a browser. From a command window, start up the WEBrick server if you do not already have it running.

```
> ruby script/server
```

Now in your browser, navigate to the index action of the home controller by typing this URL: `http://localhost:3000/home/index`. If you've followed all the steps up to this point, you should see a page similar to Figure 6.8.

Oops, it doesn't quite look like the view that was shown in Figure 6.7, does it? The good news is that the content looks correct — it's just not styled the way you'd like it to be. That can be fixed by defining some CSS styles, which you'll do shortly.

There is one other problem with the page: There is no page title in the browser title bar. Remember that in the template for this page, the title was set using an `@title` instance variable. However, in the `index` action method of the home controller, you did not set the title. Go back and set the `@title` instance variable in the `index` method to something like "Book Shelf." You can do that by modifying the `index` method of the home controller (`app/controllers/home_controller.rb`) as shown below:

```
def index
    @title = 'Book Shelf'
end
```

Now you can reload the page in your browser to see the title displayed in the browser title bar.

221

FIGURE 6.8

The basic home page without styling

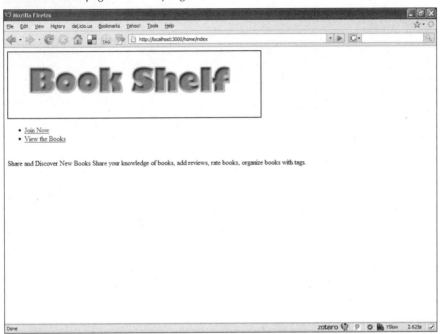

Add some style

Remember that in the layout template, you included a link to a style sheet named `style.css`. Go ahead and create that file in the `public/stylesheets` directory and edit it to contain the content shown in Listing 6.4. In this book, I won't get into the details of the CSS styles. If you want to learn more about CSS and how to style a Web application, I recommend the book, *HTML, XHTML, and CSS Bible, 4th Edition*, by Steven M. Schafer.

LISTING 6.4

Style.css

```
body {
  padding: 0;
  margin: 0;
  background-color: white;
  min-width: 700px;
  background-position: left top;
  background-repeat:repeat-x;
  font-family: Verdana, Arial, Helvetica, sans-serif;
```

```
 font-size: 80%;
}

#header {
    height: 150px;
    background: url(../images/header_bg.png) repeat-x;
}

#logo_image {
    float: left;
    position: relative;
}

#logo_image img {
    border: none;
}

#notice {
    color: red;
    font-weight: bold;
    margin-left: 30px;
    margin-bottom: 30px;
}

#error {
    color: red;
    font-weight: bold;
    margin-left: 30px;
    margin-bottom: 30px;
}

#join_now_text {
    clear: both;
    text-align: right;
}

#Content {
    margin:75px 0px 50px 220px;
    padding:5px;
}

#sidebar {
    position:absolute;
    top:230px;
    left:20px;
    width:170px;
}

#Menu {
```

continued

LISTING 6.4   *(continued)*

```
     display:block;
     float:left;
     padding:10px;
     background-color:#eee;
     border:1px dashed #999;
     line-height:17px;
     width:170px;
     margin-bottom: 20px;
}

#home_menu {
     list-style: none;
     margin: 0px;
     padding: 0px;
}

#home_menu li {
 padding-top: 20px;
 padding-bottom: 20px;
 font-size: 1.5em;
 color: blue;
}

.home_quote {
     font-family: Verdana, Arial, Helvetica, sans-serif;
     float: left;
     margin-left: 25px;
     font-size: 12pt;
 color: #777777;
 border: 3px solid #0066cc;
 width: 75%;
 padding: 15px;
 background-color: #a6cae1;
}

.home_quote.quote_title {
     display: block;
     font-size:14pt;
     font-weight:bold;
     color:gray;
     margin-bottom: 15px;
}
```

Now if you've done everything right up to this point, your home page should look like the home page shown in Figure 6.7. Your first task is nearly complete. There is just one more thing to do, and that is to add a default route to the Rails configuration.

Set up a default route

Currently, you can navigate to the home page by specifying the home controller and action name in the URL like this: `http://localhost:3000/home/index`. Since the action is named index, you could have left the action name off. Rails will look for an action named index if no action is specified in the URL. However, it is better to have the home page come up when the user routes to the top level of the Web site, for example, using the URL `http://localhost:3000`. In order to get that URL to navigate to your home controller, you need to set up a default route. You can do that in this section by editing the Rails routes configuration.

Open up the `config/routes.rb` file. Near the top of the file, you should see these lines:

```
# You can have the root of your site routed with map.root
# -- just remember to delete public/index.html
# map.root :controller => "welcome"
```

This defines a default or empty route that is used if there is not a controller or action specified in the URL. You need to uncomment the line that starts with `map.root`. This line sets up a route to match the empty pattern, `' '`. You also need to change the name of the controller from `welcome` to `home`. The route definition should look like this:

```
map.root :controller => "home"
```

After making that change, you can close the `routes.rb` file; however, if you try going to `http://localhost:3000`, you still won't get the page you are after; instead, the `index.html` page that is stored in the `public` directory will be loaded. This is the application start page that was shown in Figure 6.6. Any HTML files that are stored in the `public` directory of a Rails application will be served directly, bypassing the Rails routing mechanism. You need to either rename or delete the `public/index.html` file.

After you have either renamed or deleted the `public/index.html` file, go back to your browser, and go to `http://localhost:3000`. Now you should see the home page that you created. Because there was no controller or action specified in the URL, the empty route was used to map to the home controller.

Implementing Users

Now that you have the basic framework of the Book Shelf application started, you can implement support for users in this section. The ability to support user registration, login, and account management is a common requirement of most Web applications. This section leads you through building a system for user registration, login, and authentication. Much of what you'll learn and develop in this section is applicable to any Rails application that you will write.

Some developers would stop you at this point and suggest that instead of writing your own user authentication and login, instead you should use a Rails plug-in. There are several Rails plug-ins available that provide this functionality for you. Several of these plug-ins are described in Chapter 11 of this book. My advice is to first implement a user authentication and login system yourself at least once so that you learn how these things work in a Rails application.

Once you feel that you understand the basics of authentication and user login, it is a good idea to save yourself time and use one of the popular Rails plug-ins. Creating your own authentication system in the remainder of this chapter will be valuable experience that you can apply to existing authentication plug-ins that you want to evaluate.

The steps in this section to implement user accounts are as follows:

- Create the user model
- Implement user registration
- Implement login and logout

These steps require creating a user model, a user controller, and a few view templates. Begin with creating the user model.

Create the user model

The first thing you need to do to add user support is create the user model. However, before you create the user model, it's a good idea to think about what type of information you want to be able to store about each user. This becomes the user model design. Table 6.1 lists the fields, along with a description and a data type for each of the fields that will be used in the user model of this application.

These fields allow you to keep track of all that the application needs to know about users. Notice that you take advantage of the created_at and upated_at fields that Rails will automatically update for you each time a user record is created or updated.

TABLE 6.1

The User Model

Field	Description	Data Type
id	Primary key	integer
login	User login id	string
first_name	User's first name	string
last_name	User's last name	string
email	User's e-mail address	string
password_hash	Hashed password	string
password_salt	Salt value	string
login_count	Count of user logins	integer
last_login	Date of last login	datetime
created_at	Date user was created	datetime
updated_at	Date user was updated	datetime

Securing user passwords

The `password_hash` and `password_salt` fields allow for the secure use of passwords without storing any user's password in plain-text form. When the user submits a password, a hashing algorithm is used to create a unique hash for that password. The password hash is stored in the database. When the hash is created, a salt value is combined with the password. The salt value makes a type of attack known as a dictionary attack much more difficult for hackers. In a dictionary attack, the attacker writes a program that scans a dictionary going through every word in an attempt to guess your password.

However, by adding a Salt value to the password, the password is no longer recognizable as any dictionary word even if you used a common word as your password. With this strategy, user passwords are never stored in the database; thus, only the users know their passwords, making for a more secure system.

Generate the user model

Now that you have a good idea of what fields are used in the user model, go ahead and use the `script/generate` command to generate the user model class. Open up a command console in the `book_shelf` root directory and type this:

```
> ruby script/generate model User
 create  app/models
 exists  test/unit
 exists  test/fixtures
 create  app/models/user.rb
 create  test/unit/user_test.rb
 create  test/fixtures/users.yml
 create  db/migrate
 create  db/migrate/001_create_users.rb
```

This generates the user model class, along with a unit test file, a test fixture file, and a database migration file for the user model.

The user model class should be in the `app/models` directory and will have the filename `user.rb`. Rails uses the Ruby convention of naming class files using lowercase, underscore-separated names. The filename of any given class should be the lowercase, underscore-separated form of the class name. Open up the `user.rb` file, and you should see your `User` class similar to this:

```
class User < ActiveRecord::Base
end
```

The `User` class does not yet have any application-specific behavior, but don't forget that it has a great deal of built-in functionality as a result of extending the `ActiveRecord::Base` class. Leave the `User` class unchanged for now, and move onto creating a migration that creates the `users` database table.

Create the user migration

Each of the model classes in a Rails application is generally mapped to a database table that holds records corresponding to instances of that model type. Table names in a Rails application are lowercase and the plural form of the model class name. You need a users table to hold the Book Shelf user data that is used by the user model.

When you generated the user model, a migration file was also generated for you and placed in the db/migrate directory of the book_shelf application directory. Open up the 001_create_users.rb file, and you should see code similar to this:

```
class CreateUsers < ActiveRecord::Migration
    def self.up
        create_table :users do |t|
            t.timestamps
        end
    end

    def self.down
        drop_table :users
    end
end
```

This is an empty migration class that does not do anything useful yet, other than create a users table with two timestamp columns. Remember that the t.timestamps method call in the migration will create the updated_at and created_at columns, which Rails manages for you automatically.

The two methods, self.up and self.down, are called when the migration is applied or reversed, respectively. The self.up method is responsible for setting up the users table completely, and the self.down method should reverse any action taken by the self.up method.

You need to modify this migration so that it creates the users table with the fields that are specified in Table 6.1. Go ahead and modify the migration class to match this:

```
class CreateUsers < ActiveRecord::Migration
    def self.up
        create_table :users do |t|
            t.string :login
            t.string :first_name
            t.string :last_name
            t.string :email
            t.string :password_hash
            t.string :password_salt
            t.integer :login_count
            t.datetime :last_login
            t.timestamps
        end
```

```
        end

        def self.down
            drop_table :users
        end
    end
end
```

Now the migration creates a column for each of the required data fields. You do not have to specify the id column, as Rails will create that automatically when the migration is run.

Apply the migration with Rake

Now that you have a completed migration that specifies how the users table is built, you can go ahead and apply that migration using the Rake tool. In your project's base directory, type this:

```
> rake db:migrate
```

This runs the only migration that you have so far and creates the users table. You should see output, letting you know that the users table has been created. Running this command is also a good test of your database setup. Rake reads the database configuration information that you entered in database.yml, so if you made any mistakes when you entered that information, they will become apparent now.

Add user model validations

Rails model validations allow you to define field validations within a model class that will be automatically enforced by Rails. Using model validations, you can enforce things such as field length limits, field length content, and field uniqueness. For the Book Shelf user model, add the following validations:

- Enforce minimum and maximum length of user login.
- Enforce minimum and maximum length of user password.
- Enforce presence of login and e-mail address.
- Enforce uniqueness of login and e-mail address.
- Make sure the user enters a password and a password confirmation that contain the same value.
- Make sure the e-mail address entered conforms to a valid e-mail address format.

Each of these validations can be added using the Rails DSL that supports model validations. You won't have to create any if statements or even write any methods yourself to get these validations.

Open up the app/models/user.rb file and add the following validation code to the top of the class definition, just after the class statement.

```
validates_length_of :login, :within => 3..40
validates_length_of :password, :within => 5..40
validates_presence_of :login, :email
```

```
validates_uniqueness_of :login, :email
validates_confirmation_of :password
validates_format_of :email,

  :with => /^([^@\s]+)@((?:[-a-z0-9]+\.)+[a-z]{2,})$/i,
                  :message => "Invalid email"
```

A nice thing about using the Rails validation DSL is that the methods that you use to apply validations are very simple for you to read and understand what their function is. For example, even
someone not familiar with Rails could look at the first line, `validates_length_of :login,`
`:within => 3..40`, and understand that it validates the length of the `login` field, making sure
that it is between 3 and 40 characters in length. Similarly, the other validations are easy to read
and understand.

CROSS-REF   **If you want to learn more about the available validations, refer back to
Chapter 3.**

The last validation validates the format of the e-mail field and makes sure that it conforms to the
format of a valid e-mail address. This is probably the most complex of the validations that you
are using. This validation makes use of a regular expression. Regular expressions are text pattern
strings that are used to look for matching strings or substrings. The regular expression used in the
`:with` element is

```
/^([^@\s]+)@((?:[-a-z0-9]+\.)+[a-z]{2,})$/i
```

This regular expression will make sure that the email address conforms to a standard email address
format, including the @ sign, and a domain name containing a period, such as `yahoo.com`.

Test user validations

At this point, you should have a `users` database in place and a user model containing a handful of
field validations. Let's take a moment to test those validations using the Rails Console to verify that
they work as expected.

Start up the Rails Console from the `book_shelf` top-level directory:

```
> ruby script/console
```

This gets you into the Rails Console environment. In the Rails Console, you have full access to all
of your application classes. Go ahead and create an instance of the user model class:

```
>> user = User.new
```

The `user` object echoes back to you, showing that it currently contains `nil` values for each of the
attributes. Before you set any of the fields, see if Rails thinks it is valid as is:

```
>> user.valid?
```

After entering this command, you should see the output shown in Figure 6.9. Oops, it looks like there is a problem in your user model. Ruby is complaining that there is an undefined method, `password`. This is caused by the following two validations that you added to the user model:

```
validates_length_of :password, :within => 5..40
validates_confirmation_of :password
```

These two validations validate a password field, but if you remember when you defined the model, you did not create a field named password; instead, you just had `password_salt` and `password_hash`. This is because the password is not directly stored in the database, and so the user model does not know about this field yet.

The validation is attempting to get the value of the password field through an accessor-named password, which causes the undefined method error. Because this field is not a column in the users database table, Rails does not automatically create an accessor for this field. You can fix this problem by explicitly creating an accessor for the `password` field. You also want an accessor for a `password_confirmation` field. The second validation looks for both the `password` and `password_confirmation` accessors. Add these two accessors below the validations code in the user model, `app/models/user.rb`:

```
attr_accessor :password, :password_confirmation
```

Now go back to the command window, where you have the Rails Console running, and type **exit** to end that session. Restart the console using `ruby script/console`, create a user, and try the `valid?` method again:

```
>> user.valid?
=> false
```

FIGURE 6.9

Undefined password method

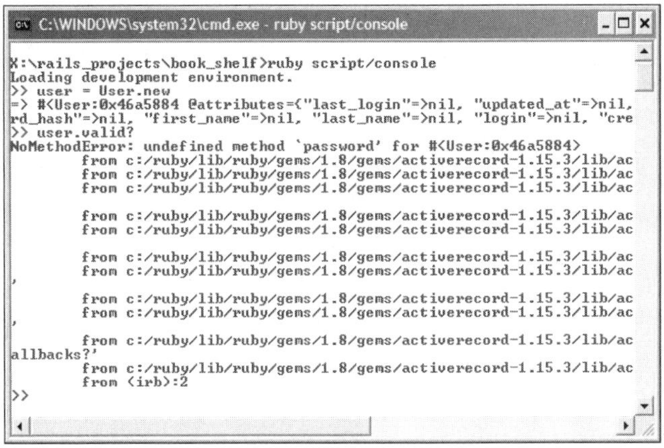

Now the method runs successfully and returns a value of `false`, indicating that the `user` object is not currently valid. This is because it does not meet the validations that you programmed for it. You can look at the problems that occurred during validation by looking at the `user.errors` object.

```
>> user.errors
```

You'll see error messages in the `user.errors` object related to the password, login, and e-mail fields. See if you can fix the problems by setting those three fields with reasonable values:

```
>> user.password = 'secret'
>> user.login = 'john'
>> user.email = 'john@doe.com'
```

Now try testing the object's validity again:

```
>> user.valid?
=> true
```

The `user` object is now valid. The values you entered for the password, login, and e-mail fields allow the `user` object to pass all of the defined validations.

Implement user registration

Now that the application has a user model class and an associated database table to support users, let's turn our attention to implementing a mechanism that will allow users to register for an account in the Book Shelf application. The tasks that need to be completed to accomplish this are as follows:

- Create a user controller.
- Handle the user password.
- Create a registration view.
- Create the user home view.

The second task deserves a brief explanation. Recall that the database stores a password hash and a password salt but not the password itself. However, the user will submit a password and a password confirmation. You need to put code somewhere to take the password and create the password hash and salt values so that they can be saved. In the second task, you will create this code to make sure that the appropriate password fields are set and stored.

Create a user controller

You've already created a user model, but right now there is not a user controller. You'll create a user controller to serve as a home for the user-related requests, such as calls related to user registration, logging in, and logging out. In the `book_shelf` directory, generate the user controller:

```
> ruby script/generate controller User
  exists app/controllers/
```

```
exists app/helpers/
create app/views/user
exists test/functional
create app/controllers/user_controller.rb
create test/functional/user_controller_test.rb
create app/helpers/user_helper.rb
```

This generates the user controller class, a functional test stub for the user controller, and a user helper class. An empty user directory is also created under app/views in which user-related view templates can be placed.

Open up the app/controllers/user_controller.rb file, which contains the source for the user controller class. It should look like this:

```
class UserController < ApplicationController
end
```

This is the class definition in which you'll add action methods to handle the user-related requests. For now, add a signup action method to handle user registration requests:

```
def signup
    @title = "Signup"
    if request.post? and params[:user]
        @user = User.new(params[:user])
        if @user.save
            session[:user] = @user
            flash[:notice] = "User #{@user.login} created!"
            redirect_to :action => "home"
        else
            flash[:error] = "Signup unsuccessful"
            @user.clear_password!
        end
    end
end
```

The signup method handles both the request to display the registration page and the request to register a user. The two types of requests are differentiated by the type of HTTP method call. A request to display the registration page is sent as an HTTP GET request. A request to register a user is sent as an HTTP POST request. In line 3 of the code, you check to see if the user parameter was posted. If so, the user registration code is executed; otherwise, you assume a simple page request.

If the method is called using a GET request, only the line that sets the @title instance variable is executed. This sets a page title for the registration page. Because there is no explicit call to render a template, Rails will look for a template named signup.html.erb in the app/views/user directory and attempt to render that view. You can create that view shortly. For now, look at the code that is executed if the method receives a POST request:

```
@user = User.new(params[:user])
if @user.save
```

```
        session[:user] = @user.id
        flash[:notice] = "User #{@user.login} created!"
        redirect_to :action => "home"
    else
        flash[:error] = "Signup unsuccessful"
        @user.clear_password!
    end
```

In this code, a new user object is created from the parameters passed from the user form. The `save` method of the `user` object is called to attempt to save the new user to the database. If the save is successful, three operations take place:

- The user's id is stored into the session with the `:user` key.
- A notice is placed in the flash message area, saying the user has been successfully created.
- The browser is redirected to the `home` action of the user controller.

Because no controller is specified in the `redirect_to` call, the current controller, `UserController`, is used. The home action should display the user's home page. Create the `home` method inside of the UserController now. Edit this file `app/controllers/user_controller.rb`:

```
def home
    @title = "BookShelf - User Home"
end
```

Right now, the home method only sets the `@title` instance variable and by default will also render a template located at `app/views/user/home.html.erb`. The `home.html.erb` template should display a user home page. You will create this template shortly. Eventually, when books are implemented in the application, this method will grow so that all of a user's books are retrieved prior to rendering the home template.

Handle the user password

Before you implement the signup and user home views, you need to add some code to properly handle the password. Because the code will set and manipulate user model fields, the correct place to put this code is in the user model, `app/models/user.rb`. You want code that will create the password hash and password salt for you whenever the `password` field is set. You can do this by creating a new setter method for the `password` field. You also create a method to generate the password hash value. Add these methods to the user model:

```
attr_protected :password_salt

def password=(pass)
    @password=pass
    self.password_salt = User.random_string(10) if !self.password_salt?
    self.password_hash = User.hash_password(@password, self.password_salt)
end
```

```
protected

def self.hash_password(pass, password_salt)
    Digest::SHA1.hexdigest(pass+password_salt)
end

def self.random_string(len)
    #generate a random password consisting of strings and digits
    chars = ("a".."z").to_a + ("A".."Z").to_a + ("0".."9").to_a
    newpass = ""
    1.upto(len) { |i| newpass << chars[rand(chars.size-1)] }
    return newpass
end
```

The `password=` method is a setter method for the `password` field. This method creates a random salt value and uses a `hash_password` method to create the `password_hash` field. As a result, each time the `password` field is set, the `password_salt` and `password_hash` fields are also set.

The salt value is generated using another method that is also defined above, the `User.random_string` class method. The `random_string` method generates a random alphanumeric string, with the length being controlled by an argument passed into the method. For the salt value, a string length of ten is used. Notice that the salt value is generated only if the `self.password_salt` value does not already exist, in other words, has a value of `nil`. This ensures that a new salt value is generated only when a user is first created.

The `hash_password` method takes a password and a password salt value as parameters and uses the SHA1 digesting algorithm to generate a unique hash value for the concatenation of the password and password salt values.

With these methods in place, the password will be correctly handled when a user submits a registration to the application. Next, you need to create the views that are used for registration and the user home page.

Create a registration view

With the user controller and user model modifications in place, let's go ahead and create the view for the user registration process. The view is placed in the `app/views/user/signup.html.erb` file to correspond to the `signup` method of the user controller. Create that file and type in the code shown in Listing 6.5.

This template uses the Rails helper `form_for` to create an HTML form to contain all of the user model fields. Each of the fields uses the `text_field` helper to generate the correct HTML for the text input fields. The two exceptions are the `password` and `password_confirmation` fields. These use the `password_field` helper to generate HTML password input fields with blocked-out character input. Near the bottom of the form, a Submit button is created using the `submit_tag` helper.

LISTING 6.5

signup.html.erb

```
<div id="signup_content">
    <span class="title">Sign-up for a BookShelf account...</span>
    <% form_for :user, @user, :url => {:action => "signup" } do |f| %>

        <%= error_messages_for 'user' %><br/>

        <div class="signup_field">
            <label for="user_login">Login:</label>
            <%= f.text_field :login %><br/>
         </div>

        <div class="signup_field">
            <label for="user_first_name">First Name:</label>
            <%= f.text_field :first_name %><br/>
        </div>

        <div class="signup_field">
            <label for="user_last_name">Last Name:</label>
            <%= f.text_field:last_name %><br/>
        </div>

        <div class="signup_field">
            <label for="user_email">Email:</label>
            <%= f.text_field:email %><br/>
        </div>

        <div class="signup_field">
            <label for="user_password">Password:</label>
            <%= f.password_field:password %><br/>
        </div>

        <div class="signup_field">

    <label for="user_password_confirmation">Password Confirmation:</
    label>
            <%= f.password_field:password_confirmation %>
        </div>

        <%= submit_tag "Signup" %>
    <% end %>
</div>
```

You're almost done with the signup page. The last task is to add some additional styles to the style sheet that you created earlier in this chapter. Add the following style definitions to the bottom of the public/stylesheets/style.css file:

```
// Implementing Registration
#signup_content {
    float: left;
    padding-left: 50px;
    width: 400px;
    text-align: right;
}

#signup_content.title, #login_content.title {
    font-weight:bold;
}

.signup_field,.login_field {
    white-space: nowrap;
    padding-bottom:.5em;
    text-align: left;
}

.signup_field label,.login_field label {
    display:block;
    float:left;
    margin-right:0.5em;
    text-align:right;
    width:12em;
}

.signup_field input,.login_field input {
    text-align: left;
}
```

The registration page should now be complete, so let's try it out. Start up the WEBrick server using the familiar ruby script/server command in the book_shelf directory, and navigate in your browser to http://localhost:3000. You should see the Book Shelf home page that you created earlier. From that page, click the Join Now link, and you should see the registration page that you just completed. It should look similar to Figure 6.10.

You can try typing some values into the text fields, but don't submit the form yet. You still have not created the user home page that is routed to after a successful user creation. Go ahead and create that page now.

FIGURE 6.10

The user registration page

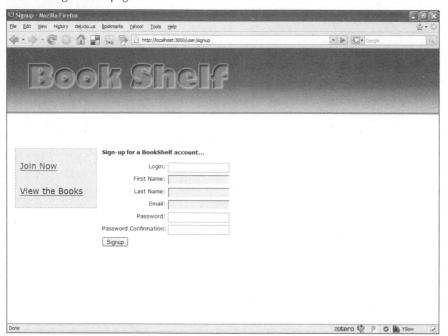

Create user home view

The last view you need to create is the template for the user home page. For now, this view will be relatively simple, but as you build out the application, you'll add more content and features to this page. Create the `home.html.erb` template in the `app/views/user` directory and just put a simple welcome message as its content for now:

```
Welcome <%= User.find(session[:user]).first_name %>
```

This displays a message that welcomes the user by first name. The user's first name is read from the user object stored in the session.

Assuming you still have the WEBrick server running, navigate back to the registration page by clicking the Join Now link if you are not already there. Fill out the registration form and click the Signup button. If all goes well, you should be taken to a user home page that looks like Figure 6.11. You should see the welcome message and the first name of the user that you signed up as.

The user home page

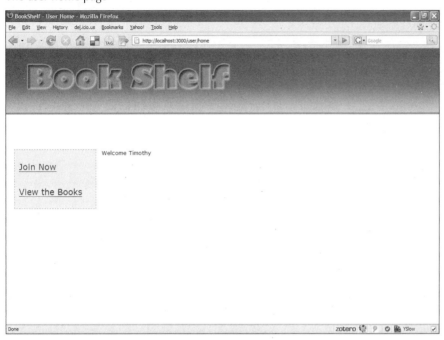

This is a good start for the user home page, but notice in the sidebar menu on the left that there is still a link that says Join Now. Because the user has already registered and has been logged into the application, it would be nicer if this link went away. That's not a difficult change to make, so go ahead and do that now.

Recall that the contents of the sidebar are defined in the view partial app/views/shared/_ sidebar.html.erb. Open up that file and make the following modifications, highlighted in bold:

```
<div id="sidebar">
    <div id="Menu">
        <ul id="home_menu">
            <% if !session[:user] %>
                <li><%= link_to 'Join Now',
                        :controller=>'user',
                        :action=>'signup' %>
                </li>
            <% end %>
```

```
        <li><%= link_to 'View the Books',
                    :controller=>'book',
                    :action=>'list' %>
        </li>
    </ul>
  </div>
  <div style="clear:both;"> </div>
</div>
```

You've added a snippet of Ruby to the sidebar partial which will cause the Join Now link to be displayed only if there is no user stored in the session. This is because when a user is logged in, a user's id is stored in the session, so the link will never appear when a user is logged in. This is the desired behavior. If you refresh the user home page, you should see that the Join Now link is now gone.

The Book Shelf application now has the ability to register new users through a simple registration form. The application also has a basic user home page, which will be extended upon in future development. Before moving on, let's return to our friend the Rails Console and make sure that the user that was created is indeed in the application development database.

Start up the console from a command window by typing **ruby script/console**. In the console, use the `find` method of the `User` class to find the first user record stored in the database. At this point, your database should contain only the user that you created using the signup page in this section.

```
>> user = User.find(:first)
>#  …
>> puts user.login
tfisher
```

If the user you registered is not found, go back and check all of your code to ensure that it matches the code in the book.

Implement login and logout

Your application now allows for users to register for an account with the Book Shelf application, but there is still not a way for existing users to log in and log out of the application. In this section, you'll add functionality to let users log in and log out. The tasks necessary to complete this functionality are to

- Create a login action method
- Create a logout action method
- Implement a login view

You'll add the two new action methods to the user controller and implement a login box that is displayed in the upper-right corner of the application whenever a user is not logged in. You can see this login box in Figure 6.1 at the beginning of this chapter.

Create login action method

First implement the `login` method in the user controller. Open up the user controller in app/ controllers/user_controller.rb and add the `login` method defined here:

```
def login

    if request.post?
        user   = User.authenticate(params[:user][:login],
                                   params[:user][:password])
        if user
            session[:user] = user.id
            flash[:notice] = "Login successful"
            redirect_to :controller=>'user', :action=>'home'
        else
            flash[:error] = "Login unsuccessful"
            redirect_to :controller=>'home'
        end
    end
end
```

The body of the method is executed only if the request is an HTTP POST. The `login` method attempts to authenticate a user using the login and password passed in as request parameters. If the authentication attempt is successful, a user id is stored in the session, a successful login notice is placed into flash, and a redirect is sent to the browser, sending the user to the user home page. If the authentication is not successful, a login error message is placed into flash, and a redirect back to the application home page is sent to the browser.

The `login` method uses the `User.authenticate` method to authenticate the user. You have not yet created this method, so go ahead and do that now. This method goes into the user model class in the app/models/user.rb file. Add this method as defined here:

```
def self.authenticate(login, pass)
    u=find(:first, :conditions=>["login = ?", login])
    return nil if u.nil?
    return u if User.hash_password(pass, u.password_salt)==u.
password_hash
    nil
end
```

The `authenticate` method takes two parameters: a login and a password. The first thing the method does is attempt to find a user that matches the login that is passed in. If a user cannot be found with a matching login, a `nil` value is returned and the method's work is done. If a user with a matching login is found, the next step is to create the password hash for the password that is passed in and see if it matches the password hash value that was stored with the user record.

If the password hashes match, the user record is returned. If the hashes do not match, the last line of the method is reached and results in the value `nil` being returned from the method. As a result, anytime an authentication is successful, a user model object for the authenticated user is returned. If the authentication fails for any reason, a `nil` value is returned.

The functionality necessary to process a user login is now complete. Next, you'll define the logout method before creating the login view.

Create the logout action method

The `logout` method handles a user's request to log out of the application. This method is very simple in comparison with the `login` method. Add the `logout` method defined below to the `app/controllers/user_controller.rb` file:

```
def logout
    session[:user] = nil
    flash[:notice] = 'Logged out'
    redirect_to :controller => 'home', :action => 'index'
end
```

To log a user out of the application, you simply have to clear the application's memory of the user. When a user is logged in, that user's id is stored in the session. This is how various methods in the application know that a user is logged in, by checking the `session[:user]` variable and seeing if it contains a user id. By setting the `session[:user]` variable to `nil`, you are effectively logging the user out of the application.

With login and logout methods completed, you can move on to implement a view template that displays the login form.

Create an application login partial

The login form is displayed in the top-right corner of any of the application's pages when a user is not logged in. You can see this in Figure 6.1. Because the login form is not a page itself, it is implemented as a partial that you can include in the application layout. Create the partial `_signin. html.erb` in the `app/views/user` directory. The content of the partial is shown in Listing 6.6. Type this into your `_signin.html.erb` partial.

The signin partial creates a form using the Rails `form_tag` helper. The controller and action that handles the form submit is passed to the `form_tag` helper method. Requests go to the `login` method of the user controller. The form contains two fields, the user login and password, and a Submit button.

The next thing you need to do is include the signin partial in the application layout template. Listing 6.7 shows the revised layout template from `app/views/layouts/application. html.erb` with the new code in bold. The code checks to see if a user is currently logged in by looking for a user id in the session. If a user is logged in, a link to the `logout` action is displayed; otherwise, the signin partial is rendered.

LISTING 6.6

_signin.html.erb partial

```
<div id="signin_section">
    <div class="signin_box">
        <div id="sign_in_title">Sign-In</div>
        <% form_tag ({:controller=> "user",
                      :action=> "login"},

   {:id=>'signin_form'}) do %>           <div class="signin_field">
                <label for="user_login">Username:</label>
                <%= text_field "user", "login", :size => 20 %>
            </div>
            <div class="signin_field">
                <label for="user_password">Password:</label>
                <%= password_field "user", "password", :size => 20 %>
            </div>
            <div id="signin_button">
                <%= submit_tag "Login" %>  
            </div>
        <% end %>
    </div>
</div>
```

LISTING 6.7

application.rhtml with signin partial

```
<!DOCTYPE html PUBLIC "-//W3C//DTD XHTML 1.0 Transitional//EN" "http://
   www.w3.org/TR/xhtml1/DTD/xhtml1-transitional.dtd">
<html xmlns="http://www.w3.org/1999/xhtml">

<head>
    <title><%= @title %></title>
    <%= stylesheet_link_tag "style" %>

    <%= javascript_include_tag :defaults %>
</head>

<body>
    <div id="header">
        <div id="logo_image">
            <%= link_to image_tag('main_logo.png'),
                {:controller=>'home', :action=>'index'} %>
        </div>
        <% if !session[:user] %>
```

continued

LISTING 6.7   *(continued)*

```
        <%= render :partial=>"user/signin" %>
    <% else %>
        <div id="user_menu"><%= link_to 'Logout',
:controller=>'user',
            :action=>'logout' %></div>
    <% end %>
    <div style="clear: both; height: 0px;"></div>
</div>

<%= render :partial=>"shared/sidebar" %>

<div id="Content">
    <% if flash[:notice] -%>
        <div id="notice"><%= flash[:notice] %></div>
    <% end -%>
    <% if flash[:error] -%>
        <div id="error"><%= flash[:error] %></div>
    <% end -%>
    <%= yield %>
</div>
</body>
</html>
```

Before you attempt to view the signup form on the application home page, you need to add a few more styles to the style.css file that you've been working with in public/stylesheets. Add the styles listed here:

```
// Implementing User Login
#user_menu {
 float:right;
 font-weight: bold;
 margin-right: 35px;
 margin-top: 15px;
}

#user_menu a, #user_menu a:visited {
 color: orange;
}

.signin_box {
 float: left;
 background: #cccccc;
 border: solid 1px #f98919;

 padding-bottom: 6px;
 padding-top: 8px;
```

```
    padding-right: 10px;
    margin-top: 10px;
    text-align: right;
    width: 250px;
    height: 100px;
}

#signin_form {
  margin: 0px;
  padding: 0px;
}

#signin_button {
  margin: 0px;
  padding: 0px;
}

#sign_in_title {

  padding-bottom: 5px;
  text-align:left;
  margin-left:20px;
  color: gray;
  font-weight: bold;
  font-size: 12pt;
}

#signin_section {
 float: right;
 margin-right: 25px;
}

.signin_field {
 margin-bottom: 8px;
 color:gray;
}
```

Now make sure the WEBrick server is running and navigate to the application home page in your browser, `http://localhost:3000`. You should see the login box appearing in the upper-right corner of the page, as shown in Figure 6.12.

Test the login and logout functionality

You should now be able to successfully log into and log out of your Book Shelf application. If you have not already created a user by following the Join Now link, do that now. Once you have created a user make sure that you are not already logged in. When you create a new user, the user will be automatically logged in after creation, so click the logout link to log the user out. Now you can test the login functionality.

FIGURE 6.12

The Book Shelf home page with login box

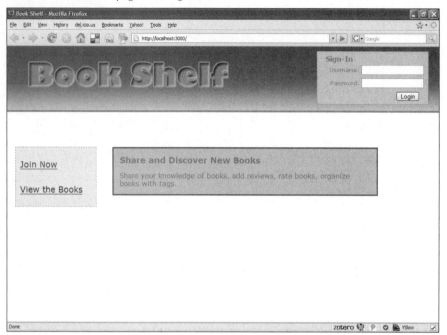

From the Book Shelf home page, enter your login and password in the login box shown in the upper right corner of the page. Click the login button and you should be successfully logged into the application. Upon successful login, the login box will be replaced with a Logout link. You should also see a welcome message and the flash text "Login successful" displayed. The Join Now link in the left-side menu will also go away when you are logged in. If you encounter any errors during login, double-check all of the code that you created in this section and verify that you have not made any mistakes.

After you are logged into the application, it is very simple to test the log out functionality. You simply have to click the Logout link in the upper right corner of your screen. This should display the flash message "Logged out" and you should be taken back to the application home page showing the login box and the Join Now menu item again.

Using a before filter to protect pages

You have a nearly complete user implementation at this point. A user is able to register for an account with the application, and log in and log out of the application. When a user is logged in, they are taken to a special user home page. What would happen if a logged-in user bookmarked that user home page in their browser and attempted to return directly to that page without logging in? You would see an application error because the application would attempt to display the user welcome message when no user is logged in. This is not the behavior that is desired. This page and other pages that are available only to logged-in users should be protected and only accessible to users that have first logged into the application. You'll use a Rails filter to implement that feature. This implementation can be broken down into the following tasks:

- Define a method in the application controller, which will be called from a filter.
- Add a login form to the signup page.

Modify the application controller

A filter in Rails allows you to have a method that you define called automatically before any methods that you specify. This will work for the requirements that you have for the current situation. Prior to handling the request to display the user home page, you want to make sure that a user is logged in. To do this, you can setup a method that will be called from a filter that will check to see if a user is logged in. If a user is not logged in, instead of processing the request for the user home page, the user will be redirected to a user login page.

To get started, edit the application controller located in `app/controllers/application.rb` and create the `login_required` method shown below.

```
def login_required
    if session[:user]
        return true
    end
    flash[:notice]='Please login to continue'
    session[:return_to]=request.request_uri
    redirect_to :controller => "user", :action => "signup"
    return false
end
```

This method will be called before any controller actions that you want to protect unlogged in users from accessing. This method checks the session to see if it contains a user id. If not, a flash notice of 'Please login to continue' is set and the user is redirected to the signup page. In just a bit, you will modify the signup page to also contain a login form for users who are already signed up. The `login_required` method is placed in the application controller class because it is not specific to any individual controller. Methods contained in the application controller can be accessed by any of your controllers because they extend the application controller.

The next thing you will need to do is setup the actual filter using another piece of Rail's intelligent Web application DSL. In this case, you will use the `before_filter` method. For now, you just want to protect the `home` action contained in the user controller. To do this, add the following line somewhere near the top of the user controller in `app/controllers/user_controller.rb`.

```
before_filter :login_required, :only=>['home']
```

This method will result in the `login_required` method being called anytime the `home` method is accessed. The `:only` parameter tells Rails to only apply the filter to the `home` method. Without the `:only` parameter, the filter would have been applied to all methods in the controller.

Add login form to the signup page

The last remaining task to complete the login filter functionality is to add a login form to the signup page. To do that, edit the signup page from `app/views/user/signup.html.erb`. Add the `login_content` div shown below above the existing `signup_content` div.

```
<div id="login_content">
    <span class="title">Existing users, login...</span>
    <% form_for :user, @user, :url => { :action => "login" } do
|f| %>
        <div class="login_field">
            <label for="user_login">Username:</label>
            <%= f.text_field :login %><br/>
        </div>

        <div class="login_field">
            <label for="user_password">Password:</label>
            <%= f.password_field :password %><br/>
        </div>

        <%= submit_tag "Login" %>

    <% end %>
</div>
```

This `div` creates a form that users can use to login from the signup page. Now if a user tries to access a page that requires a user to be logged in for, they will be redirected to the signup page which will allow a user to either signup if they do not have an account, or login if they already do have an account.

In future chapters, you will apply this same method of protecting content that should only be accessed by logged in users.

Summary

In this chapter, you started the implementation of a complete Rails application. The application will allow users to share information about books, and contains many features common in today's class of Web 2.0 applications. At this point, you have generated the application skeleton, created the database, and implemented support for user accounts for the application.

The functionality that you used to implement the user support is common to most Web applications and should be reusable by you in most other Web applications that you'll implement in Rails. Alternatively, you could use one of the third-party authentication solutions that were described in this chapter.

Even if you do use an existing solution for future applications, it was very worthwhile to have gone through the steps of implementing your own authentication solution in this chapter. The functionality you implemented in this chapter lies at the heart of the application's security model and is something that I firmly believe every developer should implement from scratch at least once before they just pull functionality from a third-party component. Having implemented your own authentication system will put you in a better position to evaluate other solutions.

Chapter 7

Developing Book Shelf: Adding the Core Functionality

In this chapter, you will continue development of the Book Shelf application that you started in Chapter 6. At this point you should have a Rails application started, with a complete user model and user authentication implemented. In this chapter, you will take the first steps toward making the application useful for sharing information about a collection of books. You will implement integration with the Amazon Web Service to look up information about books that a user wants to add to the book shelf. You will also implement the ability to add and remove books from a user's book shelf. With that functionality in place, you'll add a display of the books on a user's shelf to his home page. The last task of this chapter will be to implement a detail view for a selected book. Later chapters will build upon the detail view to add reviews and ratings.

To follow along with the development in this chapter, continue working with the code that you started in Chapter 6.

Adding Support for Books

The tasks of this chapter all relate to the ability to add books to a user's book shelf. By the end of this chapter, a user will be able to search this application for books based on keywords, add selected books to a book shelf, view books contained on the user's book shelf, delete books from a book shelf, and view a book's detail page.

The Book Shelf application gathers information about books from the Amazon catalog of books. When a user searches for a book by keyword, it is actually the Amazon catalog that is searched. The results from an Amazon search go back to the user, and the user is able to select from those books the ones that he wants to add to his shelf. If a book returned from the search is already on a user's shelf, then that is also indicated. Ten search results display at a time. If a search returns more than ten books, the user is able to page through the results.

The user's home page shows a paged view of all the books on his shelf. A user can select any book from their shelf and open up a detailed view of that book that contains information about the book. You will be adding reviews and ratings to the book detail view in the next chapter.

Just as the user support was broken down into a series of tasks for implementation, the goals of this chapter are broken down into a series of tasks that you will complete as you read through. Implementing the covered features is broken down into the following tasks:

- Refactoring the sidebar code
- Integrating with Amazon
- Implementing search capability to book shelf
- Implementing book addition and deletion to book shelf
- Displaying a user's books on their homepage
- Implementing the book detail page

As you write the code in this chapter, feel free to stop and try things out in the Rails console anytime you come across a piece of code that you don't quite understand. I've done my best to try to explain most of the code, but seeing output yourself never hurts.

Refactor the sidebar code

At the end of Chapter 6, the code contained in the sidebar view looked like this:

```
<div id="sidebar">
    <div id="Menu">
        <ul id="home_menu">
            <% if !session[:user] %>
                <li><%= link_to 'Join Now',
                            :controller=>'user',
                            :action=>'signup' %>
                </li>
            <% end %>
            <li><%= link_to 'View the Books',
                        :controller=>'book',
                        :action=>'list' %>
            </li>
        </ul>
    </div>
    <div style="clear:both;"> </div>
</div>
```

With this implementation, if there is not a user logged into the site the visitor will see two links, one to Join Now, and one to View the Books. If there is a user logged in, that user will only see one link, to View the Books. The View the Books link will show all of the books known by the application. For logged in users, we want to add an additional link that will allow the user to see only the books that are on his or her shelf.

Listing 7.1 shows the addition of the My Books link for logged in users. You'll also notice that the code has been slightly refactored into a more readable form. Update your sidebar code contained in app/views/shared/_sidebar.html.erb to match the code listing.

LISTING 7.1

Refactored _sidebar.html.erb

```erb
<div id="sidebar">
    <div id="Menu">
        <ul id="user_nav_menu">
            <% if logged_in %>
                <li>
                    <%= link_to 'My Books', :controller=>'user',
                                            :action=>'home',
                                            :user_id=>session[:user].id
    %>
                </li>
                <li>
                    <%= link_to 'All Books', :controller=>'book',
                                            :action=>'list' %>
                </li>
            <% else %>
                <ul id="home_menu">
                    <li>
                        <%= link_to 'Join Now', :controller=>'user',
                                                :action=>'signup' %>
                    </li>
                    <li>
                        <%= link_to 'View the Books',
    :controller=>'book',
                                                    :action=>'list' %>
                    </li>
                </ul>
            <% end %>
        </ul>
    </div>
    <div style="clear:both;"> </div>
</div>
```

If you looked at Listing 7.1 closely, you probably noticed one other significant difference that was sneaked in. At the end of Chapter 6 the sidebar was using this line to see if a user was logged in:

```
<% if session[:user] %>
```

This checks the session to see if a `:user` variable is set. While this works, it is a bit too closely tied to the implementation. It would be better if we had a helper method that we could use to see if a user is logged in or not. You can create that helper method now. Open up the file `app/helpers/application_helper.rb`. This methods contained in this file will be available to all of your view templates. Add the following method to this helper class:

```
def logged_in
    session[:user]?true:false
end
```

Now you have a helper method that your views can use instead of directly checking the session to see if a user is logged in. In the future, if the way you implement the user logged in status changes, you can just update this method and not worry about any checks that you have in the view templates.

Now that the sidebar contains the links you'll need to support users, let's look at how to integrate with Amazon to populate the book shelf.

Integrating with Amazon

There is a wealth of information available to an application through the Amazon Web Service (AWS). The AWS consists of a set of services that Amazon provides to Web developers. The Amazon Associates Service (A2S) is one of those services. The A2S provides an API into Amazon's huge database of information about the books and other products that it sells.

The Book Shelf application uses an open source Ruby library that encapsulates and simplifies access to the AWS. This library is called Ruby/AWS and was written by Ian MacDonald. The Ruby/AWS library hides most of the details that you need to know to use the A2S. You can read more about this library at its home page, `www.caliban.org/ruby/ruby-aws/`.

The A2S provides both a REST and a SOAP interface; Ruby/AWS uses the REST interface. Ruby/AWS uses the REXML library to parse XML responses from Amazon. You shouldn't have to do anything to install REXML, as it is included with Ruby 1.8.x or later, which is also the minimum version of Ruby that you need to use Ruby/AWS. Complete RDOC documentation for Ruby/Amazon is available at library's home page.

For the Book Shelf application, you'll create a thin class that will be put into the application's `lib` directory to encapsulate access to the Ruby/AWS library. This strategy will be used rather than making calls to Ruby/AWS directly from the Book Shelf controller or model classes. The main reasons for taking this approach are as follows:

1. If you embed the Ruby/AWS code into your model classes, they become more difficult to test independently from the Amazon interface.

2. While Ruby/AWS seems like a good choice today to provide support for accessing the AWS, you may prefer to use a different library or plug-in in the future. Therefore, if you encapsulate all Amazon interfacing into a single component class, it becomes easier to replace the Ruby/AWS plug-in in the future.

Now that you know how you are going to integrate the Book Shelf application with Amazon, let's get down to business by installing the Ruby/AWS library in your application directory.

Obtaining an Amazon Developer Token

Amazon has one of the most successful and well-known associate programs in the world. They have opened up their entire product catalog to the world through a Web service interface. Many Web sites and applications use the AWS to integrate the Amazon catalog for their own custom requirements. To use the AWS, you must sign up for an Amazon Web services account. You can sign up at https://aws-portal.amazon.com/gp/aws/developer/registration/index.html. It is an easy process to sign up and does not cost you anything. Once you have signed up, you get an Amazon Developer Token. This is the required piece of information that you need to use the Web services from within an application that you develop.

The AWS consists of several services and tools for developing Web applications. The particular service that you will use to develop the Book Shelf application is the A2S. This is the service that makes the Amazon catalog available to developers. You can read more about the A2S at www.amazon.com/E-Commerce-Service-AWS-home-page/b/ref=sc_fe_c_0_15763381_1?ie=UTF8&node=12738641. In the past, the A2S was called ECS. So, if you see references to the Amazon ECS, remember that this is the same as the A2S.

Another useful site that you can get help from for using the Amazon services is the Amazon Web Services Developer Connection site. This site provides an online AWS developer community. You can find it at http://developer.amazonwebservices.com.

You may also want to sign up for an Amazon associates account. With an associates account, you can earn a percentage of sales for any books that are purchased through Amazon links that your application creates. Signing up for an associates account is also free. You can sign up for this account at http://affiliate-program.amazon.com/gp/associates/join.

Install Ruby/Amazon

1. **Download the Ruby/Amazon library.** Go to www.caliban.org/ruby/ruby-aws/ to download the library. The library is available as a tarred and gzipped file.

2. **Download the version with the** `.tar.gz` **extension.** Depending on the version you get, this file is named something like `ruby-aws-0.3.0.tar.gz`. At the time of this writing, 0.3.0 was the current stable version of the library. Save this file to the `book_shelf/lib` directory.

3. **Extract the library archive into the** `book_shelf/lib` **directory.** If you need help extracting the `ruby-aws-0.3.0.tar.gz` on Windows see the sidebar, Extracting TAR and GZIP Files on Windows. You should see the directory structure shown in Figure 7.1 after you extract the Ruby/AWS archive.

The Ruby-AWS directory

4. **Move the contents of** `ruby-aws-0.3.0/lib` **to the** `book_shelf/lib` **directory.** The Ruby/AWS library is implemented in the files contained in the `ruby-aws-0.3.0/lib` directory. Place these in the `book_shelf/lib` directory so that they are visible to Rails and your Book Shelf application code. The `ruby-aws-0.3.0/lib` directory should contain both a file named `amazon.rb` and a directory named `amazon`. Move the `amazon.rb` file and the `amazon` directory into the `book_shelf/lib` directory.

5. **Verify the library installation.** Now open up a Rails console and include the Ruby/AWS library by using a `require` statement to verify that the library can be found. Figure 7.2 shows how you can verify that you are able to successfully see the Ruby/AWS library from your Rails environment. The `Request` object that is instantiated is part of the Ruby/AWS library. A successful instantiation of that object is a good sign that all is well with your Ruby/AWS library installation.

FIGURE 7.2

Testing the Ruby/AWS library

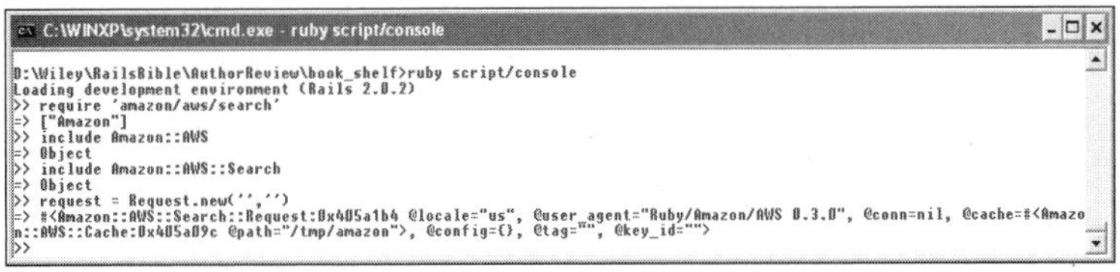

When you perform searches with the Ruby/AWS library it returns results as pages. Typically, each search query will return one page of results. At the time of this writing, there is a bug in the Ruby/AWS library that will prevent you from retrieving result pages beyond the first for searches that have more items than what is returned in a single query. Fortunately, it is very easy to fix this bug. Open up the file `/lib/amazon/aws.rb` and look at line 481. You should see this:

```
MinimumPrice OfferStatus Sort
```

Modify that line so that it also contains the keyword ItemPage. So after you modify the line, it should look like this:

```
MinimumPrice OfferStatus Sort ItemPage
```

This line and lines above it identify valid parameters to the `ItemSearch` that you will use later in this Chapter. The `ItemPage` is required to be able to get to result pages beyond the first. If you want to learn more about how the Ruby/AWS library is implemented and how it works, you should read the README file that is included with the library, and also look at the Amazon AWS documentation.

This completes the installation of the Ruby/AWS library. Now with that library in place, you have what you need to build an interface class that your application will use to read data from the Amazon library.

Extracting TAR and GZIP Files in Windows

If you are developing on a Windows computer, you may not know how to extract a tarred and gzipped archive file. The `tar` and `gzip` formats are primarily used on UNIX-based systems. UNIX includes applications to create and extract these archives with the operating system. Windows does not include built-in support for creating or extracting these files, but there is a free solution available to Windows developers. The 7-Zip application is a freeware archiving utility that supports both of these formats along with several others. You can download 7-Zip from `www.7-zip.org/` as either an `.exe` file or an `.msi` file. Once downloaded, you just have to run whichever one you've downloaded to install the 7-Zip application.

There are also commercial applications available that have free trial downloads that you may want to check out. Two of the most popular applications are WinRAR, available at `www.rarlab.com`, and WinZIP, available at `www.winzip.com`.

Implement the Book Shelf-Amazon interface

In this section, you can implement a class that encapsulates all of the Book Shelf's application access to Amazon. This class uses the Ruby/AWS API. This is also a reusable class that you can use in other applications.

In the `bookshelf/lib` directory, create a file named `amazon_interface.rb`. This is where you define the `AmazonInterface` class. Listing 7.2 contains the code that you want to enter for the `AmazonInterface` class. You want to give users the ability to search for books based on any keyword. For now, that is the only functionality you require from the Ruby/AWS library. In the `AmazonInterface` class, you'll create a method named `find_by_keyword`, which allows you to implement that search capability. You'll also use an `initialize` method to set up the interface.

The initialize method

To perform a keyword search using Ruby/AWS, you have to first create a `Request` object. The `Request` class contains the most common search methods for searching the Amazon catalog. To create a `Request` object, you pass an Amazon developer token and an Amazon associate ID. Only the developer token is required. The associate ID parameter is optional. If you do not pass an associate ID, the Ruby/AWS library contains a hard-coded associate ID that is used. However, by using your own associate ID, you earn credit for any books that are purchased from Amazon through links contained in the application. If you do not have an Amazon developer token or Amazon associate ID, see the sidebar "Obtaining an Amazon Developer Token" for information about how to get them. Both the developer token and the associate ID are available at no cost through a simple sign-up process on the Amazon Web site.

Now the `Request` object is set up and ready to use in other methods that you add to this class to perform searches against the Amazon catalog.

LISTING 7.2

AmazonInterface

```ruby
require 'amazon/aws/search'

class AmazonInterface

  # don't want to have fully qualified identifiers
  include Amazon::AWS
  include Amazon::AWS::Search

    ASSOCIATES_ID = YOUR_AMAZON_ASSOCIATE_ID
    DEV_TOKEN     = YOUR_AWS_DEV_TOKEN

  def initialize
      @request = Request.new(DEV_TOKEN, ASSOCIATES_ID)
  end

  def find_by_keyword(keyword, page)
      is = ItemSearch.new('Books', {'Keywords' => keyword })
      rg = ResponseGroup.new('Medium')
      resp = @request.search(is, rg)
      products = resp.item_search_response.items.item
  end

end
```

The find_by_keyword method

The `find_by_keyword` method takes two parameters: a keyword to search on and a page number. In order to perform a search, you use three classes from the Ruby/AWS library. The classes are `ItemSearch`, `ResponseGroup`, and the `Request` class that you instantiated in the initialize method. The first thing you do is setup the search by creating an `ItemSearch` instance like this:

```ruby
is = ItemSearch.new('Books', {'Keywords' => keyword })
```

This will tell Amazon that you want to search only for books and you want to use the keywords that have been passed into this method. For now you will ignore the page parameter. Later in this chapter when you add support for paging you will modify this setup to include the page number as well.

The next step in executing the search is to create a `ResponseGroup` instance like this:

```ruby
rg = ResponseGroup.new('Medium')
```

This tells Amazon how much information you want it to provide in the results that it returns. For the data requirements of the book shelf application, this should be Medium. Other options that you could specify here are Small and Large. For more details about using these parameters take a look at the Amazon AWS documentation at `http://docs.amazonwebservices.com/AWSECommerceService/2008-03-03/DG/`.

With the `ItemSearch` and `ResponseGroup` initialized, you are now ready to execute the search using the `search` method of the `Request` object like this:

```
resp = @request.search(is, rg)
```

You pass the `ItemSearch` and `ResponseGroup` instances that you created into the `search` method. The response that contains the search results is returned from the `search` method.

Before explaining the last line of the `find_by_keyword` method, you should understand the results that are returned from the search method. First consider the interface between Ruby/AWS and Amazon. Recall that Ruby/AWS makes requests using the Amazon REST API, so your search request might look like the following:

```
http://ecs.amazonaws.com/onca/xml?Service=AWSECommerceService
&Operation=ItemSearch&AWSAccessKeyId=[Access Key D]
&AssociateTag=[ID]&SearchIndex=Books&Keywords=ruby
```

In response to this request, Amazon will return results as XML data. Listing 7.3 is an example of what your search results might look like coming from Amazon.

This response is for a Small response group. The Medium response group follows the same format but contains much more data. Looking at just the smaller response however is good enough to understand the results that Ruby/AWS returns. The important section to understand is the set of `<Item>` elements. Each Item element specifies a book returned as part of the results.

The Ruby/AWS library converts each of the XML elements into a Ruby object. So in the response that Ruby/AWS returns, the root object will be an `ItemSearchResponse` instance. That instance will contain attributes that represent its children. The names of the attributes will be `operation_request` and `items`. When there are multiple instances of an XML element, that element is represented as an array of objects by the Ruby/AWS library. So for example, the `items` attribute of the `ItemSearchResponse` class is an instance of the `Items` class. The `items` instance will contain an array attribute named `item` which is an array of all of the individual book items.

This is enough explanation to understand the final line of the `find_by_keyword` method. This line is shown below:

```
products = resp.item_search_response.items.item
```

LISTING 7.3

Amazon Search Results

```
<ItemSearchResponse>
  <OperationRequest>
    <HTTPHeaders>
      <Header Name="UserAgent" Value="Mozilla/5.0 (X11; U; en-US;
  rv:1.8.1.13) Firefox/2.0.0.13"/>
    </HTTPHeaders>
    <RequestId>1TGEFS25LT11DF2222FFGT13</RequestId>
    <Arguments>
      <Argument Name="SearchIndex" Value="Books"/>
      <Argument Name="Service" Value="AWSECommerceService"/>
      <Argument Name="ResponseGroup" Value="Small"/>
      <Argument Name="Operation" Value="ItemSearch"/>
      <Argument Name="Version" Value="2008-03-03"/>
      <Argument Name="AssociateTag" Value="your_associate_tag"/>
      <Argument Name="Keywords" Value="Ruby"/>
      <Argument Name="AWSAccessKeyId" Value="01234567890123456789"/>
    </Arguments>
    <RequestProcessingTime>0.0731353958225256</RequestProcessingTime>
  </OperationRequest>
  <Items>
    <Request>
      <IsValid>True</IsValid>
      <ItemSearchRequest>
        <ResponseGroup>Small</ResponseGroup>
        <SearchIndex>Books</SearchIndex>
        <Title>Ruby</Title>
      </ItemSearchRequest>
    </Request>
    <TotalResults>87</TotalResults>
    <TotalPages>9</TotalPages>
    <Item>
     <ASIN>0439943663</ASIN>
     <DetailPageURL>
http://www.amazon.com/Ruby-Rails-Bible-Timothy-Fisher/dp/0470258225/
   ref=pd_bbs_sr_1?ie=UTF8&s=books&qid=1212935000&sr=8-1
     </DetailPageURL>
      <ItemAttributes>
        <Author>Timothy Fisher</Author>
        <Manufacturer>Wiley</Manufacturer>
        <ProductGroup>Book</ProductGroup>
        <Title>Ruby on Rails Bible</Title>
      </ItemAttributes>
    </Item>
```

continued

LISTING 7.3   *(continued)*

```
<Item>
  ...
</Item>
...
</Items>
</ItemSearchResponse>
```

First, you get the root element `item_search_response`. From that you grab the `items` attribute which is equivalent to the `<Items>` XML element. The `items` attribute is an instance of `Items` and contains an attribute named `item`. The `item` attribute is an array of all of the book items. This array is what you want to return from the method.

Later in the chapter, you will use the same pattern to access the data about each book. For example, to get the ASIN value of a book, you could use this code:

```
asin = resp.item_search_response.items.item[0].asin
```

This returns the ASIN of the first book returned. To get the book title there is one more level of indirection. You would first have to get the `ItemAttributes` like this:

```
title = resp.item_search_response.items.item[0].item_attributes.
    title
```

With that in mind, you should know enough about the results that you are getting from Ruby/AWS to write the rest of the Book Shelf application. Remember, to learn more about Ruby/AWS refer to its home page.

This completes the functionality that you need to start integrating the book functionality into the Book Shelf application.

NOTE The Ruby/AWS library contains a rich API of features and functionality. The Book Shelf application uses only a tiny piece of what is available to you. If you are interested in exploring all the capabilities of this library, I highly recommend looking at the API documentation, which you can find at `www.caliban.org/ruby/ruby-aws/`.

Implementing a Search

After a user logs into the Book Shelf application, they are taken to a user home page. The left column of the user home page contains a text entry field in which a user can enter a keyword, and a Search button to search for books containing that keyword, as shown in Figure 7.3. This is how the user is able to pull up a list of books that they can add to the user's shelf. In this section, you implement the keyword entry box, the Search button, the search results page, and the necessary back-end code to perform the book search using the Amazon interface that was developed in the previous section.

FIGURE 7.3

The User home page with a book search menu

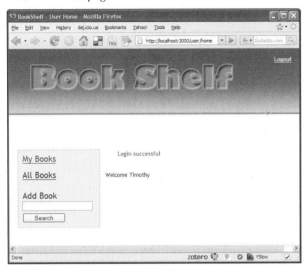

Create the book search form

Get started by adding the search feature to the left side panel. Open up the `app/views/shared/_sidebar.html.erb` file and modify it so that it looks like Listing 7.4. To implement the book search feature, add the following code to the sidebar:

```
<li>
    <% form_tag ({:controller=> "book", :action=> "search"}) do %>
        <input type="hidden" name="page" value="1" />
        <span id="add_book_title">Add Book</span>
        <%= text_field_tag "book_keyword" %>
        <%= submit_tag "Search", :id=>'search_button' %>
    <% end %>
</li>
```

The Rails helper `form_tag` creates a search form. The form contains a text field containing the keyword a user types in to search on and a submit button labeled Search. The keyword text field is created using the `text_field_tag` helper method. The parameter passed to the text field helper `book_keyword` becomes the name of the text field, as well as the name you use in the controller to retrieve the value of the keyword. The `submit_tag` helper method creates the submit button. The `submit_tag` method is passed a string that becomes the button's label, and an `id` parameter that becomes the HTML `id` attribute for the submit button.

The form tag is passed a controller and action that is called when the form is submitted. In this case, the book controller and search action are specified. Because you don't yet have a book controller or a search action, you need to implement that next (see Listing 7.4).

LISTING 7.4

The _sidebar.html.erb File with Book Search

```
<div id="sidebar">
    <div id="Menu">
        <ul id="user_nav_menu">
            <% if logged_in %>
                <li>
                    <%= link_to 'My Books', :controller=>'user',
                                            :action=>'home',
                                            :user_id=>session[:user].id
    %>
                </li>
                <li>
                    <%= link_to 'All Books', :controller=>'book',
                                             :action=>'list' %>
                </li>
                <li>

<% form_tag ({:controller=> "book", :action=> "search"}) do %>
                    <input type="hidden" name="page" value="1" />
                    <span id="add_book_title">Add Book</span>
                    <%= text_field_tag "book_keyword" %>
                    <%= submit_tag "Search", :id=>'search_button' %>
                <% end %>
                </li>
            <% else %>
                <ul id="home_menu">
                    <li>
                        <%= link_to 'Join Now', :controller=>'user',
                                                :action=>'signup' %>
                    </li>
                    <li>
                        <%= link_to 'View the Books',
    :controller=>'book',
                                                     :action=>'list' %>
                    </li>
                </ul>
            <% end %>
        </ul>
    </div>
    <div style="clear:both;"> </div>
</div>
```

You need to add a few additional styles to your application style sheet to make sure the book search form is nicely displayed. Add these styles to the `public/stylesheets/style.css` file as shown in Listing 7.5.

LISTING 7.5
_____

Styles Added to public/stylesheets/style.css File

```css
#user_nav_menu {
  list-style: none;
  margin: 0px;
  padding: 0px;
}

#user_nav_menu li {
 padding-top: 20px;
 padding-bottom: 20px;
 font-size: 1.5em;
 color: blue;
}

#user_nav_menu input {
  clear: both;
  float: left;
  width: 160px;
}

#user_nav_menu #search_button {
  width: 100px;
}

#book_search_field {
 width: 230px;
 float: left;
 margin-top: 5px;
 margin-bottom: 5px;
}

#search_button {
 float:left;
}
```

Now that you have the UI complete for requesting a book search, you need to implement the server action required to perform the search.

Generate the book controller and search action

So far, your application has a home controller and a user controller. This section leads you through adding a book controller that handles requests related to book functionality. You can generate the book controller class using the `script/generate` command:

```
> ruby script/generate controller Book

  exists app/controllers/
  exists app/helpers/
  create app/views/book
  exists test/functional/
  create app/controllers/book_controller.rb
  create test/functional/book_controller_test.rb
  create app/helpers/book_helper.rb
```

As you should expect by now, this generates not only the book controller class but also a functional test class and a view helper class. Open up the `app/controllers/book_controller.rb` file to edit the `BookController` class and add a method to handle the book search request.

```
def search
    @books = Book.search_amazon(params[:book_keyword],
                                params[:page],
                                session[:user])
    @title = "Book Shelf Search Results"
end
```

The search method calls a `search_amazon` class method of the book model class. You can write this method in the next section after you generate the book model. Three parameters are passed to the `search_amazon` method: the keyword the user is searching on, the result page being requested, and the currently logged-in user. The keyword and page parameters are passed into the `search` action from the search form that you previously created. Finally, the search action sets the `@title` instance variable so that the results page has a proper page title.

Create the book model

The book model represents a book in the Book Shelf application. As you did with the user model, start by defining what the book model should look like. Table 7.1 shows the fields that are in the book model.

The fields that contain information about a book are all fields that are populated from the results of an Amazon catalog search. Instead of storing images in the database, the application stores the URL of the book's images that are held on Amazon. The `user_id` field is a foreign key into the users table, allowing a book to be related to a particular user.

Book Model

Field Name	Description	Data Type
user_id	ID of the user who added the book	integer
title	Title of the book	string
author	Author of the book	string
release_date	Book's release date	date
description	Book description from Amazon	text
image_url_small	URL of small image from Amazon	string
image_url_medium	URL of medium image from Amazon	string
image_url_large	URL of large image from Amazon	string
amazon_url	URL of book's page on Amazon	string
isbn	Book's ISBN	string
created_at	Date and time the book was added to the shelf	datetime
updated_at	Time book record was updated	datetime

Generate the book model class

Now that the fields for the book model are defined, you can generate the book model class using the script/generate command:

```
> ruby script/generate model Book

exists app/models/
exists test/unit/
exists test/fixtures/
create app/models/book.rb
create test/unit/book_test.rb
create test/fixtures/books.yml
exists db/migrate
create db/migrate/002_create_books.rb
```

In addition to the book model class, a unit test file, a fixtures file, and a database migration class are created for the book model. The migration class is usually a good place to start when you're implementing a model. The migration class creates the model in your database.

Create the book migration

When you generated the book model, the generate script also created a migration for the books table. Edit the db/migrate/002_create_books.rb file, as shown here:

```
class CreateBooks < ActiveRecord::Migration
    def self.up
        create_table :books do |t|
            t.references :user
            t.string :title
            t.string :author
            t.date :release_date
            t.text :description
            t.string :image_url_small, :string
            t.string :image_url_medium, :string
            t.string :image_url_large, :string
            t.string :amazon_url
            t.string :isbn
            t.timestamps
        end
    end

    def self.down
        drop_table :books
    end
end
```

This creates a books table containing all the fields that were specified in the model's design from Table 7.1. Each book record also contains a primary key ID field, which is automatically created by the migration.

Run the migration

Using the `rake` tool, go ahead and run the `CreateBooks` migration:

```
> rake db:migrate
```

This creates the books table, as specified in the `CreateBooks` migration class.

Associate the book model and the user model

The book model has a many-to-many relationship with the user model. In plain English, this means that one book can belong to many users, or many users can have the same book on their shelf. Furthermore, one user can have many books on their shelf. To implement this association in Rails, you use the built-in association DSL language. Open up the `app/models/user.rb` class and add a `has_and_belongs_to_many` association by adding the following line just below the class declaration:

```
has_and_belongs_to_many :books
```

Now you have to do the same thing for the book model to implement the other side of this association. Open up the `app/models/book.rb` class and add this line just below the class declaration:

```
has_and_belongs_to_many :users
```

Because this is a many-to-many relationship, there is one more thing you need to do to make it a valid relationship that Rails understands. A many-to-many relationship needs a new relationship table that maps book IDs and user IDs. Following Rails requirements for this table, it is named `books_users`. Recall that the table is named by using the pluralized form of each model separated with an underscore and in alphabetical order, so the book's name goes first. Go ahead and manually create a migration file named `003_create_books_users.rb` in the `db/migrate` directory. The migration should look similar to what you see here:

```
class CreateBooksUsers < ActiveRecord::Migration
    def self.up
        create_table :books_users, :id => false do |t|
            t.references :book
            t.references :user
            t.timestamps
        end
    end

    def self.down
        drop_table :books_users
    end
end
```

Now go ahead and run the migrations again so that the `books_users` table is created.

```
> rake db:migrate
```

By adding these associations to the book and user models, you are now able to access the books associated with a user, or the users associated with a book through a simple instance attribute. For example, you could use the following code to get a reference to a specific user's books:

```
user = User.find(:first)
users_books = user.books
```

Implement search logic in the book model

Recall that when you completed the search action in the book controller, it contained a call to a `search_amazon` method of the book model. You can now implement that method in the book model. Listing 7.6 shows the implementation of the `search_amazon` method along with a method that is used by the `search_amazon` method, `convert_amazon_results`. The `search_amazon` method uses the `AmazonInterface` class that was implemented earlier in this chapter.

The `find_by_keyword` method of the `AmazonInterface` class returns an array of `Item` instances. Instead of returning `Item` instances, the `search_amazon` method should return an array of `Book` instances. This is the purpose of the `convert_amazon_results` method. It converts the Amazon search results into instances of the book model.

LISTING 7.6

Implementing a Search in the Book Model

```ruby
def Book.search_amazon(keyword, page, user_id)
    search = AmazonInterface.new
    results = search.find_by_keyword(keyword, page)
    return Book.convert_amazon_results(results, user_id)
end

  def Book.convert_amazon_results(results, user_id)
      user = User.find(user_id)
      converted_books = Array.new
      results.each do |result|
          book = user.books.find_by_isbn(result.asin.to_s)
          if (book)
              book.exists = true
          else
              book = Book.new
              book.exists = false
          end
          book.title = result.item_attributes[0].title[0].to_s
          if result.item_attributes[0].author
              book.author = result.item_attributes[0].author.join(',')
          end
          book.release_date =
                result.item_attributes[0].publication_date.to_s
          if result.small_image
             book.image_url_small = result.small_image.url.to_s
          end
          if result.medium_image
             book.image_url_medium = result.medium_image.url.to_s
          end
          if result.large_image
             book.image_url_large = result.large_image.url.to_s
          end
          book.isbn = result.asin.to_s
          book.amazon_url = result.detail_page_url.to_s
          converted_books.push(book)
      end
      return converted_books
  end
```

Within the `convert_amazon_results` method, notice that there is a call to `find_by_isbn` on the logged-in user's books object. The purpose of this call is to determine whether the book is already on the user's shelf. If the user already has the book, an attribute of the book instance named exists is set to true. Be sure to add an accessor for the exist property to the book model. To do that, add this line near the top of the app/models/book.rb class:

```
attr_accessor :exists
```

Also in the convert_amazon_results method you may have noticed the use of the to_s method in several places. This is because the Ruby/AWS library actually returns the attributes that you are interested in as instances of AWSObject. Fortunately, the AWSObject implements the to_s method allowing you to get the actual string value of the attribute.

Let me take a moment to say a bit more about the exists attribute before you move on. An instance of the book class can represent a book in either of these two states:

- A book that is contained in the Book Shelf application database
- A book that has been read from the Amazon catalog, but does not yet exist in the application database

The exists attribute allows you to differentiate between these types of book instances. As you will see a bit later in this Chapter, it is important to know whether or not a book is in the database when rendering views. If a book instance is created as the result of any of the Active Record methods that load data, such as the find methods, the exists attribute should always be set to true. To accomplish that, you can add an Active Record observer to the book model.

Observers are callbacks that are called by Rails when a specific action occurs. The particular observer method that helps you out here is the after_find method. If a model implements the after_find method, it is called immediately after any record is found using one of the Rails finder methods. Edit the app/models/book.rb file and add the after_find implementation shown here:

```
def after_find
    self.exists = true
end
```

The instance being created is passed to the after_find method. This implementation just sets the exists attribute to true for all records created as a result of an Active Record find method.

The converted array of book instances is what is returned from the search_amazon method. The controller action can then set this array as an instance variable to make it visible to the search results view template.

Create the search results page

With the search results action implemented in the BookController class, the next thing you should do is implement the search results page. This is the page that is rendered after the search results action is complete. Because the search action of the book controller does not specifically render a template, a template with the name search.html.erb in the app/views/book directory is rendered by default. The search action creates an instance variable named @books, which contains an array of all the books found. This instance variable is accessed from the search.html.erb template to display the search results.

Listing 7.7 shows what your `search.html.erb` template should look like. The outer `if-else` block checks to see if there are any books in the `@books` array. If the array is empty or null, a message saying "No matching books found" appears. If the `@books` array contains one or more books, the array is stepped through using the `each` method of the array. Before the `@books` array is stepped through, a variable named `first` is set to `true`. This is used as a flag to indicate the first book in the list. The first book in the list is differentiated with a different class name on the `div` that wraps the book. This allows the first book in the list to be styled slightly differently than the other books. This is useful, for example, if you want a different top margin or different padding, perhaps on the first element.

LISTING 7.7

The app/views/book/search.html.erb File

```
<% if @books && @books.size > 0 %>
    <% first = true %>
    <% @books.each do |book| %>
        <% if (first == true) %>
            <% first = false %>
            <div class="book_data_first">
        <% else %>
            <div class="book_data">
        <% end %>
            <%= render :partial=>"book_detail",
                       :locals => { :book => book, :search => true } %>
        </div>
    <% end %>
<% else %>
    <%= "No matching books found." %>
<% end %>
```

After the opening `div` statement for a book is created, a partial named `book_detail` is called to render the details of the current book of the iteration. You pass the current book and a flag named `search` as locals to the partial. The `book_detail` partial is implemented in `app/views/book/_book_detail.html.erb`. Create that file and enter the code shown in Listing 7.8.

The first line of the partial displays an image of the book. This uses the image URL that was obtained from the Amazon search. The next section of the partial shown below displays the book's title, author, release date, and ISBN. Remember that in the book model during the search, the `exists` flag is set to true for a book if it is also found on the user's shelf. The partial uses that flag to determine whether to display the title as a link to the book's record, or just text.

LISTING 7.8

The app/views/book/_book_detail.html.erb Partial

```erb
<div class="book_image"><img src="<%= book.image_url_small %>" /></div>
<div class="book_info">
    <span class="book_name">
        <% if book.exists %>
            <%= link_to book.title, { :controller => "book",
                                       :action => "show",
                                       :id => book.id } %>
        <% else %>
            <%= book.title %>
        <% end %>
    </span><br/>
    Author(s): <%= book.author %><br/>
    Release Date: <%= book.release_date %><br/>
    ISBN: <%= book.isbn %>
</div>
<% if search %>
    <div class="add_control" id="add_control_<%= book.isbn %>">
        <% if !book.exists %>
            <%= link_to_remote "Add to Shelf",
                               :update => 'add_control_' + book.isbn,
                               :url => { :controller => 'book',
                               :action => 'add',
                               :isbn => book.isbn } %><br/>
            <div id="shelf_status_<%= book.isbn %>"></div>
        <% else %>
            <%= render :partial=>'book_exists',
                       :locals => { :book => book } %>
        <% end %>
    </div>
<% else %>
    <div class="add_control">
        <% if session[:user] %>
            <%= link_to_remote "Delete from Shelf",
                               :url => { :controller => 'book',
                               :action => 'delete',
                               :isbn => book.isbn } %>
        <% end %>
        <div id="shelf_status_<%= book.isbn %>">
            <span class="users_count"><%= book.users.size %> Users</span>
        </div>
    </div>
<% end %>
```

If the book is on the user's shelf, the title appears as a link to the book's detail page.

```
<div class="book_info">
    <span class="book_name">
        <% if book.exists %>
            <%= link_to book.title, { :controller => "book",
                                       :action => "show",
                                       :id => book.id } %>
        <% else %>
            <%= book.title %>
        <% end %>
    </span><br/>
    Author(s): <%= book.author %><br/>
    Release Date: <%= book.release_date %><br/>
    ISBN: <%= book.isbn %>
</div>
```

The following portion of the partial is shown next. Recall that from the search results page, the flag `search` was passed with the value true to the partial. This section of the partial displays a link to add the book to the user's shelf if the search flag is true. The `search` flag allows you to reuse this partial when you want to display the books on a user's shelf. In that case, you do not want to show the add control, and so the `search` flag is set to false to indicate that the partial is not being called as a result of a search (see Listing 7.9).

The add control only appears if the book is not already on the user's shelf. In the third line of the above code, an `if` statement checks the `exists` field to determine if the book is already on the user's shelf. The add control consists of a remote link that uses the `link_to_remote` Ajax helper method. The `link_to_remote` method results in an Ajax request to the add action of the book controller.

The book's ISBN is also passed as a parameter. The `link_to_remote` method is also passed an update parameter that tells the method to update the add control `div` after the Ajax method is complete. Because the page will most often contain multiple books and multiple add controls, the add control `div` is given an `id` attribute that consists of the string `add_control_` with the book's ISBN appended.

If the book already exists on the user's shelf, instead of showing the add control, another partial called `book_exists` appears. The book record is passed along to that partial. You'll see details of that partial shortly.

Below the outermost `else` statement of this code block is the template that is rendered if the partial is not being called as a result of a search being performed. Instead of displaying a remote link allowing the user to add the book to her shelf, a link appears which allows the user to delete the book from her shelf. This uses the `link_to_remote` method, which creates an Ajax request, just as you use to add a book to the user's shelf. To delete a book, the `delete` action of the book controller is called, with the book's ISBN also being passed to the action.

LISTING 7.9

```
<% if search %>
    <div class="add_control" id="add_control_<%= book.isbn %>">
        <% if !book.exists %>
            <%= link_to_remote "Add to Shelf",
                                :update => 'add_control_' + book.isbn,
                                :url => { :controller => 'book',
                                :action => 'add',
                                :isbn => book.isbn } %><br/>
            <div id="shelf_status_<%= book.isbn %>"></div>
        <% else %>
            <%= render :partial=>'book_exists',
                       :locals => { :book => book } %>
        <% end %>
    </div>
<% else %>
    <div class="add_control">
        <% if session[:user] %>
            <%= link_to_remote "Delete from Shelf",
                                :url => { :controller => 'book',
                                :action => 'delete',
                                :isbn => book.isbn } %>
        <% end %>
        <div id="shelf_status_<%= book.isbn %>">
            <span class="users_count"><%= book.users.size %>
                Users
            </span>
        </div>
    </div>
<% end %>
```

Now let's create the partial that appears if the book already exists on the user's shelf. You should create this partial, called `book_exists`, in `app/views/book/_book_exists.html.erb`. Create that file and enter the code shown in Listing 7.10.

LISTING 7.10

The _book_exists Partial

```
<%= link_to_remote "Delete from Shelf",
                    :url => { :controller => 'book',
                    :action => 'delete',
                    :isbn => book.isbn } %><br/>
<div id="shelf_status_<%= book.isbn %>">
    <span class="on_shelf">On Shelf</span>
    <span class="users_count"><%= book.users.size %> Users</span>
</div>
```

This `book_exists` partial displays a remote link allowing the user to delete the book from their shelf, along with a message indicating that the book is on the shelf, and a count of the number of users who have this same book on their shelves. The `delete` function is implemented using the `link_to_remote` helper method again to create an Ajax request to the `delete` action of the book controller. You will implement the `delete` action later in this Chapter.

Stop for a moment and take a look at the progress you've made so far to make sure everything is working as planned. If you do not have the WEBrick server running, go ahead and start it using the `ruby script/server` command and go to the application's home page by navigating in your browser to `http://localhost:3000`. Log into the application or create a new user, and you should be taken to the user home page, which at this point should look similar to what is shown in Figure 7.3. From that page, enter a search term, such as "ruby programming," into the text field in the left column. Press the Search button to use the functionality you just completed in order to perform the search and display its results. You should see a search results page similar to what is shown in Figure 7.4.

The results of your search appear, but the display isn't styled quite as nicely as it could be. You need to add a few more styles to your style sheet. Go ahead and add the styles in Listing 7.11 to your `public/stylesheets/style.css` file.

FIGURE 7.4

Search results

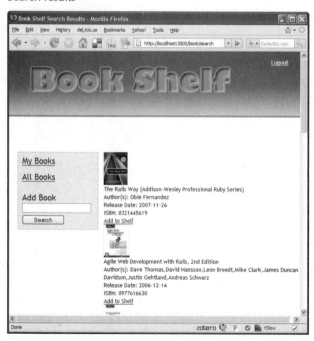

LISTING 7.11

Styles Added to public/stylesheets/style.css

```css
.book_data_first {
 float:left;
 margin-bottom: 25px;
 border: 1px solid #cccccc;
 padding: 15px;
 width: 80%;
}

.book_data {
 float:left;
 clear:both;
 margin-bottom: 25px;
 border: 1px solid #cccccc;
 padding: 15px;
 width: 80%;
}

.book_image {
    float:left;
}

#book_image {
 float: left;
    padding: 20px;
    background-color: lightblue;
    width: 130px;
}

#book_view {
    margin-left: 25px;
}

.book_info {
 float: left;
 padding-left: 15px;
 text-align: left;
 width: 70%;
}

.book_name {
 font-weight: bold;
}

.add_control {
 color: green;
```

continued

LISTING 7.11   *(continued)*

```css
  float: right;
  text-align: right;
}

#book_keyword {
    margin-top: 10px;
    margin-bottom: 10px;
}

.on_shelf {
    display: block;
    color: green;
    font-weight: bold;
    margin-top: 20px;
}

.not_on_shelf {
    display: block;
    color: red;
    margin-top: 20px;
}
```

With those styles added to your style sheet and the `style.css` file saved, reload the search results page; it should now look like Figure 7.5. I think you'll agree that this is a much nicer display of the results.

Now go ahead and try to add a book to your shelf by clicking the Add to Shelf link. Oops, you'll notice that it doesn't quite work as expected. Remember that when you created this link, you used the `link_to_remote` helper and specified the add action of the book controller to handle this request. However, you have not yet implemented the add action. That's okay for now, though, because your goal for this section is to get the search functionality working. In the next section, you'll complete the implementation of being able to add and remove books from a user's shelf.

If you use the suggested keywords of "ruby programming" for your search, and you scroll down on the search results page, you can count a total of ten books displayed. The problem is that this search actually finds more items, but you have not implemented results paging yet. Let's do that next.

Implement search results paging

Recall that a book search returns only the first ten results from the Amazon catalog. Currently, if a search finds more than ten books, there is no way to display those results beyond the first ten. The `find_by_keyword` method of the `AmazonInterface` class that you created earlier accepts a page parameter that allows you to get results beyond the first page of results. You just need to implement a way of passing a page parameter from the Web page down to this search method. Modify the search action of the book controller so that it looks like this:

```
def search
    @prev_page = params[:page].to_i - 1
    @next_page = params[:page].to_i + 1
    @books = Book.search_amazon(params[:book_keyword],
                                params[:page],
                                session[:user])
    @title = "Book Shelf Search Results"
end
```

The lines in bold print are new. These lines set two new instance variables that will be available to the search results view. The @prev_page variable holds the page number of the page previous to the one currently being viewed. The @next_page variable holds the page number of the next page of results. You use these two variables in the results view to display paging controls above the results.

FIGURE 7.5

Search results styled

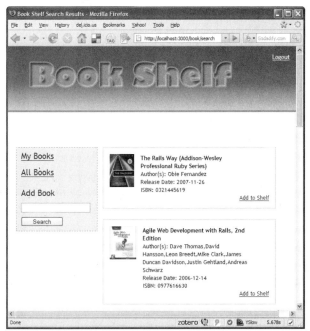

Now you need to make some small changes to the search results view contained in `app/views/book/search.html.erb`. Open that file and add this code to the very top of the template:

```
<% if @prev_page > 0 %>
    <%= link_to "Prev page", :controller=>'book',
                             :action=>'search',
                             :book_keyword=>@keyword,
                             :page=>@prev_page %>
<% end %>
<% if @books && @books.size == 10 %>
    <%= link_to "Next page", :controller=>'book',
                             :action=>'search',
                             :book_keyword=>@keyword,
                             :page=>@next_page %>
<% end %>
```

This creates a paging control that allows a user to navigate to the next page of results or back to a previous page. Notice that the `@prev_page` and the `@next_page` variables are used as the page parameter that is sent to the `search` action.

Also modify the final `else` block at the bottom of the `search.html.erb` template to display a slightly different message if you're displaying an empty page as a result of the user trying to display a next page beyond the available results.

```
<% else %>
    <%= "No matching books found." unless @prev_page > 0 %>
    <%= "No additional matching books found." unless @prev_page =
    0 %>
<% end %>
```

Listing 7.12 shows what your `search.html.erb` file should look like, complete with the paging functionality.

Assuming your server is still running, reload the Book Shelf application in your browser and navigate back to the search results page. You should now see the paging links at the top of the book results display. Perform a keyword search again using a fairly common keyword and try out the paging links. You should be able to page forward and backward through the results.

LISTING 7.12

The app/views/book/search.html.erb file with Paging

```
<% if @prev_page > 0 %>
    <%= link_to "Prev page", :controller=>'book',
                             :action=>'search',
                             :book_keyword=>@keyword,
                             :page=>@prev_page %>
<% end %>
```

```
<% if @books.size = 10 %>
    <%= link_to "Next page", :controller=>'book',
                            :action=>'search',
                            :book_keyword=>@keyword,
                            :page=>@next_page %>
<% end %>
<% if @books && @books.size > 0 %>
    <% count = 0 %>
    <% @books.each do |book| %>
        <% if (count == 0) %>
            <% count = 1 %>
            <div class="book_data_first">
        <% else %>
            <div class="book_data">
        <% end %>
        <%= render :partial=>"book_detail",
                    :locals => { :book => book, :search => true } %>
        </div>
    <% end %>
<% else %>
    <%= "No matching books found." unless @prev_page > 0 %>
    <%= "No additional matching books found." unless @prev_page = 0 %>
<% end %>
```

Implementing the Addition and Deletion of Books

Now the users have the ability to perform book searches based on any keyword. The results of the search are pulled up on a list page from which they can select a book to add to their shelf. This section guides you through implementing the functionality that allows the user to actually add a book from the results page to their shelf. After they are able to add a book, you'll continue the development by adding the capability to remove a book from a user's shelf.

Adding a book

In the previous section, when you created the book search results page, a link to add a new book to a user's shelf was added for every book found that is not currently on the user's shelf. The link uses the link_to_remote helper method.

```
<%= link_to_remote "Add to Shelf",
                    :update => 'add_control_' + book.isbn,
                    :url => { :controller => 'book',
                    :action => 'add',
                    :isbn => book.isbn } %><br/>
```

This results in an Ajax call to the `add` action of the book controller. You have not yet implemented the `add` action, so let's go ahead and implement that now. Open up the `app/controllers/book_controller.rb` file and create an `add` method using this code:

```
def add
    isbn = params[:isbn]
    book = Book.find_or_create_from_amazon(isbn, session[:user])
    if book.save
        render :partial=>'book_exists', :locals => { :book =>
  book }
    else
        render :text => 'Failed to add book'
    end
end
```

The `add` method uses the `isbn` parameter and passes that along with the id of the current logged-in user to a new method of the book model, `find_or_create_from_amazon`. The method `find_or_create_from_amazon` is responsible for either looking up the book's details from the application's database in the case when the same book is already on another user's shelf, or looking up the book's details from Amazon when it cannot be found in the application's database. In either case, a book object is returned. The book is then saved.

If the save is successful, the `book_exists` partial is rendered back to the search results page from which the Ajax call originated. If the save is not successful, a failure message is rendered back to the search results page.

Now, open up the `app/models/book.rb` file and implement the `find_or_create_from_amazon` method. Type in the following code for this method:

```
def Book.find_or_create_from_amazon(isbn, user_id)
    book = Book.find_or_create_by_isbn(isbn)
    if book.title
        book.users << User.find(user_id)
    else
        search = AmazonInterface.new
        books = search.find_by_isbn(isbn)
        book.set_from_amazon_result(books[0])
        book.users << User.find(user_id)
    end
    return book
end
```

The goal of this method is to perform one of the following tasks:

- **Find the book in the application database.** If found, add the current user to the book's users attribute.

- **Find the book in the Amazon catalog.** Create a book model object from the Amazon Item record that is returned.

The first line of the method looks up the book in the application database using the `find_or_create_by_isbn` method. This is one of the dynamic `find` methods created as a result of the book model extending `ActiveRecord::Base`. Because you are using a `find_or_create` method, the book model instance is created whether or not the book is found in the database, so you cannot simply check to see whether or not the returned record exists.

The `find_or_create_by_isbn` method is used because you need an instance of the book model class in either case. So this single line of code creates the book instance that will either be populated from the application database or later on from the result of an Amazon lookup.

To determine whether the book was found in the local database, the book's `title` attribute is checked. Because every book must have a non-blank title, this attribute is not null if the book was found in the application database. However, if the book was not found, the title attribute is null.

Remember that books and users share a many-to-many relationship. A user can be related to a book by adding the `user` instance to the book's `users` attribute. This is done if the book is found in the application database. If the book is not found in the database, the `AmazonInterface` class looks up the book in the Amazon catalog. This returns an array of `Item` records. The book with the matching ISBN is the first item in the resulting array.

Now you need to map the `Item` instance to your instance of the book class. This is done using the `set_from_amazon_result` method. After mapping the result to the book instance, the current user is associated with the book and the book is returned.

The `set_from_amazon_result` method used in the previous method is also a new method that you have to add to the `Book` model class. This is a relatively simple method that takes fields from the `Item` object and sets equivalent fields on the `book` instance object. Listing 7.13 shows the code for this method.

If you looked at the code in Listing 7.13, you probably recognized that it is very similar to code that you used in the `convert_amazon_results` method earlier in this Chapter. It would be a bad programming practice to keep both of these two nearly identical chunks of code. Code duplication is almost always a bad thing. It can often be the source of defects, and maintenance problems. In this case, there is a simple refactoring that you can perform on the `convert_amazon_results` method to remove the duplication.

Below is the refactored `convert_amazon_results` method. Notice that the duplicate code has been replaced with a call to your new `set_from_amazon_result` method.

```
def Book.convert_amazon_results(results, user_id)
    user = User.find(user_id)
    converted_books = Array.new
    results.each do |result|
        book = user.books.find_by_isbn(result.asin.to_s)
        if (book)
            book.exists = true
        else
```

```
                        book = Book.new
                        book.exists = false
                end
                book.set_from_amazon_result(result)
                converted_books.push(book)
        end
        return converted_books
    end
```

LISTING 7.13

The set_from_amazon_result method

```
def set_from_amazon_result(result)
    self.title = result.item_attributes.title.to_s
    if result.item_attributes[0].author
        self.author = result.item_attributes[0].author.join(',')
    end
    self.release_date =
            result.item_attributes[0].publication_date.to_s

    if result.small_image
        self.image_url_small = result.small_image.url.to_s
    end
    if result.medium_image
        self.image_url_medium = result.medium_image.url.to_s
    end
    if result.large_image
        self.image_url_large = result.large_image.url.to_s
    end

    self.isbn = result.asin.to_s
    self.amazon_url = result.detail_page_url.to_send
```

You are nearly finished with the add functionality. You have only one more method to add. In the find_or_create_from_amazon method, you called a find_by_isbn instance method on the AmazonInterface class. This method has not been implemented yet, so create that now.

Open up the AmazonInterface class in lib/amazon_interface.rb and add this method as shown here:

```
def find_by_isbn(isbn)

    il = ItemLookup.new( 'ASIN', { 'ItemId' => isbn } )
    rg = ResponseGroup.new('Medium')
```

```
      resp = @request.search(il, rg)
      products = resp.item_lookup_response.items.item
  end
```

In the `find_by_keyword` method, you used the `ItemSearch` class from Ruby/AWS. For this method, you use the `ItemLookup` class. The `ItemLookup` class is useful for when you have the ASIN or ISBN of a book and want to retrieve that exact book. ASIN is equivalent to an ISBN for books. However, Amazon gives every product an ASIN identifier, not just books; this why they call this field an ASIN instead of an ISBN. The ASIN is passed using the `ItemId` hash key. The rest of the method is identical to the `find_by_keyword` method. You create a `ResponseGroup`, perform the search, and return the results.

This completes the functionality required to add a book to a user's shelf. Make sure your server is running (start it if necessary), and navigate back to the search results page. Select a book returned from a search you performed and attempt to add that book to your bookshelf. If all goes well, you should see the book's listing updated, indicating that the book is now on your shelf. The results screen should look similar to Figure 7.6 after adding the book.

Instead of a link to add the book to your shelf, the link is changed to Delete from Shelf. This is also a new message indicating that the book is on your shelf, along with a count of users who have that book on their shelf.

FIGURE 7.6

Search results after adding the book

At this point, if you click on the My Books link, you'll still just see a blank page. That is because you have not yet implemented the code to display a user's books on their home page. You will do that after you implement the ability to delete a book from a user's shelf.

Deleting a book

In the previous section, you gave users the ability to add books to a personal bookshelf. In this section, you will give users the ability to delete books from their book shelf.

Earlier in this chapter, you added a delete link for books that a user adds to his shelf. That code is shown here:

```
<%= link_to_remote "Delete from Shelf",
                    :url => { :controller => 'book',
                    :action => 'delete',
                    :isbn => book.isbn } %>
```

This link is shown when the user performs a book search, and a book contained in the results is already on the user's shelf. Later in this chapter this link will also be used within the book list displayed on the user's home page.

Before you implement the functionality to delete a book, think about what should happen when the user clicks the Delete from Shelf link. From the `:url` parameter in the code above, you can assume that the `delete` method of the book controller class will be called, and the ISBN number of the book that you want to delete is passed to that action. Should you delete the book from the database in that method? Remember that the same book might also be on another user's shelf. So you would only want to delete the book from the `books` table if it is no longer on any user's shelf.

However, you do need to break the association between the selected book and the current user. To do that, you will delete the book from the `books` array attribute of the current user. Remember that the `books` array attribute contains the books that are associated with the user. By deleting the book from that array, the association record stored in the `books_users` table will also be deleted.

After you've deleted the book from the user's `books` association and deleted the book record if it is no longer associated with any other users, you need to tell the Web page to replace the Delete from Shelf link with the Add to Shelf link, so that the user is able to add the book again if she chooses to. It is also a good idea to give the user a message indicating that the delete happened successfully. You will perform the web page updates using RJS.

Add the delete action

Start the implementation now by adding the delete method to the book controller. Edit the `app/controllers/book_controller.rb` file to add the delete method shown below:

```
def delete
    @book = Book.find_by_isbn(params[:isbn])
    current_user = User.find(session[:user])
```

```
        current_user.books.delete(@book)
        if @book.users.size == 0
            Book.delete(@book.id)
        end
    end
```

In this method, you look up the book to be deleted using the `find_by_isbn` finder method. This is one of the dynamic finders that is automatically created for you by ActiveRecord. You also look up the current user using the user id stored in the session. Once you have those two items, you can break the association between the book and the user by deleting the book from the user's `books` array. Finally, in the last three lines of the method, you check to see if any other users are associated with the book. If the users count for that book is zero, you delete the book from the database using the `Book.delete` method.

Update the page with RJS

In the delete action, you performed the necessary server-side operations, now you have to make sure that the Web page is updated to reflect the current state of the book. Since it has been deleted, the user should see a link allowing him to add it again if he chooses. You also want to show the user an indication that the delete action was successful. Right now, the code that displays the Add to Shelf link is embedded within the `book_detail.html.erb` partial. The specific section of interest is shown here:

```
<%= link_to_remote    "Add to Shelf",
                      :update => 'add_control_' + book.isbn,
                      :url => { :controller => 'book',
                      :action => 'add',
                      :isbn => book.isbn } %><br/>
<div id="shelf_status_<%= book.isbn %>"></div>
```

So that you do not have to duplicate that block of code, it is a good idea to move it into a partial of its own. Create a partial and name it `_book_not_exists.html.erb`. Make sure it is in the `app/views/book` directory. After you have created that partial, go ahead and replace that block of code in the `_book_details.html.erb` partial with these two lines:

```
<%= render :partial=>'book_not_exists',
           :locals => { :book => book } %>
```

Now, you have the partial that you will display after you have deleted a book from a user's shelf. As I said a bit earlier, you will use RJS to perform the necessary page updates after the delete action. RJS allows you to perform page manipulations that you would normally do with JavaScript code. RJS actually results in JavaScript being generated.

Start by creating an RJS template in the file `app/views/book/delete.rjs`. Since this RJS template has the same name as the `delete` action, and there are no other templates with the same name, this template will be rendered automatically by the book controller. Type the code shown below into the RJS template:

```
# display book not exists partial
page['add_control_' + @book.isbn].replace_html
        :partial=>'book_not_exists', :locals => { :book => @
   book }

# display book deleted message and highlight it
page['shelf_status_' + @book.isbn].replace_html 'Book Deleted'
page['shelf_status_' + @book.isbn].visual_effect :highlight
```

You can tell from the comments, this template performs two page manipulations. First it displays the book_not_exists partial which contains the Add to Shelf link. That is done using what is called an element proxy. The code, `page ['add_control_' + @book.isbn]`, is an element proxy for the div element with the id equal to 'add_control_' followed by the isbn number of the book for which this is being displayed. That div element currently contains the Delete from Shelf link along with the On Shelf message and the user count for that book.

The second half of the template displays a Book Deleted message and uses a Scriptaculous visual effect to highlight it.

Once you have this code in place, go ahead and try adding and then deleting a book. If you have followed along closely, it should work as expected. In the next section, you'll implement a page that will display all of the book's on a user's shelf.

Displaying a User's Books

Now that users have the ability to add and remove books from a bookshelf, go ahead and modify the user's home page so that the books from the user's shelf appear on the page. The user home page template is in `app/views/user/home.html.erb`. Open the file and add this line following the welcome message line:

```
<%= render :partial=>'book/list_books', :locals=>{:books=>@books}
   %>
```

This line uses a partial to render a list of the books that are on the user's shelf. The partial `list_books` is also new and you'll implement that shortly. First, however, you have to modify the `home` action of the user controller so that it reads in the books on the user's shelf and sets them in an array instance variable named @books. Edit the home action of the user controller, `app/controllers/user_controller.rb`:

```
def home
    current_user = User.find(session[:user])
    @books = current_user.books
    @title = "BookShelf - User Home"
end
```

The lines in bold print are the new lines that you have to add to the method. These lines get the current user's books from the `books` association attribute of the user. Now you have to create the new partial for listing the books.

Create the partial at `app/views/book/_list_books.html.erb`. Type in this code for the implementation of the partial:

```
<% count = 0 %>
<% books.each do |book| %>
    <% if (count == 0) %>
        <% count = 1 %>
        <div class="book_data_first">
    <% else %>
        <div class="book_data">
    <% end %>
    <%= render :partial=>"book/book_detail",
             :locals => { :book => book, :search => false } %>
    </div>
<% end %>
<div style="clear:both"> </div>
```

That's it! The user's home page should now display any books that are on his shelf. Try it out by clicking the My Books link in the left-hand navigation panel after adding a book to your shelf. This takes you to your home page, and the newly added book should appear.

Implementing the Book Detail Page

The last task of this Chapter will be to implement a book detail page. The book detail page is a Web page that contains detailed information about a specific book stored on a shelf in the Book Shelf application. In this section, you'll implement a basic book detail page that contains information about a selected book.

CROSS-REF In Chapter 8, you can extend the book detail page to include user reviews and ratings.

In the `book_detail` partial, the title of a book appears as a link to the book's detail page for books that exist in the application database. Here is the code from that partial template:

```
<%= link_to book.title, { :controller => "book",
                          :action => "show",
                          :id => book.id } %>
```

This uses the Rails helper method `link_to` to create a regular link to the `show` action of the book controller. The `id` of the book is also passed as a parameter to the request. You have not yet implemented the `show` action, so do that now. Open up the `app/controllers/book_controller.rb` file and add the `show` action as defined here:

```
def show
    @book = Book.find(params[:id])
    @title = "Book Detail"
end
```

Use the `find` method to grab the correct book instance from the database corresponding to the passed-in id. The book instance is made available to the view template by setting it as an instance variable, `@book`. The `@title` instance variable is also set so that the book detail page has a title. Because no template is explicitly rendered, a template named `show.html.erb` (see Listing 7.14) in the `app/views/book` directory is rendered by default.

LISTING 7.14

The /app/views/book/show.html.erb File

```
<div id="book_view">
    <div id="book_view_upper">
        <div id="book_image">
            <%= image_tag @book.image_url_medium %>
        </div>
        <div id="book_summary">
            <span class="book_title"><%= @book.title %></span>
            Author: <%= @book.author %><br/>
            <div id="book_details">
                Release Date: <%= @book.release_date %><br/>
                ISBN: <%= @book.isbn %><br/><br/>
            </div>
            Users: <%= @book.users.size %><br/>
            Added to BookShelf on: <%= @book.created_at %><br/><br/>
            <%= link_to „Buy from Amazon",
                        @book.amazon_url,
                        :class=>"action_button" %><br/><br/>
        </div>
    </div>
    <div style="clear:both;"> </div>
</div>
```

This view displays details about the book in a `div` named `book_view_upper`. Later, when reviews and rating are added, there will be another `div` that follows this `div` containing the review and ratings data. The template should be very easy for you to understand. There is nothing fancy going on with this one, nor are there any partials being called.

Before you try out this page, you need to add a few more styles to your growing style sheet. Add these styles to `public/stylesheets/style.css`:

```
#book_view_upper {
  float: left;
  border: solid thin #cccccc;
```

```
    padding: 10px;
    width: 80%;
}

#book_summary {
  float: left;
  margin-left: 20px;
  line-height: 1.5em;
}

#book_summary .book_title {
  font-weight: bold;
  font-size: 12pt;
  color: #f98919;
  display: block;
  margin-bottom: 5px;
}
```

Now if you return to your browser and navigate to your user home page, either by logging in or clicking the My Books link if you are already logged in, you can click the title of a book that is on your shelf and be taken to the book detail page. You should see a book detail view similar to that shown in Figure 7.7.

FIGURE 7.7

Book detail view

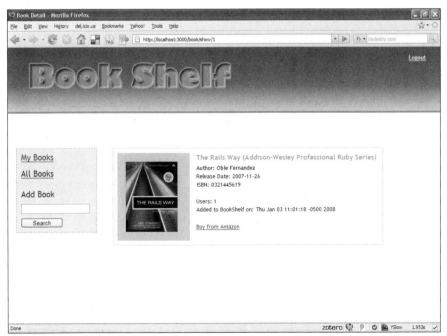

Summary

This chapter continued the development of the Book Shelf application. In the previous chapter, the user model was implemented, providing full support for user authentication. In this chapter, you added the core functionality of the application, which was the ability to add and remove books from a user's bookshelf. This functionality included integration with the Amazon A2S Web service for reading information about books that a user searches for. Significant views added to the application in this chapter were the search results page, the book display on the user's home page, and the book detail page. Each of these views will continue to grow as you complete the application in the next chapter.

As you've been following along with the development, you may have noticed ways in which you can improve upon the design or implementation of the application. That is a very good sign that you are learning well, and I highly encourage you to follow your temptations and feel free to refactor the application as you wish. The next chapter includes some refactoring for some of the previously implemented functionality after all of the core features are implemented.

Chapter 8

Developing Book Shelf: Social Support

In this chapter you will complete the development of the Book Shelf Web application. With that in mind, there is a great deal to accomplish in this chapter. In the past two chapters, you have added support for users and basic book support. A user can log in, search for books, add books to their shelf, remove books, and view a book detail page. Now you turn your focus to adding features that make the application more fun and interesting to use in a community environment. These features are commonly known as social features and are a trademark of Web 2.0 applications.

If you want to follow along with the development in this chapter, you can continue working with the code that you developed in Chapter 7, or you can download the complete Chapter 7 source code from www.rubyonrailsbible.com.

IN THIS CHAPTER

Adding social support

Implementing tagging

Implementing book reviews

Implementing book ratings

Extending the application

Adding Social Support

In this chapter, you will continue development of the Book Shelf application by adding some popular social features to the application.

- **Tagging:** Organize your books by keywords.
- **Reviews:** Give users the ability to post reviews for any books in a database.

In addition to these features, I will also get you started on how to implement a ratings system that allows users to attach a rating to a book. The good thing is that these features are common to many Web applications, and therefore you can take advantage of code that has already been written, saving yourself some time and effort. You'll use Rails plugins for the implementation of tagging and ratings. As you add each feature to the application, you'll notice a repetition of tasks that will become second nature to you as you develop more Rails applications. For each feature that you want to add to a Rails application, you generally have three tasks to implement:

- Add or modify model layer classes.
- Add methods to an existing controller or create a new controller.
- Create view templates.

Implementing Tagging

Content tagging is a popular feature of most Web 2.0 social networking applications. Tagging allows a user to associate keywords with a piece of content. Content can then be easily categorized and found by using the keywords or tags that have been applied.

For the Book Shelf application, users are allowed to create tags for books stored in the application. Each user can maintain their own unique set of tags for each book on their shelf. In the left side panel, users can view a tag cloud from which they can select a tag to view related books. The application supports two tag cloud views: one showing the current user's tags and the other showing all of the tags from all users.

The steps that you will go through to implement tagging in the Book Shelf application are as follows:

- Install a tagging plugin
- Create a migration to add tagging support to the database
- Add tagging support to the model layer
- Add tagging support to the controller layer
- Implement the view layer for tagging support

To get started, choose and install a tagging plugin, which will make the task much easier than if you were creating all of the tagging support from scratch.

Installing a tagging plugin

A Rails plugin provides the core of the tagging implementation. Because tagging is a feature that is common across many Web applications, it is likely that someone has solved this problem for you already and you can save yourself some work through reuse. In fact, if you search for a Rails tagging plugin, you'll find that it's a problem that many people have attempted to solve and provide a plugin for. Here are some of the tagging-related plugins that I came across while writing this application:

- `acts_as_taggable`

- `acts_as_taggable_on_steroids`

- `tagging`

- `acts_as_taggable_redux`

Each of the plugins supports a slightly different feature set. One of the main features that I was looking for was support for user-owned tags. This means that if two users add tags to a book, those tags can be differentiated. As a result, tags are associated with both a book and a user. Each user should be able to update the tags that they set for a book, but not change tags that other users may have applied to a book. This seems like a relatively simple requirement that you think would be useful in any tagging implementation.

However, at the time I was writing this portion of the Book Shelf application, of the four plugins listed above, only the `acts_as_taggable_redux` plugin supported user-owned tags. Because of that support and the fact that `acts_as_taggable_redux` supports all of the other tagging requirements that you have, you'll use this plugin to implement tagging in the Book Shelf application.

Install the acts_as_taggable_redux plugin

To install the `acts_as_taggable_redux` script, you will use the script/plugin command as shown in Figure 8.1.

However, this plugin is not found in one of the preconfigured standard plugin repositories, so you have to pass the URL of the plugins SVN repository to the script/plugin command so that it knows where to find the plugin.

FIGURE 8.1

Installing `acts_as_taggable_redux`

The `acts_as_taggable_redux` plugin should now be in the `vendor/plugins/acts_as_taggable_redux` directory. In the sections that follow, you'll begin to use this plugin to set up tagging in the Book Shelf application.

Setting up the database for tagging support

The `acts_as_taggable_redux` plugin that you installed includes a rake task that creates a migration for you, which in turn creates all of the necessary tables required for tagging support. To create the migration, run the rake task `acts_as_taggable:db:create` from your application root directory, like this:

```
rake acts_as_taggable:db:create
```

After running this rake task, you will have a new migration in your `db/migrate` directory. The migration will have the filename `004_acts_as_taggable_tables.rb`. The migration should look like the code in Listing 8.1.

The first thing that you might notice different about this migration is that the syntax is slightly different from that which you might be used to. This is because this migration uses the pre-Rails 2.0 migration syntax. For example, prior to Rails 2.0 to create a table column, the migration syntax would look like this:

```
t.column :name, :string
```

In a migration for Rails 2.0 or later, the syntax would look like this:

```
t.string :name
```

Fortunately, the older migration syntax still works with the current version of Rails. This plugin was created prior to the release of Rails 2.0 which is why they use the older migration syntax. However, don't let that scare you away. There are many great plugins that were created prior to the release of Rails 2.0 which are still great choices.

Let's break the migration down and look at it in several pieces. The migration class consists of two methods, the `self.up` method and the `self.down` method. The `self.down` method is by far the simpler of the two, so let's start by looking at that one. The `self.down` method drops two tables, `tags`, and `taggings`.

These are the two tables that are created in the `self.up` method.

```
def self.down
    drop_table :tags
    drop_table :taggings
end
```

LISTING 8.1

AddActsAsTaggableTables migration

```
class AddActsAsTaggableTables < ActiveRecord::Migration
  def self.up
    create_table :tags do |t|
      t.column :name, :string
      t.column :taggings_count, :integer, :default => 0, :null => false
    end
    add_index :tags, :name
    add_index :tags, :taggings_count

    create_table :taggings do |t|
      t.column :tag_id, :integer
      t.column :taggable_id, :integer
      t.column :taggable_type, :string
      t.column :user_id, :integer
    end

    # Find objects for a tag
    add_index :taggings, [:tag_id, :taggable_type]
    add_index :taggings, [:user_id, :tag_id, :taggable_type]
    # Find tags for an object
    add_index :taggings, [:taggable_id, :taggable_type]
    add_index :taggings, [:user_id, :taggable_id, :taggable_type]
  end

  def self.down
    drop_table :tags
    drop_table :taggings
  end
end
```

Next, look at the first part of the `self.up` method. It consists of these lines:

```
create_table :tags do |t|
   t.column :name, :string
   t.column :taggings_count, :integer, :default => 0, :null =>
  false
end
add_index :tags, :name
add_index :tags, :taggings_count
```

This creates the tags table. Each row in the tags table contains a name column that is a string, and a taggings_count column that is an integer. This table stores all of the tags that all of the users of the Book Shelf application create. After the table is created, you also add two indexes to the table, one for each of the columns. This improves the access, and sorting time for retrieving tags from the table.

The last part of the `self.up` method contains this code:

```
create_table :taggings do |t|
    t.column :tag_id, :integer
    t.column :taggable_id, :integer
    t.column :taggable_type, :string
    t.column :user_id, :integer
end

# Find objects for a tag
add_index :taggings, [:tag_id, :taggable_type]
add_index :taggings, [:user_id, :tag_id, :taggable_type]
# Find tags for an object
add_index :taggings, [:taggable_id, :taggable_type]
add_index :taggings, [:user_id, :taggable_id, :taggable_type]
```

Here you create the taggings table. The taggings table associates a tag with a taggable item and a user. For the Book Shelf application, the taggable items are books. The taggings table consists of the following columns:

- `tag_id`

  References a tag in the tags table.

- `taggable_id`

  References a tagged object. In the case of the Book Shelf application, this is a book object. So the `taggable_id` will be the ID of a book.

- `taggable_type`

  Describes the type of object that the `taggable_id` points to. For the Book Shelf application, this contains the string "Book" because the taggable items are books.

- `user_id`

  References a user stored in the users table.

In addition, an `id` column is added automatically. Four different indexes are also created on this table to provide more efficient data access.

With this implementation of tags, your application could support tagging of a variety of object types using the same tables. That is why the `taggable_id` and `taggable_type` columns are kept generic. They can store references to any type of objects that you might want to make taggable in your application.

Now that you have the migration created for the tagging implementation, go ahead and run that migration using rake.

```
rake db:migrate
```

Your database is now set up to handle tagging of books. The next step in implementing tagging is to add tagging support to the `Book` and `User` model classes. You'll do that next.

Adding tagging support to the models

Now that your database has the necessary tables to support tagging, the next step to implement tagging for the Book Shelf application is to make a minor change to the `Book` and `User` model classes. Open up the `app/models/book.rb` class and add this line near the top of the class, just beneath the `has_and_belongs_to_many` association statement:

```
acts_as_taggable
```

This causes a bunch of methods from the `acts_as_taggable_redux` plugin to be mixed into the book model. So you may be wondering how adding this single line can cause a bunch of new methods to be mixed into your book model. What are you actually doing in terms of Ruby code when you add the `acts_as_taggable` line shown here? You are calling a method with the name `acts_as_taggable`. Rails looks for a class method defined on either your `Book` model class or in `ActiveRecord::Base` with this name.

You know your book model doesn't contain this method; after all, you never wrote this method and you created the `Book` model class. `ActiveRecord::Base` does not know anything about tagging, so this method is not natively a part of that class either. The answer lies in how the `acts_as_taggable_redux` plugin works. Normally you won't have to worry about the details of how a plugin works as long as you know how to use it, but in this case, examine how the plugin works for educational purposes. Go ahead and open up the file located at `vendor/plugins/acts_as_taggable_redux/lib/acts_as_taggable.rb`. The top of the file looks like this:

```
module ActiveRecord
  module Acts #:nodoc:
    module Taggable #:nodoc:
      def self.included(base)
        base.extend(ClassMethods)
      end

      module ClassMethods
        def acts_as_taggable(options = {})

  has_many :taggings, :as => :taggable, :dependent => :destroy,
  :include => :tag
          has_many :tags, :through => :taggings

          after_save :update_tags

          extend ActiveRecord::Acts::Taggable::SingletonMethods
          include ActiveRecord::Acts::Taggable::InstanceMethods
        end
      end
```

The first line of the file re-opens the `ActiveRecord` module. This is a clue that the plugin is adding new methods into ActiveRecord. A few lines down, you see this line:

```
module ClassMethods
```

The methods contained in the block that follows are added to ActiveRecord as class methods. The first method you see is the method you are interested in, `acts_as_taggable`. Looking at this method, you see that it adds the necessary associations to the taggings and tags models. It also adds an `after_save` event filter that calls `update_tags` so that the tags are automatically updated anytime you perform a save on the book model.

So now you see how adding a single line that looks more like a declarative statement to your book model is actually calling a method that gives it the extra functionality required to support tagging. Ruby's support for calling methods without using parentheses is a big part of what makes this statement look like a declarative part of the language, as opposed to a method call. Methods such as `acts_as_taggable` become part of the DSL (domain-specific language) of Rails.

You also need to make a similar addition to the `user` model. Because you will be implementing tags that are associated to both a book and a specific user, the user needs to have a few methods mixed into it as well. Add the `acts_as_tagger` method shown below to the user model in `app/models/user.rb`, just beneath the `has_and_belongs_to_many` association statement:

```
acts_as_tagger
```

The `acts_as_tagger` method is also defined by the `acts_as_taggable_redux` plugin. This method adds the necessary associations to the user model.

That's it for the model classes. With those two simple one-line additions to the `Book` and `User` model classes, you've given them all that's necessary to support tagging. With the model support for tagging in place, the next thing you do is add tagging support to the book controller.

Adding tagging support to the controllers

Now that your model classes are set up to support tags, you need to add some logic to the book controller to handle the creation, display, and modification of tags. Open up the book controller in `app/controllers/book_controller.rb`. Add the following methods to this controller.

```
def tag_cloud_user
   @tags = session[:user].tags
end


def tag_cloud_all
   @tags = Tag.find(:all,
                    :limit => 100,
                    :order => ,taggings_count DESC').sort_
   by(&:name)
end


def show_for_tag
   @tag = params[:id]
   @books = Book.find_tagged_with(@tag)
```

```
   end

   def update_tags
      editor_id = params[:editorId]
      book_id = editor_id.split(,_')[-1]
      tags = params[:value]
      book = Book.find(book_id)
      book.user_id = session[:user]
      book.tag_list = tags
      book.save
      render :text=>tags
   end
```

Now let's walk through each of the methods that you added and understand the behavior that you've given this controller. The first two methods create tag cloud views. You've probably seen a tag cloud on a Web site before, even if you are not familiar with the term *tag cloud*. For example, Figure 8.2 shows a tag cloud that you can find on the popular photo-sharing site, flickr.com.

A tag cloud shows a view of an application's most popular tags in alphabetical or even random order, with popularity indicated by the font size of the tags. In the Flickr example, the tag "Wedding" is the most popular tag, meaning that this tag is the most often-used tag of those shown in the cloud. The Book Shelf application includes a tag cloud view of the tags that users apply to books. The book controller contains methods to create two kinds of tag clouds:

- A tag cloud representing the tags created by an individual user
- A tag cloud representing all tags created by all users

FIGURE 8.2

A tag cloud from flickr.com

So let's look at these two methods now.

```
def tag_cloud_user
  @tags = session[:user].tags
end


def tag_cloud_all
  @tags = Tag.find(:all,
                   :limit => 100,
                   :order => ,taggings_count DESC').sort_
    by(&:name)
end
```

The method `tag_cloud_user` gets the tags for the current user and stores them in a `@tags` instance variable that is available to a view. After you examine the last two methods that you added to the book controller, you'll create the tag-related views, which will use the `@tags` instance variable set by these methods.

The next method you look at is `show_for_tag`. This method is used to show all of the books that contain a particular tag.

```
def show_for_tag
  @tag = params[:id]
  @books = Book.find_tagged_with(@tag)
end
```

In this method, you set two instance variables, the `@tag` variable and the `@books` variable. The `@tag` instance variable contains the name of the tag that the user wants to display books for. This variable is set from the value of `params[:id]`. Recall from your knowledge of Rails routes that a URL like the following one is routed to the `show_for_tag` method of the book controller class, and the string "ruby" is set as the `id` parameter.

```
http://localhost/book/show_for_tag/ruby
```

A bit later, you'll see how to use this type of URL to provide links from tags to this controller method to show all of the books that contain the tag that is clicked.

The `@books` instance variable contains an array of all the books containing the passed-in tag name. The `Book.find_tagged_with` method is added to the book model as a result of adding the `acts_as_taggable` method call to it. The instance variables are used in the `show_for_tag` view template that you'll create in the next section.

The last method that you added to the book controller is the `update_tags` method. This method is called using an Ajax call to save updates that the user makes to tags for a particular book.

```
def update_tags
  editor_id = params[:editorId]
  book_id = editor_id.split('_')[-1]
```

```
      tags = params[:value]
      book = Book.find(book_id)
      book.user_id = session[:user]
      book.tag_list = tags
      book.save
      render :text=>tags
   end
```

This method expects two parameters to be passed:

- `editorId`

   The `editorId` parameter looks like this, `tag_list_5`, where `tag_list_` is a constant that is always present with this parameter, and 5 is a book ID. The book ID changes, depending on the book that tags are being edited for. This originates from the `id` attribute for a particular Ajax in-place editor field.

- `value`

   The `value` parameter contains the list of tags.

Using these parameters, the correct book model is looked up, and the book's tags are set from the tags that were passed in the `value` parameter. The taggings plugin requires the `user_id` to be set as an attribute on the book instance in order for the tag to be correctly associated with a user. That is why the `user_id` attribute is set on the book instance. The `save` method is then called on the book object to save the tag list. The list of tags is rendered back as text. This becomes the response to the Ajax call that initiated this method. When you see the views that correspond to tagging support, the use of this method will become clearer to you.

That completes all the changes necessary to the controller layer to support tagging for the Book Shelf application. In the next section, you'll add tagging support to the view layer.

Creating the view layer for tagging

There are several views that you will create that are related to tagging support.

In the sidebar, you'll create a tag cloud that shows the most popular tags, arranged alphabetically and styled according to tag popularity. Figure 8.3 shows what this tag cloud looks like in the sidebar. At the top are two tabs that are displayed only when a user is logged in. These tabs allow the user to display either those tags that were created by that user, or all tags.

FIGURE 8.3

Tags in the sidebar

On any page that displays a book list, such as the user home page, the tags associated with a book are displayed along with other book details in the book list view. This is also where you can edit the tags associated with a book. Clicking the tags creates an in-place editor that is used to type in tags. Figure 8.4 shows an example of a book listing showing tags. If you click the tags, you get the in-place tag editor view, shown in Figure 8.5.

FIGURE 8.4

Showing tags

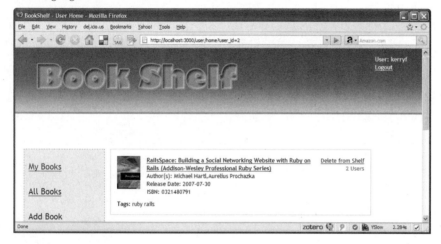

FIGURE 8.5

Editing tags

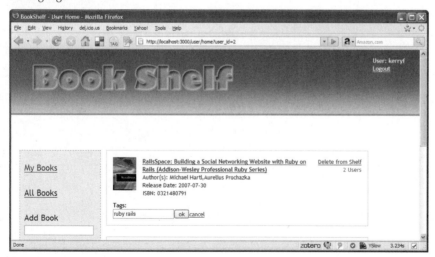

The last view related to tagging that you will create is the view that allows a user to see all of the books that have been tagged with a given tag. This is the view that renders in response to the `show_for_tag` controller action.

Implementing the sidebar tag cloud view

Let's get started with implementing the tag cloud view shown in the left sidebar of the application. The sidebar view is defined in a partial contained in the `app/views/shared` folder named `_sidebar.html.erb`. Currently, this file should look like that shown in Listing 8.2.

LISTING 8.2

_sidebar.html.erb

```
<div id="sidebar">
    <div id="Menu">
        <ul id="user_nav_menu">
            <% if logged_in %>
                <li><%= link_to 'My Books', :controller=>'user',
                                            :action=>'home',
                                            :user_id=>session[:user]
    %></li>
                <li><%= link_to 'All Books', :controller=>'book',
                                             :action=>'list' %></li>
                <li>

    <% form_tag ({:controller=> «book», :action=> «search»}) do %>
                    <input type=»hidden» name=»page» value=»1» />
                    <span id=»add_book_title»>Add Book</span>
                    <%= text_field_tag «book_keyword» %>
                    <%= submit_tag «Search», :id=>'search_button' %>
                <% end %>
                </li>
            <% else %>
                <ul id=»home_menu»>
                    <li><%= link_to 'Join Now', :controller=>'user',
                                                :action=>'signup' %></
    li>
                    <li><%= link_to 'View the Books',
    :controller=>'book',

    :action=>'list' %></li>
                </ul>
            <% end %>
        </ul>
    </div>
    <div style=»clear:both;»> </div>
</div>
```

You could add the necessary HTML and ERb code for the tag cloud directly into this file; however, this is a good opportunity to break this sidebar partial into a few additional partial files that will improve the organization, maintainability, and readability of the code. Before you add the tag cloud, let's refactor the existing sidebar partial a bit.

Create a new partial in the app/views/shared directory and call it _nav_menu.html.erb. This partial contains all of the code related to the navigation menu.

Copy the block of code shown in Listing 8.3 from the sidebar partial and put it into the new _nav_menu.html.erb file:

LISTING 8.3

_nav_menu.html.erb addition

```erb
<div id="Menu">
    <ul id="user_nav_menu">
        <% if logged_in %>
            <li><%= link_to 'My Books', :controller=>'user',
                                        :action=>'home',
                                        :user_id=>session[:user] %></li>
            <li><%= link_to 'All Books', :controller=>'book',
                                         :action=>'list' %></li>
            <li>
                <% form_tag ({:controller=> "book", :action=> "search"})
    do %>
                    <input type="hidden" name="page" value="1" />
                    <span id="add_book_title">Add Book</span>
                    <%= text_field_tag "book_keyword" %>
                    <%= submit_tag "Search", :id=>'search_button' %>
                <% end %>
            </li>
        <% else %>
            <ul id="home_menu">
                <li><%= link_to 'Join Now', :controller=>'user',
                                            :action=>'signup' %></li>
                <li><%= link_to 'View the Books', :controller=>'book',
                                                  :action=>'list' %></li>
            </ul>
        <% end %>
    </ul>
</div>
```

Now where you copied this from the _sidebar.html.erb file, replace this block of code with a call to the new partial like this:

```
<%= render :partial=>"shared/nav_menu" %>
```

Now your _sidebar.rhtml file is much more compact. It should look like this:

```
<div id="sidebar">
    <%= render :partial=>"shared/nav_menu" %>
    <div style="clear:both;"> </div>
</div>
```

With the details of the navigation menu removed from the sidebar partial, it is easy to see at a glance exactly what is contained in the sidebar. Right now it contains only the navigation menu. You'll implement the tag cloud in another partial, so go ahead and add a call to a new partial for the tag cloud just as you did for the navigation menu. With the call to the tag cloud partial, the sidebar looks like this:

```
<div id="sidebar">
    <%= render :partial=>"shared/nav_menu" %>
    <%= render :partial=>"shared/tag_cloud" %>
    <div style="clear:both;"> </div>
</div>
```

Now you can create the tag cloud partial in the file app/views/shared/_tag_cloud.html. erb. Edit it so that it contains this code:

```
<% if logged_in %>
  <%= link_to_remote 'My Tags',
      {:url   =>  {:controller => 'book', :action => 'tag_cloud_
  user'}} ,
      :class => "tag_cloud_title_current",
      :id => "my_tags_link" %>

  <%= link_to_remote 'All Tags',
      {:url   =>  {:controller => 'book', :action => 'tag_cloud_
  all'}} ,
      :class  => 'tag_cloud_title',
      :id => "all_tags_link" %>
<% end %>

<div id="cloud_view"><%= tag_cloud_revised %></div>
```

The block of code that is wrapped in the check to see whether a user is logged in, displays the tabs allowing the user to display tags specific to the logged-in user, or all of the tags in the application. Refer back to Figure 8.3 to see an example of these tabs.

Each tab is implemented as a link using the Rails helper method, `link_to_remote`. The `link_to_remote` helper method creates a link that executes an Ajax call back to the server when clicked. If the user clicks the My Tags link, the `tag_cloud_user` method of the book controller is sent the Ajax request. If the user clicks the All Tags link, the `tag_cloud_all` method of the book controller gets the Ajax request. You wrote both of these controller methods in the previous section. Each of the links is also given `class` and `id` attributes to assist with styling them to look like tabs. The two relevant controller methods are shown again here:

```
def tag_cloud_user
    @tags = User.find(session[:user]).tags
end


def tag_cloud_all
    @tags = Tag.find(:all,
                     :limit => 100,
                     :order => 'taggings_count DESC').sort_
    by(&:name)
End
```

These methods each just set an instance variable containing an array of either the tags associated with the logged-in user, or the first 100 tags contained in the application, sorted alphabetically.

Instead of rendering a view template like you usually do after a controller action, this time you use an RJS template to accomplish the update of the tag cloud with the new set of tags. Create two new RJS templates in the `app/views/book` directory and call them `tag_cloud_user.rjs` and `tag_cloud_all.rjs`. Because these RJS templates are named the same as the controller methods, they are called automatically after the controller methods execute. Remember that if no template is explicitly rendered by an action method, Rails looks for a view template with the same name as the action method. If a view template cannot be found, Rails looks for an RJS method with the same name as the action method.

The contents of the two new RJS templates are shown in Listings 8.4 and 8.5.

LISTING 8.4

tag_cloud_user.rjs

```
page[:cloud_view].replace_html tag_cloud_revised(@tags)

page[:all_tags_link].remove_class_name :tag_cloud_title_current
page[:all_tags_link].add_class_name :tag_cloud_title

page[:my_tags_link].remove_class_name :tag_cloud_title
page[:my_tags_link].add_class_name :tag_cloud_title_current
```

LISTING 8.5

tag_cloud_all.rjs

```
page[:cloud_view].replace_html tag_cloud_revised(@tags)

page[:my_tags_link].remove_class_name :tag_cloud_title_current
page[:my_tags_link].add_class_name :tag_cloud_title

page[:all_tags_link].remove_class_name :tag_cloud_title
page[:all_tags_link].add_class_name :tag_cloud_title_current
```

The first line of both of these templates is identical. The tag cloud is replaced with a new tag cloud generated using the `tag_cloud_revised` helper method and the set of tags that was created by the controller method called. This either contains the tags associated with the logged-in user, or all the tags, depending on the link that was clicked. I'll discuss the `tag_cloud_ revised` helper method in just a bit.

The last four statements of each of the templates changes the CSS class name that is associated with the `all_tags_link` and the `my_tags_link` links.

After the block inside the logged-in check, in the tag cloud partial, there is a call to the `tag_ cloud_ revised` helper method.

```
<div id="cloud_view"><%= tag_cloud_ revised %></div>
```

This line is where the actual tag cloud is created and displayed. The `tag_cloud_ revised` method is a helper method that is a slightly modified form of a `tag_cloud` helper method that is a part of the `acts_as_taggable_redux` plugin

Implement tag_cloud_revised helper method

In both of the RJS templates that you just completed and in the `_tag_cloud.html.erb` partial, you used a helper method named `tag_cloud_revised`. This is a helper method that is responsible for displaying the tag cloud. This method is a modified version of the method `tag_cloud` that is a part of the `acts_as_taggable_redux` plugin.

Let's have a look at the `tag_cloud` method. You will find the method in the file `vendor/plugins/acts_as_taggable_redux/lib/acts_as_taggable_helper.rb`. The method is shown in Listing 8.6.

LISTING 8.6

tag_cloud

```
def tag_cloud(options = {})
    # TODO: add options to specify different limits and sorts
    tags = Tag.find(:all,
                    :limit => 100,
                    :order => 'taggings_count DESC').sort_by(&:name)


    classes = %w(popular v-popular vv-popular vvv-popular vvvv-popular)

    max, min = 0, 0
    tags.each do |tag|
        max = tag.taggings_count if tag.taggings_count > max
        min = tag.taggings_count if tag.taggings_count < min
    end

    divisor = ((max - min) / classes.size) + 1

    html =    %(<div class="hTagcloud">\n)
    html <<   %(  <ul class="popularity">\n)
    tags.each do |tag|
        html << %(    <li>)
        html << link_to(tag.name,
                        tag_url(tag),
                        :class => classes[(tag.taggings_count - min) /
    divisor])
        html << %(</li> \n)
    end
    html <<   %(  </ul>\n)
    html <<   %(</div>\n)
end
```

The problem with this method is that it reads the tags itself and always reads in the first 100 tags sorted alphabetically. There is no way to pass in a set of tags, which you need to do in order to implement the user tags cloud. To meet the Book Shelf requirements, you should be able to pass an array of tags into this helper method and have it build the tag cloud with the tags that are passed in. Rather than change this existing method, I've opted to create a new method and give it the name tag_cloud_revised.

The new method is shown in Listing 8.7. Be sure to add this to the acts_as_taggable_helper.rb file.

LISTING 8.7

tag_cloud_revised

```
def tag_cloud_revised(tags = nil)
    if !tags
        tags = Tag.find(:all,
                        :limit => 100,
                        :order => 'taggings_count DESC').sort_by(&:name)
    end

    classes = %w(popular v-popular vv-popular vvv-popular vvvv-popular)

    max, min = 0, 0
    tags.each do |tag|
        max = tag.taggings_count if tag.taggings_count > max
        min = tag.taggings_count if tag.taggings_count < min
    end

    divisor = ((max - min) / classes.size) + 1

    html =    %(<div class="hTagcloud">\n)
    html <<   %(  <ul class="popularity">\n)
    tags.each do |tag|
        html << %(    <li>)
        html << link_to(tag.name,
                        '/book/show_for_tag/'+tag.name,
                        :class => classes[(tag.taggings_count - min) /
    divisor])
        html << %( </li> \n)
    end

    html <<   %(  </ul>\n)
    html <<   %(</div>\n)
end
```

The new method allows you to pass the array of tags into it. Alternatively, if you do not pass tags into it, it behaves the same as the original tag_cloud method. You may have noticed that the options parameter is omitted from the tag_cloud_revised method. That is okay as this parameter was not used at all by the original tag_cloud method either.

As indicated in the comments preceding the tag_cloud_view method, the method is inspired by this blog post: www.juixe.com/techknow/index.php/2006/07/15/acts-as-taggable-tag-cloud/.

You will make two additional small changes to the `tag_cloud_revised` method. You want the method to display each tag as a link to a page that shows all of the books that have been tagged with that specific tag. The original method uses the method `tag_url` as the URL connected to the link. You should change that to the following:

```
'/book/show_for_tag/'+tag.name
```

You will see the change in Listing 8.7. This will call the `show_for_tag` action of the book controller to display the books that are tagged with that tag word being clicked on. The tag's name is passed as a parameter.

The last change you will make is to add a non-breaking space character after each tag that is displayed. Without the space being explicitly added, the tags will be blended together without spaces. You can see the ` ` added just before the closing `</li>` in the `tag_cloud_revised` method.

Generate the tagging style sheet

At this point, you have nearly finished the tagging implementation for displaying tags in the sidebar. However, you need a bit of CSS styling to pretty things up a bit so that your tag cloud actually looks like a tag cloud. The `acts_as_taggable_redux` plugin provides you with a generator that you use to create a style sheet that is used to style the tag cloud that will be displayed. From the Book Shelf root directory, use rake to run this command:

```
rake acts_as_taggable:stylesheet:create
```

This creates `acts_as_taggable_stylesheet.css` in the `public/stylesheets` directory. This file contains the basic styles for the tag cloud. Next, you have to add a link to this style sheet to the layout template. Open up `app/views/layouts/application.html.erb` and add this link into the head section:

```
<%= stylesheet_link_tag 'acts_as_taggable_stylesheet' %>
```

Now, you just need to add a few more styles to the application style sheet. Add these style definitions to `public/stylesheets/style.css` (see Listing 8.8).

This completes the implementation for the tag cloud view; however, before you can test it, you need to complete the rest of the tagging implementation in the next section so that users have a way of creating tags.

LISTING 8.8

public/stylesheets/style.css Addition

```
.tag_cloud_title, .tag_cloud_title_current {
  float: left;
  display: block;
```

```
  background-color: #f98919;
  color: white;
  line-height: 2em;
  margin-bottom: 15px;
  padding-left: 5px;
  width: 40%;
  border-right: thin solid black;
  border-left: thin solid black;
}

.tag_cloud_title:hover {
  background-color: black;
  font-weight: bold;
}

.tag_cloud_title_current {
  background-color: green;
  font-weight: bold;
}
```

Implement the static tag view

Now that you have the tag cloud view complete, you need a way of getting tags into the application. To accomplish this, you add a display of the tags to the book listing view. This is also where a user can edit tags for a book. Refer back to Figures 8.4 and 8.5 for views of how this looks.

In previous sections, you implemented the necessary logic in the models and controllers layer. All you have to do to finish the work is to modify the view layer. The list of books is displayed using the _list_books.html.erb partial. This partial uses the _book_detail.html.erb partial to display information for each book. In order to display tags for a book, you modify the _book_detail.html.erb partial to include a display of the tags. Go ahead and open up app/views/book/_book_detail.html.erb. Listing 8.9 shows what the code should look like, with the new code appearing in bold.

LISTING 8.9

_book_detail.html.erb

```
<div class="book_image"><img src="<%= book.image_url_small %>" /></div>
<div class="book_info">
    <span class="book_name">
        <% if book.exists %>
            <%= link_to book.title, { :controller => "book",
                                       :action => "show",
                                       :id => book.id } %>
        <% else %>
```

continued

311

LISTING 8.9 *(continued)*

```erb
            <%= book.title %>
        <% end %>
    </span><br/>
    Author(s): <%= book.author %><br/>
    Release Date: <%= book.release_date %><br/>
    ISBN: <%= book.isbn %>
</div>
<% if search %>
    <div class="add_control" id="add_control_<%= book.isbn %>">
        <% if !book.exists %>
            <%= link_to_remote "Add to Shelf",
                                :update => 'add_control_' + book.isbn,
                                :url    => { :controller => 'book',
                                             :action => 'add',
                                             :isbn => book.isbn } %><br/>
            <div id="shelf_status_<%= book.isbn %>"></div>
        <% else %>

    <%= render :partial=>'book_exists', :locals => { :book => book } %>
        <% end %>
    </div>
<% else %>
    <div class="add_control">
        <% if session[:user] %>
            <%= link_to_remote "Delete from Shelf",
                                :update => 'shelf_status_' + book.isbn,
                                :url    => { :controller => 'book',
                                             :action => 'delete',
                                             :isbn => book.isbn } %>
        <% end %>
        <div id="shelf_status_<%= book.isbn %>">
            <span class="users_count"><%= book.users.size %> Users</span>
        </div>
    </div>

    <div class="tags">
        <span class="tags_title">Tags:</span>
        <% if book.tag_list.length > 0 %>
            <span class="tag_list" id="tag_list_<%= book.id %>">
                <%= book.tag_list %>
            </span>
        <% else %>
            <span class="empty_tag_list" id="tag_list_<%= book.id %>">
                (Click to add tags)
            </span>
        <% end %>
    </div>
<% end %>
```

The acts_as_taggable_redux plugin adds a tag_list instance method to the book model. The tag_list method returns an array of tags associated with the book model on which it is called. If a tag has spaces in it, that tag is wrapped in double quotes. The line <%= book.tag_list %> outputs the tags, separated by a space. If the tag list is empty, a message appears, telling the user to click it to add tags.

Make the tags editable

The list view now contains a static display of the tags associated with a book. With some help from the JavaScript libraries, Prototype and Scriptaculous, you can make the tag field editable when it's clicked. Currently, the book list view contains a static list of the tags contained within a span tag. Because a list typically contains multiple books, there are multiple instances of these span tags on the page. Each is given a unique id attribute by appending the book ID to the string "tag_list_". Now open up the app/views/book/_list_books.html.erb file and add this code to the bottom of the file.

```
<% if logged_in %>
  <script>
      document.observe('dom:loaded', function() {
         <% books.each do |book| %>

  new Ajax.InPlaceEditor('tag_list_<%= book.id %>',            '/
book/update_tags?authenticity_token=<%= form_authenticity_token() %>');
         <% end %>
      });
  </script>
<% end %>
```

This code inserts a chunk of JavaScript into the view. The function document.observe is a Prototype function that allows you to specify a function to be run in response to an event. In this case, the event being watched for is dom:loaded. This event fires immediately after the HTML document is fully loaded. So when the page is completely loaded, this code is run:

```
<% books.each do |book| %>
   new Ajax.InPlaceEditor('tag_list_<%= book.id %>',
        '/book/update_tags?authenticity_token=<%=
   form_authenticity_token() %>');
<% end %>
```

This code uses the Ajax.InPlaceEditor method, which is provided by Scriptaculous to create in-place editors for each of the books displayed on the list page. This method takes two parameters. The first parameter is the id of an element that you want to make an in-place editor of. The second parameter is a URL to which changed values are submitted.

Notice that you have to add an authenticity_token to the URL. This was added to Rails after version 2.0. This is security mechanism that is normally done for you automatically when you use the Rails form helper methods. Here you use the form_authenticity_token method to generate the required token value.

Implement the show_for_tag view

When the user clicks on a tag in the tag cloud, a page should be shown that displays all of the books that also have been tagged with that tag. You have already implemented the show_for_tag action in the book controller. Now create the view in app/views/book/show_for_tag.html.erb. For this view, enter the code shown below:

```
<span class="info_title">Books with tag <span class="tag">
<%= @tag %></span></span><br/><br/>
<%= render :partial=>'list_books', :locals=>{:books=>@books} %>
```

This view reuses the list_books partial that you created for the main book list page to display the books associated with the selected tag.

Using tags

The Book Shelf application now has a complete implementation of content tagging. Users can add tags to any book on their shelf and update those tags at any time. A tag cloud also appears in the left sidebar, giving the user an overview of tags currently in use and providing an easy way for the user to find books by tag.

Make sure that your server is running. If it is not, start it from the Book Shelf home directory using the familiar ruby script/server command. Once the server has started, navigate to your application by going to http://localhost:3000 in your browser. Once you have a few books on your shelf, go ahead and add some tags and verify that the tagging behavior is working correctly.

Implementing Book Reviews

Reviewing a book is a common way of sharing information about a book. In the Book Shelf application, users are able to view book reviews on the detail page for any book. If a user is logged in to the application, he can also create a review for any book that he is viewing. Figure 8.6 displays a view of the book detail page showing a book that has one review.

The implementation of book reviews consists of implementing the following pieces:

- Review model
- Review controller
- Review view

In the last section, when you implemented tagging, you started out by implementing the necessary model changes, followed by adding controller methods, and then creating the required view and RJS templates. To show that you don't always have to develop your code in that order, I'll do things a little differently in this section.

You should generally start by implementing the model layer, so I'll keep that step the same, but after the model, I'll implement the view layer. Then when you move to the controller layer, you'll know what methods the view layer requires.

FIGURE 8.6

A book detail page with a review

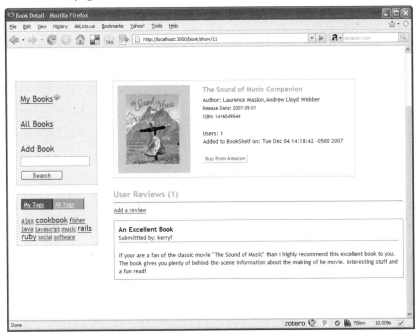

Implementing the review model

Book reviews are modeled with their own class. Use the Rails generator to create a Review model:

```
ruby script/generate model Review
```

Along with some testing files, this creates the `Review` model class for you in `app/models/ review.rb` and a migration that you will use to create the `reviews` table in `db/migrate/ 005_create_reviews.rb`.

As you've done in the past, you should start by identifying the columns that you'll want to create for the Review class. Those are identified in Table 8.1. A review is associated with both a user and a book, so you see the review model includes columns to identify the user and book. The other fields should be self-explanatory.

Now go ahead and create the migration to implement this design. Edit the file `db/ migrate/005_create_reviews.rb` so that it looks like the following:

```
class CreateReviews < ActiveRecord::Migration
    def self.up
        create_table :reviews do |t|
```

```
                    t.references :user
                    t.references :book
                    t.text :body
                    t.string :title
                    t.timestamps
                end
            end

            def self.down
                drop_table :reviews
            end
        end
```

TABLE 8.1

Review model

Field Name	Description	Data Type
user_id	ID of the user reviewing the book	integer
book_id	ID of the book being reviewed	integer
body	The body of the review	text
title	The title of the review	string
created_at	Date and time the review was created	datetime
updated_at	Date and time the review is updated	datetime

Once you have the migration completed, run it using the db:migrate command:

```
rake db:migrate
```

This will create the reviews table for you. Now you are ready to edit the Review class. Open up that class and edit it to contain the code shown in Listing 8.10.

LISTING 8.10

The review model

```
class Review < ActiveRecord::Base

    belongs_to :user
    belongs_to :book

    validates_presence_of :body, :title, :user_id, :book_id

end
```

You can see that this is a very simple model implementation. Most of its behavior comes from the fact that it extends `ActiveRecord::Base`. Each review that is created is associated with a single user and a single book. However, a user can create many reviews and thus is associated with zero or more reviews.

Also, many reviews can be written for each book. Therefore, reviews have a one-to-many relationship with both users and books. This relationship is modeled using the `ActiveRecord` method `belongs_to` in the `Review` model class. In a minute, you'll add the other side of these associations to the `User` and `Book` model classes.

When a user creates a book review, it is also a good idea to make sure that it contains a body and a title. In order for the associations to work correctly, a review also must have a `user_id` and a `book_id` set. A validator is added to the `Review` model to ensure the presence of these fields:

```
validates_presence_of :body, :title, :user_id, :book_id
```

Adding associations to the book and user models

Previously, you created one side of a one-to-many relationship between reviews and a book, and between reviews and a user. Now you need to add a line of code to each of the `User` and `Book` model classes to complete that association. Edit both the `app/models/user.rb` class and the `app/models/book.rb` class, and add the following line inside the class definition beneath the `has_and_belongs_to` association that you added to each of these classes in the last chapter:

```
has_many :reviews
```

Adding this method completes the association between reviews and users and reviews and books. A user's reviews are now accessible through the user model, and a book's reviews are accessible through the book model.

That's all of the model layer code that is required for implementation of book reviews. Next, you'll implement the view layer to support display and entry of book reviews.

Implementing the review view

There are several view pieces that you have to implement to support book reviews. These different view pieces are as follows:

- Static display of a book's reviews on the book detail page
- The book review entry form for adding new reviews

To implement these views in a user-friendly way, I'll use a bit of Ajax and some nifty helpers provided by Prototype and Scriptaculous.

Displaying reviews for a book

The book detail page shows the reviews for the book being displayed. This page is also where users can add new reviews if they are logged into the application. Initially, a book has no reviews and the reviews section of the display looks like that shown in Figure 8.7. The count of how many reviews exist for the book is in parentheses after the section title User Reviews. Because no reviews have been created yet for this book, it shows a value of zero.

Also notice that there is a link below, which says, "Be the first to review this book." This link is what a user clicks if they want to write a review for the book. Note that the link only appears if the user viewing the book is logged into the application.

If a book does have one or more reviews, those are displayed after the User Reviews heading, as shown in Figure 8.8.

Notice that the text on the link to add a new review is changed from "Be the first to review this book" to "Add a review." Also notice that the count of reviews in parentheses shows the value 1, indicating that there is one review for this book.

FIGURE 8.7

A book detail with no reviews

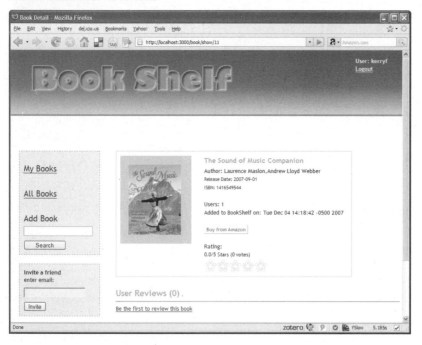

A book detail with a review

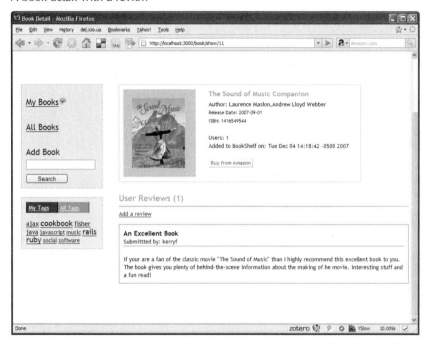

Finally, the review itself is shown with the title in bold, followed by the login name of the reviewer, and the date on which the review was submitted. The body of the review is the final piece of the review shown. Once a review is submitted, there is no way to edit the review. That is a feature briefly discussed in the final section of this chapter, but ultimately left to the reader to implement.

Okay, so now that you've seen what the views should look like, let's get started with what you need to do to implement those views. Your application already has a page that shows details for a single book when a user clicks the title of the book from the book-listing screen. This is the same page where the reviews are included.

Open up the template for that page, `app/views/book/show.html.erb`, and edit it to display book reviews by adding the content shown in bold in Listing 8.11.

The code that you added designates the work of showing the book reviews to a partial named `book_reviews`. Following the Rails standard of adding an underscore to the name, this is stored in `app/views/book/_book_reviews.html.erb`.

Go ahead and create that file now, and edit it to contain the content shown in Listing 8.12. This is a fairly large partial that implements the following pieces of the review display:

- It provides some header text with a reviews label and a count of the number of reviews that exist for the current book.

- It provides a link that a user can click to display the review entry form.

- It includes a partial to display the review entry form.

- It displays each of the reviews that exist for the current book.

LISTING 8.11

show.html.erb Template

```
<div id="book_view">
    <div id="book_view_upper">
        <div id="book_image">
            <%= image_tag @book.image_url_medium %>
        </div>
        <div id="book_summary">
            <span class="book_title"><%= @book.title %></span>
            Author: <%= @book.author %><br/>
            <div id="book_details">
                Release Date: <%= @book.release_date %><br/>
                ISBN: <%= @book.isbn %><br/><br/>
            </div>
            Users: <%= @book.users.size %><br/>
            Added to BookShelf on: <%= @book.created_at %><br/><br/>
            <%= link_to „Buy from Amazon", @book.amazon_url,
                :class=>"action_button" %><br/><br/>
        </div>
    </div>
    <div id="reviews_content">
        <%= render :partial=>'book_reviews', :locals => { :book => @book
    } %>
    </div>
    <div style="clear:both;"> </div>
</div>
```

Near the top of the partial is a span element that displays the User Reviews section title, along with a count of the reviews that are associated with the current book. Remember that books have a one-to-many relationship with reviews. In the previous section, you modeled this relationship by adding the has_many method to the book model. This makes the reviews associated with a given book available as an array instance attribute on the book model.

```
<span class="reviews_title">User Reviews (<%= book.reviews.size
    %>)</span>
```

LISTING 8.12

_book_reviews.html.erb partial

```erb
<div id="book_reviews">

    <span class="reviews_title">User Reviews (<%= book.reviews.size %>)</
    span>
    <hr/>
    <% if logged_in %>
        <div id="add_review">
            <% if book.reviews.size == 0 %>
                <% add_review_text="Be the first to review this book" %>
            <% else %>
                <% add_review_text="Add a review" %>
            <% end %>
            <span class="reviews_add">
                <%= link_to_function add_review_text, "show_add_review_
    form()" %>
            </span>
        </div>
        <div id="cancel_add_review" style="display:none;">
            <%= link_to_function "Cancel Review", "show_add_review_
    form()" %>
        </div>
        <div id="add_review_form" style="display:none;">
            <%= render :partial=>"review/add_review_form",
                        :locals => { :book => book } %>
        </div>
    <% end %>
    <div id="reviews">
        <% book.reviews.each do |review| %>
            <div class="review">
                <div class="review_header">
                    <span class="review_title"><%= review.title %></
    span>
                    <span class="review_user">
                        Submitted by: <%= review.user.login %>
                    </span>
                    <span class="review_date">
                        Submitted at: <%= review.created_at %>
                    </span>
                </div>
                <span class="review_body"><%= review.body %></span>
            </div>
        <% end %>
    </div>
    <div style="clear:both"> </div>
</div>
```

The links to add a new review and the review entry form that would become visible when clicking the link are only displayed if the user is logged in. If the user is logged in, the template sets a variable with the contents of a message that becomes the text of a link in order to display the add review form. The `link_to_function` helper method is then called to create a link to a JavaScript function.

```
<%= link_to_function add_review_text, "show_add_review_form()" %>
```

When the user clicks this link, the JavaScript function `show_add_review_form` is called. You have to create the `show_add_review_form` function. This function should cause the `add_review_form`, which is initially hidden by setting a `display:none` style on it, to show up. This is a good point for you to go ahead and implement that JavaScript function so that you don't forget it later. Open up the `public/javascripts/application.js` file, which is where you should put all of your application-specific JavaScript methods. The method that you need to create is shown here:

```
function show_add_review_form() {
    if ($('add_review_form').getStyle('display') == 'none') {
        Effect.BlindDown('add_review_form');
    }
    else {
        Effect.BlindUp('add_review_form');
    }
    Element.toggle('add_review');
    Element.toggle('cancel_add_review');
}
```

This method actually serves two purposes: It is used to show the add review form if the user clicks the add review link. It is also used to hide the add review form if the user clicks the cancel link while adding a review. The interesting pieces of this method are the use of `Effect.BlindDown`, `Effect.BlindUp`, and `Element.toggle`.

The first two methods, `Effect.BlindDown` and `Effect.BlindUp`, are provided by the Scriptaculous toolkit. These methods produce a distinct style of showing and hiding the contents of the add review form. The form gradually appears or disappears through an effect that makes the form appear to slide upward or downward, similar to the way a window blind is raised and lowered.

The method `Element.toggle` is implemented by the Prototype toolkit. This method is used to toggle the display state of the element whose `id` attribute is passed to it. In this example, the method is used twice to toggle the display state of the add review link and the cancel link. These two links are toggled in opposite directions. If the add review link is displayed, the cancel link is hidden, and vice versa.

Now turning your attention back to the `_book_reviews.html.erb` partial, you see that the add review form is rendered using another partial that you'll create in a bit. First, look at the final piece of this partial. The contents of the bottom `div` element with the ID of 'reviews' displays each of the reviews that exist for the current book. The code to display the reviews is fairly straightforward and should be easy for you to understand. The reviews for the current book are accessed using the `reviews` attribute of the book model. For each review, the review title, the review's user, the date on which it was created, and the body of the review are displayed.

Implementing the review entry form

Now implement the partial that creates the add review entry form. Because this partial is very specific to a review, you should create the partial in the `app/views/review` directory. This directory does not yet exist, so first you'll have to create the `review` directory under the `app/views` directory. Next, create the partial with the name `_add_review_form.html.erb`.

The add review entry form should allow the user to enter a title and a body for the review. At the bottom, the form should have a button that allows the user to submit the review. The form looks like what you see in Figure 8.9.

FIGURE 8.9

The review entry form

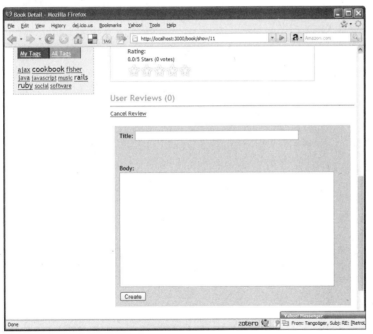

Listing 8.13 shows the code that you should enter for this partial.

LISTING 8.13
_____

_add_review_form.html.erb partial

```
<% remote_form_for :review, @review,
                   :url => { :controller => "review",
                             :action => "create" } do |f| %>
    <%= f.hidden_field(:book_id, :value=>book.id) %>
    <label>Title:</label>
    <%= f.text_field(:title, :size=>60) %><br/><br/>
    <br/><br/>
    <label>Body:</label><br/>
    <%= f.text_area(:body, :cols => 60, :rows => 15) %><br/>
    <%= submit_tag 'Create', :id=>"review_submit_btn" %>  
<% end %>
```

This code uses Rails helpers to create an HTML form that is submitted as an Ajax request to the `create` method of the review controller. The `remote_form_for` helper method is used to create the form. This helper method uses Prototype functions to create the Ajax code that submits the contents of the form as a POST request.

This completes the implementation of the view templates for now. This is a good time to implement the review controller that is called by the add review form submission. After implementing the review controller, you'll actually implement one more template, which will be an RJS template to handle the response from the form submission.

Implementing the review controller

The review controller is fairly straightforward to implement. The first thing you should do, however, is generate the controller using the following command:

```
ruby script/generate controller Review
```

Now go ahead and open up the `app/controllers/review_controller.rb` file and add the `create` method, as shown in Listing 8.14.

LISTING 8.14

ReviewController

```
class ReviewController < ApplicationController

    def create
        @review = Review.new(params[:review])
        @review.user = User.find(session[:user])
        if !@review.save
            # render error message using RJS
        end
        @book = Book.find(@review.book_id)
    end

end
```

The `create` method instantiates an instance variable, `@review`, which is populated with the contents of the review form. Because the review form does not include anything about the user and yet you know that a review is associated with a specific user, the next line sets the currently logged-in user as the `user` attribute for the `@review` instance.

The `@review` instance is saved, and if the save is not successful, a bit of RJS is rendered back to the add review form page to display an error message. If the `@review` is saved successfully, an instance variable is created, holding the book that the review is associated with. This allows the RJS template that is rendered back to the page to rebuild the reviews listing for the current book.

Now create a file to hold the RJS template in `app/views/review/create.rjs`. Because the template is given the same name as the controller method, it is rendered by default by the `create` method. Listing 8.15 shows what this template should look like.

The template replaces the content of the `reviews_content` `div` with the book reviews partial. This is the same partial that was originally rendered into that `div` when the page was first loaded, and so you are essentially just refreshing the book reviews content. This causes the newly created book review to appear and the add review form to be hidden again, thus resetting the page back to how it looks when the page is first loaded.

LISTING 8.15

create.rjs

```
page[:reviews_content].replace_html  render :partial=>'book/book_reviews',
                                              :locals => { :book => @book }
```

Adding some style

The last thing you need to do to wrap up the implementation of book reviews is to add some more styles to your style sheet. Open up `public/stylesheets/style.css` and add the new style definitions as shown in Listing 8.16.

LISTING 8.16

public/stylesheets/style.css Addition

```
#book_reviews {
    float: left;
    clear: both;
    margin-top: 25px;
    width: 100%;
}

.reviews_title {
    font-weight: bold;
    font-size: 14pt;
    color: #f98919;
}

#review_field {
    width: 200px;
}

.review {
    margin-top: 15px;
    border: solid thin gray;
    padding: 10px;
}

.review_header {
    display: block;
    border-bottom: solid thin gray;
    line-height: 1.5em;
}

.review_title {
    font-weight: bold;
    font-size: 1.2em;
}

.review_user {
    display: block;
}

.review_date {
```

```
        display: block;
}

.review_body {
    display: block;
    margin-top: 20px;
}

#add_review_form {
    margin: 10px;
    margin-top: 20px;
    margin-bottom: 40px;
    border: solid thin #cccccc;
    padding: 10px;
    background-color: #ffcc99;
}

#add_review_form label {
    font-weight: bold;
}

#review_submit_btn {
    margin-top: 10px;
}
```

Adding a book review

You have now completed the implementation of book reviews. It's time to try out everything you've done in the past few sections to make sure that the reviews work as expected. Make sure that your server is still running, or restart it again using `ruby script/server`.

Log in to the application and click the title of a book that you have added to your shelf. You should be taken to the book detail page, similar to what you see in Figure 8.7. The book has no reviews because you have not created any reviews yet. Click the `Be the first to review this book` link to create your first review. You should see the book review form drop down into view. Go ahead and fill out the form to create your review. When you are finished, click the Create button and you should see the reviews section reload, now showing the review that you just created. The view should look similar to Figure 8.8.

Here is an important point to remember: Any book can be added by more than one user to their shelves. Each time a book is added to another user's shelf, another row is added to the `books_users` table, but there is not another book record created.

Reviews are associated with the book record. So this means that any reviews that are created for a given book are shown anytime that book's detail page is shown, regardless of which user's shelf you are requesting it from. This is exactly the behavior that you want. Any reviews that I add for a book on my shelf become visible to all other users who have also added that book to their shelf.

Implementing Book Ratings

So far in this chapter, you've implemented tagging for books and book reviews. These are both popular features of social networking sites. In this section, I will provide you with an overview of how you might add another popular feature of social networking sites, ratings. Ratings allow a user to associate a simple number rating to a book. Adding a ratings system to the Book Shelf application would be a nice addition to the reviews functionality. If you've ever looked up a book on Amazon, you have probably seen the reviews and ratings system that Amazon uses. By adding a ratings feature, you can have similar functionality in Book Shelf.

There is an excellent Rails plugin available (`acts_as_rateable`) that will make implementing the ratings feature not such a difficult task. You can find more information about this plugin and download it from `http://rateableplugin.rubyforge.org/`.

The plugin will provide you with the server-side functionality to support ratings, but does not provide you will a fancy user interface for setting and viewing ratings. The most common way of allowing users to set and view ratings is through a display of stars. There is a helpful blog post available about how to implement such a system that uses the `acts_as_rateable` plugin. The blog post is available at `http://blog.aisleten.com/2007/05/03/ajax-css-star-rating-with-acts_as_rateable/`.

The approach described in that post uses Ajax, CSS, and a few images to achieve the star display of the ratings. The blog post contains step-by-step instructions for implementing the ratings feature.

A nice thing about a Rails application is that you tend to follow the same process over and over again as you add additional features to your application. To implement the ratings feature, you follow steps very similar to the steps you went through to implement tagging and reviews. To get you started on the ratings task, below is an outline of the required steps to completely implement the functionality.

- Install the `acts_as_rateable` plugin.
- Create a migration to add database support for ratings.
- Make modifications to the book model to support ratings.
- Create the ratings controller.
- Create a ratings view partial.
- Add some CSS to make it all look good.

You'll find that these are the same steps and even the same sequence of steps that is outlined in the blog post referred to previously.

Extending the Application

Over the last three chapters, you've created an application that can be very useful as is. However, there are also a great number of ways in which you could extend the application to make it even more valuable to users. In this section, you'll get an overview with some brief comments about a few enhancements that you could make to the application.

Below is a summary of the enhancements that will be discussed:

- User interface improvements
- Providing an administrator interface
- RSS feeds for a user's books
- Support for other sources of book information
- Book recommendations or suggestions
- Expanded user profiles and avatars

Improving the user interface

There are several places in the Book Shelf application where the interface is not ideal. The focus of the development in this book was to show you general concepts of implementing an application of this scope using the Rails framework. It was not a goal to provide a world-class user interface. Some of the areas that immediately come to mind that could use some fixing up are as follows:

- **Provide alternate views for the book list.** Currently, books are presented in a vertical list with a small image and some basic information about each book. It might be useful to have a view that displays only the cover images of all the books in a user's collection, or perhaps a table listing of the books in your collection without having to show the images.

- **Allow users to edit book reviews they have submitted.** Presently in the application, there is no way to edit a review once the user submits it. If the user reads it and notices a typographic error or an incorrect fact, they have no way of going back and updating the review. It would be a nice addition to allow reviews to be edited by the user who submitted them.

Implementing an administrator interface

Nearly every Web application of this style that allows for user-contributed content also includes some form of an administrator interface that can be used by the site administrator to manage the site's content. The current implementation of Book Shelf has no way for an administrator to manage the site. Some features that you might want to expose through an administrator interface include the following:

- Allow the administrator to manage the users. The administrator should be able to remove user accounts, disable user accounts, reset a password, and view a list of all users.

- Allow the administrator to access and edit or remove any of the book reviews.

- Allow the administrator to access and edit the entire collection of books along with their tags.

Adding RSS feeds to the application

Content syndication is another common feature of today's social networking applications. RSS which stands for Really Simple Syndication is the most common way of making a content from a website available to other sites and feed viewers.

RSS feeds are a common feature on user start pages such as the Google home page, and the Google Reader. Start pages and feed readers allow you to get content from all of the sites that you are interested in on one page. Syndication through RSS feeds would be a useful feature to add to the Book Shelf application. An RSS feed for the Book Shelf application could be updated anytime a book or book review is added to the site. This would allow users to keep track of what books and reviews are being added without having to visit the site everyday.

Adding support for other book information sources

Currently, the Book Shelf application looks up book information using the Amazon Web service. This is probably adequate for most users, but it is feasible that you could also extend the application to allow for different catalog providers to be plugged into the application. In addition to commercial sources of information, you could consider integrating with information provided by libraries. Many public libraries today provide online access to their inventory. You may get some ideas related to this by taking a look at the Library Lookup Project site at `http://weblog.infoworld.com/udell/stories/2002/12/11/librarylookup.html`.

Implementing recommendations and suggestions

Another feature that would give the application more of a social and community aspect would be support for book recommendations and suggestions. Give the users the ability to recommend books to friends in the application. Also, based on a user's current books, intelligence could be added to the application to look for books with similar tags and suggest those to the user. The most popular and indeed the most valuable sites today are those that provide social networking features. Today's web users want to interact with each other as much as they interact with the content that is provided. Adding more social features to the application will likely make it more useful and more valuable.

Expanding user profiles and adding avatars

Currently in the application, there is no profile information stored for a user. It would probably be a nice community type of feature to collect some profile information about users as they register. This information could be used to build user profile pages, allowing users to know a bit about each other. A common feature on profiles today is the ability for a user to have a small photo or avatar to represent him or her. Expanded user profiles would also help to facilitate more social networking features for the application.

Summary

In this chapter, you completed the implementation of a complete real-world Rails application. This chapter focused on adding social content features to the application. Many of the features that you added are common in today's popular generation of Web 2.0 applications. In the last section, you also were given some ideas on how you can expand the Book Shelf application to make it more usable and more useful to its users.

The application included many features that are common to today's most popular Web 2.0-style applications, such as content tagging and content reviews.

What you learned as you developed this application should be transferable knowledge that you can apply to other applications that you will develop using the Rails framework. Before moving away from the Book Shelf application completely, in the next chapter you will see how easy it can be to write tests for a Rails application, using the Book Shelf application as the test subject.

Chapter 9

Testing the Book Shelf Application

Testing is a critical component of any software development project. One of the best results of the rise in popularity of agile development is that it has brought unit testing to the forefront of software development. More developers regularly write unit tests today than at any time in the history of software development.

With Rails, you have no excuses not to write tests. Rails makes it easy to write and execute tests for your Rails applications. The framework comes with integrated, automated testing tools built-in. Rails provides you with the tools to write unit, functional, and integration tests. You'll use *unit tests* to validate your model classes. *Functional tests* allow you to test your controller methods and verify things like responses, redirects, and HTML. *Integration tests* allow you to test your application from the user's perspective. Integration tests cover multiple controllers and navigation across pages.

This chapter will introduce you to all of the testing capability that is built into Rails, along with some that is not built-in but is extremely useful. In this chapter, you will write tests for the Book Shelf application that was developed in Chapters 6, 7, and 8.

Why Test?

All too often in the past, developer testing was left to the end of a project, and then only minimal testing was done. For the most part, application developers relied on Quality Assurance (QA) teams to test their applications when the coding was complete. The primary reason why developers avoided testing was that it was considered a difficult and time-consuming task, with very little in the way of best practices or common patterns applied.

Fortunately, today, for many developers, their view of testing has made a dramatic shift. As agile methodologies became more popular, developer testing also saw a great rise in popularity. There are a few reasons for this:

- **Agile methodologies encourage developer refactoring of code.** *Refactoring* is a practice in which code is modified to make improvements in its design, readability, or maintainability without changing its functionality. This can be a dangerous and error-prone practice without having a safety net of unit tests that you can use to ensure that, as you refactor, you are not breaking the application.

- **About the same time agile methodologies were gaining traction, unit-testing frameworks were also being created and quickly gaining popularity due to the ease with which they made unit testing possible.** The most popular test framework to come out was the JUnit framework. JUnit is a Java unit-testing framework created by Kent Beck, one of the founders of Extreme Programming, an early agile methodology. The core features of JUnit have since been implemented in almost every other popular programming language, including .Net, Perl, PHP, and Ruby.

- **As developers have written more unit tests, they have realized that writing tests serves another less obvious purpose:** It actually makes your code better. In order to make your code easily testable, you are forced to make your methods as simple as possible, and to adhere to rules of good encapsulation and cohesion.

Developer testing has transitioned from a task that developers had shunned to a practice that developers actually enjoy. Good developers recognize the improvements to their code that can be attributed to writing tests. Without tests, developers are often afraid to make large changes in a code base for fear that something will break somewhere in the application. This, in turn, leads to developers sticking with code that they may feel is not ideal or not the best code for the job. As a result, the developer satisfaction and enjoyment of the project declines along with the quality of the code.

On the other hand, if an application includes good test coverage, the developer does not have to be afraid of making large changes to a code base. They can feel confident that any problems will be detected by running the unit tests. Therefore, the developer is able to make improvements in the code and fix design flaws. This makes for an enjoyable development experience. Those who are not yet in the practice of regularly writing unit tests may be thinking, how can I ever enjoy writing tests? My advice is to try it for a month, see what happens, and you'll probably have the answer to that question.

By making it easy to write tests, Rails' built-in test support contributes to a developer joy and higher-quality Web applications. Even if you start with a small Web application that you feel tests may not be necessary for, it is probably still a good idea to write the tests as you develop the application. All too often, those small, one-person developed applications become huge, successful Web 2.0 applications today. Rails also provides a measure of guilt for developers who do not write tests. Test files and fixtures are automatically generated for you as you generate your application's models and controllers. As a result, if you choose not to test, you're ignoring this great support that Rails has given you.

Agile methodologies have also ushered in a new way of developing, called test-driven development. *Test-driven development* (TDD) is a method of software development in which you write unit tests before you write any other code. The unit tests you write will define the minimum acceptable behavior for the code that you have to write. The general procedure you follow when doing test-driven development is as follows:

1. **Write a unit test that tests a piece of functionality that you want to implement.**

2. **Execute the unit test and verify that it fails, which it should, as you have not yet written any code corresponding to that feature.**

3. **Write the minimal code required to make the unit test pass.**

4. **Repeat the execution of the unit test and verify that the test now passes.**

5. **Repeat this procedure to add new features and functions.**

The unit tests that you write should be derived from use cases and user stories. As you build up the functionality of your application, you have complete test coverage and great freedom to refactor and improve the code that you initially wrote to minimally pass your unit tests. Test-driven development was first popularized by the Extreme Programming methodology and its creator, Kent Beck. It has since been widely used outside of Extreme Programming and is often used with other agile methodologies.

Many developers using Rails are also strong advocates of agile methodologies. As a result, while test-driven development is not something that is Rails-specific, it is a topic that you are likely to come across when you start looking for a Rails development job. The official Rails Web site wiki provides an excellent starting point for using test-driven development in a Rails application:

```
http://wiki.rubyonrails.org/rails/pages/
    HowToDoTestDrivenDevelopmentInRails
```

Test-driven development can be difficult to get started with for many developers, and it requires a lot of discipline to apply it consistently. If you choose not to do test-driven development, you should get in the practice of writing tests as soon as possible after you've developed each new feature in your application.

Do not wait until your application is completely developed before you decide to write tests. Three reasons come to mind why waiting until the end is a bad idea:

1. **The motivation to write tests after you've completed development is very low.** Most developers will not follow through with writing tests if they feel they are done with development.

2. **You will miss out on many of the benefits that writing unit tests provide you with during development, such as improved design, and freedom to refactor safely.**

3. **The longer you wait after writing a specific feature, the harder it will be to go back and fill in the tests.** This is not just because you my forget the specifics of the implementation, but also because the tighter your feedback loop between coding and testing is, the more your code will tend to be written in a way that enables testing.

Using Test::Unit

The Rails testing support uses the Ruby module Test::Unit to provide its core functionality. Test::Unit is a framework that makes it easy to write tests for any Ruby application. The framework allows you to write test methods that make assertions about the code you are testing. Whether those assertions pass or fail decides the results of a test.

Test methods can be bundled together into test classes. Test classes are bundled into a test suite. Test methods can also use test *fixtures*, which define test data to be used by your test methods. The idea is that you create a suite of test classes containing test methods that use test fixtures to test your real methods. You then run that suite of tests to get test results that tell you how many of your tests succeeded and how many failed.

Test assertions

Assertions provide the core of the testing framework. You use assertions to check your code for expected outcomes. When your code produces an unexpected outcome, that result is detected by an assertion and results in a failed test. Assertions are implemented as methods in the Test::Unit framework.

The assertion methods available in Test::Unit are described here:

- `assert(boolean, message=nil)`
  Asserts that boolean is not false or nil.

- `assert_block(message="assert_block failed.") {|| …}`
  Passes if the block yields true. This is the assertion upon which all other assertions are based.

- `assert_equal (expected, actual, message=nil)`
  Passes if expected == actual. The ordering of the elements here is important, because on failure, a helpful error message is generated for you.

- `assert_in_delta(expected_float, actual_float, delta, message="")`
  Passes if expected_float and actual_float are equal within delta tolerance.

- `assert_instance_of (some_class, object, message="")`
  Passes if object.instance_of? some_class evaluates to true.

- `assert_kind_of(some_class, object, message="")`
  Passes if object.kind_of? some_class evaluates to true.

- `assert_match(pattern, string, message="")`
  Passes if `string =~ pattern` evaluates to true.

- `assert_nil(object, message="")`
  Passes if `object` is nil.

- `assert_no_match(regexp, string, message="")`
  Passes if `regexp !~ string` evaluates to true.

- `assert_not_equal(expected, actual, message="")`
  Passes if `expected != actual` evaluates to true.

- `assert_not_nil(object, message="")`
  Passes if `!object.nil?` evaluates to true.

- `assert_not_same(expected, actual, message="")`
  Passes if `!actual.equal? expected` evaluates to true.

- `assert_nothing_raised(*args){||..}`
  Passes if the block does not raise an exception.

- `assert_nothing_thrown(message="", &proc)`
  Passes if the block does not throw anything.

- `assert_operator(object1, operator, object2, message="")`
  Compares `object1` with `object2` using `operator`.
  Passes if `object1.send(operator, object2)` is true.

- `assert_raise(*args){||..}`
  Passes if the block raises one of the given exceptions.

- `assert_raises(*args, &block)`
  Alias of `assert_raise`, deprecated in Ruby version 1.9 and to be removed in Ruby version 2.0.

- `assert_respond_to(object, method, message="")`
  Passes if `object.respond_to?` method evaluates to true.

- `assert_same(expected, actual, message="")`
  Passes if `actual.equal? expected` evaluates to true.
  This would indicate that they are the same instance.

- `assert_send(send_array, message="")`
  Passes if the method `send` returns a true value.
  The `send_array` is composed of a receiver, a method, and arguments to the method.

- `assert_throws(expected_symbol, message="", &proc)`
  Passes if the block throws `expected_symbol`.

With these assertion methods, you'll be able to write tests that check just about any condition that you can think of. You'll notice that in addition to other parameters, most of the `assert` methods take a message parameter. The message parameter is a string value that will be displayed if the test fails. This is useful when you are trying to figure out why a particular test failed.

Test fixtures

Test fixtures are a way of representing data that is used by your application. The test fixtures are used by your tests. As you'll see later in this chapter, Rails will automatically generate test fixtures for all of the model classes that you generate. Fixtures save you from having to create your own methods of inserting and cleaning up data that is necessary only for testing.

Test methods

The tests that you write will be contained in test methods. Your test methods will be contained in test classes. Test classes allow you to encapsulate groups of test methods that test a particular class or feature. All of your test classes should extend the `Test::Unit::TestCase` class. The `Test::Unit::TestCase` class includes a set of test methods that assists you in writing your tests. Two methods from this class that are often used are the `setup` and `teardown` methods. By overriding these methods in your test classes, you can specify code that should be run before and after each of your test methods are run.

As of Rails 2.0, Rails provides specific subclasses of `Test::Unit::TestCase` that perform initialization specific to the test type. Functional tests extend `ActionController::TestCase` while unit tests extend `ActiveSupport::TestCase`. Also new in Rails 2.0 is the ability to specify multiple setup and teardown blocks using the syntax:

```
setup do … end
teardown do … end
```

Below is an example of a simple test class that uses `setup` and `teardown` methods and contains two test methods.

```
require 'test/unit'

class MyTest < Test::Unit::TestCase
  def setup
    puts 'Starting a test method…'
  end

  def teardown
    puts 'Completed a test method…'
  end

  def test_one
    assert(false, 'Assertion was false.')
  end

  def test_two
    assert(true)
  end
end
```

Each test method in the example above contains one assertion. However, in general, a test method can contain multiple assertions. There is no limit to the number of assertions that you can perform in each test method. The first failed assertion in the test method will cause evaluation of that test to stop and the test system will move to the next test method. As a result, each test method should usually test one particular feature or requirement of the class you are testing.

The `test_one` method in the above example will always result in a failed test. The `assert` method passes only if the logical expression that is passed to it evaluates to true. In this case, the value `false` is passed to `assert`, and thus the assertion will always fail. A failed assertion also causes the test method that it is contained within to fail. Upon failure, the `Assertion was false.` message will also be printed. The second test, `test_two`, will always result in a successful assertion.

A new instance of your test class, `MyTest`, is created for each test method that runs. The `setup` and `teardown` methods are called for each test method that you create. As a result, the lifecycle for each test method looks like this:

1. **An instance of class `MyTest` is created.**

2. **The `setup` method is run.**

3. **The test method (`test_one` or `test_two`) is run.**

4. **The `teardown` method is run.**

5. **The test class object is destroyed.**

This lifecycle assures that each test method is independent from other test methods.

`Test::Unit` provides you with a consistent framework and style for writing your unit tests. Generally, you should follow these steps when writing tests for your application:

1. Require `'test/unit'` in your test script. Rails tests should also require `'test_helper'`, a common file provided by Rails to house shared test setup and assertion code.

2. Create a class that subclasses `Test::Unit::TestCase`, or the relevant Rails subclass.

3. Define test methods that begin with `"test_"`.

4. Make assertions in your test methods.

5. Optionally define `setup` and `teardown` methods.

6. Run your tests.

Any methods that begin with the word "test," such as the `test_one` method in the example above, will be run automatically when you run the tests. Only these methods will be run during the test suite.

> **NOTE** Tests are not run in the order that they are listed in the test class. Tests contained in a test class are run in alphabetical order.

Test runners

Now you've seen some of the basics about writing tests using the Test::Unit framework, but having done that, how do you run your tests and get the results? Test::Unit has a couple of nice utility applications for running your unit tests that will help you. These applications are called test runners.

The most common test runner built into Test::Unit is the `Test::Unit::UI::Console::Test Runner` class. This provides a console-based test runner. The console test runner is invoked automatically when you run a Ruby script that requires `test/unit`.

In the previous section, you saw a test class named `MyTest`. If that class were saved in a file called `my_test.rb`, you could run the tests contained within it by simply calling it as a Ruby script, like this:

```
> ruby my_test.rb
```

Because `my_test.rb` includes a `require` statement for `test/unit`, the tests will be run using the console test runner. You should see output similar to Figure 9.1 if you run the tests. Notice that the `Assertion was false` message is printed. This was the message parameter that you passed to the `assert` method. Also notice that the test runner tells you the exact line number in your test file on which the failure occurred.

FIGURE 9.1

Test runner output

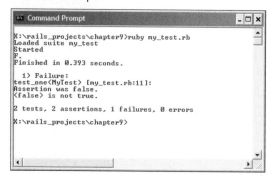

Test suites

As you write more test methods, and create more test classes, it can become burdensome to run them one class at a time. Test suites allow you to bundle multiple test classes into a single suite. A test suite can be passed to the run method of a test runner, and all of the test classes defined in the suite will be run. Below is a simple example of a test suite:

```
require 'test/unit/testsuite'
require 'module_one_tests'
require 'module_two_tests'
require 'module_three_tests'

class TS_MyTests
    def self.suite
        suite = Test::Unit::TestSuite.new
        suite << ModuleOneTests.suite
        suite << ModuleTwoTests.suite
        suite << ModuleThreeTests.suite
        return suite
    end
end
Test::Unit::UI::Console::TestRunner.run(TS_MyTests)
```

This code creates a test suite called `TS_MyTests`. The suite bundles three test classes: `ModuleOneTests`, `ModuleTwoTests`, and `ModuleThreeTests`. In the last line, the test suite is run by passing it to the run method of the console test runner.

You may have noticed that the code to create a test suite violates the DRY principle, and seems to require a lot of repetitive code. There is actually an easier way to create a test suite. The code below does the same thing as the previous test suite code:

```
require 'test/unit'
require 'module_one_tests'
require 'module_two_tests'
require 'module_three_tests'
```

Wow, much simpler to write that, isn't it? Given this set of `require` statements, Test::Unit is smart enough to find all of the test cases contained in the required files, and bundles them into a test suite for you. It will then run the suite using the console test runner.

Testing in Rails

Rails makes writing and running tests for your application very simple. As you generate models and controllers, the Rails generate script also generates test files that you can use to write tests in. Rails also uses a separate database just for testing. The test database is rebuilt each time the application's tests are run, and so you always have a consistent database when your tests are run. This keeps you from having to add test data to a production database, which you probably don't want to corrupt with test data.

Rails tests use the Ruby Test::Unit testing library, which you read about in the previous section. You'll normally run your Rails application tests using the Rake utility. Rails comes with built-in tasks that let you specify which tests you want to run. Later in this chapter, when you begin writing tests, you'll see exactly how to use Rake to run your tests.

Rails test directory

At the top level of a Rails project is a test directory that contains all of the test files that Rails generates, and which you use to build the tests for your application. Inside the test directory is the following directory structure:

```
test/
    fixtures/
    functional/
    integration/
    mocks/
        development/
        test/
    unit/
```

This directory structure maps to the three types of tests that Rails supports: functional, integration, and unit tests. Later in this chapter, you'll have the chance to write each of these types of tests for the Book Shelf application. The test directory also contains directories for fixtures and mocks. *Fixtures* are files that allow you to set up test data that can be used by your applications. Fixtures will save you a lot of time and effort when writing Rails tests.

Normally, when you write unit tests, you have to first write code that will create test data and get the database into a known populated state. Rails fixtures do most of that work for you. *Mocks* are classes that allow you to replace dependencies that are difficult to test with. For example, like the Book Shelf application, your application might have a class that accesses the Amazon Web Service or another external Web service.

In your test, if you don't want to actually make calls to Amazon, you could implement that class as a mock, and use the mock in your tests.

Rails test lifecycle

When you run your Rails application's tests, a standard lifecycle is followed each time. This lifecycle consists of the following steps:

1. **Load up test fixtures.** This clears the database tables and loads your fixture data into the database.

2. **If your test accesses data, it is read from the database.**

3. **After your tests run, the database is rolled back to its starting state.** Tests are wrapped in transactions, making this easy for Rails.

This lifecycle is carried out for you automatically by Rails each time you run your tests using the Rake command.

Setting Up a Test Database

As you've learned previously, Rails applications support several different runtime environments. One of the environments supported is a test environment. The test environment is used when you run your application's tests. You define a separate database for each of your application's environments. In this section, you will prepare a test database for the Book Shelf application that was developed in Chapters 6, 7, and 8. You can download the completed source code for the Book Shelf application at this book's Web site, www.rubyonrailsbible.com.

CAUTION Although you might be tempted to specify the same database instance for both your development and test environments, it is very important that you do not. The test database is completely erased each time you run your tests. In most cases, you do not want to erase and rebuild your development database every time you run your tests. For the same reason, it goes without saying that you should never specify the same database for both your test and production environments. That would be a quick way to lose all of your production data, if you are running unit tests periodically.

The test database that you create here will be used for all of the tests that you'll write later in this chapter.

1. **Create the test database.** To begin testing, the first thing you need to do is make sure that you have created and configured a test database. Let's go ahead and do that now for the Book Shelf application. Open a command-line and create the MySQL test database using the MySQL command-line program, as shown here:

   ```
   >mysql -u root -p create database bookshelf_test
   ```

   If you are using a MySQL username other than 'root,' make sure that you use the appropriate username in the command above.

   The command `rake db:create:all` will create all the databases specified in your `database.yml` file, including the test database.

2. **Configure the test database.** Next, you'll have to configure the test database in your `config/database.yml` file just as you configured the development database. Below is an example configuration for a test database from `database.yml`:

   ```
   test:
     adapter: mysql
     database: bookshelf_test
     username: root
     password: <<your_password>>
     host: localhost
   ```

   Open up the `config/database.yml` config file for your Book Shelf application and make sure that the test database is properly configured in it. Make sure you plug in your own local database username and password. By default, MySQL is installed with a user named "root" with an empty password. You can specify an empty password by leaving the password field blank, like this:

   ```
   password:
   ```

3. **Prepare the test database.** You can run a special Rake command to prepare the test database. This is run from the command-line in your application's root directory. Go to the `book_shelf` directory and type this:

   ```
   rake db:test:prepare
   ```

   This will copy your database schema (the tables and columns) from the development database to the test database. If you run your tests via the standard rake commands, this task is performed for you automatically. However, if you run your tests via an alternate mechanism, such as the autotest gem, you may need to periodically reset the test database.

Now you should have a test database created and ready for use. Next, you'll begin writing your first Rails tests.

Functional Tests

Functional tests are used to test an application's controller methods. When you generate a controller class using the script/generate command, Rails also generates functional test files that you will use to write functional tests. The functional test files are located in the test/functional subdirectory within your applications directory.

Look at the book_controller_test.rb file in the test/functional directory of your Book Shelf application:

In Rails 2.0 or higher, the file looks like this:

```
require 'test_helper'

class BookControllerTest < ActionController::TestCase
  # Replace this with your real tests.
  def test_truth
    assert true
  end
end
```

However, the ActionController::TestCase class encapsulates a lot of behavior that used to be included in each and every functional test file. It's helpful to know exactly what features are provided for you in a controller test, so lets take a look at the older version of this file.

```
require File.dirname(__FILE__) + '/../test_helper'
require 'book_controller'

# Re-raise errors caught by the controller.
class BookController; def rescue_action(e) raise e end; end

class BookControllerTest < Test::Unit::TestCase
  def setup
    @controller = BookController.new
    @request    = ActionController::TestRequest.new
    @response   = ActionController::TestResponse.new
  end

  # Replace this with your real tests.
  def test_truth
    assert true
  end
end
```

This is the functional test stub that was created by the generate script when you generated the book controller class. You should see similar test files for the other Book Shelf controller classes. As is, this stub is not terribly useful, but let's take a closer look at what it does contain.

The first two lines of the file require the `book_controller` class file and a `test_helper` file. The `test_helper` file is located at the top level of the tests directory, as the `test/test_helper.rb` file. You'll see how to use that file later in this chapter. It is a place where you can put methods that you want to use in more than one of your tests.

```
require File.dirname(__FILE__) + '/../test_helper'
require 'book_controller'
```

After the `require` statements, you see these two lines:

```
# Re-raise errors caught by the controller.
class BookController; def rescue_action(e) raise e end; end
```

This line ensures that any exceptions that are raised by the `BookController` class will be thrown from the test class as well, and not just silently ignored.

Next comes the definition of the book controller test class, shown here:

```
class BookControllerTest < Test::Unit::TestCase
  def setup
    @controller = BookController.new
    @request    = ActionController::TestRequest.new
    @response   = ActionController::TestResponse.new
  end

  # Replace this with your real tests.
  def test_truth
    assert true
  end
end
```

The first thing to notice about the class is that it extends the `Test::Unit::TestCase` class, which is a part of the standard Ruby unit-testing module, Test::Unit. All of the tests you write will extend this class. The Rails testing facilities are built on top of the Test::Unit module. You can use Test::Unit for unit testing in Ruby, even outside of Rails applications.

The test class is generated with two methods already defined, `setup` and `test_truth`. The `setup` method is a place where you can put code that you want to execute before each test runs. In this `setup` method, an instance of the `BookController` is created, along with `request` and `response` object instances. Each of these objects will be used within the tests that you'll write shortly.

The `test_truth` method is a simplistic test that you'll replace when you begin writing the real tests. This test uses the `assert` method to test the value `true` which will always be true, and thus the test will always pass. This is the `assert` method from the `Test::Unit::TestCase` class.

Before you write any real tests, let's look at how to run tests for a Rails application, and make sure that what is there so far gives you passing tests.

Running a test

From the `book_shelf` directory, you can run an individual test such as the book controller test, like this:

```
> ruby test/functional/book_controller_test.rb
Loaded suite test/functional/book_controller_test
Started
.
Finished in 1.068 seconds.

1 tests, 1 assertions, 0 failures, 0 errors
```

If all goes well, you should see the output shown above, indicating success. The single period that appears in the output after the line containing `'Started'` indicates that the test contained one test. A period will be output for each successful test that is run. If a test fails or results in an error, the period will instead be the letter 'F' or 'E' to indicate failure or error, respectively. The meaning of success is the most obvious, but what is the difference between a failing testing and an error test? They are defined as follows:

- **Failure:** This means that the code completed normally, but an assertion has failed. This is usually indicative of the code under test not performing as it should.

- **Error:** This means that a exception was thrown while trying to run a test, preventing the code from completing normally.

The last line of the output gives a summary of the test results. In this case, there was 1 test run and 1 assertion, with 0 failures and 0 errors.

You normally will want to run more than a single test class or a single test suite. This is where Rake comes in handy. Rails includes Rake scripts that will allow you to execute all of your tests at once. To execute all of your functional tests, try this from the `book_shelf` directory:

```
> rake test:functionals
```

You should see output similar to that shown in Figure 9.2.

FIGURE 9.2

Using Rake to run functional tests

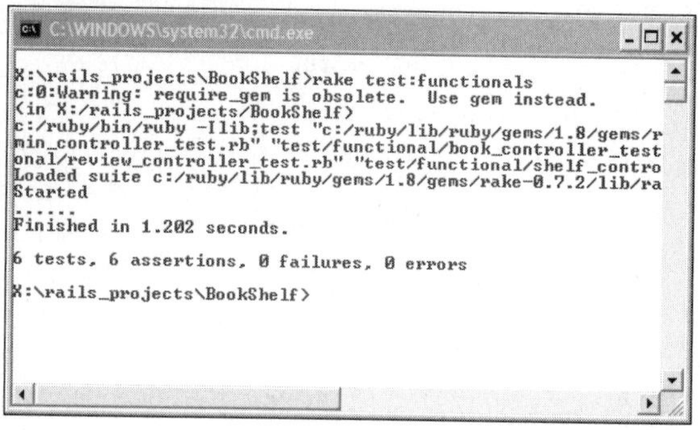

```
C:\WINDOWS\system32\cmd.exe                                    _ □ x
X:\rails_projects\BookShelf>rake test:functionals
c:0:Warning: require_gem is obsolete.  Use gem instead.
(in X:/rails_projects/BookShelf)
c:/ruby/bin/ruby -Ilib;test "c:/ruby/lib/ruby/gems/1.8/gems/r
min_controller_test.rb" "test/functional/book_controller_test
onal/review_controller_test.rb" "test/functional/shelf_contro
Loaded suite c:/ruby/lib/ruby/gems/1.8/gems/rake-0.7.2/lib/ra
Started
......
Finished in 1.202 seconds.

6 tests, 6 assertions, 0 failures, 0 errors

X:\rails_projects\BookShelf>
```

Creating a test

Go ahead now and make the `BookControllerTest` class more useful by creating some real functional tests in it. After each test is written, you rerun the tests to make sure that they still pass. The first test you write will test the `list` method of the `BookController`. The `list` method looks like this:

```
def list
  @books = Book.find(:all)
  @books.each {|book| book.exists = true}
  @title = "Book Shelf All Books"
end
```

Here is what you want to test for the `list` method:

- Simulate the user hitting the page with a GET request.
- Verify that the `list` method assigns the page title, and that it has the correct value.
- Verify that the `list` method assigns the `books` variable.
- Verify that the size of the `books` array is what is expected.
- Check for the proper HTTP response of success.
- Verify that the correct `erb` template is rendered.

Before you begin writing the test, you will want to set up some test fixtures to insert some test data into your database.

Setting up fixtures

One of the things in the list of items to verify is the size of the books array that is assigned by the list method. In order for this to be a value other than zero, you need to make sure that the test database contains a few book records.

Do you have to write code to insert book records into the database? Because of the fixture support in Rails, you do not have to write that code. *Fixtures* are simple text files that define test data using the YAML format.

If you open up the fixture that was automatically generated for book, contained in test/ fixtures/books.yml, you should see this:

```
one:
  id: 1
two:
  id: 2
```

This defines two book objects, each containing only an id field. The rest of the fields for each book record will be null. However, you can edit this file to create more realistic test data. Do that now by editing the file to look like this:

```
one:
    title: Ruby on Rails Bible
    author: Timothy Fisher
    description: A book about the Rails framework.
    release_date: May 12, 2008
    image_url_small: http://www.rubyonrailsbible.com/small.jpg
    image_url_medium: http://www.rubyonrailsbible.com/medium.jpg
    image_url_large: http://www.rubyonrailsbible.com/large.jpg
    amazon_url: http://www.rubyonrailsbible.com
two:
    title: A Test Book
    author: John Tester
    description: A book about testing.
    release_date: January 1, 2007
    image_url_small: http://www.testing.com/small.jpg
    image_url_medium: http://www.testing.com/medium.jpg
    image_url_large: http://www.testing.com/large.jpg
    amazon_url: http://www.testing.com
```

Now the books fixtures file contains two fully described book records.

Create a Fixture in CSV Format

Fixtures can also be created in CSV format. To create a CSV header file, the first line must contain the field names, comma-separated, and each subsequent line must contain a comma-separated record. For example, a simple book record fixture might be defined as follows:

```
id, title, author, description
1,Ruby on Rails Bible,Timothy Fisher,A book about the Rails framework.
2,A Test Book,John Tester,A book about testing.
```

Unlike when using the YAML format, you do not give each record a unique name in the CSV file. Instead, unique record names are automatically generated for you by combining the model name, a dash "-", and an incrementing counter value. In this example, the first record would have the name 'book-1', and the second would have the name 'book-2'.

Using Ruby in fixtures

You can also embed Ruby inside of your test fixtures, the same way you embed Ruby in `rhtml` template files. You use embedded Ruby (ERb) to put Ruby in your fixtures. You won't need this for the fixtures that you created so far, but it can be a useful thing to know. Let's cover it now.

ERb can only be used in YAML-formatted fixtures. You cannot use it with CVS fixtures. Below is an example of how you might use ERb to populate date fields in your test records:

```
current_book_entry
   title: New and Exciting Stuff
   author: Camden Fisher
   created_at: <%= (Date.today).to_s %>
   updated_at: <%= (Date.today).to_s %>

old_book_entry
   title: The World of Ruby
   author: Timmy Fisher
   created_at: <%= (Date.today - 60).to_s %>
   updated_at: <%= (Date.today - 60).to_s %>
```

In this fixture, the `created_at` and `updated_at` fields are populated using the `Date` class from Ruby. The first record, `current_book_entry`, will get the current date set for both of the fields. The second record, `old_book_entry`, will get a date 60 days in the past for both of these fields.

Another scenario that could be useful would be to use Ruby loops to generate multiple records, as in this example:

```
<% for i in 1..50 %>
item_<%= i %>
  title: Ruby Book <%= i %>
  author: Author <%= i %>
  created_at: <%= (Date.today - i).to_s %>
  updated_at: <%= (Date.today - i).to_s %>
<% end %>
```

This would save you from having to type large amounts of data when you want to simulate a lot of records in your database.

Including fixtures in your tests

Now that you have created some book records in a `books` fixture, you have to make sure that fixture is loaded by the book controller tests. To load a fixture in a test class, you have to use the `fixtures` method, followed by the names of the fixtures that you want to load. To load the `books` fixture in the book controller tests, you would modify the `BookControllerTest` class to look like this:

```
class BookControllerTest < ActionController::TestCase

    fixtures :books

end
```

You can pass the `fixtures` method either a symbol or a string value containing the name of the fixture to load. You can load multiple fixtures by passing them in a comma-separated list.

Writing a test method

Okay, now that you have your test database created, and some book records defined in a test fixture, it's finally time to write a real functional test. Open up the `book_controller_test.rb` file and add a `test_list` method that looks like this:

```
def test_list
  get :list
  title = assigns(:title)
  assert_equal "Book Shelf All Books", title
  books = assigns(:books)
  assert_equal 2, books.size
  assert_response :success
  assert_template "list"
end
```

In the first line of this method, the `get` method is called. This will simulate a GET request being routed to the `list` method of the `BookController` class. There are five request types that you can submit using these methods:

- get
- post
- put
- head
- delete

Of these, you will most often be using the `get` and `post` methods. These are the most commonly used HTTP request methods. You can also pass parameters to these methods by adding extra parameters to the method call. For example, if you wanted to make a GET request and pass an `id` parameter, you could use this line of code:

```
get :list, :id => 1
```

In the second line of the test method, you see this code: `title = assigns(:title)`. The `assigns` method is provided by Rails. This method looks for an instance variable defined in your controller's action method with the name passed in. In this line, `title = assigns(:title)`, the value of the instance variable `@title` which was assigned by the `list` action is placed into the local variable, `title`.

The next line of the test method asserts that the title contains the value you expect. Then, you grab the value of the `@books` instance variable and assert that it contains two elements, by using the `size` method of the `Array` class. Recall that two is the correct number of books to expect because you added two book records to the `books` fixture.

There is another way to get the values of instance variables assigned by your action methods. Rails makes available four hashes that contain information that you might want to inspect. The four hashes that you can use are:

- **assigns:** Instance variables assigned in the action that are available for the view
- **cookies:** Holds any cookies sent to the user on this request
- **flash:** Used to access messages stored in the flash area
- **session:** Holds objects stored in the session

Each of these hashes is also available as a method call -- in other words, you can do either of `assigns["person"]` or `assigns(:person)`. In the specific case of `assigns`, the hash version takes string keys, while the method version takes symbol keys, which is admittedly a little odd. You'll see some of these hashes used later in this chapter.

The last two lines of the `test_list` method make use of two assertions that you have not seen before: `assert_response` and `assert_template`. In the next section, you'll learn about these and some additional assertions that Rails makes available specifically for testing your controller methods.

More assertion methods

The `assert_response` and `assert_template` assertions used by the `test_list` method are not a part of the Test::Unit framework. These methods are defined by the ActionController module of Rails. Rails adds the following assertions for use in testing your controllers:

- `assert_dom_equal(expected, actual, message="")`
  Compares two HTML strings, `expected` and `actual`, to see if they are equivalent. Details that do not affect the HTML meaning of the string, such as order of attributes, will not break the equivalence.

- `assert_dom_not_equal(expected, actual, message="")`
  Compares two HTML strings, `expected` and `actual`, to see if they are not equivalent. Details that do not affect the HTML meaning of the string, such as order of attributes, will not break the equivalence.

- `assert_generates(expected_path, options, defaults={}, extras={}, message=nil)`
  Asserts that the provided options can be used to generate the provided path, passed in as a string.

- `assert_no_tag(*opts)`
  Asserts that the specified tag does not exist. The options are exactly as in `assert_tag`. In Rails 2.x, `assert_select` is preferred.

- `assert_recognizes(expected_options, path, extras={}, message=nil)`
  Asserts that the expected options, which is a hash of the form to be passed to `url_for`, result in the string passed into the path argument. If the route requires a specific HTTP action, then the `path` argument is a hash of the form `{:path => 'the/path', :method => :post}`.

  Any query options that you want to test need to be passed in the extras hash, rather than including them as part of the path string.

- `assert_redirected_to(options={}, message=nil)`
  Asserts that the redirection options passed in as `options` match those of the redirect that was the result of the last action. You do not have to specify all of the options for a successful match, only specified conditions are tested.

  For example, the assertion `assert_redirected_to(:controller => "book")` will match the redirect of `redirect_to(:controller=>"book", :action=>"show")`.

- `assert_response(type, message=nil)`
  Asserts that the response is one of the following types:

  - `:success`

    Status code was 200

  - `:redirect`

    Status code was in the 300-399 range

- :missing

  Status code was 404

- :error

  Status code was in the 500-599 range

You can also pass an integer as the argument, in which case the response code must match exactly.

- `assert_routing(path, options, defaults={}, extras={}, message=nil)`

  Asserts that the URL generated from `options` must be the same value as `path`, and that the options recognized from `path` are the same as `options`. In other words, it performs both the `assert_recognizes` and the `assert_generate` tests in one fell swoop.

- `assert_select(element, selector, equality?, message)`

  The preferred Rails 2.0 mechanism for testing HTML output. In general, it returns true if there is an HTML tag matching the selector and the equality test is chosen. There are a few details as seen in the sidebar "assert_select In Depth."

- `assert_select_email`

  Allows you to perform tests inside the body of an e-mail that would have been sent by the controller action. This method takes no regular arguments; all tests performed on the body are passed as a block argument. If there is more than one delivery in the action being tested, this assertion will be run against each of them.

- `assert_select_encoded(element) { |elements| ... }`

  Typically called inside an `assert_select`, assumes that the element is encoded HTML (as might be passed inside an XML document, for example), decodes it, and allows you to run further tests on the decoded element.

- `assert_select_rjs(id?) {block}`

- `assert_select_rjs(statement, id?) {block}`

- `assert_select_rjs(:insert, position, id?) {block}`

  The Ajax version of `assert_select`. As with the HTML version, if the test is written without a block then the test just asserts the existence of a specific RJS call. If a block is specified, then further assertions can be made on the HTML passed as part of the RJS call, as in an `insert_html call` call. This includes further `assert_select` calls on the generated HTML.

  In the one argument form, the test checks to see if any RJS statements have been made against the DOM id specified. In the two argument form, it checks for the specific RJS method of the same name and the DOM id specified. The three argument form is specific to RJS insert calls and specifies the position within the DOM element where the insertion is expected to take place.

assert_select In Depth

The selector argument specifies a set of HTML tags using CSS selector syntax, normally a string, but also possibly an `HTML::Selector` object. The first part of the selector is the HTML tag being searched for. Additions to the selector narrow the scope of the match, using standard CSS syntax to specify a CSS class (`tag.class`), a DOM id (`tag#id`), or an arbitrary attribute of the HTML tag (`a[selected="true"]`).

The equality test can also use `*=` meaning that the attribute contains the value `^=` to test for an attribute that starts with the value and `$=` to test for an attribute that ends with the value.

There is also a series of pseudo-elements that allow you to specify a tag from the list of matching tags, such as `form:first-child`, `form:last-child`, `form:nth-child(n)`, `form:nth-last-child(n)`. Also the normal CSS specifiers for tag relationships, such as `h1 > div`, work as they do in a CSS page.

If no equality test is specified, then the test will pass if there is at least one HTML tag in the response body of the controller action that matches the selector. You can get some behavior if the equality argument is true. If the equality argument is false, you get the opposite behavior, testing that the specified tag is not in the output.

If the equality argument is an integer, the test passes if that exact number of HTML tags matches the selector. If the argument is a range, the test passes if the number of HTML tags is in the range. If the argument is a string, the test passes if at least one matching HTML tag has inner text that matches the text. If it's a regular expression, then at least one matching HTML tag must have inner text that matches the expression.

If you want to do more than one test on the same selector, you can pass a hash of equality tests. Pass string or regex arguments with the key `:text` or `:html`. The integer argument can be passes as `:count`, and the range argument is passed in two parts as `:minimum` and `:maximum`.

The following example searches for `li` elements that are direct descendants of `ul` elements and have the CSS class bold. It verifies that there is exactly one such tag, and that its contents are `Fred`:

```
assert_select("ul>li.bold", :text => "Fred", :count => 1
```

The fourth argument form that starts with an element limits the test to that element and its children. Normally, you would not call that form directly but rather implicitly invoke it via a block argument to another `assert_select`. For example:

```
assert_select "form", 1 do
  assert_select "input[type="hidden"], 1
end
```

In this snippet, the inner `assert_select` call will only match elements that are inside the element matched by the outer call.

- `assert_tag(*opts)`

  Asserts that there is a tag/node/element in the body of the response that meets all of the given conditions (see the sidebar "assert_tag(*opts) Conditions"). The `assert_select` test is preferred.

- `assert_template(expected=nil, message=nil)`

  Asserts that the request was rendered with the appropriate template file.

- `assert_valid(record)`

  Asserts that the passed-in record is valid according to Active Record — that is, it passes all of a model's validations.

For further details and examples using all of these assertions, see the Ruby on Rails documentation.

Verifying your test

The `test_list` method has accomplished what I set out to test. Here were the things that I wanted to test for the `list` method, along with a brief description of how they were tested:

- **Simulate the user accessing the page with a GET request.** This is accomplished using the `get` method.
- **Verify that the `list` method assigns the page title, and that it has the correct value.** This is completed using the `assigns` hash and the `assert_equal` method.
- **Verify that the `list` method assigns the `books` variable.** This is completed using the `assigns` method.
- **Verify the size of the `books` array.** This is completed with an `assert_equal` method.
- **Check for the proper HTTP response of success.** This is verified using the `assert_response` method.
- **Verify that the correct ERb template is rendered.** This is verified using the `assert_template` method.

At this point, you think the method is well tested, but you have not run the test yet to see if it works. Let's do that now. You should use Rake to run the functional tests and verify that your new book controller test passes.

If you do not get passing test results, go back and look at your test code closely and make sure that you did not make any errors.

Adding more tests

That's one test down, but let's keep going and add a test for the `show` method of the `BookController`. The show method looks like this:

assert_tag(*opts) Conditions

The `conditions` parameter must be a hash of any of the following keys (all are optional):

- `:tag`

  The node type must match the corresponding value.

- `:attributes`

  A hash. The node's attributes must match the corresponding values in the hash.

- `:parent`

  A hash. The node's parent must match the corresponding hash.

- `:child`

  A hash. At least one of the node's immediate children must meet the criteria described by the hash.

- `:ancestor`

  A hash. At least one of the node's ancestors must meet the criteria described by the hash.

- `:descendant`

  A hash. At least on of the node's descendants must meet the criteria described by the hash.

- `:sibling`

  A hash. At least one of the node's siblings must meet the criteria described by the hash.

- `:after`

  A hash. The node must be after any sibling meeting the criteria described by the hash and at least one sibling must match.

- `:before`

  A hash. The node must be before any sibling meeting the criteria described by the hash must match.

- `:children`

  A hash for counting children of a node. It accepts the following keys:

  - `:count`

    Either a number or a range that must equal or include the number of children that match.

  - `:less_than`

    The number of matching children must be less than this number.

  - `:greater_than`

    The number of matching children must be greater than this number.

  - `:only`

    Another hash consisting of keys to use to match the children; only matching children will be counted.

```
def show
  @book = Book.find(params[:id])
  @title = "Book Detail"
end
```

For the show method, you'll want to verify that the @book instance variable set does indeed point to the expected book. In this test, you'll also see how you can verify the actual contents of the page that is rendered.

Add the test_show method to the book_controller_test.rb file:

```
def test_show
  get :show, :id=>'1'
  book = assigns(:book)
  assert_equal "Ruby on Rails Bible", book.title
  title = assigns(:title)
  assert_equal "Book Detail", title
  assert_response :success
  assert_template "show"
end
```

So far in the test_show method, you see basic testing being done as you saw for the test_list method. There is nothing new here yet. You have verified that the correct template is rendered, but it would be much better if you could also verify that the rendered template displays the data that you expect. That is where the assert_select method comes in handy.

With assert_select, you can verify the contents of the template that is returned. Edit the test_show method to add a few tag assertions, like this:

```
def test_show
  get :show, :id=>'1'
  book = assigns(:book)
  assert_equal "Ruby on Rails Bible", book.title
  title = assigns(:title)
  assert_equal "Book Detail", title
  assert_response :success
  assert_template "show"
  assert_select "div#book_image"
  assert_select "div#book_summary"
  assert_select "div#book_reivews"
end
```

Now there are three assert_select calls. Each of these calls looks for a different element of the page that is rendered. The first assert_select will verify that the page contains a div tag containing an id attribute with the value book_image.

The next two assertions verify the presence of a `div` tag with the `id` attribute containing the value `book_summary`, and a `div` tag with the `id` attribute containing the value `book_reviews`. With these three assertions, you have verified that the rendered page contains the correct basic structure, and thus is most likely the correct page. Of course, you could go further and assert each element on the page to make certain that it is built correctly.

Add some reviews

The book show page shows a book's reviews in addition to details about the book. When the `show` action of the book controller is called, books are retrieved from the database. Because books contain a has_many relationship to reviews, the corresponding reviews should also be returned. It's a good idea to further extend the `test_show` method to verify that those book reviews are indeed returned and properly displayed on the book show page.

So far, you've created fixtures only for book records. The test database will not contain any review records. Go ahead and add some reviews to the test database by adding some review fixtures. Open up `test/fixtures/reviews.yml` and edit it to look like this. Each review specifies the name of the user and book fixtures to which it is related — the user and book fixtures must also exist:

```
one:
  user: valid_user
  book: one
  body: This is a test review.
  title: Test Review 1
two:
  user: valid_user
  book: one
  body: Another test review.
  title: Test Review 2
```

Now the first book defined in the books fixture will have two reviews associated with it. Let's verify that the has_many association on the book model is working by making sure that the book with id = 1 also has an array of two book reviews. After adding an assertion (the bold text in the following code) to verify the size of the book reviews array, the `test_show` method will now look like this:

```
def test_show
  get :show, :id=>'1'
  book = assigns(:book)
  assert_equal "Ruby on Rails Bible", book.title
  assert_equal 2, book.reviews.size
  title = assigns(:title)
  assert_equal "Book Detail", title
  assert_response :success
  assert_template "show"
  assert_select "div#book_image"
  assert_select "div#book_summary"
  assert_select "div#book_reivews"
end
```

The last thing you'll do to finish the `test_show` method is to add a few more `assert_select` methods to verify that the book reviews are rendered as expected. Listing 9.1 shows the final form of the `test_show` method.

LISTING 9.1

Final test_show Method

```
def test_show
  get :show, :id=>'1'
  book = assigns(:book)
  assert_equal"Ruby on Rails Bible", book.title
  assert_equal 2, book.reviews.size
  title = assigns(:title)
  assert_equal "Book Detail", title
  assert_response :success
  assert_template "show"
  assert_select "div#book_image"
  assert_select "div#book_summary"
  assert_select "div#book_reievws"
  assert_select "div#reivews" do
    assert_select "div.review", 2 do
      assert_select "span.review_title"
      assert_select "span.review_user"
      assert_select "span.review_body"
    end
  end
end
```

The first new assert that is added deserves a bit of explanation, as it is more complicated than the previous uses of `assert_select`. This assertion looks for a `div` tag containing an `id` attribute named `reviews`. That much you've seen before, but there is more. In order to match, the `div` tag must also contain two child `div` tags, each with a `class` attribute named `review`. The last four assertions will assure that the rendered page correctly contains the review information.

Verify the tests again

With the completed `test_list` and `test_show` methods, let's run the functional tests again to verify that the new tests pass. If all goes well, you will have no failures.

In a real project, you would ideally have been writing these tests either before you wrote the code or shortly after you wrote the code. All of the controllers would have a suite of tests providing full functional test coverage for the application. Full test coverage is not shown in this book, but if you download the Book Shelf application from this book's Web site, you can look through a full suite of tests that are included.

Unit Tests

Unit tests are used to test methods contained in your model classes. These tests are used to test the majority of your business logic, which should be in your models. Unit testing is also the most popular form of testing that Rails supports.

While not everyone is familiar with writing functional and integration tests, most good developers today do have some practice writing unit tests. I strongly encourage you to write all three types of tests, but at a minimum, you should write unit tests for your applications.

Take a look at one of the unit test files that was generated for you while you were developing the Book Shelf application. The code below is the current unit test file for the user model, contained in `test/unit/user_test.rb`:

```
require File.dirname(__FILE__) + '/../test_helper'

class UserTest < ActiveSuport::TestCase
  fixtures :users

  # Replace this with your real tests.
  def test_truth
    assert true
  end
end
```

So far, the unit test contains only a dummy test method that will always succeed. Listing 9.2 shows the user model code that you'll write unit tests for.

LISTING 9.2

User Model Code

```
require 'digest/sha1'

class User < ActiveRecord::Base

    has_and_belongs_to_many :books

    validates_length_of :login, :within => 3..40
    validates_length_of :password, :within => 5..40
    validates_presence_of :login, :email, :password, :password_
  confirmation, :password_salt
    validates_uniqueness_of :login, :email
    validates_confirmation_of :password
    validates_format_of :email, :with => /^([^@\s]+)@((?:[-a-z0-
  9]+\.)+[a-z]{2,})$/i, :message => "Invalid email"
```

continued

361

LISTING 9.2 *(continued)*

```
  attr_protected :id, :password_salt

  attr_accessor :password, :password_confirmation

def self.authenticate(login, pass)
  u=find(:first, :conditions=>["login = ?", login])
  return nil if u.nil?
  return u if User.encrypt(pass, u.password_salt)==u.password_hash
  nil
end

def password=(pass)
  @password=pass
  self.password_salt = User.random_string(10) if !self.password_salt?
  self.password_hash = User.encrypt(@password, self.password_salt)
end

def send_new_password
  new_pass = User.random_string(10)
  self.password = self.password_confirmation = new_pass
  self.save
  Notifications.deliver_forgot_password(self.email, self.login, new_
pass)
end

protected

def self.encrypt(pass, password_salt)
  Digest::SHA1.hexdigest(pass+password_salt)
end

def self.random_string(len)
  #generate a random password consisting of strings and digits
  chars = ("a".."z").to_a + ("A".."Z").to_a + ("0".."9").to_a
  newpass = ""
  1.upto(len) { |i| newpass << chars[rand(chars.size-1)] }
  return newpass
  end
end
```

The User class contains the following methods, which you'll want to test:

- `self.authenticate`
- `password`

- `self.encrypt`
- `self.random_string`

Before you write any tests, the first thing you'll want to do is set up some user fixtures so that you have user records to test with.

Setting up user fixtures

As you did when writing functional tests, you should first be thinking about the test data that you will use. Because you will be testing the user model, it makes sense that you will need some sample user test records. Edit the `users` fixture, located in `test/fixtures/users.yml`. Add a single user to the fixture, as defined below:

```
valid_user:
    login: clark
    email: clark@dailyplanet.com
    password_salt: 123
    password_hash: f2b14f68eb995facb3a1c35287b778d5bd785511 #secret
```

This record represents a valid user of the Book Shelf application. Because a password hash is a common element of most authentication systems, let's talk about how the password hash test value was determined. Using the Book Shelf user model and the handy Rails Console application, you can find the hash for any password and salt combination that you want.

Let's walk through the steps:

1. **Start up the Rails Console in the** `book_shelf` **directory.**

    ```
    > ruby script/console
    ```

2. **Call the** `User.encrypt` **method to calculate a password hash.**

    ```
    >> hash = User.encrypt('secret','123')
    => f2b14f68eb995facb3a1c35287b778d5bd785511
    ```

    The `User.encrypt` method calculates the password hash for the password and salt values passed in, and returns it. You can then plug this value into a user fixture. This is the same method that the Book Shelf application will use when it calculates password hashes at run-time.

Test authentication

Now that you have a user fixture defined, you have all you need to begin writing unit tests. Start by writing a unit test for the `authenticate` method. The `authenticate` method is a class method of the `User` class. It takes a login and password and returns a `User` object if the following conditions are satisfied:

- A user exists in the database with a login matching the login value passed in.

- The correct password value for that user is passed in.

Because you added a user to the `users` fixture, when these tests are run, there will be a valid user in the test database. You can test using a valid login and password by passing in the login and password that was used in the fixture record, `"clark"` and `"secret"`. Start the `test_authenticate` method with that test case:

```
def test_authenticate
  # check with a valid login and password
  assert_equal @valid_user, User.authenticate("clark", "secret")
end
```

When you write unit tests, keep in mind that you should not only test for positive conditions, such as whether a method works when it receives data that it expects, but you should also verify that the method behaves as expected when it receives input that will not result in a good or passing condition. In the case of the `authenticate` method, you should also verify that it works when you pass in an invalid login, an invalid password, or both. Add those test cases to the `test_authenticate` method so that it now looks like this:

```
def test_authenticate
  # check with a valid login and password
  assert_equal @valid_user, User.authenticate("clark", "secret")

  # check with incorrect login, correct password
  assert_nil User.authenticate("badlogin", "secret")

  # check with incorrect password, correct login
  assert_nil User.authenticate("clark", "badpassword")

  # check with incorrect login and password
  assert_nil User.authenticate("badlogin", "badpassword")
end
```

With those additions, you have a more thorough test for the `authenticate` method. The test will make sure that `authenticate` returns a valid user object when it should, and it will make sure that it does not return a user instance when it should not.

With the `test_authenticate` method complete, it's time to run the unit tests to make sure that everything works as expected. All of your unit tests can be run with a special Rake command, just like you used to run the functional tests. Run the `rake test:units` command and verify that you receive output similar to that shown in Figure 9.3.

FIGURE 9.3

Running unit tests, part 1

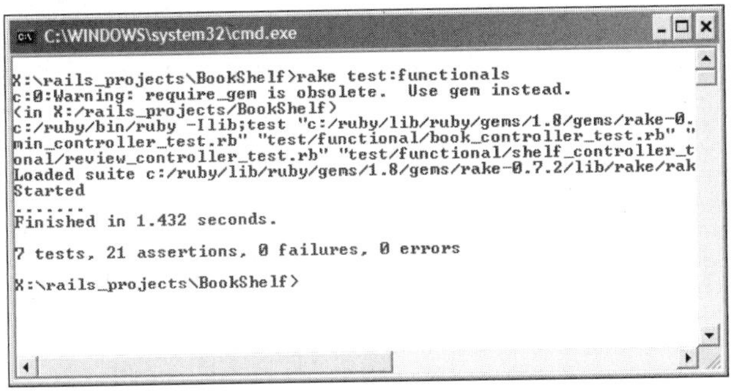

Test validations

Now that you have a test to validate the `authenticate` method, the next thing that you probably want to validate with some unit tests is the validations in the user model. Recall that in the user model the following validations were defined:

```ruby
validates_length_of :login, :within => 3..40
validates_length_of :password, :within => 5..40
validates_presence_of :login, :email
validates_uniqueness_of :login, :email
validates_confirmation_of :password
validates_format_of :email,
                    :with => /^([^@\s]+)@((?:[-a-z0-9]+\.)+[a-z]
  {2,})$/i,
                    :message => "Invalid email"
```

These validations deal with three attributes of the user model: `password`, `login`, and `email`. You'll write tests to check that each of these attributes are properly validated.

Test valid password

The `password` attribute has a minimum and maximum length constraint, and a password confirmation constraint. The `validates_confirmation_of` validation will make sure that in order to create a valid user, both a `password` and a `password_confirmation` attribute must be present. If you consider all of these constraints, you can create the following possible password scenarios:

- Password is too short

- Password is too long

- Password is empty

- Password confirmation is empty

- Password is valid

The `test_valid_password` method should then test each of these scenarios and verify the correct behavior. Add the `test_valid_password` method to the `UserTest`:

```
def test_valid_password
  u = User.new
  u.login = "tim"
  u.email = "tim@timothyfisher.com"

  # password too short
  u.password = u.password_confirmation = "a"
  assert !u.save
  assert u.errors.invalid?('password')

  # password too long
  u.password = u.password_confirmation =
      "123456789012345678901234567890123456789012345"
  assert !u.save
  assert u.errors.invalid?('password')

  # empty password
  u.password = u.password_confirmation = ""
  assert !u.save
  assert u.errors.invalid?('password')

  # empty confirmation
  u.password = "password"
  assert !u.save
  assert u.errors.invalid?('password_confirmation')

  # valid password
  u.password = u.password_confirmation = "tims_password"
  assert u.save
  assert u.errors.empty?
end
```

Notice the lines that look similar to this one:

```
assert u.errors.invalid?('password')
```

This line looks at the errors that are a result of validating the user object's attributes. The `invalid?` method will check to see if the attribute name that is passed in is invalid. If it is invalid, based on having run the validation, a value of `true` will be returned. If the field passed into `invalid?` is actually valid after having run the validation, a value of `false` is returned. Therefore, these assertions will pass only if the field names passed into the `invalid?` method are determined to be invalid, based on the validations of the user model.

With these tests in place, you can be fairly confident that the password validations work as expected if all the tests pass. Check that now by running the unit tests again. Once again, use the `rake test:units` command from the `book_shelf` directory, and expect the output shown in Figure 9.4.

Running unit tests, part 2

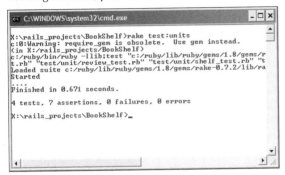

Test valid login

Just as you were able to create a set of scenarios for passwords that could be submitted, let's do the same thing for the possible login values that can be submitted. The `login` attribute has an additional constraint in that it must be unique. You cannot use a login that has already been used by another user in the database. The possible login value scenarios are as follows:

- Login is too short
- Login is too long
- Login is empty
- Login is not unique
- Login is valid

The `test_valid_login` method will test each of these scenarios and verify the correct behavior. Add the `test_valid_login` method to the `UserTest`:

```
def test_valid_login
  u = User.new
  u.password = u.password_confirmation = "cams_password"
  u.email = "camden@fisherfamily.com"

  # login too short
  u.login = "a"
  assert !u.save
  assert u.errors.invalid?('login')

  # login too long
  u.login = "12345678901234567890123456789012345"
  assert !u.save
  assert u.errors.invalid?('login')
```

```
# empty login
u.login = ""
assert !u.save
assert u.errors.invalid?('login')

# non-unique login
u.login = «clark»
u.password = u.password_confirmation = «my_password»
assert !u.save

# valid login
u.login = "camden"
assert u.save
assert u.errors.empty?
end
```

After you've completed the `test_valid_login` method, turn to the now-familiar Rake utility and make sure that all of these tests pass as expected. The expected output is shown in Figure 9.5.

Running unit tests, part 3

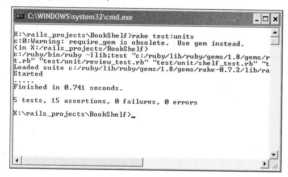

Looking at the test results, you have now created 24 assertions, with one more set of validations to write tests for.

Test valid e-mail

To test the e-mail validations, you'll again start by compiling a list of possible e-mail scenarios. For the e-mail field, there are really only three possible scenarios, defined here:

- E-mail is empty
- E-mail is invalid format
- E-mail is valid

The `test_valid_email` method will test each of these scenarios and verify the correct behavior. Add the `test_valid_email` method to the `UserTest`:

```
def test_valid_email
  u = User.new
  u.password = u.password_confirmation = "cams_password"
  u.login = "camden"

  # no email
  u.email = nil
  assert !u.save
  assert u.errors.invalid?('email')

  # invalid email
  u.email='camatfisherfamily.com'
  assert !u.save
  assert u.errors.invalid?('email')

  # valid email
  u.email="camden@fisherfamily.com"
  assert u.save
  assert u.errors.empty?
end
```

With the completion of the e-mail validation testing, you have now written unit tests to make sure that all of the validations on the Book Shelf user model are indeed working as expected. Now's a good time to run the unit tests a final time to make sure that they all work as expected. Figure 9.6 shows the results you should see when you run the unit tests.

FIGURE 9.6

Running unit tests, part 4

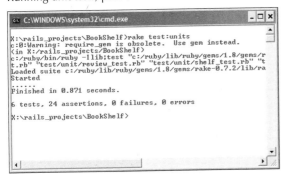

As with functional testing, you were walked through the process of writing unit tests for the Book Shelf application. However, the test coverage is far from complete at this point.

I encourage you to continue this process and write unit tests for the remaining user model methods, and then move on to the other models. At the very least, download the Book Shelf source code from this book's Web site and look at the complete suite of unit tests.

In the next section, you'll see the final type of testing that Rails supports, integration tests.

Integration Tests

Integration tests allow you to test the interaction between multiple controllers. These tests allow you to test out more complete user scenarios, or use cases from your requirements. Another way of thinking about integration tests is that they allow you to simulate a user clicking around and accessing various pages that make up your application.

In this section, you'll write an integration test for the Book Shelf application to test the scenario of having a new user register for the site. Integration tests are the only type of test for which you do not get any starting-point files generated for you by Rails as you generate your models and controllers. However, there is a `generate` method available that you will use to create a starting point for your integration tests.

Start by creating an integration test called `new_user`:

```
> ruby script/generate integration_test new_user
```

This will create a single file, `new_user_test.rb`, in the `test/integration` directory. You will create the integration test in this new file. If you open up this test file, you'll see what has been created for you:

```
require "#{File.dirname(__FILE__)}/../test_helper"

class NewUserTest < ActionController::IntegrationTest
  # fixtures :your, :models

  # Replace this with your real tests.
  def test_truth
    assert true
  end
end
```

You'll create a test called `test_new_user` that will test the process of a new user signing up for the site. You'll start with the user going to the application home page and clicking the Join Now link:

```
def test_new_user
  get "home"
  assert_response :success
  assert_template "index"
```

```
      get "/user/signup"
      assert_response :success
      assert_template "signup"
   end
```

This looks pretty simple and very similar to test assertions that you have used in the functional tests that you wrote. The first three lines request the application home page and verify that a successful response is returned with the correct template rendered.

The next three lines simulate the user having clicked the "Join Now" link by requesting the signup page. Again, the response and template rendered are checked with assertions.

After accessing the user signup page, the next thing the user would do is fill out the registration form and click a Signup button to have the form submitted. Add code to the test to simulate that process:

```
   def test_new_user
      get "home"
      assert_response :success
      assert_template "index"

      get "/user/signup"
      assert_response :success
      assert_template "signup"

      post "/user/signup", :user => {:login => 'tfisher',
        :first_name => 'tom', :last_name => 'fisher',
        :email => 'tom@fisher.com', :password => 'password',
        :password_confirmation => 'password'}
      assert_response :redirect
      follow_redirect!
      assert_template "user/home"
      assert session[:user]
   end
```

Instead of using the get method to request a page, in this new code, the post method is used to submit form parameters to the signup action of the user controller. For the form parameters, you specify a user with all of the fields that are displayed on the signup page filled out. Let's take a look at the signup action to see what should be expected next:

```
   def signup
      @title = "Signup"
      if param_posted?(:user)
        @user = User.new(params[:user])
        if @user.save
          session[:user] = @user
          flash[:notice] = "User #{@user.login} created!"
          redirect_to :action => "home"
        else
```

```
            flash[:error] = "Signup unsuccessful"
            @user.clear_password!
        end
      end
    end
```

By looking at this method, you can see that if a user is saved successfully, a redirect to the home action of the user controller occurs. Looking back at the test method, after the post is issued, you verify that the response returned is a redirect using the `assert_response :redirect` statement.

The next line tells the test framework to follow the redirect. After following the redirect to the home action of the user controller, the `user/home` template should be rendered, and so that is verified with another `assert_template` call. In the last line of the method, you see `assert session[:user]`. This assertion verifies that the user has been stored in the session.

With the test as is, you have verified that the user is able to reach the home page, move to the user signup page, and submit new user information to create a new user account. With assertions along the way, you have verified that the correct responses and templates are received at each step.

At this point, do you know for sure that the user was successfully created? Based on having received successful responses and the correct pages being rendered, you'd like to think so, but it would probably be an even better idea to extend the test to have the new user log out and then log in again. This will verify that the user is successfully able to log in to the new account.

With that complete, you should be satisfied that the new user was successfully created. Add the following lines after the last assertion of the `test_new_user` method:

```
get "/user/logout"
assert_response :redirect
follow_redirect!
assert_template "home/index"
assert !session[:user]
```

You've seen all of these methods and assertions before, and so this code should be pretty straightforward. In the last line, notice that you are making sure that the user is no longer stored in the session. Now go ahead and simulate the user logging back in using the new account to verify that it is successful. Add these lines to the end of the method again:

```
post "user/login, :user => {:login=>'tfisher',
    :password=>'password'}
assert_response :redirect
follow_redirect!
assert_template "user/home"
assert session[:user]
```

The `post` method is used to submit the user login details to the login action of the user controller. You then verify that the correct template is rendered, and you ensure that the user is stored in the session as expected.

With that, you have a complete and useful integration test. The completed integration test is shown in Listing 9.3. Notice that in the integration tests, you did not dive deep into details of the pages and instance variables with assertions. Verifying those details is the job of the functional tests for each controller. The purpose of the integration test is to verify the flow of the application at a higher level and across controllers.

LISTING 9.3

Complete integration test

```
def test_new_user
  # visit the application home page
  get "home"
  assert_response :success
  assert_template "index"

  # request user signup form
  get "/user/signup"
  assert_response :success
assert_template "signup"

  # complete new user form and submit it
post "/user/signup", :user => {:login => 'tfisher',
                      :first_name => 'tom',
                      :last_name => 'fisher',
                      :email => 'tom@fisher.com',
                      :password => 'password',
                      :password_confirmation => 'password'}
assert_response :redirect
follow_redirect!
assert_template "user/home"
assert session[:user]

  # log user out
  get "/user/logout"
  assert_response :redirect
  follow_redirect!
  assert_template "home/index"
  assert !session[:user]

  # log user back in
  post "user/login, :user => {:login=>'tfisher', :password=>'password'}
  assert_response :redirect
  follow_redirect!
  assert_template "user/home"
  assert session[:user]
end
```

Running All Tests

At this point, if you've been diligently following along with writing the tests for the Book Shelf application, or if you simply downloaded the application with complete tests, then you have tests of each type — functional, unit, and integration. While you were developing these tests, you saw how to run each type independently.

There is also an easy way to run all of the automated tests for your application at once. In fact, the way in which you run all tests will show you how important the Rails developers felt testing was to development. If you run the Rake utility with no arguments, all of the tests will be run. The default task for Rake is to run all of the tests.

Try running all tests now, and verify that you get output similar to that shown in Figure 9.7.

```
> rake
```

FIGURE 9.7

Running all tests

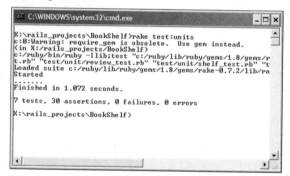

Test Coverage

In this chapter, you have written a handful of tests for the Book Shelf application. However, if you consider all of the code that you wrote in Chapters 6, 7, and 8, there is still plenty of code for which no tests exist. A measure of how well the application code base is covered by tests is called the *test coverage*. Test coverage can be a good metric to maintain over a development project.

Test coverage is a measure of how much of your code is actually exercised by your test suite. The coverage tool runs your tests and counts which lines of code are actually touched when running the tests and which are ignored. By definition, lines of code not touched by any of your tests are not being properly tested.

The standard Ruby tool for measuring test coverage is called rcov. It is available as a ruby gem or as a native exception. If you can, install the native exception version, it's about 100 times faster. Instructions for downloading and installing rcov differ based on operating system, and can be found at `http://eigenclass.org/hiki.rb?rcov`.

To integrate rcov with rails, you also need the `rails_rcov` plugin, which can be installed using the command:

```
./script/plugin install http://svn.codahale.com/rails_rcov
```

With both of those installations taken care of, you now have the extra rake tasks `test:units:rcov`, `test:functionals:rcov` and `test:integrations:rcov`. Invoking one of these tests runs the rcov coverage test against the relevant test suite.

The output of these rake tasks is a series of HTML files. The main one, `index.html`, contains a list of all files touched by the code suite. For each file, rcov reports the percentage of total lines touched and the percentage of actual code lines touched. Ideally you are at 100 percent on both measures. Clicking on a file name shows the source for that file color-coded — green lines are actually touched in the code, while red ones are not.

Code coverage is a necessary, but not sufficient, condition of a good test suite. The coverage tool does not know whether the lines are actually involved in an assertion against them, or if the test just happens to run the line without verifying it's functionality. You still need to write good tests, the coverage tool will just show you places that need more focus.

If you want a really involved test of your suite coverage, look up a Ruby gem called Heckle. Heckle will take a model or controller in your system, make a random change to it, and verify that you then have a code failure. If you have true complete coverage, than any change in your code should trigger a test failure somewhere.

Debugging Techniques

Debugging is a process closely related to testing, and Rails also provides you with some special support for debugging your Rails applications.

The Rails log files

Rails automatically generates and writes to log files as your application runs. The log files are located in the application's top-level `log` directory. The information written to these files can be one of your greatest resources in debugging problems in your application.

Each of the three environments that Rails defines — development, production, and test — has a separate log file. These files are named `development.log`, `production.log`, and `test.log`. As you develop your Rails applications, the `development.log` file will be the file that you are primarily interested in. This is also the log file that contains the greatest level of detail.

The information written to the development log files includes the following:

- Incoming request details, including any parameters that are sent.
- Any SQL queries that are performed by the application.
- The results of requests, such as page renders or redirects.
- Any information you write to the log file using the logger object.

If you are developing on a UNIX-based system, such as Linux, the `tail` command is very useful for watching the log file as your Rails application runs. Using the `tail` command like this from your application's root directory will cause the log contents to be written to the console in which this command is executed:

```
tail -f log/development.log
```

Although the `tail` command is not a part of Windows natively, you can install a Windows version of tail by downloading this free version from Bare Metal Software:

```
www.baremetalso ft.com/baretail
```

Console-based

The Rails Console is perhaps the most useful debugging tool and probably the tool that you will use the most often to debug, test, and try things out while you are coding. The Rails Console provides an interactive environment based on the Ruby irb utility.

In addition to being a command-line parser for Ruby, like irb, Rails loads your application environment. You can use all of your Rails classes, including models and controllers within the Console.

Using the debugger

Most developers are familiar with using a debugger, either a command-line debugger or a graphical debugger that has been integrated into an IDE. In Rails 2.0, Rails uses the ruby-debug gem to create a debugger. With the gem installed, start the server using the option –debugger or –u. Place the command debugger at the breakpoint in your application.

The console that runs the server will enter the debugger, giving you commands to execute expressions, check out the stack state, and step through the program. More details are available at www.datanoise.com/ruby-debug. You should also be able to similarly invoke the debugger during tests.

Summary

In this chapter, you've learned how easy Rails makes it to write tests for your Rails Web applications. Hopefully, you have also gained an appreciation for the value of writing those tests. Whether or not a developer regularly writes unit tests for the code they write, is increasingly considered a measure of how good a developer is. The best developers make it a regular practice to write unit tests while they are writing the code for their applications.

You learned that Rails has built-in support for three types of testing for your applications: unit, functional, and integration tests. Each type tests different aspects of your application and is important to your overall testing strategy.

Debugging is a process that is closely related to testing. Ideally, the better you become with writing tests, the less debugging you'll have to perform. However, you will always encounter situations where you need to debug some problems that occur with your application. Rails provides a number of features that help you debug while you are developing an application. In this chapter, you learned how to use Rails log files, the Rails Console, and the breakpointer utility to assist with debugging.

Part IV

Advanced Rails

Chapter 10

Using Prototype and script.aculo.us

oday's browser-based applications are becoming more dynamic, more interactive, and richer than they have ever been before. Alternative Web application solutions such as Flash have increased user expectations of what is possible in a Web application. If HTML applications are to remain a viable solution for developing rich Internet applications, then web developers need to use all the power of JavaScript in ways it has never been used before.

This chapter will introduce you to the JavaScript libraries Prototype and script.aculo.us, and you'll see how you can use those libraries to develop highly interactive and rich Web 2.0-style applications built on the Rails framework. Just as using Rails can increase your productivity when developing server-side code for your Web applications, using Prototype and script.aculo.us will increase your productivity in writing client-side JavaScript.

Rails provides a number of useful helpers for integrating these libraries using Ruby code, however at some point you will reach the limits of what is possible using RJS, and it'll be time for you to work directly in JavaScript. Knowing the details of these libraries will help you make your application unique.

Prototype, script.aculo.us, and Rails

The Prototype and script.aculo.us JavaScript libraries are included with the Rails distribution. When you install Rails, you also get these libraries with nothing more to install. Rails support for these libraries doesn't stop there, though.

Rails also includes built-in helper methods that make using these libraries in a Rails application very simple; in fact, some developers use these libraries without even realizing it. Many of the Rails form and Ajax helper methods use Prototype in their implementation.

The Rails development team has done a good job of seamlessly integrating these libraries into the Rails view layer. However, it is important to realize that even though these libraries are included with the Rails distribution, they are not dependent on Rails, nor is their development tied to Rails. Each of the libraries can also be used in non-Rails applications. They can be, and are, used with applications written in Java, PHP, Python, .Net, or any other back-end language that you choose.

The reason for having two JavaScript libraries is that each of the libraries provides functionality at a different level. The Prototype library provides lower-level functionality such as extensions to the JavaScript language, event handling, form handling, and Ajax support. script.aculo.us provides higher-level functionality that is aimed more at developers who want to create rich and spectacular browser-based applications.

script.aculo.us provides functionality to help with visual effects, drag and drop, auto-completion, element sorting, in-place editing, and rich controls. script.aculo.us is built on top of the Prototype library. You can use Prototype on its own without script.aculo.us, but if you are using script.aculo.us, you must also be using Prototype.

The official Web sites for each of these libraries can be found here:

- `www.prototypejs.org`
- `http://script.aculo.us/`

Using Prototype and script.aculo.us from Rails

If you've looked around in the `public/javascripts` directory of any Rails application, you've probably come across these Prototype and script.aculo.us library files:

- `prototype.js`
- `scriptaculous.js`
- `builder.js`
- `effects.js`
- `dragdrop.js`
- `slider.js`
- `controls.js`

Only the `prototype.js` file is a Prototype library file. The rest of the `.js` files are parts of the script.aculo.us library. When you include the default JavaScript files in a Rails application by using the following line in the HTML header section of your layout, the Prototype and script.aculo.us libraries are automatically included and available in all of your template files:

```
<%= javascript_include_tag :defaults %>
```

Typically you would put this line in a layout file, such as the global layout file, `application.html.erb`. This gives you access to the libraries from any of your view templates that use the layout.

In the sections that follow, you'll learn more about how Prototype and script.aculo.us can help you create a fantastic Web application and allow you to write cleaner and more readable JavaScript. As you're learning, keep in mind that this chapter is geared toward using these libraries with Rails, and does not provide a full reference to either of these libraries.

Rails provides helpers for many of the Prototype and script.aculo.us methods and classes. The Rails helpers generate JavaScript that uses Prototype and script.aculo.us, and so in many cases you get the power of these libraries without having to directly use them. Where Rails helpers are available, it is these helpers that you will primarily use in this chapter, rather than Prototype and script.aculo.us methods directly.

Create a Rails project

Before you move, it's a good time to create another Rails application that you can use throughout this chapter to test the code that you'll be learning.

1. **Create a new Rails project.** Go into your projects directory and run the Rails command:

   ```
   > rails dynamic_app
   ```

2. **Generate a home controller.** Navigate to the `dynamic_app` directory and generate a home controller:

   ```
   > ruby script/generate controller Home
   ```

You'll use this application and its home controller to display pages that contain code that you'll write throughout this chapter, to demonstrate the power of the Prototype and script.aculo.us libraries.

Include the Prototype and script.aculo.us files

You have to add an `include` tag to your application layout template so that the Prototype and script.aculo.us libraries are available to your view templates. Create the layout template `application.html.erb` in `dynamic_app/app/views/layout` and include this code:

```
<!DOCTYPE html PUBLIC "-//W3C//DTD XHTML 1.0 Transitional//EN"
    "http://www.w3.org/TR/xhtml1/DTD/xhtml1-transitional.dtd">
<html>
```

```
<head>
    <title>Dynamic App</title>
    <%=  stylesheet_link_tag "style" %>
    <%= javascript_include_tag :defaults %>
</head>

<body>
    <%= yield %>
</body>
</html>
```

By passing the `:defaults` parameter to the `javascript_include_tag`, you are telling Rails to include a standard set of JavaScript libraries in the template. The standard set of JavaScript files includes the following:

- `application.js`

  A file that you use to place your custom JavaScript code in.

- `prototype.js`

  Implements the Prototype library.

- `controls.js`

  Implements the Controls functionality of the script.aculo.us library.

- `dragdrop.js`

  Implements the drag-and-drop functionality from script.aculo.us.

- `effects.js`

  Implements the visual effects functionality from script.aculo.us.

Prototype Overview

Just a few years ago, JavaScript was generally looked down upon as one of the least powerful of programming languages, in part because complex tool support, such as editors and debuggers, was lacking. Most developers usually avoided writing much JavaScript, preferring to do as much as possible on the server-side. Much of the JavaScript that was created was poorly written, and hard to read and maintain. JavaScript is a powerful language that not many people took the time to properly learn or make use of its full power.

With the advent of Web 2.0-style applications, with their richer and more interactive browser-based features, the necessity to use JavaScript and implement more complex behavior with it has grown. Fortunately, some developers recognized the need for libraries that could help them write better and more powerful JavaScript. Just as there are many libraries to help you on the back end, there are now many library choices on the front end as well. The Prototype library was spun off from Rails and was first released as a standalone library in 2005.

Considering the great deal of functionality in Prototype, it remains relatively small in physical size. The entire library is contained in a single JavaScript file called `prototype.js`. It is approximately 120KB in size, or less than 30KB if it is gzipped. Within that relatively small library, Prototype packs a great deal of functionality.

To cover all of its functionality would require a great deal more than a single chapter of a book. There are entire books available that cover Prototype and script.aculo.us. In this chapter, you focus on a selection of the functionality that you'll find most useful in implementing a Rails application.

Ruby's influence on Prototype

Prototype was inspired by Ruby and can often feel like Ruby when you use it. Many of the additions and extensions that Prototype makes to JavaScript have a Ruby-style syntax. This makes using Prototype even easier for Ruby developers, who find the syntax of Prototype very intuitive and familiar.

What is Prototype?

Prototype is a JavaScript library designed to make it easier to write good JavaScript. The prototype library provides features in these main areas:

- Extensions to JavaScript
- DOM manipulation
- Event handling
- Forms
- Ajax

Of these areas, this chapter covers extensions to JavaScript, event handling, and Ajax.

As it is important to understand what Prototype provides you as a developer, it is just as important to understand what Prototype is not. Prototype does not provide widgets, drag and drop, or other rich interface components. Rather, it provides the layer between a rich UI JavaScript toolkit and raw JavaScript. Many higher-level JavaScript libraries, including script.aculo.us, use Prototype.

At the time of this book's writing, the current version of Prototype is 1.6.0.2. This is the version that is bundled with Rails 2.0.

Extensions to JavaScript

The Prototype library includes features that essentially extend the JavaScript language, providing a great deal of utility functionality that you'll use with your JavaScript.

One of the ways in which Prototype extends JavaScript is by enhancing JavaScript's OOP support. Prototype makes it easy to build classes and extend classes through inheritance. OOP in native JavaScript uses a slightly different paradigm than most other Object-Oriented languages (prototype instance, rather than class instance) and has been avoided by most developers.

Simplifying JavaScript with the dollar sign

Prototype offers a set of utility functions that provide shortcuts for some extremely useful methods that you will use on a regular basis. These methods all have very short names that begin with the dollar sign ($). The most often-used of these methods is the $ method. The other methods consist of the $ followed by a single additional character. Table 10.1 summarizes these methods.

TABLE 10.1

Prototype's $ Methods

Method Name	Description	Sample Usage
$	Element selector, essentially equivalent to `getElementById`. Returns elements with prototype DOM extensions.	`$('sidebar')`
$$	Selects all elements that contain the ID passed in using CSS3 selectors, in the order they exist in the document.	`$$('content_section')`
$A	Converts array-compatible items to an array.	`$A(arguments)`
$w	Splits a string into an array of words.	`$w('one two three four')`
$F	Extracts the current value of a form field selected by ID.	`$F('phone_number')`
$H	Shortcut for creating new hashes.	`state_codes = $H`
$R	Creates a range.	`$R (1,10)`

Selecting elements with $

The $ method is the most frequently used method in all of Prototype. The $ method replaces the longer `document.getElementById(id)` standard method. You use the $ method like this:

```
content_element = $('content')
```

Besides being a much shorter method to type, a big advantage of using the $ method over `document.getElementById()` is that the $ method returns a a DOM element that has Prototype extensions included. This means that the element returned by $ has access to all the additional methods that Prototype adds to elements. These extensions include several dozen methods that can be called on any element that has been accessed via $.

Table 10.2 contains a list of some of the most interesting methods.

TABLE 10.2

Methods to Call on Any Element Accessed by $

Method	Description
element.addClassName(ccsClass)	Adds the CSS class to the element.
element.ancestors()	Returns all of the element's ancestors as an array. The ancestors all contain the Prototype extensions.
element.childElements()	Returns all of the element's children as an array. The ancestors all contain the Prototype extensions.
element.descendents()	Returns all of the element's descendants as an array. The ancestors all contain the Prototype extensions.
element.empty	Returns true if the element only contains white space.
element.fire(event)	Fires a custom event for the element.
element.getStyle(property)	Returns the value of the CSS property specified.
element.hide	Hides the element.
element.insert(content) element.insert({position: content})	Inserts the content in the element at the specified position. The position properties are as in the Rails RJS helper.
element.remove()	Removes the element from the dom.
element.replace(html)	Replaces the element with the HTML content specified. This includes the tag itself.
element.show()	Shows the element.

In most cases, the $ method can take either the ID of a DOM element, however you can also pass the method an normal DOM element, in which case, the Prototype extensions will be added to the element.

Selecting elements with $$

The $$ method allows you to select all elements on a page that match a condition that you can use a CSS3 selector to specify. Even if the browser in which a user is running your application does not support CSS3, these selectors still work. This is because Prototype has implemented the CSS3 selectors itself.

The current version of Prototype supports the selectors described here:

- **Type:** Select using tag names, such as `div`.

```
$$('div')
// selects all DIVs in the document and returns them as
   extended elements in
// an array.
```

■ **Descendant:** Allows you to select descendents of a tag, as in this example:

```
$$('#content a')    // selects all link elements contained
    within the
// #content element.
```

■ **Attribute:** Allows you to select elements based on the presence of attributes. The full set of CSS3 attribute selectors is supported. Some examples are shown here:

```
$$('div[class]')  // selects all div elements that contain a
    class attribute.

$$('div[class=box]') // selects all div elements that contain a
    class attribute
                    // containing the value of box.
```

Additional CSS3 attribute selectors allow you to select attributes that contain a given substring, attributes that start or end with a given value, attributes that do not have a given value, and more. For the full set of CSS3 attribute selectors, see www.w3.org/TR/css3-selectors/#attribute-selectors.

■ **Class:** Allows you to select all elements that contain a given CSS class name.

```
$$('.odd_row') // selects all elements that contain the CSS
    class odd_row.
```

■ **Child:** Similar to the descendant selector, except that the child selector selects only direct children.

```
$$('#content>div') // selects div elements that are direct
    children of the
                    // #content element.
```

■ **Sibling:** The selector matches a pair of elements that both have the same parent if the first tag comes earlier in the document than the second.

```
$$('li.first + li.second')
```

The following CSS pseudo-classes have the same meaning in Prototype as they do in the CSS specification:

■ :nth:

■ :first:

■ :last

■ :empty:

■ :enabled, :disabled, :checked:

Creating arrays with $A

The $A method converts any iterable set of items into a JavaScript Array object. You want to do this because Prototype extends the Array class significantly, as discussed later in this chapter.

```
$A(document.getElementsByTagName('li');
```

Splitting strings with $w

The $w method is used to convert a string into an array. It's the same as Ruby's %w mechanism.

```
$w('one two three four')
// creates an array that looks like this:
//    ['one','two','three','four']
```

The string that you pass to the $w method is split on white space. It does not properly convert a comma-delimited string of values.

Getting form field values with $F

The $F method allows you to retrieve the current value of any form field within a document. To retrieve a value, you pass the ID of a form field to the $F method.

```
$F('first_name_field')
```

Remember that you must pass the ID of a form field. Passing a form field's name does not work.

Creating hashes with $H

The $H method is a shortcut for creating Prototype Hash objects. The other way of creating a Prototype Hash object is to use the standard Hash.new() method.

Creating ranges with $R

Ranges are a programming structure that many developers are first exposed to when they learn Ruby. The $R method allows you to create ranges in JavaScript similar to the way you create ranges in Ruby code. You pass start and end integer values to the $R method to create a range that spans those values.

```
$R(1,10)
```

This creates a range of integers starting at one and ending with ten. By default, the range contains the ending number, but if the optional third argument is true, then the range does not contain the ending value. Prototype ranges implement Prototype's Enumerable module, and also have a method include that takes an argument and returns true if that argument is in the range.

More powerful arrays

The JavaScript Array object is probably one of the most useful objects in JavaScript. Prototype adds to the usefulness of JavaScript arrays by adding 35 additional methods to an array. Many of these methods come through Prototype's implementation of an Enumerable module, which behaves very similar to Ruby's enumerable functionality. Table 10.3 lists methods that are added to JavaScript arrays by Prototype.

Enumerating an array

Prototype mixes the Enumerable module into JavaScript Array objects. The most common method that is gained from Enumerable is the each method. Using the each method, you can step through each element of an array and take action on it using a function that you pass as a parameter.

```
list = ['tim', 'kerry', 'camden', 'timmy'];
list.each(function(val) {
        alert(val)
    });
```

You'll recognize this as being very similar to the each method available in Ruby. The other Enumerable methods are not listed in the below table but are very similar to the methods provided by Ruby's Enumerable method.

TABLE 10.3

Prototype's Array Methods

Method	Description
Array.from	Converts an iterable item into an Array object. Equivalent to $A().
clear	Clears the array of all values.
clone	Returns a duplicate of the array.
compact	Returns a copy of an array with any null or undefined elements removed
each	Iterates through each element of an array
first	Returns the first element of the array
flatten	Returns a one-dimensional version of the array, with multi-dimensional elements occurring in the same relative order.
indexOf	Returns the index of an element passed in, or -1 if the element is not found
inspect	Returns a string representing the values in the array
intersect	Returns a new array consisting of any elements that exist both in the current array and the one passed as a parameter
last	Returns the last element of the array
lastIndexOf	Returns the index of the last occurrence of the element passed in, or -1 if the element is not found
reduce	If the array has just one element, returns that element, otherwise return the array unchanged. Turns a nested array into a flat single-level array
reverse	Reverses the contents of an array
size	The size of the array as an integer
toJSON	Returns the array as a JSON string representation.
uniq	Creates a new array with any duplicate items removed
without	Returns a new array that does not contain any of the passed arguments

JSON support

If you've developed a rich browser-based application that uses Ajax, then you are probably familiar with JSON, which stands for *JavaScript Object Notation*. JSON is a method of representing objects or text using standard JavaScript syntax. Using JSON, you can represent an arbitrary object structure including objects, strings, arrays, Booleans, or other value types as a simple string value. This is useful for passing structured data and objects across an interface, such as when you make an Ajax call. The use of JSON is growing, and it is rapidly displacing XML as the preferred format for sending and receiving complex data when using Ajax.

Prototype provides the following methods for encoding JavaScript data using JSON:

```
Object.toJSON(obj)
array.toJSON()
date.toJSON()
hash.toJSON()
number.toJSON()
string.toJSON()
```

The first method, `Object.toJSON`, is a static method that converts whatever object you pass into it to JSON format. The other `toJSON` methods are instance methods that are provided for specific object types: `Array`, `Date`, `Hash`, `Number`, and `String`.

If you already have a JSON-encoded string, Prototype provides you with a way to decode that back into JavaScript object structures using this method:

```
jsonString.evalJSON([sanitize = false])
```

The `evalJSON` method returns a JavaScript object. The method takes a single optional parameter named `sanitize`. This parameter provides a measure of security for JavaScript that you are attempting to evaluate. By setting this parameter to true, the method makes sure that the JSON string contains only JavaScript that follows accepted syntax.

Let's take a look at a practical example of converting a JavaScript array to JSON and back:

```
var book = {title: 'Ruby on Rails Bible',
            publisher: 'Wiley',
            keywords: ['ruby', 'rails', 'programming'],
            pubDate: new Date(2008, 5,12)};
json_val = Object.toJSON(book);

// json_val =
// '{"title":"Ruby on Rails Bible", "publisher","Wiley",
//   "keywords":["ruby","rails","programming"],"pubDate":"2008-05-
     12T00:00"}'
```

In this example, the `book` object contains two string value attributes, an array attribute, and a date attribute. Each of these are converted to JSON and represented in the `json_val` string. The `json_val` string is returned as a single-line string. It is only shown on multiple lines in the example to make a readable display.

Notice that objects or hashes are represented in JSON as data enclosed within curly brackets. Hash keys or object attribute names are enclosed in double quotes and separated from their values with a colon. Arrays are represented in JSON as comma-separated lists enclosed in square brackets.

OOP with Prototype

Object oriented programming (OOP) has always been possible with raw JavaScript, but Prototype makes it easier to use OOP in all of your JavaScript code.

Defining classes and inheritance

JavaScript's object model is a bit unusual, and may be difficult to fully understand if you are used to more traditional class-based object-oriented structures. Object features are much more informal in JavaScript — an object is little more than a hash associating keys with data and functions. Any set of data and functions can be classified as an object at any time. Objects can be extended at any time, and new instances can be created using existing images as a template.

The JavaScript object model is amazingly flexible, but one side effect is that class creation and definition is not necessarily confined to one particular place in the code (this is also true of Ruby, but Ruby is slightly more explicit about delimiting when a class definition starts and ends). In particular, traditional JavaScript style requires you to create the constructor for an object separately from its definition:

```
function Person(name) {
    this.name = name;
}
Person.prototype={
  say: function(message) {return this.name + ': ' + message;}
}
```

Compare that with the way you can create a class using support provided by Prototype. Prototype provides the Class.create function that generates an object and its own instance method. The same class definition in Prototype would look like the following:

```
var Person = Class.create({
    initialize: function(name) {
        this.name = name;
    },
    say: function(message) {
        return this.name + ': ' + message;
    }
});
```

To create a person, you would then do something like this:

```
var person = new Person("Fred Flintstone");
```

Implementing class inheritance with Prototype

There are two ways to implement a traditional class inheritance style in Prototype. The older mechanism is the method `Object.extend(dest, src)`. The destination argument is a JavaScript object, which will receive any new data or methods defined in the source object, which is typically a hash of some kind. This can be combined with either the traditional JavaScript class creation mechanisms or the Prototype `Class.create`.

```
var Student = Class.create();
Student.prototype = Object.extend(new Person(), {
    initialize: function(name, grade) {
        $super(name);
        this.grade = grade;
    }
}
```

However, there's a preferred way in Prototype 1.6 and higher. The `Class.create()` method takes an optional first argument that is the class being overridden or the module being mixed in.

```
var Student = Class.create(Person, {
    initialize: function(name, grade) {
        $super(name);
        this.grade = grade;
    }
}
```

The second mechanism is a little bit cleaner and easier to manage.

Event Handling

Prototype provides a simple, cross-browser way to bind a function to a user event. The method is `Event.observe`, which takes three arguments. The first is a DOM element, or, more likely, the string ID of a DOM element. This is the element being observed. The second is the string name of the event you want to watch for, typically the name of the in-tag handler minus the "on," such as `click` or `change`. The final argument is the function you want to invoke when the event is observed. This can be a predefined function or an anonymous function defined in-line.

```
Event.observe('class_name_menu', "change",
    function() {alert("the name changed");};
```

If for some reason the function being invoked needs to access the `this` variable of the current object (if perhaps you are doing form validation), then the function object needs to be call the Prototype utility `bindAsEventListener`:

```
Event.observe('element', "click",
    observer_func.bindAsEventHandler(obj));
```

The resulting compound function places the object handling the event as the first argument to the outer function.

Ajax

If you regularly develop Web applications, you have probably heard of Ajax over the last year or three. Ajax has been used to create responsive Web applications that feel more like desktop applications. The term Ajax was coined by Jesse James Garret in 2005. *Ajax* stands for Asynchronous JavaScript and XML. A simple explanation of Ajax is that it is a technology that allows you to send requests to a Web server and receive responses without going through the normal full page load mechanism.

One of the Web applications that first gave rise to the current popularity of Ajax is the Google Maps application. Google Maps allows the user to scroll around a map and continuously receive updated map data without performing any page loads. When you scroll a map in Google Maps, asynchronous requests are being submitted to the Google server, and responses of updated map data are returned to the browser. This happens without the user realizing that any client-to-server communication is even taking place.

Another common use of Ajax that you may have come across is the live search feature. When you begin typing a keyword in a text box that is enabled with live search, you immediately begin seeing possible matches for your keyword with each new keystroke that you type. The matches are retrieved through asynchronous calls to the server, with current matches being returned.

When you use only JavaScript, implementing Ajax can be a challenge. Prototype makes using Ajax extremely easy, and Ajax support is one of the most often-used features of Prototype. When you use Prototype and Rails together, writing Ajax calls becomes even easier. Rails includes helper methods that generate the Prototype JavaScript calls that are necessary to communicate with the server through Ajax. I'll walk you through some sample Ajax implementation scenarios in this section.

Ajax links

With a Rails helper, creating an Ajax-enabled link is not much more difficult than creating a regular link. Let's take a look at a simple example:

```
<%= link_to_remote "Get Current Date and Time",
    :update => 'time_and_date',
    :url => { :action => 'get_date_time' } %>
<div id="time_and_date"></div>
```

This example creates a "Get Current Date and Time" link that sends an Ajax call to a server method named `get_date_time`. The `time_and_date` DIV is updated with the result of the Ajax call. The `:update` argument is optional, if it's not there, the assumption is that the server call will trigger an RJS page that will handle more than a single DOM element update.

Ajax link options

You can create powerful and perhaps more useful Ajax-powered links using more of the options that are available to the `link_to_remote` helper method. These options include the following. Note that many of these options can more elegantly handled in an RJS script:

- `:condition`

    A JavaScript expression evaluated when the user intiates the request. It must return true, or the request is cancelled.

- `:before`, `:after`

    These options allow you to specify a function or JavaScript function that is called before or after the Ajax call occurs.

- `:success`, `:failure`

    These options allow you to specify a JavaScript function that is called after the Ajax method returns either successfully or with a failure. This allows you to gracefully handle Ajax failures and perform the intended action only on successful calls. You can also use a specific response code as a an argument, as in `404 => alertNotFound();`

- `:complete`

    A JavaScript expression evaluated when the Ajax request is fully complete, whether it succeeded or failed. This takes place after the success or failure option.

- `:loading`

    Called while the Ajax request is ongoing, typically this is a progress bar or busy cursor.

- `:loaded`

    Called after the remote content has been loaded.

- `:interactive`

    Called if the user can interact with the remote document while it is loading.

- `:confirm`

    The value is a string used as an alert dialog that the user must okay before the Ajax request happens.

- `:submit`

    The parent of the form elements being submitted, if a form submit is happening, and if the parent is not the current form.

- `:with`

    A JavaScript expression that returns a string suitable for appending on the end of the query string of the URL request.

script.aculo.us Overview

The script.aculo.us library is developed in close concert with the Prototype library. Its syntax and usage is very similar to Prototype, and, like Prototype, you will notice its Ruby influence. script.aculo.us extends the functionality of the Prototype library by providing features in the following categories:

- Animation framework
- Drag and drop
- Ajax controls
- DOM utilities
- Unit testing

While Prototype provides relatively low-level functionality that extends JavaScript and makes JavaScript code easier to write and maintain, script.aculo.us provides functionality much closer to the UI layer, allowing you to create exciting and dynamic interface elements for your Web applications.

At the time of this book's writing, the current version of script.aculo.us is 1.8.1. This is the version that is bundled with Rails 2.0.2.

Visual Effects

The visual effects provided by script.aculo.us are probably the most often-used part of the library. They allow you to attach cinematic or animated effects to your JavaScript events. These effects can be used to add visual appeal to your application and create interfaces that traditionally were only seen in richer Flash-based applications.

Rails provides a helper method, and an RJS method to assist you in creating visual effects for DOM elements on your Web page. Try out some of the effects that you can achieve with script.aculo.us by creating a Web page that you can experiment on. Within the `dynamic_app` that you created earlier, create a new view template in `app/views/home` and call it `effects.erb.html`. In the template, type this code:

```
<div id="red_box">Effects</div>
<%= link_to_function "Fade", visual_effect(:fade, :red_box) %>
```

You also need to add a style to your application style sheet in `public/stylesheets/style.css`, as follows:

```
#red_box {
  width: 150px;
  height: 150px;
  background-color: red;
  color: white;
}
```

Now make sure your Web server is running for the `dynamic_app` and navigate to the effects page by going to `http://localhost:3000/home/effects`. You should see a page similar to Figure 10.1, containing a red box and a link with the label Fade. If you click the Fade link, the red box slowly fades away. When it is completely faded from view, it is removed and the Fade link moves up on the page into the space previously occupied by the red box.

FIGURE 10.1

A Fade effect using script.aculo.us

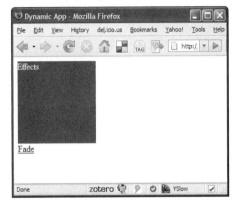

script.aculo.us effects

Fade is just one of many effects that are made available to you by script.aculo.us. Each of these effects is described below. Some of the effects are describe in pairs because they provide opposite effects. You'll understand that better after you read the descriptions. Up-to-date listing and demos of the effects are available at `http://wiki.script.aculo.us/scriptaculous/show/CombinationEffectsDemo`.

- **Fade, Appear:** Gradually decreases or increases an element's opacity until the element is either completely visible or invisible. If the element becomes invisible, its display property is also set to `none`, causing the other page elements to reflow and occupy space that the faded element previously occupied.

- **BlindUp, BlindDown:** Gradually changes the height of an element while leaving the element's content fixed.

- **SlideUp, SlideDown:** Gradually changes the height of an element, where the content appears to be sliding up or down as the height changes. To use this, you must have a wrapper DIV surrounding the content of the target DIV.

- **Shrink, Grow:** Resizes an element from its center point.

- **Highlight:** Temporarily changes the background color of an element to a specified color, or pale yellow by default. This effect is often used to draw the user's attention to a targeted page element.

- **Shake:** Causes an element to shake back and forth horizontally several times. This effect is commonly used to indicate that the targeted element is invalid, such as if you are attempting to drop a draggable element on an invalid drop point.

- **Pulsate:** Rapidly fades an element in and out several times. This can be used to achieve a blinking effect on the targeted item.

- **Dropout:** Fades an element and also slides it downward so that it appears to drop off the page.

- **SwitchOff:** Simulates an old television being shut off. It provides a quick flicker of the element, and then the element collapses into a vertical line.

- **Puff:** Makes an element increase in size while also decreasing in opacity. The effect makes the targeted element seem to disappear in a cloud.

- **Squish:** Resizes an element while maintaining the position of the element's top-left corner.

- **Fold:** Reduces an element's height to a thin line and then reduces its width until the element disappears.

Effect options

Most of the script.aculo.us effects can take options that modify the behavior of the effect. Here are some common options that you'll find useful:

- **duration:** Specifies the duration in seconds for the effect. You pass the duration as a float value. The default duration time is 1 second. An example of setting the duration from the Rails `visual_effect` helper taken from the Rails API is shown here:

```
<%= link_to_remote "Reload", :update => "posts",
        :url => { :action => "reload" },

    :complete => visual_effect(:highlight, "posts", :duration =>
    0.5)
```

This is an example that uses Ajax with a visual effect that is executed upon completion of the Ajax call. The visual effect applies the highlight effect to the DIV with the ID of `posts`. The highlight effect is applied for 0.5 seconds.

- **fps:** Specifies the frames per second for an effect. The fps value defaults to 25 and can be set to any integer value up to a maximum of 100.

- **transition:** Sets a function that modifies the current point of animation, which is between 0 and 1. Several transitions are available out-of-the-box, including the following:

    - `Effect.Transitions.sinoidal`

    - `Effect.Transitions.linear`

    - `Effect.Transitions.reverse`

- ▓ `Effect.Transitions.wobble`
- ▓ `Effect.Transitions.flicker`

The behavior of each of these transition types is best understood by experimenting with them, which I recommend so that you can get a feel for how these transitions modify a particular effect.

- ■ **from:** Used to specify the starting point of a transition as a float value between 0.0 and 1.0. The default value is 0.

- ■ **to:** Sets the end point of a transition to a float value between 0.0 and 1.0. The default value is 1.0.

Using combination effects

script.aculo.us effects can be used together to create even more interesting visual effects. This is accomplished through the `Effect.Parallel` object, which takes an array of other effects as it's main argument. There isn't as much direct Rails support for using parallel effects.

```
new Effect.parallel(
    [new Effect.Shake(element), new Effect.Fade(element)]);
```

Controls

In addition to effects, script.aculo.us provides widget-like components that you can easily integrate into your Web pages. In this section you'll learn how to use three controls provided by script.aculo.us:

- ■ Sliders
- ■ Auto-completion
- ■ In-place editing

Sliders

Sliders are vertical or horizontal UI elements that let you set a value by sliding a visible control along the slider element. Figure 10.2 shows you an example of several sliders implemented using script.aculo.us.

The basic creation of a slider involves creating the slider object, the HTML DOM objects that will interact, and the CSS that will enable them to look something like a slider. The Javascript part looks like this:

```
new Control.Slider('thumb', 'axis', {});
```

FIGURE 10.2

Sliders in script.aculo.us

The two arguments are the DOM ids of the two parts of the slider, the third argument takes any of a number of options that can effect behavior. Generally the DOM elements being referred to are a set of `div` tags, one inside the other.

```
<div id="axis"><div id="thumb"></div></div>
```

Each of those elements needs CSS styles to show up, typically you use the width and height properties to size the elements, and the various color or image elements to make it look pretty. For example:

```
#axis {
    width: 250px;
    height: 10px;
    background-color: black;
}
#thumb {
    width: 5px;
    height: 20px;
    background-color: yellow;
}
```

At this point, the axis and thumb would be drawn on the page and the thumb would move as you'd expect.

The options passed in the creation of the JavaScript slider object control many aspects of its behavior, here are some of them:

- **axis:** Can be either `horizontal` (the default) or `vertical`.
- **range:** The range of slider values, as normally defined using $R.
- **sliderValue:** The initial value of the control.

- **onChange:** An event handler when controls value changes. The function invoked takes one argument, the new value of the slider.
- **onSlide:** Similar to `onChange`, but called when the thumb is dragged.

Auto-completion

The use of auto-completion is gaining popularity for implementing searches within a Web application. Auto-completion refers to a feature that attempts to complete a word or phrase that the user has begun typing in a text field. For example, when auto-completion is implemented in a search box, as the user types characters for the search keyword, the application presents the user with a list of matches based on the characters that are currently entered. As each new character is typed, the list of matches changes to reflect the new partial keyword entry.

script.aculo.us makes implementing auto-completion relatively painless. The script.aculo.us class that you use to implement auto-completion is `Ajax.Autocompleter`. The general syntax of a call to this method is as follows:

```
new Ajax.Autocompleter(text_field_id, div_to_populate_id, url,
    options);
```

The `text_field_id` contains the ID of a text field in which the user types text that is auto-completed. The `div_to_populate_id` contains the ID of a DIV that contains matches based on the text that the user types. The `url` field points to a method on the server that handles the Ajax calls to get matches based on the user's current text. The last parameter, `options`, can contain options that allow you to customize the behavior of the autocompleter.

In Rails, the `auto_complete` plugin is available from `http://svn.rubyonrails.org/rails/plugins/auto_complete` (prior to Rails 2.0 it was part of the core). As I write this, it doesn't seem like the Rails plugins have moved to github with the rest of Rails. Anyway, using the plugin is simplicity itself.

On the view side, the form tag:

```
<%= text_field_with_auto_complete :object, :method %>
```

will create the autocomplete editor (yes, it will also work within `form_for` tags). The method takes a number of optional tags. The most useful are listed in Table 10.4.

On the controller side, the controller declaration looks like this:

```
auto_complete_for :object, :method
```

Further options are sent as the options hash to the `find` command inside that method to customize SQL behavior. The default behavior is to do a `LIKE "%<entry>%"` critera on the selected field, meaning that a match will be counted if the user-typed string appears anywhere in the database entry. Both the entry and the database field are converted to lower case, meaning the search will be case insensitive.

If you want to just match the start of the field or otherwise customize the behavior, override the method `auto_complete_for_#{object}_#{method}`. The output needs to be an HTML `ul` tag. The value input is in `params[object][method]`.

TABLE 10.4

Optional Tags for autocomplete Editor

Option	Description
`after_update_element`	A JavaScript expression that is called after the user makes their selection. It must be a function object that takes two arguments — the DOM id of the autocomplete field, and the value of the user's selection.
`frequency`	Time to wait after a keystroke for the Ajax request to be initiated.
`indicator`	The DOM id of an element to show while the autocomplete request is in progress.
`method`	HTTP action of the Ajax request, defaults to POST.
`min_chars`	The minimum number of characters typed by the user before the control will initiate an Ajax request.
`tokens`	A character set that acts as a delimiter for the user input, allowing the user to auto complete multiple values, as in the tag field of a social networking site.
`with`	As in `link_to_remote`, a JavaScript expression that returns a query string to be sent as part of the Ajax request.

In-place editing

In-place editing is a relatively recent addition to the toolset of a good Web developer. It is now commonplace in many Web 2.0 applications. An in-place editor allows you to dynamically transform a static text field into an editable text area in response to a user action. For example, on a form that shows user information, you might implement in-place editing to allow for easy updating of any of the fields, simply by clicking them. See Figures 10.3 and 10.4 for an example of a form that uses in-place editing, both before and after a field has been clicked.

If you were to implement this task using raw JavaScript, it would take more code and effort that you may think it is worth, and in many cases a developer might end up choosing another way of editing a form, such as by using a pop-up window or even a completely different edit page.

While those can be good solutions, depending on the particular application and the target audience, in-place editing can offer a more user-friendly way of editing simple fields in a quick manner. Fortunately, script.aculo.us makes implementing this functionality relatively easy.

> **NOTE**   If you've heard negative feedback about the script.aculo.us in-place editor in the past, you'll be interested to know that the in-place editor implemented in the 1.8 version of script.aculo.us is nearly a complete rewrite of the code. The problems with the previous version have been cleaned up, and the API has also changed a bit; as a result, the in-place editor code you see here will probably not be compatible with earlier versions of script.aculo.us.

IGURE 10.3

FIGURE 10.3

In-place editing, before clicking a field

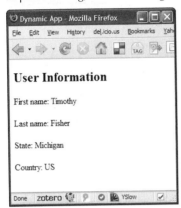

FIGURE 10.4

In-place editing, after clicking a field

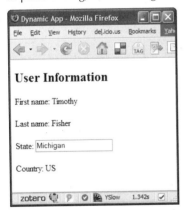

Implementing a single value in-place editor

script.aculo.us supports two basic types of in-place editors. These use two different script.aculo.us objects, `Ajax.InPlaceEditor` and `Ajax.InPlaceCollectionEditor`. The former one is used to create editors for text fields, and the latter one allows you to create editors for drop-down selection lists. Here are the steps required to implement the in-place editor for a single text field:

1. **Start by creating a new view template named** `inplaceedit.rhtml`. Make sure you put the view template into the `app/views/home` directory. Edit the view template to contain this code:

```
<h2>User Information</h2>
<label>First name:</label>
<span id="first_name">Timothy</span>

<script>
    document.observe('dom:loaded', function() {
        new Ajax.InPlaceEditor('first_name', '/home/update');
    });
</script>
```

The view contains a single field that is currently hardcoded in the page. You implement an in-place editor on this field so that you are able to change its value by clicking it, entering a new text value, and pressing Return.

2. **Create a controller method to handle an Ajax update call.** Open the app/controllers/home_controller.rb file and add this method:

```
def update
    render :text => params[:value]
End
```

Make sure the Rails server is running for the dynamic_app and load the page http://local host:3000/home/inplaceedit. You see the single static text field containing the value Timothy. Notice that if you hover over the word Timothy, it becomes highlighted with a pale yellow background. You also see a tooltip that says, "Click to Edit."

If you move off the text, the highlighting slowly fades and the tooltip is removed. If you click the Timothy text, it is replaced with an editable text field, an OK button, and a cancel link. This editable view is shown in Figure 10.5.

FIGURE 10.5

An in-place editor with a single text field

Pressing the cancel link closes the editable text box and returns you to the original, unmodified static text field. If you want to change the text field, you click it, enter a new value, and then press the OK button.

When you press the OK button, an Ajax call is made to the URL that you passed as the second parameter to the `Ajax.InPlaceEditor` method, `/home/update`. This calls the `update` action off the home controller. The `update` action simply gets the new text field value and renders that as text. This is stored back into the original text field on the page.

Building the editor in Rails

Rails also provides a simple in-place editing plugin at http://svn.rubyonrails.org/rails/plugins/in_place_editing. It is very similar to the autocomplete plugin. In the view, use the helper method:

```
<%= in_place_editor_field :object, :method %>
```

Table 10.5 lists the most useful options.

TABLE 10.5

Options for Rails' In-place Editing Plugin

Option	Description
cancel_text	The text for the editing form's cancel button, defaults to "Cancel."
click_to_edit_text	Default text displayed on mouse over of the control in non-edit mode. Default is "Click To Edit."
cols	Number of columns in the edit control, as in an HTML text control.
loading_text	Text displayed while the control is retrieving data from the server via Ajax call.
load_text_url	URL to retrieve the edit data, if for some reason it's different then the default URL. Any structure acceptable by `url_for` is okay here.
options	Any options you want passed along to the Prototype `Ajax.Updater` object.
rows	Number of rows to display. If greater than one, then an HTML text area is used.
save_text	Text for the edit form's save button. Defaults to "ok."
script	If true, then the control will evaluate the result of the Ajax call loading the text as JavaScript.
with	JavaScript expression returning a query string to be appended onto the Ajax request.

And in the controller:

```
in_place_edit_for :object, :method
```

The normal behavior is to update the object with the edited value, and change the method display back to the plain text. Again, if you want custom behavior, directly implement `in_place_edit_for_#{object}_#{method}`, and have it render the text being displayed when the editor is not in use.

Drag and Drop

Desktop applications have used drag-and-drop techniques to manipulate on-screen objects, making the user interface easier and more appealing for many years now. Until recently, drag-and-drop features were rarely seen in a Web application, except perhaps in Flash-based applications.

The JavaScript and DOM manipulation necessary to simulate this type of technique was considered too complex and difficult to write for most developers to accomplish and achieve acceptable performance with. script.aculo.us gives you the ability to add drag-and-drop capability to your Web applications using simple JavaScript methods.

Creating draggable elements

Rails provides you with a convenient helper method for turning any standard DOM element contained on your page into a draggable object. Using the `dynamic_app` project you created, you'll see how you can use Rails helpers to make creating draggable areas simple. In your `dynamic_app`, create a template called `dragndrop.erb.html` in the `app/views/home` directory. Edit the view to contain this code:

```
<div id="drag_me" class="drag_box">Drag Me</div>
<%= draggable_element :drag_me %>
```

You also need to add a new style to your `style.css` stylesheet contained in the `public/stylesheets` directory:

```
.drag_box {
  width: 150px;
  height: 150px;
  background-color: red;
  color: white;
}
```

Save the files, and start up the server for your `dynamic_app` using `ruby script/server`. Navigate to this page by going to `http://localhost:3000/home/dragndrop`. You should see a red box that you can drag around the screen, as shown in Figure 10.6.

You have to admit that was pretty easy. With the power of Rails helpers and script.aculo.us, creating elements that you can drag has now become a very simple task.

FIGURE 10.6

A draggable box

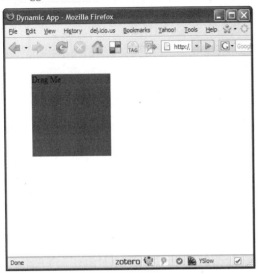

Draggable options

There are several options available for specifying the behavior of draggable elements. Options can be passed to the `draggable_element` helper like this:

```
<%= draggable_element("my_image", :revert => true)
```

In this example, the `:revert` option is passed. This reverts the draggable element to its original position after being dropped. This is useful, for example, if you want to denote dragging an item to something like a shopping cart, but also keeping the element available in the main list of items.

The other options available to draggable elements are as follows:

- **ghosting:** With this option set to true, the original element is left in place and you drag a cloned copy of it.

- **handle:** This option allows you to specify a sub-element to be used as a drag handle. So, instead of dragging an element anywhere, you have to click and drag the element's handle.

```
<div id="drag_box">
    <span id="handle">Drag me</span>
</div>
<%= draggable_element :drag_box, :handle => "'handle'" %>
```

Notice that there are two sets of quotes, double and single, on the handle value. That is not a typographic error. The handle value should be a JavaScript expression that evaluates to an element ID, or an element reference. So, instead of `handle`, you could pass any valid JavaScript expression that evaluated to a handle ID in its place.

- **change:** This option can be set to a function that is called every time the draggable element is moved while dragging. The function gets the draggable element as a parameter. Here is an example:

```
<div id="drag_box">Change Sample</div>
<%= draggable_element :drag_box, :change =>
   "function(draggable) {
draggable.element.innerHTML=draggable.currentDelta()}" %>
```

This example displays the current amount by which the draggable DIV has been dragged.

- **constraint:** This option can be set to `horizontal` or `vertical` and constrains the drag to that dimension.

- **snap:** This option allows you to specify a grid value that causes the draggable element to snap to a grid. For the snap value you can pass an integer, an array of the form [x,y], or a function that is passed the current x,y coordinates of the draggable element. If you pass an integer *n*, the draggable element snaps to a grid of *n* pixels.

If you pass an x,y array, the grid can have different vertical and horizontal dimensions, as specified by the values of x and y. If you pass a function, the coordinates passed to it are offsets from the draggable element's starting position. The function must return the snapped coordinates.

Here are a few examples showing the various uses of snap:

```
<div id="drag_box">Snaps to a grid of 10 pixels</div>
<%= draggable_element :drag_box, :snap => 10 %>

<div id="drag_box">Snaps to a grid of 10 pixels by 20 pixels</
   div>
<%= draggable_element :drag_box, :snap => '[10,20]' %>

<div id="drag_box">Snaps to a grid determined by a function</
   div>
<%= draggable_element :drag_box, :snap => "function(x,y) {
            Return [x<0 ? 0 : (x>100 ? 100 : x),
            Y<0 ? 0 : (y>100 ? 100 : y];
}" %>
```

In the last example, which uses the function to determine the snap coordinates, the technique shown applies boundaries to the drag region. In fact, this is the only way to apply boundaries to a drag region. In this example, the drag region is constrained to a 100-pixel-wide box.

Creating droppable elements

Just like you created a draggable element out of a DOM element, you can create a droppable element from a standard DOM element. Droppable elements provide regions in which you can drop a draggable element.

When a draggable element is dropped on a droppable element, you would typically perform some action. Creating a droppable element is no more difficult than creating a draggable element. Rails provides you with a helper that makes it easy. Add a droppable element to your `dragndrop.erb.html` file with the following code:

```
<div id="drop_here" class="drop_box">Drop here</div
<%= drop_receiving_element :drop_here, :hoverclass => 'hover' %>
```

Droppable options

In the previous example, you saw one option that you can use when creating a droppable element. You used the `hoverclass` option to specify a class that is assigned to the droppable element when a draggable item is hovered over it.

Table 10.6 shows a list of additional options that you can pass to the `drop_receiving_element` helper method. The most important option is :url, which takes a `url_for` compatible destination, and triggers an Ajax call to that location when the drop takes place. The other elements are passed directly through to the script.aculo.us control.

TABLE 10.6

Additional Options to Pass to drop_receiving_element

Method	Description
accept	A string or array of strings, representing the names of CSS classes. If set, those classes are the only objects the droppable will accept.
containment	Like accept, but the droppable will only except items contained by these classes.
greedy	Boolean, default is false. If true, stops the search for further droppables at the drop point.
hoverclass	A CSS class whose properties are added to the droppable when a valid draggable is over it. For highlighting purposes.
overlap	Can be set to horizontal or vertical, controls in which direction the draggable must be more than halfway into the droppable before the drop counts.

Sortable lists

Often, you want to provide a user with the ability to sort a list of items. In the past this has often been implemented by having a set of buttons adjacent to a list that allow you to move a selected item up or down in the list. That type of implementation still exists in many applications today.

A more elegant way of allowing users to sort a list is to enable them to select an element, drag it to the place in the list where it should go, and then drop it there. script.aculo.us assists you in building this type of drag-and-drop enabled sortable lists.

In order to create a sortable list, you need a view that contains an HTML list — either an ordered or unordered list will do. Inside that list, you need to have a series of items. It also helps if you have some way to store or some reason to care about the order in which these items are displayed. Each item needs to have a DOM ID of the form <name>_<id>, and they all need to have the same name. You might also want to have the whole thing surrounded by a div container. A sample view list might look like this:

```
<div id="sortable_container">
  <ul id="sortable">
    <% gizmos.each.sort_by(&:position) do |gizmo| %>
      <li id="gizmo_<%= gizmo.id %>"><%= gizmo.name %></li>
    <% end %>
  </ul>
</div>
```

Then you need a Rails helper to create the script.aculo.us object that manages the sorting. The setup here is very similar to the droppable setup. You want to give the helper the DOM id of the list, as well as a URL for the Ajax callback.

```
<%= sortable_element "sortable", :url => {:action => :sorting} %>
```

At this point, you can drag the list elements around to change their order. The URL is called every time the order changes. In the controller method, the variable params[:sortable_list] contains an array of the IDs of the list elements as they appear in the DOM ids for the li tags.

Within the controller method, you are free to do hatever you want. Commonly, the items are updated in the database with their new position. You can choose to redraw the list based on the new positions, but you don't have to. The control will maintain its own list of items client-side.

Further options that you can pass to the sortable control include but are not limited to the options shown in Table 10.7

TABLE 10.7

Options to Pass to the Sortable Control

Option	Description
constraint	As the option for draggables.
format	A regular expression that controls the split between name and id in the sortable list item DOM IDs. The expression must have two groups with the first representing the group name, and the second representing the item id.

Option	Description
handle	As for draggables.
hoverclass	As for droppables
only	As the accepts option for droppables
overlap	As for droppables
tag	The type of tag being sorted — for a normal list, this would be `li`.

JavaScript Testing

Testing should be important to any developer, but it tends to be especially important to Rails developers, as it is well supported for all of the Ruby code that you will write in creating a Rails application. JavaScript is often the most under-tested piece of a Web application. Sometimes JavaScript is not tested at all.

script.aculo.us includes a unit-testing framework for Java that can help you test your JavaScript. Unfortunately (in my opinion), the standard Rails distribution leaves out the JavaScript file that implements the unit test framework. However, by downloading the script.aculo.us distribution from `http://script.aculo.us` you can get the `unittest.js` file that implements the unit-testing framework.

An alternate way of obtaining the unit test framework is by installing it as a plug-in. From your `dynamic_app` directory, you can install the plug-in by using the `script/plugin` command, as follows:

```
> ruby script/plugin install http://dev.rubyonrails.org/svn/rails/plugins/
    javascript_test
```

In addition to the unit test library, this plug-in includes a generator that allows you to generate unit test files for any of your application-specific JavaScript files, such as `application.js`. A rake task that allows you to run all of your JavaScript tests is also included.

Creating JavaScript unit tests

With the plugin installed, you can generate a JavaScript test file by running the following generate command:

```
> ruby script/generate javascript_test application
```

This generates a test stub that you can use to write unit tests for your JavaScript methods contained in `application.js`. The test stub is placed into `test/javascript/application_test.html`.

Open up the application_test.html file, and you should see a test stub that looks similar to Listing 10.1.

LISTING 10.1

A JavaScript Test Stub

```
<!DOCTYPE html PUBLIC "-//W3C//DTD XHTML 1.0 Transitional//EN"
        "http://www.w3.org/TR/xhtml1/DTD/xhtml1-transitional.dtd">
<html xmlns="http://www.w3.org/1999/xhtml" xml:lang="en" lang="en">
<head>
  <title>JavaScript unit test file</title>
  <meta http-equiv="content-type" content="text/html; charset=utf-8" />
  <script src="assets/prototype.js" type="text/javascript"></script>
  <script src="assets/unittest.js" type="text/javascript"></script>

  <script src="../../public/javascripts/application.js" type="text/
   javascript"></script>

  <link rel=»stylesheet» href=»assets/unittest.css» type=»text/css» />
</head>
<body>

<div id=»content»>

  <div id=»header»>
    <h1>JavaScript unit test file</h1>
    <p>
      This file tests <strong>application.js</strong>.
    </p>
  </div>

  <!-- Log output -->
  <div id=»testlog»> </div>

</div>

<script type=»text/javascript»>
// <![CDATA[

  new Test.Unit.Runner({

    // replace this with your real tests

    setup: function() {

    },
```

```
    teardown: function() {

    },

    testTruth: function() { with(this) {
      assert(true);
    }}

  }, «testlog»);
// ]]>
</script>
</body>
</html>
```

The structure of this test stub is very similar to the structure of the unit tests that you wrote for your Ruby code. The test file contains `setup` and `teardown` methods, and as many test methods as you want to define. Each test method can contain any number of `assert` statements that make assertions about your JavaScript code.

Running JavaScript unit tests

The plugin creates the rake task

```
rake test:javascripts
```

This task will run all test files in your `test/javascripts` directory in the supported browser set for your developer operating system. Meaning Windows users get IE and Firefox, Mac OS X users get Safari and Firefox, Linux users get Firefox and Konqueror. The browser windows are opened automatically, but you have to close them yourself.

You can also run an individual test file by creating a symbolic link between the plugin's asset directory and your `test/javascripts`.

```
ln -s vendor/plugin/javascript_test/assets test/javascript/assets
```

With that done, you can open your JavaScript test HTML files in the browser of your choice.

Summary

This chapter provided an overview of the functionality available in the Prototype and script.aculo.us JavaScript libraries. Both of these libraries are included with the Rails distribution. Rails includes a number of helper methods that make direct use of these libraries to assist you in creating rich and dynamic Web applications.

You also saw how to make use of a JavaScript framework that is included with script.aculo.us and that allows you to write unit tests for your JavaScript that look and behave very similar to the unit tests you should already have in place for your Ruby code. This helps to fill the often unmet need of testing your application's JavaScript code.

Both Prototype and script.aculo.us provide a great deal more functionality than what I was able to cover in this single chapter. These are powerful libraries that will make you a better JavaScript developer and give you the power that you need to create rich, dynamic Web applications. I encourage you to continue to learn and explore each of these libraries and make use of their rich set of features within your own applications.

Chapter 11

Extending Rails

A strong belief held by the creator of the Rails framework is that the framework should be kept limited in features and focused on the core technology related to developing database-backed Web applications. What is core technology consists of in a Web application is something that has been and will continue to be debated by Web users and programmers, both in person and across the Internet. However, you are not likely to see things like login systems, message boards, image management, or other application-level features built into any future versions of Rails. That said, if you develop more than one Rails application, you are likely to come across chunks of functionality that you find yourself repeating in every application you write. These chunks of functionality, which are not core to Rails but are common to most of the applications you write, can be leveraged as extensions to the Rails framework using Rails generators, plugins, and engines.

Rails supports an excellent model for extensibility that makes it easy to add the specific features you want as extensions to Rails. You can then easily reuse those extensions in your other applications, as well as make them available to the public at large.

Beyond the Core

Rails extensions often grow out of a feature that you originally implemented inside one or more applications prior to recognizing the value of such a feature as a reusable component. It is rare that you can plan upfront what all of the plugins for an application will be. Often your plugins will evolve out of your code base. In this chapter, you'll learn about various ways of extending the Rails framework with reusable components that you develop. You can also find many reusable extensions to Rails on the Internet. I'll point you to some resources for finding those extensions in this chapter.

The primary ways of extending Rails are through the following extension types:

- **Generators:** Allow you to easily generate classes, migrations, views, or other code using the built-in `script/generate` command.
- **Plugins:** Are the most popular way to extend Rails with custom functionality and features.
- **Engines:** Allow you to add a complete slice of functionality, including models, views, and controllers, to an application.

In earlier version of Rails, prior to Rails 2.0, there was actually another reusable code type, known as a *component*. Components were officially deprecated with the Rails 2.0 release. Components were never really used to a great extent, and those who did use them often complained about how slow they were. Because they are deprecated and not recommended to be used, even in earlier versions of Rails that do support them, they are not covered in this book.

Generators

Generators are used in a Rails application to automatically generate code. You are already familiar with generating models, views, and controllers using generators that come standard with Rails. To generate those objects, you use the `script/generate` command. In this section you will learn how to create your own generators that you will be able to run using the `script/generate` command.

If you or your team develop multiple Rails applications and you find yourself repeatedly creating common pieces of code, or copying code from one project to another, then custom generators may be a great thing for your project. However, before you make the decision to create your own generators, make sure you also understand what a Rails plugin is. You may decide that a plugin is a better choice for what you are doing than a generator. In the next section, you'll learn all about writing your own Rails plugins. Generators are usually preferable if you are creating boilerplate code or code that you will be modifying and extending with additional custom code. Common features that you use across applications without having to modify the code are usually better candidates for plugins. Plugins often include generators as part of their feature set.

The Ruby on Rails wiki, located at `http://wiki.rubyonrails.org/rails/pages/AvailableGenerators`, lists some generators that are available. However, you may be writing generators that are specific to your organization. In the next section, you will see how to write your own Rails generator.

In this section, you'll create your own generator. To use a real-world example of code that might end up in a generator, you'll use the authentication code that was developed for the Book Shelf application in Chapter 6. You'll implement a generator that can be used to automatically generate the models and controllers necessary to implement user authentication.

The generator directory structure

The code that makes up a generator is placed into a consistent directory structure. The structure of a generator is shown here:

```
generator_name/
    |-- USAGE
    |-- generator_name_generator.rb
    |-- templates/
            |-- INSTALL
            |-- controllers/
            |-- lib/
            |-- migrate/
            |-- models/
            |-- test/
            |-- views/
```

Let's look at the elements shown in this directory structure. At the top level, you have a directory with the name of the generator. That directory contains three elements: a USAGE file, a Ruby script file, and a `templates` subdirectory. The contents of the USAGE file are printed automatically if the user calls the generator with the –h or –help option as an argument. The Ruby script file contains the name of the generator with the "_generator.rb" suffix. This script contains the generator's instructions for generating the target code.

The `templates` subdirectory contains the templates for all of the code that your generator will generate. You generator could generate controllers, `lib` files, migrations, models, tests, or views. When you write your generator, you will create a template for what the outputted code will look like, and that will be placed in the subdirectory of template that corresponds to the type of file it is.

There are two choices for where you would put your generator code. If you want your generator to be available to multiple Rails applications, you would put it in a place where Rails looks for generators. Rails automatically looks for generators that are put into a directory named `.rails` inside of your user home directory. So on a UNIX-based system, this would be something like `/user/timothyf/.rails`. On Windows, the directory would be in `C:\Documents and Settings\timothyf\.rails`. If you want your generator to be available to just a single application, you can put it in the application's `lib/generators` directory. Generators that are part of a plugin go in the plugin's `lib/generators` directory. If you are sharing a generator among multiple projects, I'd recommend packaging it in a plugin before putting it in a `.rails` directory.

Writing generator code

After you set up the appropriate directory structure for your generator, the next thing that you'll typically want to do is to write the _generator.rb Ruby script file containing the instructions for your generator. You do this by creating a class that extends one of the following:

- `Rails::Generator::Base`
- `Rails::Generator::NamedBase`

The `Rails::Generator::Base` class is the more generic class to extend for general-purpose generators. The `Rails::Generator::NamedBase` class assumes that your generator takes a single class name as its first parameter, followed by a list of actions. For example, think of the way the generators for controllers work; you pass the name of the controller that you want to generate, followed by a list of action methods that you want to be created within that controller. If you want to follow that same pattern with your generator, you would extend the `Rails::Generator::NamedBase` class.

To create the authentication generator, you will extend the `Rails::Generator::Base` class. The first thing you need to think about when writing your generator script is: what are all of the tasks that you want your generator to perform? Let's list those for the authentication generator:

- Create a User model
- Create a User controller
- Create a User migration
- Create tests and fixtures

This list gives you a pretty good start at having a complete authentication system. You could also consider generating the view templates for login and registration within this generator, but since the view layer tends to be more application-specific, it will be left out of this exercise. However, if you were developing an authentication generator for your organization, you may also want to include the views, so that your applications have a common look to their login and registration features.

With the tasks in mind that you want the generator to perform, you can start writing the generator script. The complete generator script for the authentication generator is shown in Listing 11.1. Let's walk through this script.

LISTING 11.1

authentication_generator.rb

```
class AuthenticationGenerator < Rails::Generator::Base

  def initialize(runtime_args, runtime_options = {})
    super(runtime_args, runtime_options)
    @attributes = @args.select {|a| a.include?(":")}.map do |attribute|
```

```
        Rails::Generator::GeneratedAttribute.new(*attribute.split(":"))
    end
end

def manifest
    record do |m|

            # Controller
            m.file "controllers/user_controller.rb",
                    "app/controllers/user_controller.rb"

            # Models
            m.file "models/user.rb", "app/models/user.rb"

            # Migration
            m.migration_template "migrate/create_users.rb", "db/
    migrate",
                    :assigns => {:attributes => @attributes}

            # Tests
            m.file "test/unit/user_test.rb", "test/unit/user_test.rb"
            m.file "test/functional/user_controller_test.rb",
                    "test/functional/user_controller_test.rb"
            m.file "test/fixtures/users.yml", "test/fixtures/users.yml"

            m.readme "INSTALL"
        end
    end

def file_name
    "create_users"
    end
end
```

The `initialize` method of the generator takes two arguments rolled up from the command line as specified by the user. The `runtime_args` is the normal arguments, as a list, and the `runtime_options` are the command options as specified with flags (such as `-c` or `−svn`, which adds newly generated files to Subversion).

The default behavior of the `initialize` method is to place those arguments in instance methods `@args` and `@opts`. This method further parses the arguments, searching for `key:value` pairs and turning them into attribute objects. This allows the user to specify further arguments that can get added to the user table of the form `firstname:string`, and is consistent with other generators in Rails.

The main thing to notice about the generator script is that it always contains a method named `manifest`. The `manifest` method is the block of code that copies files from the `templates` directory to destination directories within the Rails application. In every generator that you write, you will always implement the `manifest` method. This is the method called when your generator is run. Within the `manifest` method, you'll notice that the method `m.file` is used over and over again. The `m.file` method simply copies a file from the `templates` directory to a destination directory. For example, look at the following line:

```
m.file "models/user.rb", "app/models/user.rb"
```

You can see that this line is copying the file located in `templates/models/user.rb` to the destination location, `app/models/user.rb`. The next method that you probably don't recognize is the `m.migration_template` method. This method creates a new migration using the first parameter as the source template, and the second parameter as the destination for the migration file. The migration is created using the correct name, which includes a migration number — that is, `001_create_users.rb` (in Rails 2.1 and up, the number is a timestamp) — based on migrations that already exist and the migration number that you are currently up to. The migration_template method evaluates its template as an ERb file, with local variables passed as the `:assigns` option.

That leaves one other method to explain in the script, the method `m.readme`. This method just prints the contents of a file. It is used to give the user additional instructions after the generator is complete.

Table 11.1 lists all the commands that you can call in the main block of a generator file.

TABLE 11.1

Commands to Call in a Generator File's Main Block

Method	Description
class_collisions(*class_names)	Takes a list of potential class names and raises an exception if any of the name match Rails core classes.
directory(path)	Creates a new directory. The pathname is relative to the rails root.
file(source, dest, options = {})	Copies the file. The method takes an optional block with the file as the block argument, allowing for some manipulation before the file is saved.
migration_template(template, dest, options = {})	Parses the template as an ERb file, generates the next possible migration file in db/migrate.
readme(source)	Displays the contents of the file.
route_resources(*resources)	Adds the listed resources as RESTful routes in the routes.rb file.
template(template, dest, options = {})	Coverts the template file via ERb before copying to the destination. Values in an :assigns option are available to the template during parsing.

Creating the templates

After you are done with the generator script, the next step is to create the templates that the generator uses as source material. For this plugin, you'll need a template for each of the following:

- `user_controller.rb` controller
- `user.rb` model
- `create_users.rb` migration
- `user_test.rb` unit test
- `user_controller_test.rb` functional test
- `users.yml` fixture

The controller and model implementations that you will use are those that were developed in Chapter 6 for the Book Shelf application. Listing 11.2 shows what your `user_controller.rb` template should look like. The user controller contains three methods: `signup`, `login`, and `logout`. Those methods will provide the necessary logic for implementing user authentication in your application.

LISTING 11.2

user_controller.rb Template

```
class UserController < ApplicationController

    def signup
        @title = "Signup"
        if param_posted?(:user)
            @user = User.new(params[:user])
            if @user.save
                session[:user] = @user
                flash[:notice] = "User #{@user.login} created!"
                redirect_to :action => "home"
            else
                flash[:error] = "Signup unsuccessful"
                @user.clear_password!
            end
        end
    end

    def login
        if request.post?
            if session[:user] = User.authenticate(params[:user][:login],
                                                    params[:user]
[:password])
                flash[:notice]  = "Login successful"
```

continued

LISTING 11.2   *(continued)*

```
                    redirect_to_stored
              else
                    flash[:error] = "Login unsuccessful"
                    redirect_to :controller=>'home'
              end
        end
    end

    def logout
        session[:user] = nil
        flash[:notice] = 'Logged out'
        redirect_to :controller => 'home', :action => 'index'
    end
end
```

The next template you'll need is the User model template. The template for the User model is shown in Listing 11.3, in the user.rb file.

LISTING 11.3

user.rb Template

```
class User < ActiveRecord::Base

    validates_length_of :login, :within => 3..40
    validates_length_of :password, :within => 5..40
    validates_presence_of :login, :e-mail
    validates_uniqueness_of :login, :e-mail
    validates_confirmation_of :password
    validates_format_of :e-mail,
                        :with => /^([^@\s]+)@((?:[-a-z0-9]+\.)+[a-z]
    {2,})$/i,
                        :message => "Invalid e-mail"

    attr_accessor :password, :password_confirmation
    attr_protected :password_salt


    def password=(pass)
        @password=pass
        self.password_salt = User.random_string(10) if !self.password_
    salt?

    self.password_hash = User.hash_password(@password, self.password_
    salt)
```

```
    end

    protected

    def self.hash_password(pass, password_salt)
        Digest::SHA1.hexdigest(pass+password_salt)
    end

    def self.random_string(len)
        #generate a random password consisting of strings and digits
        chars = ("a".."z").to_a + ("A".."Z").to_a + ("0".."9").to_a
        newpass = ""
        1.upto(len) { |i| newpass << chars[rand(chars.size-1)] }
        return newpass
    end

    def self.authenticate(login, pass)
        u=find(:first, :conditions=>["login = ?", login])
        return nil if u.nil?

    return u if User.hash_password(pass, u.password_salt)==u.password_
    hash
        nil
    end
end
```

This model contains some validations for the `login`, `password`, and e-mail fields, and the methods necessary to create a hashed password and to authenticate a user. For a complete explanation of the methods and attributes in this model, see Chapter 6, where it was used within the Book Shelf application.

The `create_users.rb` template is shown in Listing 11.4. This template is used to create a migration for the users table. The template contains only the fields that are essential to the authentication model. This template shows how to use the extra arguments passed as the command line by taking advantage of the ERb parser. You could enhance the migration after it is generated to include any additional fields that you want your User model to have.

LISTING 11.4

create_users.rb migration Template

```
class CreateUsers < ActiveRecord::Migration
    def self.up
        create_table :users do |t|
            t.string :login
```

continued

LISTING 11.4   *(continued)*

```
                t.string :e-mail
                t.string :password_hash
                t.string :password_salt
                <% attributes.each do |attribute| %>
                  t.<%= attribute.type %> :<%= attribute.name %>
                  <% end %>
                t.timestamps
            end
        end

        def self.down
            drop_table :users
        end
    end
end
```

Once you have completed the migration template, the remaining templates are the test- and fixture-related templates. Rather than providing just test stubs like those created by the standard generators, your authentication generator should create complete tests that provide full test coverage for the functionality created by the generator. It is a good practice to remember that code should always be accompanied by tests, no matter where that code is coming from. A generator should include tests for code that it provides, a plugin should include tests for code that it creates, and you should always write tests for the code that you write directly.

Running the new authentication generator

Once you have the generator script and the code templates all completed, you have a complete Rails generator. You can run your generator the same way you would run one of the standard Rails generators. Create an empty project that you will use to test the new generator.

```
> rails test_proj
```

After this is complete and you have your new `test_proj` directory structure set up, go ahead and copy the generator code that you just wrote into the `test_proj/lib/generators` directory. This makes the generator available to the application. Using the `script/generate` command, try running your new generator. You should see the following output:

```
> ruby script/generator authentication
  create app/controllers/user_controller.rb
  create app/models/user.rb
  create db/migrate
  create db/migrate/001_create_users.rb
  create test/unit/user_test.rb
  create test/functional/user_controller_test.rb
  create test/fixtures/users.yml
  readme INSTALL
Contents of INSTALL file printed here
```

The generator creates the files that you expected and places them into the appropriate places within the application's directory structure. After the files are copied into location, the contents of the INSTALL file are printed to the screen.

Extending Rails::Generator::NamedBase

In this example, you build the generator script by extending `Rails::Generator::Base`. In other cases, you may want to extend the class `Rails::Generator::NamedBase` instead. When you use `Rails::Generator::NamedBase`, your generator takes a class name as its first parameter, followed by a list of actions. You are able to use that class name passed in, both in your generator script and within your templates.

Plugins

Once you've learned how to write your own generators, plugins are the next tool that you should learn to use in your projects. Plugins are the primary Rails mechanism for extending the Rails framework to implement features that you might find useful in more than one Rails application. There are currently hundreds of plugins available for Rails, and there are a few different places where you can find online directories of plugins. Check out some of these sites to get started:

- `http://agilewebdevelopment.com/plugins`
- `http://wiki.rubyonrails.org/rails/pages/Plugins`
- `http://www.railslodge.com/`

Figure 11.1 shows you the home page of the agilewebdevelopment.com/plugins site. At this site, you can find an RSS feed to keep track of plugins as they are added to the directory. On the site, you can view the highest-rated plugins and the recently added plugins. You are also able to view plugins by category, as follows:

- Assets
- Controllers
- Internationalization
- Misc. Enhancements
- Model
- Searching and Queries
- Security
- Statistics and Logs
- Testing
- View Extensions

FIGURE 11.1

`agilewebdevelopment.com/plugins`

These categories make it easy to find exactly the kind of plugin that you are looking for. New plugins are being developed and added to the directories often, and so if you don't find what you are looking for today, be sure to keep an eye on the directories or search around on Google to locate anyone who might be developing the plugin you are interested in. If you are not able to find an existing plugin that meets your requirements, you can write your own plugin. You will learn how to do that a bit later in this chapter.

Using the Plugin script

Throughout this book, you've used the `script/plugin` command to install plugins as needed. The `script/plugin` command can also be used with a number of other options to do the following tasks:

- Get a list of available plugins
- Get a list of plugin sources
- Add and remove plugin sources
- Discover new plugin sources
- Install plugins

- Remove plugins
- Update plugins

Several of the `plugin` commands use or modify a list of plugin sources sites. Plugin sources are configured URLs which maintain a list of plugins can be found and downloaded from that site. The `plugin` script automatically searches the configured sources for any plugins that you attempt to install. This means that if you are attempting to install a plugin and it can be found at a plugin source site, you do not have to specify a full URL to install it. For example, you could install the `acts_as_list` plugin using this command, which would place the plugin source in vendor/rails/acts_as_list:

```
> ruby script/plugin install acts_as_list
```

The `acts_as_list` plugin is located in one of the standard repositories that are configured as a plugin source out-of-the-box with Rails. If you find yourself using plugins from other sources that are not already configured as plugin sources, you can easily add those repositories as plugin sources. In just a bit, you will see how to do that. Most plugins, however, are described and documented with the full URL of their host server, and if you have that URL, using the exact location is preferable to just using the plugin name.

List available plugins

You can get a list of all the plugins that are currently available using the `script/plugin list` command. This shows you the plugins that are available at the sources that Rails currently knows about.

```
> ruby script/plugin list
acts_as_tree http://dev.rubyonrails.com/svn/rails/plugins/acts_
    as_tree/
atom_feed_helper http://dev.rubyonrails.com/svn/rails/plugins/
    atom_feed_helper/
auto_complete http://dev.rubyonrails.com/svn/rails/plugins/auto_
    complete/
...
```

The results that are returned give you the name of the plugin, along with the repository in which it can be found. All of the plugins in the list above are in the `http://dev.rubyonrails.com/svn/rails/plugins/` repository.

List plugin sources

To get a list of the plugin sources that are currently configured, you can use the `script/plugin sources` command.

```
> ruby script/plugin sources
http://dev.rubyonrails.com/svn/rails/plugins
```

When you first install Rails, there is only a single plugin source configured: `http://dev.ruby onrails.com/svn/rails/plugin` URL. This is why the previous `list` command listed only plugins that were in that repository.

Adding and removing plugin sources

You may find that you are using several plugins from a particular source, or your internal organization may have an internal source of Rails plugins. In either case, you can tell Rails about new plugin sources using the `script/plugin source` command.

```
> ruby script/plugin source http://svn.techno-weenie.net/projects/
    plugins
Added 1 repositories.
```

This command adds the popular `svn.techno-weenie.net` source to your configured list of plugin sources. The `svn.techno-weenie.net` source hosts more than 30 plugins, including some of the most popular Rails plugins, such as `acts_as_authenticated`, `attachment_fu`, and `restful_authentication`. These plugins were all developed by one of the community's most prolific plugin developers, Rick Olson. Rick is also a member of the Rails core development team. You can generally count on consistent quality with his plugins. After adding the `svn.techno-weenie.net` source, you can view the plugins that it offers by running a `script/plugin list` command.

Removing a configured plugin source is just as easy. You use the command, `script/plugin unsource`, to remove a source. You can remove the previously added `svn.techno-weenie.net` source using this command:

```
> ruby script/plugin unsource http://svn.techno-weenie.net/
    projects/plugins
removed: http://svn.techno-weenie.net/projects/plugins/
Removed 1 repositories.
```

Discover new plugin sources

Sometimes you may not be able to find the plugin you are looking for. Rails can help you discover new sources of plugins to find exactly what you want. The `script/plugin discover` command looks on the Internet for new plugins and lets you add new plugin sources to your source list. The plugins are discovered by parsing the HTML from the the plugins page of the Rails wiki, searching for the string "plugin" inside of any HTTP or Subversion URL. You are prompted as to whether you want to add each plugin source that is discovered.

```
> ruby script/plugin discover
Add http://agilewebdevelopment.com/plugins/? [Y/n]
Add svn://rubyforge.org/var/svn/expressica/plugins/? [Y/n]
Add http://soen.ca/svn/projects/rails/plugins/? [Y/n]
Add http://technoweenie.stikipad.com/plugins/? [Y/n]
Add http://svn.techno-weenie.net/projects/plugins/? [Y/n]
Add http://svn.recentrambles.com/plugins/? [Y/n]
```

```
Add http://opensvn.csie.org/rails_file_column/plugins/? [Y/n]
Add http://svn.protocool.com/public/plugins/? [Y/n]
...
```

You can also use a page of your choosing as the page that is scraped when searching for new plugin sources. This can be particularly useful if your team maintains an internal wiki page that describes plugins of interest to your team. To discover sources from your own page, simply pass its URL to the `discover` command like this: `ruby script/plugin discover http://www.mycompany.com/railsplugins`.

Rails then attempts to parse the page at the URL you passed and prompts you to add any URL plugin sources that it finds, just like it did when scraping the standard Rails wiki page.

Installing, removing, and updating plugins

If you implemented the Book Shelf application that was developed in Chapters 6 to 8 of this book, you have already used the plugin script to install plugins into your Rails application. The `install` option is the option you will use most often with the `plugin` command. To install a plugin, you use the `script/plugin install` command with the name of the plugin that you want to install.

```
ruby script/plugin install acts_as_list
```

This causes Rails to search through the list of configured plugin sources to find a plugin with the name you passed in. That plugin is installed into the current application if it is found. You can also install a plugin that is not available at a configured plugin source by passing a complete URL to the `install` command.

```
ruby script/plugin install
http://svn.techno-weenie.net/projects/plugins/acts_as_
    authenticated
```

If you know the repository URL for a plugin that you are trying to install, it's usually a good idea to just go ahead and specify it, rather than hope that the plugin will be found in a configured plugin source repository.

If you are using Subversion as your source control, then the `-x` option adds the plugin to your repository as a Subversion external, meaning that the only a link to the plugin host is stored in your repository, and the plugin is updated locally any time you update your repository. Plugins can also be managed using a tool called Piston, which allows you to store plugin source locally, but still get easy update behavior.

To remove an installed plugin, use the `script/plugin remove` command. This command deletes the plugin from the `vendor/plugins` directory and also runs the plugin's `uninstall.rb` script if it has one.

```
> ruby script/plugin remove acts_as_taggable
Removing 'vendor/plugins/acts_as_taggable'
```

429

You have now learned how easy it is to manage the plugins that your Rails application has available to it. In the next section you will learn how to write your own plugins.

Writing a plugin

Now that you've seen how easy it is to add plugins to a Rails application, let's look at what it takes to create your own Rails plugin.

To start writing your own plugin, just as with an application, Rails gives you an easy-to-use generator for creating the structure of your new plugin. Just run the plugin generator:

```
> ruby script/generate plugin my_plugin
  create vendor/plugins/my_plugin/lib
  create vendor/plugins/my_plugin/tasks
  create vendor/plugins/my_plugin/test
  create vendor/plugins/my_plugin/README
  create vendor/plugins/my_plugin/MIT-LICENSE
  create vendor/plugins/my_plugin/Rakefile
  create vendor/plugins/my_plugin/init.rb
  create vendor/plugins/my_plugin/install.rb
  create vendor/plugins/my_plugin/uninstall.rb
  create vendor/plugins/my_plugin/lib/my_plugin.rb
  create vendor/plugins/my_plugin/tasks/my_plugin_tasks.rake
  create vendor/plugins/my_plugin/test/my_plugin_test.rb
```

You pass the name of the plugin that you want to create as a parameter to `script/generate plugin`. In the above example, the plugin would be named `'my_plugin'`.

You now have a directory structure set up for writing your plugin. Let's take a closer look at the directories and files that make up a plugin. Here is a representation of a standard plugin:

```
plugin_name/
      |-- init.rb
      |-- install.rb
      |-- uninstall.rb
      |-- Rakefile
      |-- README
      |-- MIT-LICENSE
      |-- lib/
           |-- plugin_name.rb
      |-- tasks/
           |-- plugin_name_tasks.rb
      |-- test/
           |-- plugin_name_test.rb
```

Although this is the standard structure of a plugin and you will find many plugins that contain each of these components, you might be surprised to find out that none of these components are actually required. Your plugin could be nothing but a `tasks` directory, or perhaps a `lib` directory. So with that in mind, let's examine what each of the components of a plugin is used for.

- The `init.rb` file runs every time the Rails application in which the plugin is installed is started. This is useful for situations where you want to dynamically modify some other piece of code prior to your application running, such as mixing in a helper module that all of your views can take advantage of.

- The `install.rb` file runs one time only when the plugin is installed into your application. You can use this script to copy files into desired locations and print additional setup directions to the screen.

- The `uninstall.rb` file runs one time when you uninstall a plugin. This can be used to remove files or to take other actions to clean up after a plugin.

- The `Rakefile` is commonly used to generate documentation and run tests for the plugin.

- The `README` file should contain information that describes your plugin and provides installation instructions for users. RDoc format is common, but not in any way required.

- The `MIT-LICENSE` file contains a copy of the MIT License, which is the default license for your plugin. If you prefer a different license for your plugin, just delete or replace this file with a description of your preferred license.

- The `lib` directory contains Ruby classes that are available to your application.

- The `tasks` directory can contain `.rake` files that extend your application with new rake tasks. By default you get a test task and a documentation task.

- The `test` directory contains tests that test the functionality of your plugin. Just as with any other code that you write, you should have a full suite of tests providing complete test coverage for your plugin.

It is important to note that the `install.rb` file only runs if you install the plugin using the `script/plugin install` command. If you install a plugin into your Rails application by manually copying its files into your application's `vendor/plugins` directory, the `install.rb` file does not automatically run. The same holds true for the `uninstall.rb` file. If you manually delete a plugin, the `uninstall.rb` file does not run. The proper way to uninstall a plugin is to use the `script/plugin remove` command.

Write a new plugin

To show you how easy it is to write a plugin, I will walk you through the development of a simple plugin that adds a feature to all of your ActiveRecord models, allowing you to retrieve a random record from the database.

Because you want to add the random finder feature to all of your ActiveRecord models, you'll implement the feature with a module that will be mixed into the `ActiveRecord::Base` class, which all of your ActiveRecord models inherit from. To get started, create a new Rails application and generate a plugin named `random_finder`.

```
rails chapter11
cd chapter11
ruby script/generate plugin random_finder
```

431

After the `generate` script is complete, the files related to your new plugin are in the `vendor/plugins/random_finder` directory. Assume this to be the root path for files are referred to in this section.

Start by opening the file `lib/random_finder.rb`. In this file is where you will put the new finder method that you want to expose to all of your ActiveRecord models. To do this, you'll implement the method in a module that can later be mixed into the `ActiveRecord::Base` class.

Listing 11.5 shows what your completed `random_finder.rb` file should look like.

LISTING 11.5

random_finder.rb Plugin

```
module RubyOnRailsBible
    module RandomFinder

        def self.included(mod)
            mod.extend(ClassMethods)
        end

        module ClassMethods
            def find_random
                find(:first, :order => 'rand()')
            end
        end
    end
end
```

The `RandomFinder` module is created inside another module called `RubyOnRailsBible`. This is done for name-scoping purposes. By creating a higher-level module with your organization or company name, you can avoid naming conflicts in your plugins. The first method in the `RandomFinder` module is as follows:

```
def self.included(mod)
    mod.extend(ClassMethods)
end
```

The `self.included` method is automatically called by Rails when this module is included in another class or module. The module that this module is being included in is passed as an argument to `self.included`.

The module including `RubyOnRails::RandomFinder` is then extended with the methods from `RubyOnRails::RandomFinder::ClassMethods`. The `extend` call takes all instance methods of the `ClassMethods` module and adds them as class methods of the `mod` module. This enables you to include class level methods along with instance level methods.

The `RubyOnRails::RandomFinder::ClassMethods` module includes a single method, `find_random`. The method `find_random` uses the following line to return a random record:

```
find(:first, :order => 'rand()')
```

This line says to get the first record when the records are sorted in a random order. This results in a random record being returned. However, there is a significant limitation to this code. The `rand()` function that is being passed in the order clause only works with MySQL databases. If your database is something other than MySQL, this code does not work. You won't solve the database independence problem here, but if you are interested in a plugin with this functionality that does work with more databases than MySQL, check out the `random_finders` plugin written by Daniel Morrison. You can get information about the `random_finders` plugin at `http://agilewebdevelopment.com/plugins/random_finders`.

The last thing you need to do in order to make the `random_finder` plugin functional is to edit the plugin's `init.rb` file so that the `RubyOnRailsBible::RandomFinder` module is automatically included in `ActiveRecord::Base`. The complete implementation of `init.rb` is shown here.

```
require 'random_finder'
ActiveRecord::Base.send(:include, RubyOnRailsBible::RandomFinder)
```

The `RubyOnRailsBible::RandomFinder` module is included in `ActiveRecord::Base` by calling the `ActiveRecord::Base.send` method, and passing the `:include` argument along with the name of the module you want included, which triggers an `include` call from `ActiveRecord::Base`.

Try out the new plugin

You have now implemented the essential code for a functioning Rails plugin. You can test your new plugin within the `chapter11` Rails project that you created at the start of this section. First, make sure that you have a local development database configured in the application's `config/database.yml` file, like this:

```
defaults: &defaults
  adapter: mysql
  username: root
  password:

development:
  database: chapter11_development
  <<: *defaults
```

For this exercise there is no need to create a test or production database, and so only the development database is specified. Go ahead and use rake to create the database.

```
rake db:create:all
```

With your database set up, the next step is to create a simple model on which you can try out the random finder method.

```
ruby script/generate model Post title:string body:text
```

When the model generation is complete, go ahead and run the migration to create the posts table in your database.

```
rake db:migrate
```

The next thing you have to do is to set up some test data that you can find with the random finder method. Go into the Rails console to create some Post records like this — the bold lines you type, the the other lines are the console response:

```
ruby script/console
Loading development environment (Rails 2.0.2)
>> Post.create :title=>"Title 1", :body=>"This is my body"
=> #<Post id: 1, title: "Title 1", body: "This is my body">
>> Post.create :title=>"Title 2", :body=>"Oh, another body"
=> #<Post id: 1, title: "Title 2", body: "Oh, another body">
>> Post.create :title=>"Title 3", :body=>"Yet another body"
=> #<Post id: 1, title: "Title 3", body: "Yet another body">
```

There are now three unique Post records in your database. This should be adequate to test the find_random method created by the random_finder plugin. When your Rails application is started, the plugin's init.rb script is run, which causes the find_random method to become available to any models that extend ActiveRecord::Base, such as your Post model. From within the Rails console, try calling the find_random method a few times, again the commands you type are in bold:

```
>> Post.find_random
=> #<Post id: 1, title: "Title 2", body: "Oh, another body">
>> Post.find_random
=> #<Post id: 1, title: "Title 1", body: "This is my body">
>> Post.find_random
=> #<Post id: 1, title: "Title 2", body: "Oh, another body">
>> Post.find_random
=> #<Post id: 1, title: "Title 3", body: "Yet another body">
```

Because the find_random method returns a random Post instance, your results will not be identical to the results you see above. However, you should notice randomness in the results that are returned.

Congratulations, you've now written your first Rails plugin. When you break it down into simple steps as I did here, you see that writing a plugin is not very difficult. Although I didn't include any tests for this plugin, you should not forget to include tests with any plugins that you write. Tests are an important part of any plugin, especially if you want to release the plugin into the wild. Many developers do not trust a plugin that does not have any tests. In the next section you will learn some common techniques that are often used to develop plugins.

Common techniques used to develop plugins

Now that you've seen how to develop a plugin of your own, in this section you'll see an overview of some of the common techniques that can be used to develop a plugin. Because of Ruby's dynamic nature, it is an ideal language for implementing an extension mechanism such as what you get with Rails plugins. Many Rails plugins take advantage of Ruby's dynamism to add new features by extending or modifying existing classes. The techniques that you will find the most valuable when you write plugins include the following:

- **Extending the functionality of an existing class using modules.** This is also known as the mixin technique.

- **Opening a class or module and adding new methods, or overriding existing methods.**

- **Extending existing code dynamically through callbacks and hooks.** These techniques include implementing methods such as `method_missing`, `Class#inherited`, `Module#const_missing`, and `Module#included`.

- **Using code generation to add new functionality.**

These techniques do not have to be used independently. Quite often, a plugin will use more than one of these techniques to implement a single plugin. In the following subsections, you'll see examples of how each of these techniques can be used in the development of a plugin.

Extending classes with mixins

A mixin is a module that defines one or more methods. The mixin is then included into another class, and the module's methods become available to the class in which it is included. Using this technique, you can add new functionality to existing classes. The class extended most often by plugins is the `ActiveRecord::Base` class. `ActiveRecord::Base` is the class from which most of your application's model classes extend. So by extending this class, you can effectively add to or change the behavior of all of your application's model classes.

Take a look at an example of how that `ActiveRecord::Base` is extended through a mixin in the `acts_as_rateable` plugin. This is the same technique that you used in the previous section to write your own plugin, the `random_finder` plugin.

First, look at the `init.rb` file for `acts_as_rateable`. The `init.rb` file is executed automatically when the Rails application, which includes `acts_as_rateable`, is started. The code in `init.rb` will include the `Juixe::Acts::Rateable` module in the `ActiveRecord::Base` module.

```
require 'acts_as_rateable'
ActiveRecord::Base.send(:include, Juixe::Acts::Rateable)
```

Now take a look at the plugin's `lib/acts_as_rateable.rb` code, shown in Listing 11.6. The first key method to understand here is the `self.included` method of the `Juixe::Acts::Rateable` module. This method is called when the module is included in another class or module. So when the module is included in `ActiveRecord::Base` as a result of the `init.rb` script executing, this method extends `ActiveRecord::Base` with the methods contained in the `ClassMethods` module.

The `ClassMethods` module contains a single method, `acts_as_rateable`. So now the method `acts_as_rateable` becomes available to any of your models that extend `ActiveRecord::Base`.

LISTING 11.6

acts_as_rateable.rb

```
module Juixe
    module Acts #:nodoc:
        module Rateable #:nodoc:

            def self.included(base)
                base.extend ClassMethods
            end

            module ClassMethods
                def acts_as_rateable
                    has_many :ratings, :as => :rateable, :dependent =>
    true

                    include Juixe::Acts::Rateable::InstanceMethods
                    extend Juixe::Acts::Rateable::SingletonMethods
                end
            end

            module SingletonMethods
                ...
            end

            module InstanceMethods
                ...
    end
            end
        end
end
```

Next, let's see what happens when a model calls the `acts_as_rateable` method. The first line of the method adds a `has_many` association to the model that calls it. The association associates ratings with the calling model. The next two lines add more methods to the calling model. In the second line, some additional instance methods are included by including the `Juixe::Acts::Rateable::InstanceMethods` module. That module is defined further down in the file.

In Listing 11.6, the methods of the `InstanceMethods` module are left out for brevity. The last line of the `acts_as_rateable` method adds new singleton methods to the calling model by extending the calling class with the `Juixe::Acts::Rateable::SingletonMethods` module. This module is also defined further down in the file, with the methods left out of the listing for brevity.

The end result is that you can add a call to `acts_as_rateable` to any of your model classes, and as a result, the model gains a new `has_many` association, along with new instance and singleton methods related to ratings functionality. The singleton methods behave as class methods, but only in class that actually include `acts_as_rateable`.

So by looking at the code from the `acts_as_rateable` plugin, you've seen a good example of how your plugins can use mixin modules to enhance existing code. You can use the techniques shown in this section to extend your model classes with all sorts of specialized behavior.

Opening a class

This technique has an end effect similar to the previous technique of using module mixins. You end up with an existing class having new or changed behavior. So, for example, you could add a method to `ActiveRecord::Base` as follows:

```
module ActiveRecord
  class Base
    def self.find_random
      find(:first, :order => 'rand()')
    end
  end
end
```

The `init.rb` for this plugin would only need to require the file defining this method and the new method is available to all `ActiveRecord::Base` subclasses. This technique is more direct than the mixin technique, which is a strength and a weakness. It's much easier to understand, and exceptionally well suited to utility methods that you actually do want every instance of that class to share.

On the other hand, it's much less flexible — the typical acts_as plugin makes the addition of most of its functionality conditional on calling the original method. That can't easily be done through just opening a class. Opening a class is also more susceptible to name collisions between two methods with the same name.

Dynamic extension with callbacks and hooks

Rails has an excellent event model with callback and hook methods allowing you to dynamically tie into the framework in quite a few different places. Use of these methods provides another common style of implementing plugins. The plugin `acts_as_taggable_redux`, which was used in Chapter 8 to add tagging functionality to the Book Shelf application, provides an excellent example of this technique in a plugin.

Listing 11.7 shows the top portion of the file `acts_as_taggable.rb` from the `acts_as_taggable_redux` plugin.

LISTING 11.7

acts_as_taggable.rb

```
module ActiveRecord
    module Acts #:nodoc:
        module Taggable #:nodoc:
            def self.included(base)
                base.extend(ClassMethods)
            end

            module ClassMethods
                def acts_as_taggable(options = {})
                    has_many :taggings, :as => :taggable,
                            :dependent => :destroy, :include => :tag
                    has_many :tags, :through => :taggings

                    after_save :update_tags

                    extend ActiveRecord::Acts::Taggable::SingletonMethod
s
                    include ActiveRecord::Acts::Taggable::InstanceMethod
s
                end
            end
            ...
```

At first glance, you will probably recognize elements of the mixin technique described in the previous section. This plugin makes use of several common techniques for adding functionality to your application. What you should pay closer attention to for this section is the `after_save` method call. That line of code tells Rails to always call the `update_tags` method after saving any model that uses the `acts_as_taggable` method. This is how the plugin keeps tags updated every time you make changes to a model instance without requiring any manual code modifications on your part.

The `update_tags` method that is called is shown in Listing 11.8. This is added as an instance method of the class that calls `acts_as_taggable` (meaning that it's in the `InstanceMethods` module included when the plugin is invoked).

So now you've seen another technique that developers use to add functionality to an application dynamically. This example shows how you can hook into an application with the `after_save` event method. Rails has a bunch of these event methods that allow you to hook into the Rails

ActiveRecord processing cycle. For more information about these methods, refer to the Rails documentation for ActiveRecord callback methods at `http://api.rubyonrails.org/classes/ActiveRecord/Callbacks.html`.

LISTING 11.8

update_tags method

```
def update_tags
    if @new_tag_list
        Tag.transaction do
            unless @new_user_id
                taggings.destroy_all
            else
                taggings.find(:all,
                    :conditions => "user_id = #{@new_user_id}").each do
    |tagging|
                        tagging.destroy
                  end
            end

            Tag.parse(@new_tag_list).each do |name|
                Tag.find_or_create_by_name(name).tag(self, @new_user_id)
            end

            tags.reset
            taggings.reset
            @new_tag_list = nil
        end
    end
end
```

Using code generation

Earlier in this chapter, you learned how to write a Rails code generator. Generators can also be included within a plugin. The use of generators provides another mechanism for a plugin to add to your existing code base and provide you with new functionality. Because you saw how to create a generator earlier in this chapter, I will not walk you through the details again here. Just know that a plugin can include multiple generators. You would place those generators inside of the plugins `lib/generators` directory.

Managing plugins with Piston

One awkward thing about Rails plugins is that it's somewhat challenging to keep them up to date. Piston is a Ruby program that manages plugin information for you. Piston allows you to update all your plugins on command, and also to freeze plugins at a specfic version. The 1.x version of Piston assumes that your repository and the plugin respository are both Subversion, however the 2.x versions (in beta as of this writing) allows either side of the relationship to be managed using git.

Piston is a Ruby gem; acquire it by typing:

```
gem install —include-dependencies piston
```

If you already have plugins managed using as Subversion externals (this includes Rails itself), you can convert them over to Piston using the command:

```
piston update
```

This should go through all your externals and convert them to be managed by piston. This will break the external relationship, and the code files will actually be exported to your local repository — you'll need to commit the changes to your repository when this is complete.

New plugins, or plugins that are not run as externals are imported using a command like this — this one works on Rails itself (or did, before Rails moved to git).

```
piston import http://dev.rubyonrails.org/svn/rails/trunk vendor/
    rails
```

The first argument is the remote host of the plugin, the second is the target directory. Unlike Rails managed plugin loading, you must specify the directory explicitly. Also, the `install.rb` of the plugin is not run, so you'll have to run that manually.

Once all your plugins have been pistonized, the command

```
piston update
```

Will check all managed plugins for updates. If you only want to check a specific plugin, specify it's directoy as an argument to the command.

When you are convinced that your application is near launch and you want to stop getting updates on a specific plugin, use the command.

```
piston lock vendor/plugins/plugin_to_lock
```

Obviously, the directory can be any plugin directory or Rails itself. A locked plugin is not updated even if a general update is requested. The piston unlock command removes the lock.

Summary of Useful Plugins

There is a large number of useful plugins already developed that you can install and use within your applications today. These plugins can shave significant time off the development of your custom Web applications. Every Rails developer should have some familiarity with the plugins that are available in the open source community. In this section, you'll learn about some of the most useful and popular plugins.

The following plugins are listed here:

- `acts_as_rateable`
- `will_paginate`
- `acts_as_state_machine`
- `annotate_models`
- `exception_notifier`
- resource_controller
- Authentication plugins
  - `restful_authentication`
- Enhanced Scaffolding
  - `streamlined`
  - `AutoAdmin`
  - `ExtJS Scaffold`
  - `Lispsi`
  - `ActiveScaffold`
- Content Tagging
  - `acts_as_taggable_redux`, `acts_as_taggable_on_steroids`
  - `has_many_polymorphs`
- File Uploads
  - `attachment_fu`

acts_as_rateable

You have probably come across many Web sites that use those fancy-looking stars or other cute graphics for a rating system. You hover over the stars and they change color, indicating the rating score that you want to submit. Ratings are a very useful feature of Web 2.0 applications. They let you share with others your opinion of a product or service. If you are looking for a product or service, a rating gives you some quick feedback as to how other users feel about it. There are a few plugins available that make adding this kind of rating system to a Rails application quite easy. The most popular plugin for ratings is probably the `acts_as_rateable` plugin.

Using `acts_as_rateable`, you can add ratings to any model. Once you have ratings associated with a model, you can then search and sort, based on the ratings. The home page for this plugin is at `http://rateableplugin.rubyforge.org/`. Going there takes you to the Rdoc documentation for the plugin. If you want to see a practical example of how to use this plugin, see Chapter 8. The `acts_as_rateable` plugin is used to add ratings to books for the Book Shelf application.

Pagination

In most real-world Web applications, you are storing some type of data in a database. Often, you have a lot of records of a particular type, perhaps thousands of book entries, thousands of user records, or thousands of recipes. Whatever it is that your application deals with, you need to display that information to the user. If you have thousands of records, you probably do not want to dump them into a single Web page all at once. This would take a very long time to load and would not be a very user-friendly experience, forcing them to scroll through a huge list of data.

A common solution to this problem is to paginate data that you are presenting to the user. This means that you return a page containing a set number of records, and additional records are retrieved when the user chooses to view another page of records. With this type of interface, the user is typically able to page back and forth through these pages of data records. The implementation of this style of interface for presenting large amounts of data, and the backend logic to process it, is what I am referring to when I say pagination.

Prior to Rails 2.0, there was a built-in mechanism for getting pagination of your model object data. However, the built-in mechanism had a very bad reputation and many faults, the first of which was poor performance. Pagination is no longer included in Rails as of version 2.0. Fortunately, there is are two very good and easy-to-use plugins, `will_paginate`, and `paginating_find`, which allow you to get easy pagination of your model data. I'll cover `will_paginate` here; `paginating_find` is similar.

Installing will_paginate

You can install `will_paginate` using the `script/plugin install` command.

```
ruby script/plugin install svn://errtheblog.com/svn/plugins/will_paginate
```

Adding pagination to your application

After you have the plugin installed, it's very easy to add the pagination functionality to your application. I'll look at an example where I want to add pagination to a Post model. To implement pagination in your application, you'll implement these three tasks:

- Define the `per_page` class variable in your model
- Retrieve model instances in the controller method using `Post.paginate`
- Use the `will_paginate` helper in view to display pagination controls

To add pagination to a Post model, you would start by defining how many posts you want to appear on a single page by first defining the `per_page` class attribute inside of the Post model, `app/models/post.rb`.

```
class Post < ActiveRecord::Base
    cattr_reader :per_page
    ⊥_page = 10
end
```

Defining the `per_page` attribute is actually optional; if you do not define it, a default value of 30 items per page is used. The next step is to modify your posts controller method that retrieves posts for display to use the `Post.paginate` method instead of the standard `Post.find` method. A modified `index` method of `app/controllers/posts_controller.rb` would look like this:

```
def index
    @posts = Post.paginate :page => params[:page]
end
```

The `Post.paginate` method retrieves one page of results and sets them in the `@posts` variable. The parameter being passed to `Post.paginate` is the page number of results. If you want to order your posts, you can easily add an order parameter to the method like this:

```
def index
    @posts = Post.paginate :page => params[:page], :order =>
    'created_at DESC'
end
```

As another alternative to setting the `per_page` attribute in your Post model, you could also pass the per_page count directly to the `Post.paginate` method, as follows:

```
def index
    @posts = Post.paginate :page => params[:page] , :per_page => 20
end
```

Just as you are able to use other forms of the `find` method, such as `find_by_name`, you can also use different forms of paginate in order to retrieve a filtered set of posts.

```
@posts = Post.paginate_by_blog_id @blog.id, :page =>
    params[:page]
```

This example would retrieve only those posts having a `blog_id` attribute matching the `@blog.id` attribute passed in. In general, if you want to page your results, you use the `paginate` method just as you would normally use the `find` method when you are not doing paging.

The last step to implementing paging is to use the `will_paginate` helper method in the view that displays your paged results. Continuing with the posts example, because the controller method used is the `index` method, the template rendered is the `app/views/posts/index.html.erb` template. Add a call to the `will_paginate` helper where you would like the pagination controls to appear.

```
<p>My Posts</p>
<%= render :partial => 'post', :collection => @posts %>
<%= will_paginate @posts %>
```

In this example, the pagination controls appear following the list of posts. The pagination controls allow you to navigate back and forth across pages.

With that, you now have an easy method of implementing paging across any of your model objects. By applying some CSS styling to your data display, and pagination controls, you will have a nice looking display of your model data.

acts_as_state_machine

In any large application, a common requirement is to be able to support one or more of your models having multiple states. This is especially true in any application that supports some form of workflow. For example, a common feature of Web sites today is that when a user registers for the site, their account is placed into an unvalidated state and the user has to confirm the registration by replying to an e-mail that is automatically sent to them. Once they have replied to the e-mail (or clicked a link contained in the e-mail), their account is placed into the active state.

The `acts_as_state_machine` plugin allows you to easily add this type of state machine behavior to your models.

Installing acts_as_state_machine

To install the `acts_as_state_machine` plugin, use the `script/plugin` install command:

```
ruby script/plugin install http://elitists.textdriven.com/svn/plugins/acts_
    as_state_machine
```

Using acts_as_state_machine

Listing 11.9 shows a common way of using the functionality of `acts_as_state_machine` with a User model.

LISTING 11.9

User Model with acts_as_state_machine

```
class User < ActiveRecord::Base

    acts_as_state_machine :initial => :pending, :column => 'status'

    # States for the User model
    state :passive
    state :pending, :enter=>:make_activation_code
    state :valid, :enter=>:do_validate
    state :suspended
    state :deleted, :enter=>:do_delete

    event :register do
        transitions :from=>:passive,
                    :to=>:pending,
                    :guard=>Proc.new do
                      |u| !(u.crypted_password.blank? && u.password.blank?)
```

```
                    end
    end

    event :activate do
        transitions :from=>:pending, :to=>:active
    end

    event :suspend do
        transitions :from=>[:passive,:pending,:active], :to=>:suspended
    end

    event :delete do
        transitions :from=>[:passive,:pending,:active, :suspended],
                    :to=>:deleted
    end


    def make_activation_code
            self.deleted_at = nil
            self.activation_code = Digest::SHA1.hexdigest(
                                    Time.now.to_s.split(//).sort_by {rand}.join)
        end
    end
```

Let's take this one step at a time. At the top of the model, the method `acts_as_state_machine` is called, which sets up various instance variables and methods for the state machine to work. There's a required option, `:initial`, which is starting state of the machine. The optional argument is `:column`, which is the database column where the current state of each model is stored. The default is `state`.

Next up, a series of `state` definitions, corresponding to the valid states of the system. Each state is pretty much just a name, there are three optional callbacks for each state, `:enter`, `:after`, and `:exit`. Each callback takes a method name or block.

The enter block is called for the state being entered, before the state is updated and the record is saved, while the exit block is called for the state being left, and after the record is saved. The after block is called on the block being entered, after the enter block. The behavior for a new object is slightly different, so it's best not to depend on the exact timing if you can avoid it.

At this point, you've defined a number of states, but no events that cause the model to move between states. That's next, with the series of calls to `event`. Each event takes a symbol as its name and a block. Inside the block you define a number of transitions. Each transition goes `:from` one or more states `:to` a single state. An optional `:guard` clause takes a method name or block which must return true for the transition to fire.

Note that these blocks are invoked exactly once, at load time, and the transitions are extracted from them at that point — if you want to have other behavior accompany the state transition, use the state before and after callbacks.

A number of helpful instance methods are created from your states and events to help move your model through the state machine. Each state automatically creates a boolean method of the form pending? which returns true if the model is in that state. Each event generates an action method of the form suspend! which triggers the appropriate state transitions and callbacks.

The action method also updates and saves the record back to the database. The method is supposed to return true if the transition performs appropriately, but as of this writing, it can fail silently under certain conditions. Using the action methods, you can guide the model through its life cycle.

The plugin also generates a couple of class level methods. You can use find_in_state(:all, state, *args) to find all records in a given state — any optional arguments are passed through to the regular find method. Similarly, count_in_state(state, *args) and calculate_in_state(stage, *args) mimic the plain ActiveRecord versions.

annotate_models

Because of the magic of ActiveRecord, your model classes are kept very clean and free of the typical getters and setters and attribute definitions that you would likely see in a different framework. As nice as this is, there can be a downside to not having your model's attributes visible anywhere in your model classes.

Often when you are working with a project, you want to quickly have a reminder of what a particular model object's attributes are. However, in a typical Rails application, to find out what a model's attributes are, you have to look in the database, look at your migrations, or look in the schema.rb file that is created for you when you run migrations. While this is not that big of a deal, it can slow you down if you are writing code in a model and just want to look up the attributes of that model. This is a scenario in which the annotate_models plugin becomes useful. The annotate_models plugin adds a comment summarizing the current schema to the top of each ActiveRecord model source file.

Installing annotate_models

To install the annotate_models plugin, use the script/plugin install command:

```
ruby script/plugin install http://repo.pragprog.com/svn/Public/
    plugins/annotate_models
```

Using annotate_models

The functionality of annotate_models is provided through a rake task. To have the annotations generated for all of your model classes, run the annotate_models rake task:

```
> rake annotate_models
```

This adds a schema description comment to the top of each of your model classes. Consider a Post model created with the following migration:

```
class CreatePosts < ActiveRecord::Migration
    def self.up
        create_table :posts do |t|
            t.string :title
            t.text :body
            t.timestamps
        end
    end

    def self.down
        drop_table :posts
    end
end
```

After running the `annotate_models` rake task, the following comment is added to the top of the `app/models/post.rb` file:

```
# == Schema Information
# Schema version: 1
#
# Table name: posts
#
#  id         :integer           not null, primary key
#  title      :string(255)
#  body       :text
#  created_at :datetime
#  updated_at :datetime
#
```

As you can see in the comments, you get the schema version, the table name, and the name and data type of each attribute for the model. Now if I am working on code in a specific model class, I only have to look at the top of the class file to see a complete description of the model's attributes.

If you run the `annotate_models` task each time you run your migrations, you always have up-to-date model annotations. Each time you run the `annotate_models` task, the schema description comments are completely rewritten at the top of each of your model files. So, if you added any of your own comments into the annotation comments, they would be lost the next time you generate the annotations with the `annotate_models` task.

exception_notifier

Error handling is an important part of any application. With a Web application, errors can happen at any time. It would be nice to have an easy mechanism that could notify you when errors occur in your live applications. That is exactly what the `exception_notifier` plugin does for you. It adds a mailer object that sends you e-mail notifications when errors occur in your Rails application.

The e-mail that is sent out includes a backtrace of the exception that occurred, along with information about the current request, session, and environment. Through configuration, you can set the following parameters for the exception_notifier:

- Sender e-mail address
- Recipient e-mail addresses
- Subject line prefix text

Installing exception_notifier

To install the exception_notifier plugin, use the script/plugin install command:

```
ruby script/plugin install http://dev.rubyonrails.org/svn/rails/
    plugins/exception_notification/
```

Using exception_notifier

After you have installed the plugin, the first thing you need to do is to add the ExceptionNotifiable mixin to the controller in which you want to generate error e-mails.

```
class ApplicationController < ActionController::Base
    include ExceptionNotifiable
end
```

The next step is to add the e-mail recipients into your applications configuration in config/environment.rb.

```
ExceptionNotifier.exception_recipients = %w(tim@fisher.com kerry@
    fisher.com)
```

The recipients are the only mandatory configuration that you have to add, but you can also define the sender address and a prefix for the e-mail title like this:

```
# defaults to exception.notifier@default.com
ExceptionNotifier.sender_address = %("Application Error" <app.
    error@myapp.com>)

# defaults to "[ERROR] "
ExceptionNotifier.e-mail_prefix = "[APP] "
```

The plugin only sends out e-mail messages if the server IP address is not local. Local is normally defined by the local IP of the server or 127.0.0.1, but you can add a custom IP address or range in your controllers:

```
consider_local "1.2.3.4"
```

The string is converted to an Ruby IPAddr object, so network ranges are legal.

You can customize the actual message by placing a partial file in the app/views/exception_notifier directory. The sections you can override are named _request, _session, _environment, and _backtrace. You can add your own sections by setting Exception Notifier.sections value — the expected array is made up of lower-case strings. You would then write a partial to match any new sections you might add.

Your custom partials have access to the instance variables shown in Table 11.2.

Instance Variables

Variable	Description
@backtrace	The backtrace of the exception, with file names cleaned to their absolute versions.
@controller	The controller object in which the error happened
@data	Optional data in the mailer object.
@exception	The raised exception
@host	The requesting hostname
@rails_root	The Rails root directory, in canonical form.
@request	The request object
@sections	The list of sections written by the mailer

resource_controller

If you've done a lot of RESTful resource creation, you've probably noticed that Rails creates the same boilerplate code for each controller you ask it to build. Technically, this would seem to be a violation of the Don't Repeat Yourself (DRY) principle.

There have been a couple of attempts to make a controller structure that does not repeat itself for each an every new controller. The resource_controller plugin, created and maintained by James Golick, is probably the most widely used plugin in this category.

Installing resource_controller

The most recent stable version of resource_controller is available at:

```
script/plugin install svn.jamesgolick.com/resource_controller/
    tags/stable
```

The cutting edge version is:

```
script/plugin install svn.jamesgolick.com/resource_controller/
    tags/trunk
```

Using resource_controller

Take any old controller that you want to make RESTful. Change it's parent class like so:

```
class UsersController < ResourceController::Base
end
```

449

An alternate syntax is available if you need your controller to have a specific different parent class.

```
class UsersController
  restful_controller
end
```

Both versions are identical, as long as the `restful_controller` method call is the first thing in your controller class.

And hey, that's it, as long as you want to use all the defaults. Which you probably don't. Luckily, it's really easy to customize your controller, and it helps to be able to focus on what is unique about your controller, rather than having to wade through all the code that is identical to other RESTful controllers.

For each of the basic RESTful actions you can create a `before` or `after` block invoked either before or after the actual action:

```
save.before do
  logger.debug "about to save"
end
```

One quick note — one of the RESTful actions is `new` — Ruby doesn't like it if you use that all by itself, so the new action is referred to as `new_action`.

Each action has several optional methods you can call to customize its behavior, as shown in Table 11.3.

TABLE 11.3

Optional Methods to Customize Action Behavior

Hook	Description
after	Takes a block, which is invoked after the action completes.
before	Takes a block, which is invoked before the action starts.
failure	Scopes any other block to specifically be invoked if the action fails, such as `create.failure.flash = "Oops"`.
flash	A string placed in the flash by the action.
response	Takes a block which replaces the entire `respond_to` block for the action.
success	Scopes for actions that have succeeded. The default for methods that are not explicitly scoped as failure.
wants	Adds an individual line to the respond_to block for the action, such as `new_action.wants.js { render :partial => "javascript" }`.

If you have several changes for the same action, they can all go in one block:

```
update do
  flash = "something flashy"
  wants.xml { render :xml, @user }
end
```

The plugin also allows you to handle alternate mechanisms for loading your objects or collections, nested resources, polymorphic connections, and the like.

Adding user authentication

In most applications that you will write, you will likely have the concept of users. Typically you will give users the ability to log into your application to gain access to protected features or functionality, or to provide a personalized user experience. In order to support the ability for users to log in and log out from your application, you need to implement some form of user authentication. User authentication allows you to confirm that a user is who they claim to be, usually by verifying a password that the user submits.

User authentication is a very important piece of your application to get right, as it lies at the heart of your application's security. Fortunately, there are several authentication plugins available that have been used in many applications and can be trusted to work well.

Whether you choose to implement user authentication for your application by using one of these plugins, another plugin, or create your own, I believe it is important that you take a look at what you are getting and that you take the time to understand the code. Authentication is such a key component of your application that it is a good idea to take the time to understand how it works. I think you'll find that once you understand it, authentication and its implementation are not that complex.

The `restful_authentication` plugin has become the most commonly used authentication plugin in Rails 2.0.2. What's nice about this plugin is the way that it provides a simple core of functionality that is easily extended to the specific needs of your application. You can even use this plugin to manage e-mail based authentication of new users.

Installing restful_authentication

Installing the plugin is normal:

```
script/plugin install http://svn.techno-weenie.net/projects/
    plugins/restful_authentication/
```

To start using the basic features, run the generator:

```
./script/generate authenticated user sessions
```

The first argument is the name of the model to use for user information, the second is the name of the controller to use for managing login and logout.

The migration gives you a bunch of files:

- Two library files, `authenticated_system`, and `authenticated_test_helper` that provide system wide functionality.
- A controller that has a new method (the login screen), a create method (authentication), and destroy (logout)
- A user model and migration
- A controller to manage CRUD for the user model
- Test files for the controllers and migration. Tests will be in RSpec if that's what your project seems to be using.
- If you add e-mail authentication with the generator option `-include_activation`, you'll also get a mailer object.

Be sure to run the new migrations before continuing.

Using restful_authentication

The overwhelming majority of `restful_authentication` functionality is in it's controllers and in the `authenticated_system` library file.

To add authentication to any controller, create a before filter that forces a user to be logged in.

```
before_filter :login_required
```

This causes the controller to require an authenticated user or else it redirects to `sessions/new`, which is the login page. You can use the `:only` option to limit access to only a listed set of controller actions. If you want different behavior when a user is not logged in, override the method `access_denied`. Override the method `authorized?` if you want a fancier check — for one thing, `restful_controller` does not handle differing levels of user access out of the box. The currently logged in user is available using the method `current_user`, assuming you specified `user` as the name of the model.

The user model and controller provide a form for adding new users with a login, e-mail, password, and password confirmation. The passwords are stored in the database encrypted according to accepted best practices, including a separate random "salt" added to the password before encryption. You can then augment the user model according to your own needs.

The session controller handles displaying the password challenge, verifying credentials, and saving the current user into the session if the password authenticates.

Enhanced scaffolding

There are several useful Rails plugins that you can use as a replacement for the out-of-the-box scaffold generating that you get with Rails. These plugins provide a much richer user interface for interacting with your Active Record models. We'll discuss two of the most popular plugins here.

Streamlined

Like the default scaffolding, Streamlined allows you to quickly generate interfaces for your Active Record models. According to their Web site, Streamlined aims to bring the declarative goodness of Active Record to the view layer. It manages the presentation, creation, and editing of instances of your models, with full-featured scaffolds that include relationship management.

The current version of Streamlined is a Rails plugin; however, earlier versions were released as a generator. The official Web site for Streamlined is at `http://streamlinedframework.org`.

Following are some of the features that Streamlined presents:

- Zero-configuration relationship management
- Ajax-powered widgets and transitions
- Live data filtering
- Out-of-the-box sortable lists and pagination
- Exporting to XML, CSV, and JSON
- Declarative and easily-customizable UI development
- Cross-browser support, including Firefox, Internet Explorer, and Safari
- Pluggable CSS styling

Installing Streamlined

You can install the latest stable branch of Streamlined using this command from the root of your Rails application:

```
ruby script/plugin install http://svn.streamlinedframework.org/
    branches/stable/streamlined
```

Using Streamlined

Let's walk through a simple example of using Streamlined with a very simple Rails application. This example will not show you all of the features of Streamlined, but you will get an idea of how easy it is to create a quick interface for managing your model instances. For this example, consider an application with two models, where one is classes and the other is students. This allows you to also see how Streamlined handles associations in the user interface.

To get started, generate a new rails application and call it students.

```
rails students
```

Next, go into the `students` directory and install the plugin.

```
ruby script/plugin install http://svn.streamlinedframework.org/
    branches/stable/streamlined
```

After that, generate models for students and classes. Also generate a controller for each.

```
ruby script/generate model student name:string year:string
    birthdate:date
ruby script/generate model course name:string capacity:integer
ruby script/generate controller courses
ruby script/generate controller students
```

We had to use course instead of class, because "class" is a reserved keyword in Ruby, Rails does not let you use it as a class name.

As a result of generating the student and course models, the migrations shown in Listings 11.10 and 11.11 should have been automatically created for you. We're still in standard Rails mode — nothing Streamline specific has happened yet.

LISTING 11.10

001_create_students.rb Migration

```
class CreateStudents < ActiveRecord::Migration
  def self.up
    create_table :students do |t|
      t.string :name
      t.string :year
      t.date :birthdate

      t.timestamps
    end
  end

  def self.down
    drop_table :students
  end
end
```

LISTING 11.11

002_create_courses.rb Migration

```
class CreateCourses < ActiveRecord::Migration
  def self.up
    create_table :courses do |t|
      t.string :name
```

```
      t.integer :capacity

      t.timestamps
    end
  end

  def self.down
    drop_table :courses
  end
end
```

Make sure that you have your database running (in Rails 2.0.2 and higher, the default project created here will use SQLite), and use the following commands to generate the databases for this project. After generating the database, go ahead and run the migrations.

```
> rake db:create:all
> rake db:migrate
```

Then let's quickly add a many to many relationship between students and courses.

```
class Student < ActiveRecord::Base
    has_and_belongs_to_many :courses
end
class Course < ActiveRecord::Base
    has_and_belongs_to_many :students
end
```

Because you are using the has_and_belongs_to_many association to create a many-to-many relationship between your two models, you also need to create a mapping table in the database to make this type of relationship work. You do not need a model class for this new table, so you can generate just a stand-alone migration file. Use the Rails generator to create the new migration, as follows:

```
ruby script/generate migration CreateCoursesStudents
```

This creates another migration file at db/migrate/003_create_courses_students.rb. Open up that file and edit it to look like Listing 11.12. This migration creates the mapping table with two columns, a reference to a course, and a reference to a student. These reference columns are translated to a column for course_id, and a column for student_id. Also notice that the ID column is explicitly left out of this table by passing the :id=>false parameter to the create_table method. Recall that for mapping tables, the mapping table does not require an ID column.

003_create_courses_students.rb Migration

```
class CreateCoursesStudents < ActiveRecord::Migration
  def self.up
    create_table :courses_students, :id => false do |t|
      t.references :course
      t.references :student
    end
  end

  def self.down
    drop_table :courses_students
  end
end
```

Because you have a new migration, you have to run the migrations again to get this new table created. Go ahead and do that now.

```
rake db:migrate
```

Now you make the controllers `streamlined` enabled by specifying a special streamlined layout and a method call to `acts_as_streamlined`. Add these two statements to both controllers like this:

```
class CoursesController < ApplicationController
    layout "streamlined"
    acts_as_streamlined
end
```

And away we go. Starting the server and hitting `courses`, should give you something similar to Figure 11.2:

This figure shows the basic Streamlined look and feel

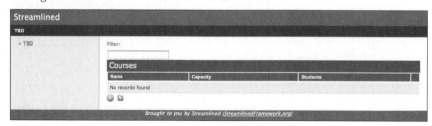

So far, you've invested two lines of code in Streamlined. For that investement, you've got a nice looking CSS sheet. You've got a top navigation and a side navigation, both of which are currently marked "TBD". The columns of our model are listed accurately, of course there aren't any courses in there to view yet. What you can't see from the screen shot is that the table is sortable by any column by clicking on the header.

The filter text box does an Ajax filter of the items in the table. Below the table, one button takes you to a form to add a new course, the other pops up a list of options to export the courses as XML, CSV, JSON, or YAML. The new course form has a nice table layout, and automatically generates based on the model fields. When courses are listed in the index page, each course has nice icons for show/edit/destroy, and an Ajax edit in the students column to let you connect courses and students. All in all, quite a return on two lines of code.

Naturally, there are several ways to customize this layout. The side and top menus are set via helper methods. Application wide ones can be placed in the top level application helper, versions in the helpers for specific controllers will override. The method names are `streamlined_top_menus` and `streamlined_side_menus`. The return value of these methods is a two-dimensional array. Each entry in the array is a two-element list of the form `[caption, url]`. For example:

```
def streamlined_top_menus
  [["Courses", courses_path]]
end
```

The first element is a string, the second is anything that can be used as a URL — a url_for hash, or a named route method (the example given assumes that courses has been added as a RESTful resource in the `routes.rb` file.

Further customizations go in the Streamlined UI file, which you can create with a rake task:

```
rake streamlined:model MODEL=Course
```

This creates the directory app/`streamlined` and the file `course_ui.rb`. The file contains the following:

```
module CourseAdditions

end
Course.class_eval { include CourseAdditions }

Streamlined.ui_for(Course) do

end
```

Any method in the `CourseAdditions` module gets mixed in as a class method of the `Course` model, this is a way to keep UI related decorators and helper modules separate, while still making them available to the model class in Streamlined.

One design goal of Streamlined was to give the view layer the same simple declarative syntax style that ActiveRecord has, and the UI block in this file is where the declarations go. Inside the UI block, the declaration:

```
user_columns :students, :capacity, :name
```

Sets the columns that are visible from any view. The `pagination` method specifies various options for the index display, such as `pagination :per_page => 50`. And so on, check out the Streamlined documentation for the complete list of the numerous ways that a Streamlined application can be customized.

ActiveScaffold

Like Streamlined, ActiveScaffold is another Rails plugin that provides a method for quickly generating an administrative interface for interacting with your model instances. It has a different structure and technique than Streamlined.

Go back to the same minimal application, course model, student model, two controllers, and the join table. Just remove the Streamlined plugin and replace it with ActiveScaffold:

```
script/plugin install  http://activescaffold.googlecode.com/svn/
    tags/active_scaffold
```

Where Streamlined created it's own layout file, ActiveScaffold works within your already existing layout file. This means you need to create a file there, in `app/views/layouts/application.html.erb`. For the moment, the minimal layout file is perfectly fine:

```
<!DOCTYPE html PUBLIC "-//W3C//DTD XHTML 1.0 Transitional//EN"
        "http://www.w3.org/TR/xhtml1/DTD/xhtml1-transitional.dtd">

<html xmlns="http://www.w3.org/1999/xhtml" xml:lang="en"
    lang="en">
<head>
 <meta http-equiv="content-type" content="text/
   html;charset=UTF-8" />
 <title>Your Title Here</title>
 <%= javascript_include_tag :defaults %>
 <%= active_scaffold_includes %>
</head>
<body>

<%= yield  %>

</body>
</html>
```

The important parts to include are the default JavaScripts, the `active_scaffold_includes` helper tag, and, of course, the `yield`.

You then add ActiveScaffold to a controller like so:

```
class StudentsController < ApplicationController
  active_scaffold
end
```

The `active_scaffold` call assumes that the associated model will have the expected name, if not, then use the model name as an argument to the call. The resulting display looks like Figure 11.3 — I'm showing it with the Ajax new entry form displayed.

FIGURE 11.3

ActiveScaffold in action

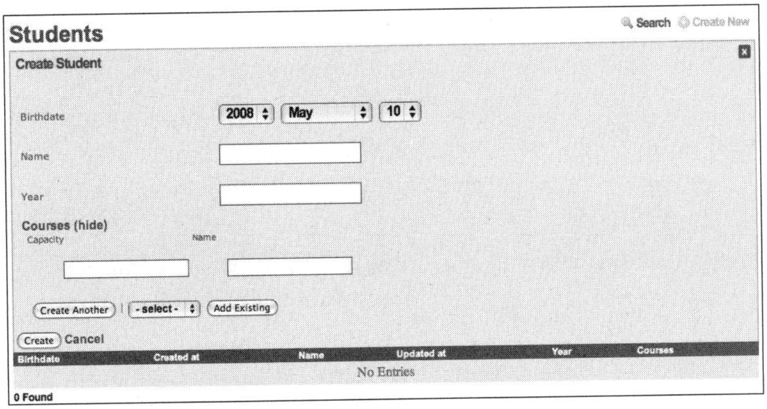

This has the same basic feature set as Streamlined — display, search, view, even an Ajax view to associate related objects.

Customizing ActiveScaffold is done via a global block placed in the ApplicationController, and then controller specific blocks placed in each individual controller. The global one looks like this:

```
ActiveScaffold.set_defaults do |config|

  config.ignore_columns.add [:created_at, :updated_at]

end
```

In this case, you are telling ActiveScaffold to not display the timestamp columns. Individual controller customizations are actually in a block argument to the `active_scaffold` call, and would go something like this:

```
active_scaffold do |config|
  config.label = "Students"
  list.sorting = {:name => "ASC"}
```

```
    columns[:name].label = "Full Name"
  end
```

Naturally, this just scratches the surface of what you can do with ActiveScaffold, check it's online documentation for more details.

Implementing content tagging

Tagging has become a critical part of user-created content in Web 2.0, allowing for flexible classification and more accurate search. Originally, a Rails plugin from the core team called `acts_as_taggable` managed tagging in Rails applications, however over time several plugins have augmented or re-implemented the behavior.

The basic taggable functionality involves a table of tags that can have a polymorphic relationship with any other object. This allows any object in the system to be associated with one or more tags. Typically, there is functionality to find items by tag and also to create tag counts for the purposes of building tag clouds.

The `acts_as_taggable_redux` plugin adds a helpful piece of functionality, specifically the ability to associate tags to a specific user. Grab the plugin via the normal method:

```
script/plguin install http://svn.devjavu.com/geemus/rails/
    plugins/acts_as_taggable_redux
```

To use the plugin, you need to create a database migration:

```
rake acts_as_taggable:db:create
```

This migration creates two tables, the Tags table, which is essentially just the name of the tag, and a Taggings table, which is a polymorphic join table associating with another object, and also containing an optional user id. After running the migration, you can make any model class taggable by adding the following line to the model:

```
acts_as_tagger
```

With that line in place, you can then get and set the list of tags associated with the object using the pseudo-attribute `tag_list`. You can set a text field to `tag_list` in a form, and the entered data will be parsed and associated with the object. If you also want to associate the tags with a user id, then the getter takes the `user_id` as an optional argument. In the setter, `user_id` is a separate attribute added to added to taggable objects, both the user and the tags need to be set for the tags to be associated with the specific user.

For finding items with a specific tag, the plugin adds the class method `find_tagged_with`, which takes a list of tags as its argument. There are two important optional arguments. The first, `:method` is `:any` by default, causing an object to be selected if it matches any of the tags, it can also be set to `:all`, which changes the behavior to only select objects that match all the tags. The other option, `:user`, is a user id to match tags against.

If no user is specified, you will get all tags (not just all tags not associated with a user), so if you are doing user-based tagging, you need to be consistent about passing in the user id.

Finally, the plugin includes a couple of helper methods for creating tag clouds, include

```
<%= tag_cloud %>
```

in a view to get an entire cloud. The plugin contains a CSS sheet you can install to get a tag cloud like look. You'll also need a tags controller, which will be the destination for any link created in the cloud.

Handling file uploads

With the growing popularity of content sharing that Web 2.0 sites such as `flickr.com` and `youtube.com` have contributed to, file uploading has become a requirement that is common to many of the applications you will write. Because this is a common feature that many applications require, this is the perfect example of a great feature to turn into a plugin. There are several plugins available for dealing with file uploads, and one in particular has been extremely well received and implemented in many Rails applications. The plugin I am talking about is `attachement_fu`.

attachment_fu

The `attachment_fu` plugin has become the most popular Rails plugin for dealing with image uploads. This plugin makes implementing image uploads a simple and painless task. The `attachment_fu` plugin lets you upload the images to your file system, your database, or the Amazon S3 hosting cloud.

In order to use `attachment_fu`, you'll need to have one of the three major Ruby image processing libraries installed: RMagick, Minimagick, or ImageScience. These libraries all depend on native image processing libraries — RMagick and Minimagick depend on ImageMagick, while ImageScience depends on FreeImage. The details of installing the native package depend on your operating system, the documentation for the libraries should have full information.

Assuming that you have one of those libraries installed, you can get attachment_fu via:

```
script/plugin install http://svn.techno-weenie.net/projects/
    plugins/attachment_fu/
```

To use `attachment_fu`, you need a data model for image metadata with some specific fields, which you can add to any migration — the table name is arbitrary, but the field names are specific.

```
create_table :images do |t|
  t.string  :filename
  t.string  :content_type
  t.integer :size
  t.integer :height
  t.integer :width
  t.integer :parent_id
```

```
      t.integer :thumbnail
      t.timestamps
   end
```

Most of those should be self-explanatory — the `size` is the file size of the image, and `parent_id` and `thumbnail` manage the relationship between the original image and any thumbnails automatically created by `attachment_fu`.

Usually, images uploaded with `attachment_fu` are associated with a model, it's the picture of that thing you are selling, or the user's buddy icon or something like that. So, in order to user `attachment_fu`, you'll also need to set up that relationship in a migration, either by including a foreign key in the images table, or by including a key to that table in your model.

Of course, the images table itself implies a model, and it's this model that gets the details that -specify the attachment:

```
class Image < ActiveRecord::Base
  has_attachment :content_type => :image,
                 :size => (1.kilobyte..10.megabytes),
                 :storage => :file_system,
                 :thumbnails => {:thumb => "57x57>"}

  validates_as_attachment
  # also place the relationship with the data model
end
```

The `:content_type` field can also be a specific MIME type, or a list of MIME types, the `:image` symbol used, causes any image to be allowed. The `:size` argument takes a range, with values in bytes, the Rails helpers are useful here. If you only want to set one bound, you can use either of the options `:min_size` or `:max_size` instead. The `:storage` option, as specified, puts the files in the `public/<table>` directory of your server. Images can also go to the `:db_file`, which requires the database table to have a BLOB field to put the image in. You can also specify `:s3`, which uses Amazon.

The `:thumbnails` option specifies one or more thumbnails to create, the hash key is appended to the image name to create the thumbnail image name, and the value is the size of the thumbnail, the value can also be a two-element list [width, height] instead of the string. The `:resize_to` option changes the size of the actual image, again it takes a string or a two-element list. Finally, the `validates_as_attachment` method ensures that uploaded files intended for this class match the parameters for content and size.

To upload a file via attachment_fu, ensure that the form being used is multipart, and use the `fields_for` helper to embed the image model in your data form. This form assumes the data object has an image field representing the relationship between data and image.

```
<% form_for @data, :html => {:multipart => true} do |f| %>
  <%# data things #%>
  <% fields_for :image do |img| %>
```

```
    <b>Upload</b>
    <%= img.file_field :upload_data %>
  <% end %>
<% end %>
```

The `file_field` uses the ordinary Rails helper, the field name `upload_data` is mandated by attachment_fu. Given an ordinary save controller on the server, this form will upload the file, and attachment_fu will save the file and the metadata.

The image class is given an attribute `public_filename` that can be used to display the image.

Engines

Rails engines provide another way to extend Rails. Engines are actually implemented as another Rails plugin. They were created by Dr. James Adam, an active member of the Ruby community. There is an official Web site for Rails engines at `http://rails-engines.org/`.

According to the front page of the engines site, "[t]he engines plugin enhances Rails plugins - allowing sharing of code, views and other aspects of your application in a clear and managed way."

Basically, an engine is a plugin that is meant to handle an entire MVC vertical slice of an application. Whereas typical Rails plugins only touch the Model layer of an application, engines provide controllers, models, and views related to a specific aspect of an application. If you find yourself implementing the same feature over and over again in your applications, creating a Rails engine may be a good option for you. A directory of Rails engines can be found online at the same site that lists the Rails plugins. You can get a listing of some available engines at `http://agileweb development.com/plugins/category/10`.

There are not nearly as many engines available as there are plugins. Because engines implement a full MVC slice of an application, including controller, model, and even view code, they tend to be more specific to a particular organization's implementation style, and from that standpoint are probably less reusable than Rails plugins. This explains why there are relatively few of them that have been released publicly. However, internal to a single organization, you may find that engines are an even better mechanism to achieve reuse than plugins.

The Engines plugin was recently updated to work with Rails 2.0. Engines 2.0 is the most recent version of the Rails Engines plugin at the time of this writing.

The most common recommended strategy for writing your own engine is to first write the functionality of your engine as a stand-alone Rails application. This makes it easier to test and convert into an engine when you are comfortable with the way it works. Because an engine represents a complete MVC slice of an application, this strategy seems like a good one.

The scope of an engine can vary wildly, from the implementation of a single logical feature such as user authentication, to a nearly complete application, such as the substruct and tableau that engines provide. Substruct is an e-commerce engine for Rails, and Tableau is a photo gallery engine. You won't write a complete application in this section, but instead, I'll show you the steps required to turn code that has been developed as a standard Rails application into a Rails engine. The steps that you will go through can be broken down as follows:

- Install the engines plugin
- Generate the engine skeleton for your engine
- Move your application files into the engine directory
- Modify `config/environment.rb` to start your engine
- Include your engine in the application controller and helper classes

Install the Engines plugin

You install the Engines plugin exactly the same way that you install any other plugin. In fact, the Engines plugin is just a standard plugin. It is what is enabled by the Engines plugin that goes beyond the features of standard plugins.

```
ruby script/plugin install http://svn.rails-engines.org/plugins/
    engines
```

Generate the engine skeleton

After you've installed the Engines plugin, you have an engine generator available that you can use to generate the skeleton of a new engine. Use that generator to create a directory that you will use to put your engine code into.

```
ruby script/generate engine MyEngine
/my_engine/
/my_engine/app
/my_engine/db
/my_engine/lib
/my_engine/public
/my_engine/tasks
/my_engine/test
/my_engine/init_engine.rb
/my_engine/install.rb
/my_engine/README
```

Move your application files into the engine

After you've generated the engine directory, the next thing to do is to move your application files from the main `app` directory of your project into the `vendor/plugins/my_engine` directory. You'll want to move the following files into your engine directory:

- Move the files you want in the engine from inside of your main `app` directory into `vendor/plugins/my_engine/app`.

- Move any migrations you have from `db/migrate` to `vendor/plugins/my_engine/db/migrate`.
- Move any library files you have in the `lib` directory into `vendor/plugins/my_engine/lib`.
- Move your static files from `public` into `vendor/plugins/my_engine/lib`.
- Move your tests from `test` into `vendor/plugins/my_engine/test`.

Modify your environment

After you've copied your application files into the engine directory, the next step is to modify the `config/environment.rb` file to start up your new engine.

```
Engines.start :my_engine
```

This starts up your engine when the enclosing Rails application is started.

Include your engine in your application

The final step in setting up your new engine is to include the engine in your application controller and helper files.

```
class ApplicationController < ActionController::Base
    include MyEngine
end

module ApplicationHelper
    include MyEngine
end
```

At this point the application behaves as before, but the engine has been extracted and is available to be used in another application.

Summary

Ruby on Rails is one of the most innovative and productive Web development frameworks in existence. Something that has kept Rails simple, elegant, and easy to use is the core team's reluctance to pile on features that may not be useful to Web applications in general. Rails sticks with core features of Web development and lets developers build the rest of an application around the framework. In this chapter, you learned about three different ways in which you can extend the Rails framework with reusable components of your own. These three styles of extending Rails are:

- Generators
- Plugins
- Engines

Each is useful in different situations. As you develop your own Rails applications, you should always be considering what functionality you could package as one of these extensions to make the current application easier to read and more maintainable, or to make development of future applications easier. Think about this in terms of development within your own organization, but also, if you think you have developed an extension that would be useful to the Rails community at large, consider distributing this code as open-source. That is a great way to get some recognition for yourself or your organization and to promote more Rails development.

Chapter 12

Advanced Topics

I n this final chapter of the Ruby on Rails Bible, you'll learn some additional Rails techniques that haven't been covered yet in previous chapters. While this chapter is named Advanced Topics, you should find the time to master the topics covered here, as many of them are extremely useful for most Rails projects.

Beyond the Basics

If you've been reading this book from the beginning, throughout the course of the book you've learned all of the basic information you need to begin developing real applications with Rails. However, there is still more to say about the power and elegance of Rails. In this chapter you'll explore some additional technologies that you might use in a Rails application, and some that you will most likely want to use in all of your Rails applications.

The topics that you'll learn about in this chapter are the following:

- RESTful Rails
- Web services with Rails
- Working with legacy databases
- ActionMailer
- Deploying with Capistrano

IN THIS CHAPTER

Beyond the basics

RESTful Rails

Working with legacy databases

Using ActionMailer

ActiveResource and XML

Deploying with Capistrano

RESTful Rails

One of the things that any good developer strives for in the development of a Web application, or any application for that matter, is a well-organized code base with consistent use of patterns and naming conventions. This contributes a great deal to the overall maintainability of an application. However, maintaining a well-defined organization and consistency in a code base, especially one that is being worked on by multiple developers, is not an easy task. In Web development, there have never been any widely accepted patterns for how to name models, controllers, and their action methods. While Rails imposes a certain level of standards on the naming of classes, it doesn't do much for the structure inside controllers. Developers are often not sure when looking at a code base where they should put a new action method and how that method should be named. If this is a problem that you've faced, RESTful development is definitely something that you should be interested in.

Recently, there has been a surge in popularity for a development pattern known as Representational State Transfer (REST), and Rails has fueled its popularity. The creator of the Rails framework, David Heinemeier Hansson, is a great proponent of RESTful development. Hansson introduced RESTful development to the Rails community in his RailsConf keynote address of 2006, titled "A World of Resources." In that keynote, he challenged developers to embrace the constraints of RESTful development. With the release of version 2 of the Rails framework, RESTful development has become the standard way of creating a Rails application.. Before I dive into how you implement REST in a Rails application, let's explore the question of what RESTful development is and why developers are excited about it.

> **NOTE** You can download David Heinemeier Hansson's "A World of Resources" presentation from `http://media.rubyonrails.org/presentations/worldofre-sources.pdf`.

The term REST was coined by Roy Fielding in his Ph.D. dissertation. Roy Fielding was also one of the creators of the HTTP protocol. REST describes a method of architecting software, built around the concept of resources, rather than the concept of actions. REST happens to be a very good fit for Web application development. Although REST itself is not explicitly tied to the Web or Web application development, it is within the context of the Web and Web applications that I will discuss it. Within the REST architecture, requests from the browser use a standard set HTTP methods to manipulate an application's resources.

Most Web developers are familiar with just two of the available HTTP methods, the GET and POST methods. However, the HTTP protocol defines eight methods: GET, POST, PUT, DELETE, HEAD, TRACE, OPTIONS, and CONNECT. REST is concerned with the first four of these methods, GET, POST, PUT, and DELETE. These are the methods that a RESTful Web application uses to manipulate resources. REST happens to be a very good fit for database-backed Web applications. In a database-backed Web application, resources map well to models, which in turn map well to database tables.

In his dissertation, Roy Fielding also discusses Stateless Communication as being a constraint of a REST architecture. However, nearly every Web application relies on maintaining state to some extent. State is typically stored in cookies and sessions in a Web application. Any Web application that relies on state is officially not completely compliant with REST; however, that doesn't stop most people from referring to these techniques as REST-based, even though they are not 100 percent true to the REST architecture.

In a traditional Web application developed in a framework such as Rails, a request would specify an action and a resource to perform the action on. For example, the following is a common URL found in a Rails application:

```
http://www.myapp.com/book/show/5
```

This URL tells the Rails backend to use the show method of the book controller to display the book resource that has an ID of 5. An application developed using REST would not specify the action in the URL. Instead, the URL would specify only the resource. The action is determined by the HTTP method with which the request is submitted. For example, a RESTful equivalent of the above URL would be the following:

```
http://www.myapp.com/book/5
```

This request would be submitted using the HTTP GET method and routed to the correct method, show, based on having come from a GET request. Let's expand on the example of manipulating a book resource, and look at how you would perform other actions on a book resource using RESTful development. Table 12.1 shows how various actions performed on a resource are mapped to URLs and HTTP methods.

TABLE 12.1

Actions and HTTP Methods in a RESTful Application

Action	URL	HTTP Method
show	www.myapp.com/book/5	GET
destroy	www.myapp.com/book/5	DELETE
update	www.myapp.com/book/5	POST
create	www.myapp.com/book	PUT

Notice that the URL for performing show, destroy, and update on a resource is identical. These requests are routed to the correct controller action based on a combination of the URL and the HTTP method that is used to submit them.

So the idea is that you would apply this pattern throughout your Web application's architecture. Every controller would consist of the same standard set of methods, show, destroy, update, and create... (index, edit and new also get their own standard URLs). The application framework routes to the correct method, based on looking at both the URL and the HTTP method used for incoming requests. Suddenly, you have great consistency in your Web applications.

All of your controllers are implemented in the same style and contain the same set of methods. You may be thinking about now that it is not very likely that you can actually implement an entire Web application using just resources with matched controllers and that small set of controller actions. You may find that you need a few additional controller methods, but you will be surprised at how far you can get by consistently following the RESTful pattern. You will find that this architecture also cleans up your controller and model designs.

In addition, keep in mind as you develop that not every resource is necessarily backed by a database table. You may have resources that are not stored in the database as models, yet you still follow this same resource/model matched with a controller implementation pattern — for example, the Session resource in the RESTful Authentication plugin described in Chapter 11, or search, which is often implemented as a separate search RESTful controller even if searches are not stored in the database.

Some advantages of RESTful architecture

So what are some of the advantages that you get from using this RESTful development approach?

- **Well-defined and consistent application design:** RESTful architecture defines a standard way of implementing controllers and access to models in a Web application. Applications that consistently follow this architecture end up with a very clean, very maintainable code base that is also easy to read and understand.

  Traditionally, when you have a Web development project that is worked on by several people, maybe not all concurrently, each may bring their own style of how they use controllers, what names they give to controller methods, what they determine are models, and so on. The RESTful approach makes it much easier for every developer that comes onto a project to maintain a very consistent implementation style, and thus preserve a solid architecture across the application.

  With a RESTful architecture, you know where to put your code. Every application that implements a RESTful architecture has a consistent design, and developers know exactly where to put code.

- **CRUD-based controllers:** Controllers can map one-to-one to a model. Each controller contains the code necessary to manipulate a specific model through the standard CRUD methods, create, show, update, and destroy.

- **Clean URLs:** Because URLs used in a RESTful application represent resources and not actions, they are less verbose and always follow a consistent format of a controller followed by the ID of a resource to manipulate.

■ **Ease of integration:** Because of the application's consistent API with pre-defined resource and action method names, it becomes easier for third-party applications to integrate with your RESTful application through a REST-based Web service.

REST as a Web service architecture

While REST is an excellent fit for database-backed Web applications, it is probably an even stronger fit for Web services. The REST architecture provides an excellent platform for providing services. After all, Web services are essentially APIs that let you manipulate some form of resource. Rather than create another layer on top of HTTP, as the SOAP Web service protocol does, REST-based Web services rely on the existing functionality of HTTP to provide Web services.

Because REST uses what is already built into HTTP, rather than layering another semantic layer on top of it as SOAP does, REST is a much simpler architecture for implementing Web services. The most popular consumer-facing Web services, such as those provided by Amazon, Google, Yahoo, and others, all offer a REST-based interface. REST is more popular than SOAP today for implementing commercial Web services. Considering the book example again, you could easily imagine a Web service API that used URLs identical to those that a browser uses to get HTML content — in Rails, the same RESTful controller actions with `xml` at the end of the request URL is enough to get you full XML Web service responsiveness. This gets into the next topic of interest related to REST, that of representation.

REST and representations

When you request a page using a RESTful architecture, the page that is returned can be considered a representation of the resource that you are requesting. However, think of an HTML page as just one possible representation of any given resource. Other representations might include an XML document, a text document, or a block of JSON-encoded JavaScript.

Using the RESTful architecture, you would request a different representation of a resource using the same method, but by passing a different piece of metadata to the server, thus indicating the representation that you would like to have returned. For example, the following two requests would both be routed to the same controller and action method:

```
http://www.myapp.com/book/5
http://www.myapp.com/book/5.xml
```

The first request would return an HTML representation of the book resource. The second request would return an XML representation of the book resource — Chapter 5 showed the Rails mechanism for easily managing this. The ease of adding output mechanisms is another advantage of a RESTful architecture. The same controllers and actions can be used to deliver a variety of response representations — including HTML, RSS, and XML. This makes implementing Web services in a RESTful architecture extremely easy, and again maintains a consistent design style.

Writing a RESTful application with Rails

As I mentioned earlier, with the release of Rails 2.0, REST has been adopted as the standard architecture for a Rails application. What does that mean? Rails provides a set of tools that makes building RESTful-style applications easy for the developer.

When you use the `scaffold` generator to automatically create the CRUD skeleton of your application for a given resource, the controller and action methods generated are RESTful. In versions of Rails that supported REST prior to version 2.0, you had to explicitly say that you wanted your scaffolding to be REST-based by using the `scaffold_resource` generator. In just a bit, you'll get a chance to use the `scaffold` generator to create a REST implementation for a resource in a real Rails application.

Rails routing and REST

In Table 12.1, you saw how REST uses a URL and an HTTP method to route to a specific action method. That table actually doesn't give you the complete story for how Rails maps URLs and HTTP methods to actions and controllers. In a standard RESTful Rails application, each controller has not just four, but seven actions. These actions are `show`, `update`, `destroy`, `index`, `create`, `edit`, and `new`.

Here is a description of the purpose for each of these actions. These map directly to CRUD actions for an ActiveRecord model, but RESTful resources may also interpret these categories a little more loosely for implicit server resources that aren't directly in the database:

- `show`

  This action is used to display a specific instance of a resource.

- `update`

  This action is used to perform an update on a resource.

- `destroy`

  This action is used to delete an instance of a resource.

- `index`

  This action displays a list of all of the resources of a given type.

- `create`

  This action creates a new instance of a resource.

- `edit`

  This action returns a page that allows the user to make updates to a resource.

- `new`

  This action returns a page that allows the user to create a new instance of a resource.

The new and `create` actions together are used to create a new resource instance. The new action presents you with the form that you use to create the resource, and the `create` action handles the form submission to actually create the new resource in the database. Similarly, the edit and update actions are used to update an existing resource. The edit action presents you with the form that you can use to make changes to the resource, and the update action handles the form submission, saving updates to the database.

However, Rails still just uses the same four HTTP methods, GET, POST, PUT, and DELETE, to route to the seven supported actions. To accomplish this, Rails actually uses the GET method for multiple actions.

Table 12.2 shows how URLs and HTTP methods are routed to specific actions in a Rails application.

Rails also creates dynamic methods for the routes. In addition, methods such as link_to and form_for will infer the path from the resource, so link_to(@book), will be assumed to be a show action on the books controller.

TABLE 12.2

RESTful Routes in a Rails Application

Action	URL	HTTP Method	Named Method
show	www.myapp.com/books/1	GET	book_path(@book)
update	www.myapp.com/books/1	PUT	book_path(@book)
destroy	www.myapp.com/books/1	DELETE	book_path(@book)
index	www.myapp.com/books	GET	destroy_book_path(@book)
create	www.myapp.com/books	POST	books_path
edit	www.myapp.com/books/1/edit	GET	edit_book_path(@book)
new	www.myapp.com/books/new	GET	new_book_path

Notice that the show, index, edit, and new actions all use the GET method. However, they are each differentiated in Rails by the URL that is used. To support the edit and new methods, the pureness of RESTful URLs is actually broken a bit, as these actions require that the action name be used in the URL so that they can be differentiated from the show and index actions.

You can also add your custom actions to a restful controller, which gives you a custom named method matching that action. There's a purity vs. practicality tradeoff here — I find extra actions useful for, say, Ajax actions that update partial forms that don't quite justify their own controller.

PUT and DELETE full disclosure

So far, I've talked about using four HTTP methods in combination with specific URLs to route to a set of standard action methods. There is, however, one problem in the actual implementation of the system that I've described. The current generation of Web browsers does not handle the PUT and DELETE methods. This means that in the real world, you are stuck with using only GET and

POST. The good news is that this does not change anything for you as a developer of a Rails application. As far as you are concerned, the URLs and HTTP methods and routes described in Table 12.2 are still completely valid.

Rails simulates the PUT and DELETE methods by inserting a hidden field called _method set to either put or delete. The Rails routing mechanism gets these requests and properly routes them to the actions that are shown in Table 12.2, just as if these were coming in as PUT or DELETE requests. There is nothing that you, as a developer, have to do to handle these requests any differently.

Generate a RESTful resource

In this section, you'll create the start of a RESTful Rails application. To get started, create a Rails application and call it restful_cookbook.

```
> rails restful_cookbook
```

This gives you the standard skeleton for a Rails application. So far, there is nothing RESTful about this application. Because this is a cookbook application, it is easy to imagine what some of its model or resource objects will be. Rails provides you with two generators that allow you to create a RESTful resource:

- scaffold: The scaffold generator creates an entire resource, including all the code that is necessary to perform the basic CRUD operations on it in a RESTful way. Specific files that are created include a model, a migration, a controller, views, and a full test suite.

- resource: The resource generator creates a model, migration, controller, and test stubs, but does not provide the code necessary to perform the CRUD operations. Also, no views are generated.

Let's use the scaffold generator to create a resource named Recipe.

```
> cd restful_cookbook
> ruby script/generate scaffold Recipe
    exists  app/models/
    exists  app/controllers/
    exists  app/helpers/
    create  app/views/recipes
    exists  app/views/layouts
    exists  test/functional
    exists  test/unit
    create  app/views/recipes/index.html.erb
    create  app/views/recipes/show.html.erb
    create  app/views/recipes/new.html.erb
    create  app/views/recipes/edit.html.erb
    create  app/views/layouts/recipes.html.erb
 identical  public/stylesheets/scaffold.css
dependency  model
    exists  app/models/
    exists  test/unit/
```

```
exists test/fixtures/
create app/models/recipe.rb
create test/unit/recipe_test.rb
create test/fixtures/recipes.yml
exists db/migrate
create db/migrate/001_create_recipes.rb
create app/controllers/recipes_controller.rb
create test/functional/recipes_controller_test.rb
create app/helpers/recipes_helper.rb
 route map.resources :recipes
```

Looking through the output printed to the screen, you can see all of the files that have been generated by the `scaffold` generator. You should see the model, controller, views, and test suite files. In just a bit, you'll take a look at some of those, but let's start with the last line of the output above — the line that says:

```
route map.resources :recipes
```

This line causes a single line to be added to the `config/routes.rb` file. The line added is

```
map.resources :recipes
```

This single line automatically creates the entire routing schema necessary to handle the CRUD methods in a RESTful manner. The RESTful routes shown in Table 12.2 are enabled for the Recipe resource by this line.

Without any further arguments, the resources call creates routing for the seven basic RESTful methods in Table 12.2. However, the method takes several optional arguments that allow you to create custom behavior and actions. Which argument you choose depends on what kind of action you want to create.

For typical controller actions that would manage a single object (such as edit), you use the argument `:member`. An action created with this option will have a URL based on the singular name of the controller and will expect an object id, as in `recipe/print/32`. Actions which, like `index`, manage on a list of objects are created with the `:collection` option, these URLs use the plural form of the controller name as in `recipes/search_results`. Finally, alternate actions that work with new objects are created using the `:new` option and create a URL of the form `recipes/new/from_scratch`.

The value you should pass to all these arguments is the same: a hash where the keys are the name of the new actions and the values are the HTTP method used to access them, for example, `:member => {:print => :get}`. You'll also get a helper method like `recipe_print_url`, `recipes_search_results_url`, or `recipes_new_from_scratch_url`.

Note that to use additional actions in your RESTful controller using REST helpers, they must be declared in the `routes.rb` file — however, you can always fall back on the more traditional `controller/action` URL format even within an otherwise RESTful controller. I personally find that Ajax callbacks to update part of a display don't always fit easily in the RESTful structure.

There are two variations on the ordinary `map.resources` call. If the resource in question doesn't have meaningful group behavior and is a true singleton, you should declare it using the singular call `map.resource`. The singular resource call will create all the RESTful routes and helpers except the index and index-related ones. For example, the RESTful Authentication plugin uses a singular resource to manage the session controller.

Sometimes you will have a resource that only makes sense as a part of a parent resource. For example, in a project management application, a task may only exist as part of a project. You can express that relationship in a RESTful system by nesting the child resource inside the parent like so:

```
map.resources :projects do |project|
  project.resources :tasks
end
```

Nesting a resource makes no difference in what is generated for the parent resource, however all the child helper methods now take an instance of the parent resource as an argument. So while the show helper method for a project is still `project_url(@project)`, the method for a task is `project_task_url(@project, @task)`. If you are attempting to infer the URL within a `link_to` or `form_for` helper, again the parent syntax is unchanged, `link_to("show project", @project)`, while a link to the child resource requires a parent, `link_to("show task", [@project, @task])`.

Custom actions can be added to either the parent or the child resource, using the syntax already described. Overall, nested resources are a powerful way to specify a relationship within your application, but since they do impose a fairly strong constraint on access to the child resource, you need to be sure that the relationship between the two models is consistent and constant. I also find the nested path names tend to quickly lose the value of being a shortcut.

The `resources` method can be customized in a couple of further ways. If, for some reason, the controller attached to your resource is different than the name of the resource in the code, you can specify the controller name with the `:controller` option — I believe this was added to support foreign language URL names.

The `:name_prefix` option allows you to change the prefix used in the helper methods, if you don't want it to match the resource name. The option `:path_prefix` is sort of the generic version of nesting resources, allowing you to specify a string that will be part of the URL before the part that controls the routing.

Now, take a look at the controller generated for the RESTful scaffolding of your recipes resource. Open up `app/controllers/recipes_controller.rb`. You should see code similar to Listing 12.1.

The first thing you should notice is that methods have been created for all of the standard RESTful CRUD actions: `index`, `show`, `new`, `edit`, `create`, `update`, and `destroy`. Comments before the definition of each of these methods show you how the action is called from a URL.

Also, notice that at the bottom of each of the methods is a `respond_to` block. The `respond_to` block, described in Chapter 5 allows you to handle requests for different response formats within the same method. The generated code includes handling of both HTML and XML response requests.

The `scaffold` generator also created all of the views necessary for the CRUD actions. The views created are `edit.html.erb`, `index.html.erb`, `new.html.erb`, and `show.html.erb`. The views are shown in Listings 12.2 through 12.5.

For the most part, there is nothing unique or different about these views. However, there are some URL helpers that are used within links. These are the URL helpers that were created by the `map.resources` method in the routes configuration, for example `form_for(@recipe)` in the edit view.

LISTING 12.1

recipes_controller.rb

```
class RecipesController < ApplicationController
    # GET /recipes
    # GET /recipes.xml
    def index
        @recipes = Recipe.find(:all)

        respond_to do |format|
            format.html # index.html.erb
            format.xml  { render :xml => @recipes }
        end
    end

    # GET /recipes/1
    # GET /recipes/1.xml
    def show
        @recipe = Recipe.find(params[:id])

        respond_to do |format|
            format.html # show.html.erb
            format.xml  { render :xml => @recipe }
        end
    end

    # GET /recipes/new
    # GET /recipes/new.xml
    def new
        @recipe = Recipe.new

        respond_to do |format|
```

continued

LISTING 12.1   *(continued)*

```
            format.html # new.html.erb
            format.xml  { render :xml => @recipe }
      end
   end

   # GET /recipes/1/edit
   def edit
      @recipe = Recipe.find(params[:id])
   end

   # POST /recipes
   # POST /recipes.xml
   def create
      @recipe = Recipe.new(params[:recipe])

      respond_to do |format|
         if @recipe.save
            flash[:notice] = 'Recipe was successfully created.'
            format.html {redirect_to(@recipe) }
            format.xml  {render :xml => @recipe,
                                   :status => :created,
                                   :location => @recipe }
         else
            format.html {render :action => "new" }
            format.xml  {render :xml => @recipe.errors,
                                   :status => :unprocessable_entity }
         end
      end
   end

   # PUT /recipes/1
   # PUT /recipes/1.xml
   def update
      @recipe = Recipe.find(params[:id])

      respond_to do |format|
         if @recipe.update_attributes(params[:recipe])
            flash[:notice] = 'Recipe was successfully updated.'
            format.html {redirect_to(@recipe) }
            format.xml  {head :ok }
         else
            format.html {render :action => "edit" }
            format.xml  {render :xml => @recipe.errors,
                                   :status => :unprocessable_entity }
         end
      end
   end
```

```
    # DELETE /recipes/1
    # DELETE /recipes/1.xml
    def destroy
        @recipe = Recipe.find(params[:id])
        @recipe.destroy

        respond_to do |format|
            format.html { redirect_to(recipes_url) }
            format.xml  { head :ok }
        end
    end
end
```

LISTING 12.2

edit.html.erb

```
<h1>Editing recipe</h1>

<%= error_messages_for :recipe %>

<% form_for(@recipe) do |f| %>
  <p>
    <%= f.submit "Update" %>
  </p>
<% end %>

<%= link_to 'Show', @recipe %> |
<%= link_to 'Back', recipes_path %>
```

LISTING 12.3

index.html.erb

```
<h1>Listing recipes</h1>

<table>
  <tr>
  </tr>

<% for recipe in @recipes %>
  <tr>
```

continued

LISTING 12.3 *(continued)*

```
    <td><%= link_to 'Show', recipe %></td>
    <td><%= link_to 'Edit', edit_recipe_path(recipe) %></td>
    <td><%= link_to 'Destroy', recipe, :confirm => 'Are you sure?',
  :method => :delete %></td>
  </tr>
<% end %>
</table>

<br />

<%= link_to 'New recipe', new_recipe_path %>
```

Unlike many code generation techniques from the past, all of the code that has been generated by the `scaffold` controller follows a consistent design pattern and gives you a very usable code base to build your application from.

REST is clearly the application structure of the future within Rails, since it is now the default structure for generated scaffolding. That said, there still is, as I write this, less than a year of experience with REST as the official, blessed Rails architecture (it was available as a plugin for some time before Rails 2.0 was released). I think it's fair to say that the best-practice usage of REST within a complex Web application is still being developed.

LISTING 12.4

new.html.erb

```
<h1>New recipe</h1>

<%= error_messages_for :recipe %>

<% form_for(@recipe) do |f| %>
  <p>
    <%= f.submit "Create" %>
  </p>
<% end %>

<%= link_to 'Back', recipes_path %>
```

LISTING 12.5

show.html.erb

```
<%= link_to 'Edit', edit_recipe_path(@recipe) %> |
<%= link_to 'Back', recipes_path %>
```

Within the context of the seven actions that it defines, the consistency and clarity of the REST architecture is great to work with. As I've alluded to, I've had some issues trying to adapt functionality into the REST structure — sometimes with really elegant results, sometimes less so. REST does encourage a thin controller/fat model structure that is in keeping with solid practice for Rails applications.

Using REST is recommended for the basic CRUD actions, and it's often worth the time to see what other functionality can be considered in terms of basic actions in it's own resource.

Working with Legacy Databases

Ideally, you'll have the opportunity to design your application's database when you create a new Rails application. By using standard naming and schema conventions, you can save yourself work. However, in the real world, especially in large organizations, you will often have to write an application that works with an existing or legacy database.

The database may use table and column names that are very different from what Rails expects to see by default. In that case, is Rails a bad framework choice? Fortunately, the answer to that question is no, having to work with a legacy database does not make Rails a bad choice of framework. There are still plenty of useful features in Rails that make it worth having to do a bit of additional work to configure the framework to work with your legacy database.

The main problem with dealing with a Legacy database is the main strength of using Rails — convention over configuration. Rails has a specific set of conventions that it imposes on database table and column structure.

A database created without the intent of being used in a Rails application is unlikely to be consistent with those conventions. In particular, a database created under what you might call a typical classic IT department style will not match Rails default structure. Happily, while Rails does have strong opinions on default structure, it is also simple to override the defaults to support whatever the legacy database wants to throw at you.

In particular, Rails allows you to:

- Override default database table names
- Override primary key field names
- Override foreign key field names

If your application is going to generate new data models that need to be stored in a database, you have the additional decision as to whether to create a second database for your new data. This decision may be made by outside forces — for instance, you may not have the access or permission needed to add new tables to the legacy database, or your Rails application may be seen as the eventual successor to the legacy database.

In any case, Rails can manage multiple database connections in a single application with a little bit of code.

Starting with the assumption that you are only using the one legacy database, exactly how you set up the `database.yml` file depends on how you can use the existing database. Presumably the production version of your application would connect to the production version of the database.

You'll likely want just the schema of the legacy database to support a test database for unit tests. If the database is relatively small, a copy of the data (or a subset of the data) may be appropriate for the development version. Otherwise, you might have to start with the schema and seed it with some basic data to support development. You never want to use the real production database for development.

Override database table and field names

Rails naming conventions for databases and models can be summarized as follows:

- Database tables have plural names, and their associated model class has the singular form of the same name.
- The primary key of every database table is expected to be named `id`.
- A column with a name of the form `model_id` is expected to represent a foreign key for the model table.
- A join table is expected to have the name of the two database tables being joined (in other words, the plural names) in alphabetical order.

It's not just legacy databases that violate this naming structure, by the way. Most commonly, a Rails database might use a non-standard name for a foreign key where the tables have multiple links, or where the connection has a more specific logical name in the context of the relationship then the foreign model has in general.

If your legacy database has more egregious departure from Rails' expectations, you can modify where Rails looks for database information at two different levels. The ActiveRecord::Base class has a couple of properties that allow you to change database defaults throughout your application (see Table 12.3. This is useful if you are only using the legacy database (or, I suppose, if you are creating a new database, but don't like Rails conventions). These properties are most usefully set in the `environment.rb` file so they take effect when your application is loaded.

TABLE 12.3

ActiveRecord::Base Properties

Property	Description
pluralize_tablenames	Manages the default naming of databse tables. If explicitly set to false, then Rails will assume that database table names are singular.
primary_key_prefix_table	Set this property to one of two preset values to capture common naming conventions for primary keys. If the value is :table_name, then primary keys are of the form `bookid`. If the value is :table_name_with_underscore, then primary keys are globally assumed to be of the form `book_id`.
table_name_prefix	A global prefix to all table names that should not be included when searching for an associated model.
table_name_suffix	A global suffix to all table names that should not be included when searching for an associated model.

However, there are many circumstances where changing global defaults will not be effective in mapping the legacy database. Your alternative option is to set the table names and primary keys on a model by model basis.

Within each model, the class properties `set_table_name` and `set_primary_key` can be used to customize the naming convention mapping that model to a database table. A sample usage would look like this:

```
class Book < ActiveRecord::Base
  set_table_name "book_data"
  set_primary_key "book_key"
end
```

Remember, the use of these properties is not limited to dealing with legacy databases, but with any naming oddities you choose to impose on databases you create.

Non-standard choices in the naming of foreign keys is noted in the declaration of the relationship in the ActiveRecord classes — the naming changes need to be noted on both sides of the relationship. The options for each kind of relationship are listed in Table 12.4.

TABLE 12.4	

Relationship Options

Relationship	Customization Options
belongs_to	:class_name If the name of the other model is not the expected form based on the name of the association.
	:foreign_key The name of the foreign key column in this databse table, if it isn't of the form association_id.
has_and_belongs_to_many	:association_foreign_key The name of the foreign key column in the join table pointing at the other end of the relationship.
	:class_name If the name of the other model is not the expected form based on the name of the association.
	:finder_sql A manual SQL statement used to retriev the associated models.
	:foreign_key The name of the foreign key column pointing to this model in the join table.
	:join_table The name of the join table.
	Note that both ends of the relationship must be consistently named
has_many	:class_name If the name of the other model is not the expected form based on the name of the association.
	:finder_sql A manual SQL statement used to retriev the associated models.
	:foreign_key The name of the foreign key in the other table pointing at this model.
has_one	:class_name If the name of the other model is not the expected form based on the name of the association.
	:foreign_key The name of the foreign key in the other table pointing at this model.

This set of methods, options, and properties should allow you to link up with any database that gets thrown at you.

Side by side with the legacy database

Even if you are working with a legacy database, you may still want to create a second database using Rails conventions for data that is specific to your Rails application. Just to name one possible situation, the legacy database could be an existing book catalog shared by many different applications, and it might make sense to keep your user information in a database specific to your Web application. Rails can manage the case where there is more then one database in the system, but there are some tricks to managing it properly.

In the `database.yml` file, set up your new Rails database as the default development, test, and production environments, and set up the legacy database with a differently named set of environments. Continuing with the assumption that the legacy is some kind of centralized catalog, that would give you `catalog_development`, `catalog_production`, and `catalog_test`, all pointing to some version of the legacy database.

Now, each ActiveRecord model in your application will point to a exactly one table in one of the two databases. The models that point to the Rails database don't need any special treatment, but the models that point to the legacy database are going to need to explicitly mention to Rails. The best way to handle this if you have multiple legacy ActiveRecords is to create a common parent class for all of them. The parent class only needs to contain the line of code that establish the connection, for example:

```
class LegacyBase < ActiveRecord::Base
  self.abstract_class = true
  establish_connection "catalog_#{RAILS_ENV}"
end
```

There are two additional things to note. The `abstract_class` line is there to tell Rails that `LegacyBase` really is an abstract class that will have no instances, specifically that keeps ActiveRecord from searching the database for a table named `legacy_bases`. In the next line, the `#{RAILS_ENV}` within the string ensures that the Rails application will always connect to the appropriate version of the database for the environment, whether you are in production, development, or test mode.

You do lose a couple of Rails automation features when using a second database, whether or not it's legacy. The automatic features of the Rails test environment assume the regular database connections. This means, for example, that the `rake test:prepare` task which automatically reloads the database from the schema won't run on your second database. You also won't get automatic loading of fixtures. The fixture loading is also kind of balky in any case where the table name does not match the ActiveRecord model name — meaning any case where you've changed the naming default.

You can work around this by changing the naming defaults in the test classes. I recommend doing this all at once in the `test_helper.rb` file:

```
def self.set_fixture_classes
  set_fixture_class :legacy_database_table => LegacyClassName
end
```

You can include as many table/class pairs as you want in the call to `set_fixture_class`. To actually load the fixtures in the legacy test database, you need to explicitly load them. Again, include the following method in the `test_helper.rb` file:

```
def load_external_fixtures(*tables)
  fixture_root = File.join(RAILS_ROOT, 'test', 'fixtures')
  Fixtures.create_fixtures(fixture_root, tables) do
    LegacyBase.connection
  end
end
```

This works in all ways, except that you don't get the special helper methods that Rails uses to allow direct access to fixtures, you'll need to explicitly find the data from the database. Also, you need to be a little careful with the ordering of the tables — if there's a hard foreign key constraint you'll need to put the required class before the class that requires it.

You'll also need to explicitly remove the classes, again in the test helper. Foreign key constraints will need to be in the reverse order for teardown then for load.

```
def teardown_fixture_data(*classes)
  classes.each do |klass|
    klass.delete_all
  end
end
```

Then you need to explicitly call this in your test classes:

```
class LegacyTest < ActiveSupport::TestCase
  set_fixture_classes

  def setup
    load_external_fixtures("table_1", "table_2")
  end

  def teardown
    cleanup(Class2, Class2)
  end
end
```

The reason why you want to do the declaration in the helper rather than in the individual classes is simply that a single test will likely load multiple fixture classes, and it's easier to only have to type the messy table/class pairs once. You should also be able to explicitly call the `set_fixture_class` at the class level in the test helper, rather than just inside a method.

It is actually possible to define a relationship between two ActiveRecord models that live in different databases, as long as ActiveRecord does not need to perform an SQL JOIN command to mange the data. In practice, this means that one-to-one or one-to-many relationships are fine, but many-to-many relationships are problematic.

You can work around this limitation by creating a proxy object in your local database. The local table would only generally only have one column, the remote ID of the legacy model. You also need a join table that joins the proxy id to the legacy model id. That lets you set up a structure like this (these class declarations would of course normally be in their respective `app/model` files):

```
class LegacyProxy
  belongs_to :legacy_model
end

class LegacyModel
  has_one :legacy_proxy
end
```

This sets up an ordinary one-to-one relationship between the proxy in your local database, and the actual model in the legacy database. Now, a class that wants to have a many-to-many relationship with the legacy model can declare a relationship with the proxy — the join table here is whatever name you give to the join table:

```
class LegacyModelGroup
  has_and_belongs_to_many :legacy_proxies,
      :join_table => "legacy_join_table"

    def legacy_models
      legacy_proxies.collect {|p| p.legacy_model}
    end
end
```

Long term, you might want to make your life easier by defining accessors on the proxy object that defer to the legacy model, but you certainly don't need to do that to make this setup useful.

Using ActionMailer

Even with all of the emerging technologies for interacting and collaborating with those around you, one of the Internet's first technologies, e-mail, is still the most popular way of communicating online. Sending and receiving e-mail is also a common requirement of most Web applications that you will develop. Some of the uses for e-mail in Web applications are:

- To provide a confirmation step as part of a user registration process.
- As a notification channel when something goes wrong with the application.
- To provide a lost password reminder.

Rails provides built-in support for sending and receiving e-mail. In this section, you'll see how easy it is to include e-mail in a Rails application. The steps I'll cover are:

- Configuring your Rails application for e-mail support.
- Generating a mailer model.
- Writing code to send e-mail.
- Writing code to receive e-mail.
- Handling e-mail attachments.

Configuring a Rails application for e-mail support

Rails has built-in support for sending outbound e-mails using either SMTP or SendMail. You can configure the mechanism you prefer by adding a single line to your application's `config/environment.rb` file. If you want to use SMTP, add this line to your `environment.rb` file:

```
config.action_mailer.delivery_method = :smtp
```

Or, if you want to use SendMail for your outbound e-mails, add this line:

```
config.action_mailer.delivery_method = :sendmail
```

The `config.action_mailer` call will actually trigger a class method on `ActionMailer::Base`. In most cases, you won't want to put this setting in the global `environment.rb` file.

Your email settings will probably change for each Rails environment — your production mail server is probably not accessible during development, and you probably don't want to be sending live emails during testing. Place the mailer configuration in the `conifg/environment` directory in the file corresponding to the environment you want to configure.

If you choose SMTP, you also have to add some additional code to configure your SMTP settings. You will add a block of code similar to the following to set up your SMTP options:

```
config.action_mailer.server_settings = {
    :address => "my.smtpserver.com",
    :port => 25,
    :domain => "My Domain",
    :authentication => :login,
    :user_name => "username",
    :password => "password"
}
```

By default the test environment in `config/environment/test.rb` sets the mail settings like this:

```
config.action_mailer.delivery_method = :test
```

This prevents test mails from being sent out, and instead puts the mail messages in a class property of each ActionMailer class, named `deliveries`.

You can also configure whether Rails will consider it an error if the mail message can't be sent, this setting is off in the development environment:

```
config.action_mailer.raise_delivery_errors = false
```

Generating a mailer model

After you have your e-mail server properly configured in the `environment.rb` file, the next step in adding e-mail support to your application is to generate a mailer model using the `script/generate mailer` command.

```
> ruby script/generate mailer RegistrationNotice
    exists app/models/
    create app/views/registration_notice
    exists test/unit/
    create test/fixtures/registration_notice
    create app/models/registration_notice.rb
    create test/unit/registration_notice_test.rb
```

If you look at the model that is generated, you see that it is very similar to `ActiveRecord`-based models. It should look like this:

```
class RegistrationNotice < ActionMailer::Base
end
```

As with the `ActiveRecord` model classes, this class extends a Rails class, `ActionMailer::Base`, which provides the core of the class's functionality. The unit test file that is created is a simple stub, similar to what you get with the `ActiveRecord` generator.

Writing code to send e-mail

Now that you have a `RegistrationNotice` mailer, you have the classes that you need to begin writing the e-mail code. Within the `RegistrationNotice` class, you add mailer methods that correspond to individual e-mail types that you want to support. In the mailer method, you set up the e-mail message by assigning values to variables representing attributes of the email to be sent. Let's look at an example of what a user registration e-mail mailer method might look like in the `RegistrationNotice` model that was created in the previous step:

```
def user_registered(user)
  recipients user.email
  subject = "Activate your Account"
  from = "site@myWeb.com"
  body :recipient => user.name
end
```

In this method, you are setting four variables related to the e-mail message: the recipients, subject, from, and body. There are actually many more options that can be set for an e-mail, as described below:

- **attachment:** Use this option to specify a file attachment. You can call this multiple times to specify more than one attachment for an e-mail message. The argument to this method is a hash with keys like `:content_type` and `:body`.

- **bcc:** Use this to specify a blind carbon-copy recipient for an e-mail message. You can pass a recipient parameter as a string for a single e-mail address, or an array of addresses.

- **body:** This variable is used to define the body of the e-mail message. You can pass either a string or a hash value for the body. If you pass a string, the string's value becomes the actual text of the e-mail message. If you pass a hash, the hash should contain variables that will be passed to an e-mail template. The hash variables will be merged with the template to create the text of the e-mail message. You'll see more about this when I discuss e-mail templates a bit later.

- **cc:** Use this to specify a carbon-copy recipient for an e-mail message. You can pass a recipient parameter as a string for a single e-mail address, or an array of addresses.

- **charset:** Use this to specify the character set for the e-mail message. You can set a `default_charset` setting for the `ActionMailer::Base` class that will be the default value for the character set.

- **content_type:** Use this to specify the content type of the e-mail message. If not specified, the content type defaults to `text/plain`. A global default can be set in the environment configuration.

- **from:** Use this to specify the from address for the e-mail message. The address is specified as a string value.

- **headers:** You can use this to specify additional headers that you want to be added to the e-mail message. The additional headers are specified in a hash value.

- **implicit_parts_order:** This is used to specify the order in which the parts of a multi-part e-mail should be sorted. You specify the sort order as an array of content types. The default sort order is: [`"text/html"`, `"text/enriched"`, `"text/plain"`]. The default sort order can be set with the `default_implicit_parts_order` variable on the `ActionMailer::Base` class.

- **mailer_name:** You can use this to override the default mailer name. This name tells Rails where it can find the mailer's templates. By default, the name used will be an inflected version of the mailer's class name.

- **mime_version:** This is used to specify the MIME version you want to use. This defaults to version 1.0.

- **part:** Can be used to specify a single part of a multipart message, options include :content_type, and :body.

- **recipients:** The email or list of email addresses to which the message will be sent.

- **sent_on:** The date the email was sent, as shown in the recipient's browser. You don't need to set this unless you are doing something weird, normally, it'll be sent by the mail server when the message is sent.

- **subject:** The subject of the message.

In order to actually generate the message and send it, you don't call the mailer method directly — Rails creates a couple of wrapper methods that use the mailer method as part of the creation and delivery of the actual email message. These messages are of the form `create_user_registered` and `deliver_user_registered`. The create version merely creates the email message object, while the deliver version creates the object and immediately sends it.

If you use the create version, you then send it using a structure like the following:

```
email = RegistrationNotice.create_user_notified(user)
RegistrationNotice.deliver(email)
```

This allows you to further process the email object before delivery if you want. Otherwise, the one line version just looks like this:

```
email = RegistrationNotice.deliver_user_notified(user)
```

If the body attribute of your mailer method is a hash, then Rails expects the actual body of the mail message to be in an ERb template located at `app/views/registration_notice/user_notfied.html.erb`. That's if you are sending an HTML email, the file name of the template for a text email would more properly end `.text.erb` or `.plain.erb`.

Rails will implicitly set the outgoing context type of the mail message to match the type extension of the ERb file, so choose wisely. Rails also allows you to have multiple templates for a single message, for example, both `user_notified.text.erb` and `user_notified.html.erb`. If Rails notices multiple templates, the mailer will assemble the message into a multi-part message, and let the user's client sort it out, giving the user control over whether to view the message in HTML or plain text.

This works nicely with attachments, which are specified in the mailer method using the `attachment` method. The `:content_type` is the MIME type of the attachment, the `:body` is the actual data, often acquired via `File.read`, and the `:filename` can also be specified. Multiple attachments can be added to a single message.

Writing code to receive e-mail

Writing code to receive e-mails through Rails is not any more difficult than it is to send e-mails. In fact, because there are fewer options to specify, it is probably easier to write the code to receive e-mails. Within an `ActionMailer::Base` subclass, if you specify a method named `receive`, it will be called with the email message already parsed into an email object exactly like the ones you would create in order to send an email. For example, the following snippet takes in a message and adds it to the database attached to the person who sent it.

```
def receive(email)
  person = Person.find_by_email(email.to.first)
  person.emails.create(:subject => email.subject, :body => email.
    body)
end
```

The tricky part is coaxing your email server to cause this method to be invoked when an email is received. The general form of this problem is well out of scope, however if you can access the email address you will be watching via IMAP, you can use the Ruby Net::IMAP library to fetch mail. The following code was adapted from the Rails wiki:

```
require 'net/imap'
imap = Net::IMAP.new('email_host_name')
imap.authenticate('LOGIN', username, password)
imap.select('INBOX')
imap.search(['ALL']).each do |id|
  message = imap.fetch(id, 'RFC822')[0].attr['RFC822']
  RegistrationNotice.receive(message)
  imap.store(message_id, "+FLAGS", [:Deleted])
end
imap.expunge()
```

491

A similar script could use NET::POP3. All you need to do is use a cron job or something similar to run this script periodically — note this script deletes emails as it reads them, which you might want to modify if you think you'll need access to the messages later on.

ActiveResource and XML

ActiveResource is the client-side complement to REST. A server using REST allows for a consistent interface to resources on the server, and makes it trivially easy to send out resource data as XML. Well, if you can send that data out, you'd also like to have some way to read the data and convert it from XML to a useful object. This is where ActiveResource comes in.

ActiveResource makes interacting with a remote Web service easier in almost exactly the same way as ActiveRecord makes interacting with a relational database easier. It provides a consistent interface for finding, updating, creating, and removing resources exposed by the Web service, all in a stateless system that uses existing Web standards and is fairly easy to implement.

You would use ActiveResource as part of a Web-services architecture. For example, a book buying application might receive information about individual books from a Web application provided by a publisher or distributor. If that Web application exposes a RESTful interface that returns HTML, than your Web application can use ActiveResource to easily read that data.

ActiveResource is not tied to the rest of Rails however, you could also use it in the context of a command line or GUI application. For example, Twitter is, as of this writing, one of the most heavily trafficked Ruby on Rails applications going. Its external API is largely RESTful, and therefore a potential Ruby-based desktop client for Twitter could use ActiveResource to take the API results and turn them into objects.

The most basic ActiveResource script looks something like this:

```
require 'active_resource'

class Book < ActiveResource::Base
  self.site = http://remote.restfulsite.com
end
```

That's all you need to do to set up the ActiveResource object. Note that the require statement assumes that ActiveResource is in your path somehow, normally it lives at `<rails>/activeresource/lib/active_resource.rb` where `<rails>` is either the `vendor/rails` directory of a Rails application or the root of the Rails gem in your Ruby home directory. Then you declare the Resource class as a subclass of `ActiveResource::Base`. This is different from any ActiveRecord class you might have named `Book`.

At the risk of repeating myself, this book class is backed by the RESTful server, not by the database. The `site` property specifies exactly which RESTful server will back this particular resource. If all your resources come from the same site, then you can specify the remote URL globally by setting `ActiveResource::Base.site`.

So far, this code has accomplished nothing other than setting up a connection. But actually using the connection is pretty simple. You can try the following:

```
books = Book.find(:all)
```

In the background, this line makes a remote HTTP call to `http://remote.restfulsite.com/books.xml`, parses the returned XML and converts it into ActiveResource objects. You have more or less the same implicit attributes that you would have in an ActiveRecord object, so you could do something like `books.map(&:title)`, but based on the attributes included in the XML output.

The find functionality in ActiveResource is much less extensive than ActiveRecord. This makes sense, since the expressiveness of a relational database is much greater than that of a RESTful server — in a database there is more of an ability to set filters and sort and the like. In a RESTful server, you basically have:

```
Book.find(:all)
Book.find(12)
Book.find(:first)
Book.find(:one)
```

The first line, as seen earlier, returns all books as delineated by the `index` method of the remote server. The second line takes a single resource ID, and calls the `show` method on the remote server, returning XML data for a single item. The `:first` option retrieves all data from the index method, but only returns the first element, it's not clear in what circumstance that's actually very useful. The `:one` modifier is largely used with custom actions as a signal to ActiveRecord that exactly one record will be returned.

Beyond that, you're somewhat at the mercy of what the server implementation has provided. Any key/value pairs you add to any of the find methods are added to the URL as part of the query string, so if the server methods allow you to specify, say, sort order, or a limit, or the like, you can access that functionality from ActiveResource. You can also use the option `:from` to specify a specific URL for that one find query. This is the mechanism for sending a request to a custom action defined on the server.

```
Book.find(:one, :from => "remote.restfulsite.com/book/best_
    seller.xml")
```

Again, though, you're limited to what the server has chosen to implement.

Once you've gotten your resource, you can use it like any other Rails object. Remember, though, that it is not the server-side ActiveRecord object, and any functionality built into that model will not exist on the client-side ActiveResource unless you explicitly put it there. If you are writing both sides of the client-server application, it's probably a good idea to take the functionality that could potentially be of use to both ActiveRecord and ActiveResource flavors of your model and put them in a common module that could be included by both.

The downloaded resource will not, by default, include information about any related classes, again, even when there are specific ActiveRecord relationship defined server-side. The server could choose to include related objects in the XML being retrieved, but that's not the basic feature set. Ordinarily, recovering the related objects requires an additional call back to the server.

You can also perform the rest of the basic CRUD family of actions from your active resource. You can save the item back via the `save` method, which triggers an update call on the remote server, you can also use the `create` method in the same way as you would in ActiveRecord, to instantiate a new resource and save it back to the data store, in this case, by triggering a `create` call on the remote server.

Although you cannot automatically do client-side validation of your resource, the normal ActiveRecord validation will be performed server-side when the object is saved. Deletion is managed similarly to ActiveRecord, via a class level `delete(id)` method, or an instance level `destroy` method.

Deploying with Capistrano

For a long time, the deployment was the most difficult part of creating a working Rails application. Part of this pain was caused by the difficulty in getting a Rails application to run consistently in a shared hosting environment, which, due to their low cost, is where most developers who are new to Rails start off. While the number of shared hosting providers that support Rails applications is growing, it is still low, and those that do, have had plenty of issues with application performance and reliability. However, the new `mod_rails` Apache module, in early release as of this writing, may go a long way toward improving Rails performance on shared hosts.

General deployment has become much easier using a tool named Capistrano. Capistrano was created by Rails developer Jamis Buck, who originally gave it the name Switchtower. Just as Rails itself was extracted from a real project and was developed to fulfill real project needs, Capistrano was originally created by Buck to support the Basecamp application for 37 Signals.

Capistrano can be used to automate the deployment of your Web application. It was developed for use with Rails applications, but there is actually nothing to prevent you from using Capistrano as a deployment tool for Web applications that are not Rails applications. Capistrano's greatest strengths are it's ability to manage simultaneous deployment to multiple servers at once, even if the servers have different roles, and also it's ability to quickly roll the deployment back to a previous known state in case of emergency.

The basic structure of Capistrano is for the developer to initiate a task on the local development box — either a predefined task, or one written using a task syntax similar to Rake. To run the task, Capistrano makes a remote connection to one, some, or all of the servers it knows about, and runs some set of tasks on that remote server. These tasks might include retrieving source code, running a database migration, or restarting the Web server.

Installing and setting up Capistrano

Capistrano is distributed as a Ruby gem. As of this writing, the current version is 2.3.

```
> gem install Capistrano
```

To use Capistrano, certain things need to be true about your development and deployment environments. You need to be using some kind of source control, Subversion is the default, but many other popular systems are also supported, including Git, CVS, Mercruial, and Perforce.

NOTE   Technically, Capistrano recently added a no-source control mode, but that's intended just for emergencies and is not recommended for regular use. Capistrano interfaces with your source control system to perform a clean checkout of your code every time you request a deployment, this prevents issues with the previous deployment from bleeding into the newest version.

On the server side, you need at least one server to start, and you need a network address that can access that server. Obviously, the server needs to be able to run Rails. Less obviously, the server needs to be able to communicate via SSH. Capistrano sends commands to servers via a standard Unix SSH shell. The preferred target of a Capistrano deploy is Linux, although Mac OS X servers also should meet the standard. If your server is running MS Windows, you'll need to run Cygwin or some other Unix shell program to be able to use Capistrano. Capistrano prefers to have the login to the remote machines managed with public keys, although you can use password access if you'd prefer. If you have multiple servers, the same password must work on all of them.

Once Capistrano is installed, you start using it by typing the command `capify .` from your Rails root directory.

```
capify .
[add] writing './Capfile'
[add] writing './config/deploy.rb'
 [done] capified!
```

As you can see from the snippet, Capistrano will create two files, the `Capfile`'s primary purpose is to load the `deploy.rb` file, which contains the actual deployment recipe. The Capistrano deployment file is just a Ruby file, with some custom structure behind it to allow you to create your own build tasks in addition to the standard ones.

The standard deployment file has a number of different settings and variables you'll need to adapt to the specifics of your application. The two most important are right at the top:

```
set :application, "set your application name here"
set :repository,  "set your repository location here"
```

The application name is arbitrary, but is used as the root directory of your application files on the servers being deployed to. The repository variable has a URL for the code repository, which must be visible from the server being deployed to, not the development machine being deployed from.

You can also specify the remote directory location and the source control system being used, but Capistrano provides a default value for both (the default source control system is Subversion).

If you need to specify the username or password to your Subversion repository, you can use the same `set` syntax the attribute names are `:svn_user` and `:svn_password`. Instead of taking a string as the value of the property, you can also pass a block, which enables the following work-around if you don't want to place the Subversion password in the text file.

```
set :svn_password, Proc.new do
  Capistrano::CLI.password_prompt('enter password: ')
end
```

The next most important thing you need to tell Capistrano is the location and types of your servers. The default in the file looks like this:

```
role :app, "your app-server here"
role :web, "your web-server here"
role :db,  "your db-server here", :primary => true
```

Capistrano allows you to group your servers into roles. The naming of the roles is basically arbitrary, but the default convention separates your application into Web servers and database servers, or application servers that manage both. Normally, you'd start with on server, place it's address in the `:app` role, and comment out the other two lines. As your deployment gets bigger, you'd add additional servers to that line.

When you get to the point where different servers are playing different roles, then you split the list as needed. Capistrano's normal behavior is to run a command on all servers listed in all roles. Specific tasks, however, can be customized to run for a specific role or roles — it would make no sense to run database migrations on a server that didn't have a database, for example.

A role named `:gateway`, if it exists, is expected to have a single server, and Capistrano will route access to all other servers through that machine.

Running basic Capistrano tasks

The first thing you need to do when you add a new server to your deployment is run the Capistrano setup task:

```
cap deploy:setup
```

The general form of a Capistrano command is very similar to a Rake command, `cap` is invoked, the first argument is the task to run, further options pass various options to the command.

The setup command creates a directory structure for your application. Figure 12.1 shows the directory structure.

FIGURE 12.1

Directory structure for your application

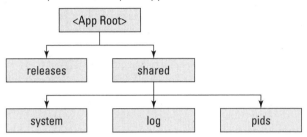

Each deployment you make to a server using Capistrano gets it's own new directory under `releases`. The top level directory has a symbolic link called `current` that always points to the most recent release directory. Files that would be shared across deployments are placed in the shared directory — Capistrano also manages the appropriate links from each deployment to the shared directories.

The setup command must be run on any server before you can deploy to it, however there is no harm from running it on servers that have already been set up.

Assuming you are starting from a basic, single server deployment, the first deploy task you run is a cold deploy, meaning that a Web server is not already running on the server.

```
cap deploy:cold
```

This performs three tasks, each of which can also be triggered as separate Capistrano tasks:

- `deploy:update`

  Retrieves a current checkout from your source control system and manages the symbolic linc manipulation

- `deploy:migrate`

  Runs a `rake db:migrate` on the remote server. This will fail if the `database.yml` file is not properly configured for production mode. In a complicated deployment, it's a common practice to dynamically generate the `database.yml` file from a custom Capistrano task.

- `deploy:start`

  Starts the Web server. This task assumes that there is a script in your application's `script` directory named `spin`. This script will be run to start the server — a simple way to start is just to defer to the standard `script/process/spawner`, which starts a small mongrel cluster. If you're fine with just a normal mongrel deployment, which is plausible for a staging server, I guess, you can override the command using something like this:

```
namespace :deploy do
  task :start, :roles => :app do
    invoke_command "mongrel_rails start -C #{mongrel_file}",
        :via => run_method
  end
end
```

Once you have the Web server running on the remote box, then you've entered the realm of hot deployment:

```
cap deploy
```

A hot deployment is the same as a cold deploy except that the database migrations are not performed (you need cap `deploy:migrations` to specifically do a hot deploy with database migrations. Also, instead of `deploy:start`, it calls `deploy:restart`, , which calls the standard Rails script/process/reaper. This should stop anything that looks a Rails server process, then start them up again. It's designed to work with the spawner script. Again, you can customize behavior to match your own needs.

Should you notice a problem in the deploy and you need to go back to the previous known state, you run the following command:

```
cap rollback
```

This command deletes the current codebase, and points the `current` symbolic link back to the previous version, then restarts the Web server using the same `deploy:restart` task used in a hot deployment.

This section has covered the most commonly used Capistrano commands, here are a couple of others that you might find useful:

- `deploy:check`

  Tests for a series of prerequisites on the remote machine including the directory structure. You can add tests by adding commands to your deploy file of the form `depend :type name`. The type can be one of `:gem`, `:command`, or `:directory`, and any further options are used to specify the name of the dependency being checked, like `depend :gem "chronic"`.

- `deploy:cleanup`

  Removes all but the last five non-current deploys from the remote server.

- `deploy:upload`

  A one-off task that uploads all the files and directories in a comma-delimited list stored in the `FILES` environment variable, as in `cap deploy:upload FILES="db/schema.rb"`.

- `invoke`

  Runs an arbitrary command, stored in the `COMMAND` environment variable.

Customizing Capistrano

There are two ways to customize Capistrano's behavior, setting variables and creating your own tasks. Many tasks depend on variables that can be set either at the command line or in your Capistrano recipe. Capistrano variables are either environment variables or Capistrano variables. Environment variables are declared in your script using the following syntax:

```
ENV["FILES"] = "app/views, app/models"
```

And are added at the command line using the syntax:

```
cap invoke COMMAND="script/process/reaper"
```

Capistrano variables are set in the recipe as follows:

```
set :svn_user, "hmason"
```

Such variables are set at the command line using one of the two forms:

```
cap deploy -s svn_user=hmason
cap deploy -S svn user=hmason
```

The difference between the two forms is when the variable set is applied. The lower-case form is applied after the recipe file loads, so that the command line setting overrides any setting in the actual recipe script. The upper-case form loads the command line variables first, so any setting in the script overrides the command line.

Setting variables is nice, but the real power of Capistrano comes in the ability to write your own custom tasks and assign them as dependencies to any Capistrano task. The syntax for writing a new task is extremely similar to Rake. Here's a sample task that generates a database.yml file — it assumes you have some way of specifying the database host for each server and that YAML has been loaded:

```
desc "create database.yml"
task :create_database_yml, :roles => [:app, :db] do
  yaml = {
      :production => {
          :adapter => mysql
          :database => my_production
          :host => find_host($HOSTNAME)  ## This is your method to
   write
          :username => 'fred'
          :password => 'dref'
      }
  }
  put YAML::dump(buffer), "#{release_path}/config/databse.yml",
      :mode => 0664
end
```

As in Rake, the `desc` method sets the comment for the next task definition to come down the pike. Unlike Rake, task dependencies are not set in the task definition. Instead, the task definition allows you to optionally specify which server roles the task applies to — in this case, the task only applies to servers that have database. Also, whereas if you define a Rake task multiple times, it will combine the definitions, a second definition of a Capistrano task will completely override the original task.

Capistrano has a couple of handy helper methods that manage server side activities, the previous snippet shows `put`, which places content in a file. Another commonly used one is `run`, which runs a shell command on all the servers affected by the task.

As with any build system, it's helpful to automatically set up dependencies so that a task will always run before or after another task. In Capistrano, this is done by placing a declaration to that effect in the recipe script. The general form is one of the following

```
after 'existing_task', 'new_task'
before 'existing_task', 'new_task'
```

You can include more than one new task by continuing to add the tasks as further arguments to the command. As is probably clear, new tasks specified as `before` are guaranteed to run before the actual task, and new tasks specified as `after` will always run after the existing task. You can have both a before and after on the same task, and the before and after declarations do compose, so you can have more than one of them for the same task and they will not override each other. Instead of a list of tasks, you can also pass a block.

This just scratches the surface of what you can do with Capistrano, each deployment is different, and getting your needs exactly right is not trivial. Check out Capistrano online for more complex details.

Summary

In this chapter, I covered some topics that are important to developing an application with Rails that had not yet been covered in previous chapters.

Representational State Transfer (REST) is a pattern for structuring your Web application that is rapidly becoming standard for Rails. For a Rails programmer, REST simplifies the URL and action structure of your controllers, and provides for a consistent interface to the resources reached via the controller.

REST also enables your application to act as a Web service. A Rails application can act as the consumer of a RESTful Web service using the ActiveResource library, which provides an ActiveRecord style interface to a remote resource.

Sometimes you will be forced to use a legacy database that does not conform to Rails naming conventions. Rails provides hook methods to override standard naming to match whatever you have. You can also maintain multiple databases from within the same application.

Applications can send email using the ActionMailer library, which is something of a mashup between a model and view, and which allows you to specify the details of an email message. You can even use ERb syntax to create a template defining the message. The email message can also have a file attachment.

Capistrano has become the default tool for specifying the details of Rails deployments to remote servers. It allows you to run the same deployment script transparently across multiple servers. You have a wide range of customization options to adapt the script to the needs of your deployment.

Part V

Appendixes

Appendix A

Ruby Quick Reference

Basic Ruby Syntax

The Ruby language is made up of expressions. Each expression returns a value. Even elements that are just statements in other languages, such as if and for, are expressions in Ruby that return values.

Ruby is a pure object-oriented language. Every variable or constant in Ruby is an object, and there are no basic non-object types. Every variable or literal responds to the basic method call syntax.

A simple Ruby expression is one of the following:

- **A literal.** Ruby has literal syntax for arrays, hashes, numbers, ranges, regular expressions, strings, and symbols.

- **The name of an existing variable or constant.**

- **A method call, which combines the name of an existing variable or constant with a method name.** The basic form of a method call is <receiver>.<method>(<arguments>). Variants on this form will be discussed later.

- **One of several special expressions invoked by the use of a keyword such as** if, case, **or** while.

Complex expressions can be built using Ruby operators. Variable assignment using = is considered to be a type of operator. Most expressions can also have arbitrarily complex expressions within them — for example, the arguments of a method call are all themselves expressions.

A Ruby expression ends with a line break unless the Ruby interpreter has a reason to believe the expression is intended to continue. The expression continues if there is an open delimiter such as a quotation mark, parenthesis, bracket, or brace. The expression also continues if the last character in the line is a comma or operator. A complex expression such as an `if` statement is usually expected to cross over multiple lines. An expression can be forced to continue to the next line by ending a line with a backslash character.

Multiple expressions can be placed on the same line by separating the expressions with a semicolon.

Literal expressions

Ruby has several different mechanisms to create literal objects. In addition to expected literals for number and string, Ruby literals can also create arrays, Booleans , hashes, ranges, regular expressions, and symbols.

Arrays

A literal array is created by enclosing the elements in brackets. Inside the brackets, the elements are separated by commas. Each element can be an arbitrarily complex Ruby expression. The result is an instance of the class `Array`. For example, lool at the array defined here:

```
x = [1, "hello", fred]
```

It contains three elements: a number, a string, and a variable.

If the elements of the array are all strings, Ruby provides a shortcut syntax, using the notation %w followed by an arbitrary delimiter. Elements in the array are separated by a space, and the strings are interpreted as literals. A backslash character can be used to insert a space inside an element, rather than treat the space as a delimiter.

```
>> %w{zot jenny max butch peabody}
=> ["zot", "jenny", "max", "butch", "peabody"]

>> %w(zot jenny max butch peabody arthur\ dekker)
=> ["zot", "jenny", "max", "butch", "peabody", "arthur dekker"]
```

A second form, with a capital `%W`, allows for string interpolation rules to be obeyed inside the array — it's the equivalent of a double-quoted string. See the Strings section for full details.

```
>> %W(a b #{1 + 1} c)
=> ["a", "b", "2", "c"]
```

Adding elements to the end of an array is managed with the `push` method or the following operator:

```
<<.[1, 2, 3].push(4)
[1, 3, 3] << 4
```

Removing the last element from the array is managed with the method pop. The methods shift and unshift provide similar functionality for the beginning of the array.

An arbitrary element in the array can be accessed using index lookup. The first element of the array is at index 0. A positive integer indicates the index from the start of the array, returning nil if the integer is greater than the size of the array. The index -1 is the last element of the array; other negative integers are counted from the end of the array.

The expression inside the brackets can be a Ruby range, in which case the sub-array corresponding to the indexes in the range is returned. Less commonly, the index expression can be two integers separated by a comma [index, length], which returns a sub-array starting at the index for the given length.

```
[1, 2, 3][0] = 1
[1, 2, 3][-1] = 3
[1, 2, 3][0..1] = [1, 2]
[1, 2, 3][0, 1] = [1]
```

Arrays provide a number of different methods that allow enumeration over the contents of the array. Many of these are provided by the Enumerable module. The methods include each, which iterates over the contents of the array, map, which applies a block to each element of the array and returns the resulting list, and select, which applies a block to each element of the array and returns those elements for which the result is true.

Boolean literals

Ruby defines the special variables true and false, which correspond to the expected Boolean values. They are the sole instances of the classes TrueClass and FalseClass. Ruby also defines the special value nil, which is the sole instance of the class NilClass.

The value nil also evaluates to false when evaluated in a Boolean expression. Unlike other scripting languages, no other values in Ruby are treated as false. All values other than false and nil are considered to be logically true.

Hashes

A hash literal contains a series of key/value pairs inside braces. The key and value are separated by => and each pair is separated by a comma. The key and value can be arbitrary Ruby expressions.

```
>> {:a => 1, "b" => "fred"}
=> {:a=>1, "b"=>"fred"}
```

The => sequence can be replaced by a comma; this should only be done if you don't want anybody to read your code. The created object is an instance of the class Hash. Ideally, a hash key is an immutable object, such as a symbol or number.

Hash elements are accessed and set through bracket index lookup: hash[key]. The methods keys and values return a list of the appropriate elements, and the method has_key? returns true if the key is in the hash.

Numbers

Ruby's number literals are straightforward. An integer is any sequence of digits. A sign character can be the first character. Integer literals can be written to other bases by starting the numbers with a leading 0 for octal, a 0x for hexadecimal, and a 0b for binary. Decimal numbers can also be indicated with 0d. Underscore characters are ignored in integer literals and therefore are often used as group separators. Integer literals create instances of the class `Fixnum`, unless the literal is outside the range of `Fixnum`, in which case the literal is of type `Bignum`.

```
>> 100      => 100
>> -100     => -100
>> 0100     => 64
>> 0x100    => 256
>> 0b100    => 4
>> 987_123 => 987123
```

Floating point literals are a sequence of digits containing a decimal point. There must be at least one digit on either side of the decimal point, or else you get a syntax error. A floating point literal is converted to an instance of the class `Float`.

```
>> 1.3   => 1.3
>> 1.3e2 => 130.0
```

Ranges

A Ruby range literal can be indicated in one of two ways. The range consists of two expressions separated by either two or three dots. The two-dot version creates a range that includes the value in the second expression, while the three-dot version excludes the final value.

Ranges are normally used as compact storage for a long sequence of consecutive values, which can be iterated over and converted to arrays. The following example shows the difference between the two- and three-dot versions by showing the difference in the array that is created from the range.

```
>> x = 1..10   => 1..10
>> x.to_a      => [1, 2, 3, 4, 5, 6, 7, 8, 9, 10]
>> y = 1...10 => 1...10
>> y.to_a      => [1, 2, 3, 4, 5, 6, 7, 8, 9]
```

The expressions that make up the two ends of the range can be arbitrarily complex. The range ends are most commonly integers, but any class that implements the method `succ` can act as a range boundary.

 Dates and strings are also often used as range boundaries.

Regular expressions

A regular expression literal can be created by placing a regular expression pattern inside a pair of forward slashes, as follows:

```
/ab*d/
```

Ruby also offers an arbitrary delimiter marker for regular expressions %r, which is often used if the expression pattern itself contains a lot of slashes.

```
%r{ab*d}
```

Regular expression literals are converted to instances of the class Regexp. Regular expressions are used to perform complex pattern matches against strings. In Ruby, these matches are performed using either the operator =~ or the method Regexp.match. Most characters in the regular expression match against the same character in the test string; however, several special character forms augment the basic behavior.

After the ending delimiter of the literal, one or more characters can be used to indicate optional regular expression behavior. The three most common options are as follows:

i   The pattern match is case sensitive

m   The pattern match is assumed to encompass multiple lines. Practically, this means that the dot special character matches newline characters.

x   Literal white space in the pattern is ignored, allowing you to use spacing to make the expression easier to read. Spaces in the pattern can be included by using a special pattern such as \s.

Regular expression literals are converted to instances of the class Regexp.

Within a regular expression literal, the following 14 characters have special meaning:

```
( ) [ ] { } . * ? | + \ $ ^
```

To actually include one of those characters literally in the pattern, they must be escaped using a backslash, as in * or \\. Each of the delimiter pairs indicates something different within a regular expression.

Parentheses have their normal function of grouping elements to indicate the scope of operators. For example, /face*/ matches the string faceeee, while /(face)*/ matches the string facefaceface. In addition, parentheses cause a portion of the matched string to be saved for use either within the regular expression pattern or after the match is complete. The groups can be referred to using special variables of the form \1 and \2 during the pattern, and $1 and $2 after the match, as in the following example:

```
>> /(.*)c(.*)/ =~ "abcde" => 0
>> $1 => "ab"
>> $2 => "de"
```

Variables are numbered based on the position of the opening parenthesis — in the pattern /((.*)c)(.*)/, the variable $1 includes c.

Brackets are used to mark a set of characters that can match the string at that point, so /[abcd]/ matches a, b, c, or d. That pattern could also be written /[a-d]/; the hyphen indicates an inclusive sequence of characters.

Multiple sequences can be in one set, and so /[a-zA-z]/ matches any upper- or lowercase letter. If the set starts with a ^, then the pattern matches only characters that are not in the set, so /[^a-zA-z]/ matches non-alphabetic characters. Also, within brackets, all special characters, except the right bracket and hyphen, can appear without being escaped.

Braces are used to indicate the number of times a sub-pattern must exist in the match. The basic form is /[a-z]{3}/, which would indicate that exactly three characters must be in the matching string. A range can be indicated with {3,5}, and a minimum value can be indicated with the form {3,}. Braces are also used as part of the #{expr} interpolation, which is the same in regular expressions as it is in double-quoted strings.

There are three shortcuts for indicating commonly used ranges for a match. The character *means "zero or more," and so the regex /a[a-z]*/ matches any string that contains an a followed by zero or more lowercase letters. The character + means "one or more" and the character ? means "zero or one."

By default, the * and + characters are "greedy," meaning that they match as much of the string as they can. This can be an issue if there is more than one potential stopping place for the sub-pattern. You can change the default behavior by putting a ? after the * or +. In the first example following, the [a-z]* pattern matches past the first b and stops at the last possible point, before the second b. In the second, non-greedy example, the pattern stops at the first point, before the first b.

```
>> /a([a-z]*)b/ =~ "aabceb" => 0
>> $1  => "abce"
>> /a([a-z]*?)b/ =~ "aabceb" => 0
>> $1 => "a"
```

There are several shortcuts to denote common character sequences. The special character ^ matches the beginning of the string, while $ matches the end. Many programmers prefer to use the slightly less cryptic synonyms \A and \z. The variant \Z matches the entire string except for a trailing newline character. The sequence \b matches a word boundary; \d matches any digit and is the same as [0-9].

The sequence \s matches the white space characters space, tab, newline, carriage return, and line feed; it is the same as [\f\n\r\t]. The sequence \w matches "word" characters, meaning [a-zA-Z0-9_]. All four of these sequences are negated by replacing the lowercase character with an uppercase one, and so \D matches any non-digit, or [^0-9].

Finally, the pipe character indicates a logical or, and so /a|b/ matches a or b.

Strings

There are several different ways to write literal strings in Ruby. The simplest is to use single quotation marks. Within a single-quoted string literal, only two interpolations are performed. A \' is used to insert a literal single quote, and a \\ is used to insert a literal backslash.

```
>> 'hello'      =>  "hello"
>> isn\'t'      => "isn't"
```

```
>> 'nip\\tuck'  => "nip\\tuck"
>> 'nip\\tuck'.size => 8
```

In a single quoted string, backslashes that are not used as an escape are treated as literals, but converted to the escape format in the irb output, so the third and fourth examples evaluate to the same result. In the final example, the irb output preserves the escape sequence in the return value — the resulting string only has one backslash, as shown by the `size` method.)

With a double-quoted string literal, the full complement of escape characters, such as \n for newline and \t for tab, are substituted (backslashes that are not part of an escape sequence are ignored). In addition, the sequence #{expr} is replaced in the string by the value of the expression; the value is converted to a string if needed. For example,

```
>> "ab#{1 + 1}c"  => "ab2c"
```

There are generic delimiter forms for both string forms, %q for single-quote and %Q for double-quote. The double-quote form can also be written as just %, as in the following example:

```
>> %q(ab#{1 + 1}c)   => "ab\#{1 + 1}c"
>> %Q(ab#{1 + 1}c)   => "ab2c"
>> %(ab#{1 + 1}c)    => "ab2c"
```

Ruby also supports Perl-style here docs. A here doc starts with << and an identifier, and continues over multiple lines until the identifier is reached.

```
<<DOC
all this is
in the here
doc string
DOC
```

If there is a hyphen before the identifier, then the closing identifier can be indented;

```
<<-DOC
        this can be indentd
    DOC
```

Otherwise, it must start at the beginning of a line. By default, the string is interpreted according to double-quote rules; however, if the identifier is encased in quotation marks, then the here doc is interpreted according to the style of quotation marks used.

Symbols

A symbol in Ruby is an immutable string, similar to an interned string in other languages. In addition, all instances of a symbol with the same value are guaranteed to point to the same internal object. Symbols are used by Ruby as the internal representation of method and variable names. Because they are immutable, they are commonly used as hash keys.

A symbol is formed by a colon, followed by a name or string literal. The string literal is interpreted according to the normal string rules. It does not matter how the symbol is constructed in determining its value; all three of the following are the same symbol:

```
:person2person
:'person2person'
:"person#{1+1}person"
```

One important note about symbols: the `Symbol` class does not implement the `<=>` operator, meaning that a list of symbols cannot be sorted using the `sort` method alone.

Variable and method names

Ruby variable names are typical of identifiers and consist of lowercase letters, uppercase letters, digits, and the underscore character, with the following restrictions:

- **A local variable name must begin with either a lowercase letter or (much more rarely) an underscore.** By convention, local variables use underscores to separate words (as in `this_is_a_name`), rather than interCaps.

- **An instance variable for an object starts with an @ sign, as in** `@thingy`. By convention, instance variables are lowercase and use underscores to separate words.

- **Class variables for objects start with @@, and are otherwise identical to instance variables.**

- **Constant values must start with a capital letter.** By convention, constants that have normal object values are in all capitals with underscores to separate words. The capitalized initial letter is a marker to Ruby that the value is constant.

- **Class and module names are a special case of constant values.** Class and module names must also begin with a capital letter. By convention, class and module names are mixed case.

- **Ruby has global variables, which begin with** `$`. Normally, global variables are rarely used within a Ruby program; however, there are several standard global variables, of which perhaps the most commonly used are `$1`, `$2`, and so on, which contain regular expression matches.

Ruby method names come in two forms. The main form is similar to a local variable, starting with a lowercase letter or underscore, and conventionally having underscores separating words. Unlike a local variable, a method name may end with a question mark (`?`) or exclamation point (`!`).

By convention, a method ending with a question mark, such as `nil?`, returns a Boolean value. An exclamation point is usually used to indicate a variant of a method that changes the receiving object in place, rather than returning a changed copy, for example `sort` and `sort!`. An exclamation point is sometimes used more generally to indicate any method that makes a destructive change on the receiving object.

Method names can also end with an equals sign (=). This is interpreted to mean that the method is a setter method and is called as the left side of an assignment statement, rather than through a normal method call. So, a method defined as `def name=` would be called in a line of code as follows:

```
obj.full_name = "Scott McCloud"
```

It is possible for a method and a local variable with the same name to co-exist in the same scope. Under normal circumstances, Ruby does a fine job of resolving ambiguity. The most common confusing case is something similar to the previous example, but without an explicit receiver, as follows:

```
full_name = "Perry Mason"
```

Ruby interprets this as an assignment to a new local variable called `full_name`. However, you might want it to call the setter method `full_name=` for the current value of `self`. In this one case, you must include the `self` value explicitly to invoke the setter, as follows:

```
self.full_name = "Perry Mason"
```

Method names can also be the symbols of one of the operators that is listed in the following section as capable of being overridden. The method declaration is just the symbol for the operator, as follows:

```
def +(other)
```

Therefore, the following line

```
a + b
```

calls the + method for object `a` if it exists (if the method doesn't exist, you get an error). Many of the operators are defined at the `Object` level, and are valid for all Ruby objects.

Operators

Ruby operators include the typical set, as well as a few Ruby-specific ones. Following is the list, from highest to lowest priority. However, if you are depending on the details of the priority list in your code, you're probably writing hard-to-read code. Throw in a couple of parentheses.

Table A.1 shows the Ruby operators and their meanings in commonly used classes. All elements in the same table row have the same priority. Unless otherwise indicated, the operators can be overridden as Ruby methods using the same symbol.

TABLE A.1

Ruby Operators and Their Meanings

Operator	Definition
: :	Module and class scope resolution. This operator cannot be overridden.
[ ]	Array or hash element lookup, overridden by directories to indicate file globbing, as in dir[file"file.*"].
[ ]=	Array or hash element assignment.
**	Raising to a power. For example, 2 ** 3 = 8.
~	Bitwise complement for numbers. Pattern negation for regular expressions and strings.
!	Logical negation.
+	Unary plus. When overriding this method, use the method name +@, as in def +@.
–	Unary minus. When overriding this method, use the method name -@, as in def -@.
*	Multiplication. Overridden for arrays and strings to indicate repetition; for example, [a, b] * 3 = [a, b, a, b, a, b] "fred" * 2 = "fredfred".
/	Division. If both operands are integers, then so is the result.
%	Modulus. Overridden by strings to provide `sprintf` formatting.
+	Binary addition. For arrays and strings indicates concatenation.
–	Binary subtraction. For arrays, implements set difference.
<<	Bitwise left shift. Left shift is overridden by Array to implement `push`, by String to implement append, and by `IO` objects to indicate writing to the output.
>>	Bitwise right shift.
&	Logical and for Booleans; bitwise and for integers. For arrays, overridden to mean set intersection.
^	Exclusive logical or for Booleans; exclusive bitwise or for integers.
|	Inclusive logical or for Booleans; inclusive bitwise or for integers. For arrays indicates set union.
>	Greater than. For most objects, all the comparison methods are defined in terms of <=> by mixing in the `Comparable` module.
>=	Greater than or equal to. For most objects, all the comparison methods are defined in terms of <=> by mixing in the `Comparable` module.
<	Less than. For most objects, all the comparison methods are defined in terms of <=> by mixing in the `Comparable` module.
<=	Less than or equal to. For most objects, all the comparison methods are defined in terms of <=> by mixing in the `Comparable` module.
<=>	Comparison operator. Returns -1, 0, or 1 depending on relationship between operands.
==	Equal.

Operator	Definition
!=	Not equal. Implemented in terms of ==. May not be overridden as a method.
===	Equal for purposes of case statement.
=~	Pattern match.
!~	Not pattern match. Implemented in terms of =~; may not be overridden.
&&	Logical and. May not be overridden as a method.
||	Logical or. May not be overridden.
..	Inclusive range operator. Cannot be overridden.
...	Exclusive range operator. Cannot be overridden.
? :	Ternary operator. May not be overridden.
=	Assignment. Variant forms are /=, *=, %=, +=, -= , |=, &=, ||=, &&=, **=, >>=, <<=. None of these may be overridden as such, but the variant forms are defined in terms of their other operators.
defined?	Returns Boolean true if the symbol is defined, as in x defined?
not	Logical not. May not be overridden.
and, or	Logical operators. May not be overridden.

Method calls

The basic form of a Ruby method call is as follows:

```
receiver.method
```

This indicates that the method is called on the receiver. See the "Objects and Classes" section for a discussion of how the class structure is searched to find the method.

There are a number of optional elements in the method call. The receiver can be omitted, in which case self is assumed for the current context. As a matter of convention, self is only explicitly used as a receiver where it is necessary to avoid ambiguity.

Arguments can be passed to the method; they are placed in a comma-delimited list.

```
receiver.method(arg1, arg2)
```

The parentheses may be omitted if doing so does not introduce ambiguity. By convention, empty pairs of parentheses are always omitted.

There are a few special argument forms, the calling forms will be discussed here. The "Defining Methods" section will discuss their meaning when responding to a call with special arguments. After the explicit arguments, a series of key/value pairs can be added:

```
receiver.method(arg1, arg2, key1 => val1, key2 => val2)
```

The key/value pairs are merged into a single hash object before being passed to the receiver.

An array can also be added with the * syntax.

```
x = [3, 4]
receiver.method(arg1, arg2, *x)
```

In this case, the array is unrolled and the elements of the array are passed to the receiver as individual arguments — the receiver in this case would get four arguments. Technically, the array rollup can only appear after the key/value pairs; however, it's almost unheard of for a method to have both.

The final optional argument to the method is a block, which can be defined in three different ways. First, the block can be an instance of the class Proc, in which case the argument must be preceded with an ampersand:

```
receiver.method(arg1, arg2, &proc)
```

The second and third ways define the block outside the argument list using either of the following syntax forms:

```
receiver.method(arg1, arg2) {|block_arg| ...}
receiver.method(arg1, arg2) do |block_arg| end
```

The technical difference between the braces and the do/end syntax is that the braces have higher priority. However, that is unlikely to be an issue in typical Ruby code. By convention, the do/end form is used for multiline blocks, and the braces are used for single-line blocks.

NOTE   You will occasionally see the convention that braces are used in any case where you intend to chain the return value of the method call with the block, regardless of how many lines the block takes.

See the "Defining Methods" section for information on how these argument types are defined and used within objects.

Special keyword expressions

Much of Ruby's control flow is managed by special expressions based on keywords. This section will discuss them.

The if expression

An if expression allows for conditional evaluation. The most basic form of the expression is as follows:

```
if <boolean expression>
  <body...>
end
```

If the Boolean expression evaluates to `true`, then the body expressions are evaluated.

An `if` expression can be written on a single line, in which case the keyword `then` must separate the Boolean expression and the body.

```
if <boolean expression> then <body...> end
```

The `if` expression takes an optional `else` clause, which is evaluated if the Boolean expression evaluates to `false`.

```
if <boolean expression>
  <body...>
else
  <else body...>
end
```

If there are multiple `else` clauses, then the keyword for separating them is `elsif`. The body corresponding to the first Boolean expression to return true is executed. If none of the Boolean expressions return true, then the `else` clause is evaluated if one has been included.

```
if <boolean expression>
  <body...>
elsif <another boolean>
  <another body>
elsif <yet again>
  <yet again body>
else
  <else body>
end
```

The `if` expression as a whole returns the value of the final expression of the evaluated block. This means that an `if` expression is commonly used as a more-readable replacement for the ternary operator:

```
result = if <boolean> then <true exp> else <false exp> end
```

An `if` expression can also be used after another expression, in which case the expression is only evaluated when the `if` expression is true. In the following line of code, the expression is completely skipped if the Boolean is false.

```
<expression> if <boolean>
```

This version is commonly used as a guard clause at the top of a method, as follows:

```
return if foo.nil?
```

The unless expression

Ruby provides an `unless` expression as a shortcut for `if not`. The `unless` expression is the exact opposite of an `if`; the body is only evaluated if the Boolean expression is false.

```
unless <boolean expression>
  <body>
end
```

In normal usage, the `unless` expression is preferred to a simple `if not`. The `unless` expression allows for an optional `else` statement, but that usage is not recommended. There is no `unless` equivalent to an `elsif` clause.

The `unless` expression also has a modifier form, which evaluates its attached expression only when the Boolean is false.

```
<expression> unless <boolean>
```

The case expression

Ruby has a very flexible `case` statement. The basic form is as follows:

```
case <value expression>
when <expression1>
  <expression1 body>
when <expression2>
  <expression2 body>
end
```

The value expression is evaluated and compared to each when expression. The first when expression to be case-equal to the value expression has its body executed. No other clauses are executed. (Note the indentation style — the when clauses are at the same indent level as the `case` line.) The when clause and the body can be on the same line, but they must be separated by the keyword `then`.

The equality test for a `case` expression is unusual. The special operator `===` is used to evaluate whether two clauses are equivalent for the purposes of a `case` statement. For most objects, the `===` operator is equivalent to the `==` operator, but there are three standard classes that override `===` in an interesting way.

The Range class overrides `===` to match any number in the range, allowing you to write the following:

```
case bowling_score
when 0..100 then "Not very good"
when 101..200 then "Good"
when 200..299 then "Very Good"
when 300 then "Perfect"
end
```

The `Regexp` class overrides `===` to perform a string match, allowing you to write the following:

```
case name
when /$A[A-M]/ then "In first half of alphabet"
when /$A[N-Z]/ then "In last half of alphabet"
end
```

Somewhat less interestingly, `Module` and `Class` override the `===` operator to indicate that the value class is either equal to or a subclass of the class in the `when` clause.

As with the `if` and `unless` expressions, the value of the `case` expression is the value of the last expression evaluated in the chosen clause.

Ruby allows you to place an `else` clause at the end of the `case` expression, which is evaluated if none of the other clauses match.

```
case name
when "fred" then "Hi Fred"
when "barney" then "Hi Barney"
else "Hi"
end
```

You can also place multiple matching expressions in a single `when` clause, separated by a comma. The associated expressions are evaluated if any of the expressions in the list match the initial value:

```
when "fred", "barney" then "Hi Guy"
```

Finally, you can also have a `case` statement without an initial value in the `case` clause. In this situation, each `when` clause contains one or more complete Boolean expressions; if any of them are true, then the associated expressions are evaluated.

```
case
when obj.nil?, obj.size > 3 then "do something"
when obj.size = 5 then "do something else"
else "shrug your shoulders"
end
```

The for expression

Ruby has a basic `for` loop expression.

```
for <loop variable> in <enumerable exp>
  <body expressions>
end
```

The loop variable is any valid local variable name. The expression must evaluate to an object that responds to the method `each`, which includes an array or any Ruby `Enumerable`. The body of the loop is evaluated once for each element in the enumerable expression, with the loop variable being set to each element in turn. This is almost exactly equivalent to the `each` method with a block (except for one minor detail: local variables created inside the body of the `for` expression are available outside it, while local variables created in an `each` block are not). In normal Ruby practice, calling the `each` method is preferred.

If the elements of the enumerable expression are themselves enumerable, they can all be assigned separately in the declaration of the `for` expression:

```
for x, y in [[1, 2], [3, 4]]
  p "(#{x}, #{y})"
end
```

The entire `for` expression can be placed on a single line, in which case the list is separated from the body by the keyword `do`.

```
for x in [1, 2, 3] do p x ** 2 end
```

The while expression

Ruby's `while` expression is extremely simple.

```
while <boolean expression>
  <body>
end
```

The Boolean expression is evaluated first; if it is true, then the body is evaluated. The body continues to be evaluated until the Boolean expression is false at the end of a loop (or until the loop is exited through a loop control keyword).

The entire expression can be placed on a single line, in which case the Boolean expression and the body must be separated by the keyword `do`.

```
while obj.incomplete? do obj.task end
```

The `while` expression also has a modifier version that comes at the end of an expression. The preceding expression is evaluated repeatedly until the Boolean expression is false.

```
obj.task while obj.incomplete?
```

If the preceding expression is a block denoted by a `begin`/`end` pair, then the block is always evaluated at least once, regardless of the value of the Boolean expression:

```
begin
  obj.task1
  obj.task2
end while obj.incomplete?
```

The return value for a normally exited `while` expression is `nil`.

The until expression

Ruby offers the `until` expression, which is the exact opposite of the `while` expression, looping over the body of the loop as long as the Boolean expression is false:

```
until <boolean-expression>
  <body>
end
```

The single line and modifier versions of the `until` expression have the same syntax as the `while` versions.

Loop control keywords

Any Ruby loop can be controlled from within the loop with one of the following four keywords: `break`, `next`, `redo`, and `retry`. These keywords work within `for` loops, `while` loops, and `until` loops, as well as `Enumerable` each loops and their variants.

The keyword `break` ends the loop at the point it is evaluated. The `break` keyword may take an optional argument. Within a `for`, `while`, or `until` loop (but not in an `each` loop), the value of that argument is returned as the value of the loop, allowing you to distinguish an exit that was the result of a `break` from a normal exit.

The keyword `next` causes the next iteration of the loop to start immediately. The keyword `redo` causes the current iteration of the loop to start again from the top of the loop. The keyword `retry` starts the entire loop over, returning the Boolean or list expression to its initial value.

Assignment

There are a couple of nuances to Ruby assignment that you should know. The most basic form of assignment has a variable name on the left and an expression on the right.

```
score = 27
```

From that point, the name takes the value of the right-hand expression. Technically, it takes a reference to the object that is the result of the right-hand expression.

You can make multiple assignments in the same line:

```
score, location = 27, "Soldier Field"
```

The right side can also be an array with the same meaning — in fact, the previous form is converted internally into the following form:

```
score, location = [27, "Soldier Field"]
```

This can also include variable swapping:

```
x, y = y, x
```

If the two sides are unbalanced, extra names on the left side are set to `nil`, and extra names on the right side are ignored. The last value on the left can have an asterisk preceding it, in which case it behaves like it would in a method argument list and takes any and all extra values on the right side as an array. The last value on the right side can also be prefixed with an asterisk, in which case it behaves like a method call and unrolls its values out of the array to be assigned one by one.

If the left-hand value is an object attribute, then Ruby looks for an appropriate setter method for that object. In the following example, Ruby calls the method `score=` on the instance `obj` with the argument 27.

```
obj.score = 27
```

Similarly, a bracket reference on the left side triggers a call to the appropriate `[ ]=` method. The arguments to that method are, in order, any value that appears inside the brackets and then the value on the right side of the assignment.

File input and output

A file can be opened by calling the method `File.new`.

```
File.new(filename, mode)
```

The method returns an instance of class `File`. The mode is a short string that indicates what operations can be performed on the file. If the mode is `r`, then the file is read-only. This is the default mode value if none is specified. If the mode is `w`, then the file is opened for writing. A non-existent file is created and an existing file is emptied. Somewhat less common is `a`, which opens an existing file for writing at the end; a non-existent file is still created.

To write string data to a file, you use the method `write`, or the shortcut operator `<<`. Note that you have to explicitly include the newline characters. If the expression being written is not a string, then it is converted before being written.

```
f.write("log file\n")
f << "the next thing\n"
```

Files implement the method `each`, which enumerates over the file line-by-line. The use of `each` allows all the methods of `Enumerable` to be used for files.

To read the data, you can use the method `readline`, which returns a whole line, the method `readchar` which reads a single character, or the method `read(int)`, which reads an arbitrary number of bytes.

When you are done with the file, close it with the method `close`. The "open, then do something, then close" structure is so common that Ruby provides a shortcut.

```
File.open(filename, mode) do |f|
   ## f is the File object, do things with it
end
```

The `open` method takes a block. The requested file is opened before the block is executed and closed when the block is complete.

Exceptions

Raising an exception in Ruby is done by calling the method `raise`, which is of the class `Kernel`, and is thus available anywhere in a Ruby program. The common usage of the method takes as an argument either one of the following:

- The class `Exception` or one of its subclasses
- An instance of the class `Exception` or one of its subclasses

An optional second argument is a string message for the exception; an optional third argument is a stack trace.

Handling an exception can take place inside any method without explicitly entering an exception-aware block. The keywords `begin` and `end` also denote the borders of a block that can handle exceptions. To actually handle an exception, use the keyword `rescue` to start a block that will be invoked when an exception is raised

```
def this_method_could_break
  <normal method body>
rescue
  <exceptional code>
end
```

Note the indentation — the `rescue` clause is outdented to the same level as the `def` or `begin` statement.

The `rescue` keyword takes an optional list of `Exception` classes that are handled by the `rescue` clause. If no classes are specified, then `StandardError` is the default class, which catches nearly all errors in typical usage. Multiple `rescue` clauses may be specified, each with its own response block of code. The `rescue` keyword and the associated code may be on the same line, in which case they must be separated with the keyword `then`.

If specific exception lists are specified, then the list of exceptions can be ended with the phrase `=> varname`, in which case the variable name is assigned the value of the exception. Even if a variable is not specified, the current exception is always available in the global variable `$!`.

After all the `rescue` clauses, there are two optional clauses that may be added. The keyword `else` is used to introduce code that is invoked if no exceptions are raised in the main body of the code. The keyword `ensure` marks code that is always executed at the end of the method or block, regardless of whether or not an exception was raised.

```
def method
  <body>
rescue
```

```
    <exception>
else
    <no exception>
ensure
    <always>
end
```

Objects and Classes

Every value in Ruby is an object, including classes and methods. In this section, you will see how methods, classes, and modules are defined and how they relate to one another.

Defining methods

Methods are defined using the keyword `def`. The most basic form is as follows:

```
def <methodname>
    <body>
end
```

The limitations on the method name are described in the previous section on variable names. A method defined in this way inside a class or module definition creates an instance method for that class or module. A method defined outside a class or module definition is effectively global to the Ruby program. Technically, it's a method of the class `Object`.

The return value of a method is the value of the last expression evaluated. You can exit the method at any time by using the keyword `return` with an optional value. If no value is specified, then the return value is `nil`. Most Ruby programmers do not explicitly use `return` in places where it would be redundant. In the following example, the method explicitly returns 0 if the argument is `nil`; otherwise, it implicitly returns two times the argument.

```
def example(argument)
    return 0 if argument.nil?
    argument * 2
end
```

The first variant to the structure involves placing a constant or expression before the method name, separated by a dot. This form is most often used to create class methods:

```
class User
    def self.total_count
        <method body>
    end
end
```

With the preceding definition, you can then call the method `User.total_count`. Generically, this structure binds the method to the object preceding the method name and with that object alone — only that one object can invoke the method definition. In the previous case, within the class definition, `self` is set to the class `User`, and so the method `total_count` is uniquely associated with the class (the declaration `def User.total_count` would have the same affect). However, you can also use the form to define a method that is specific to a single instance of a class.

```
ted = User.new
robin = User.new

def ted.go_to_work
  <body>
end
```

After this definition, the method call `ted.go_to_work` is successful, while the method call `robin.go_to_work` is not.

Method arguments are normally defined in a comma-delimited list:

```
def method(arg1, arg2, arg3)
```

Any argument can have an optional default value, which can be a constant or expression. The default value is used if the calling argument list doesn't contain all the arguments. Normally, arguments with default values are placed after all the arguments that don't have default values. The following method can be called with one, two, or three arguments.

```
def method(arg1, arg2 = 7, arg3 = 2)
  p "#{arg1} #{arg2} #{arg3}"
end
method(1)         ==>  "1 7 2"
method(1, 2)      ==>  "1 2 2"
method(1, 2, 3)   ==>  "1 2 3"
```

The default value expression can use any argument name defined earlier in the list, meaning that, in the previous example, the default for `arg3` could be defined as, say, `arg2 * 3`.

The final argument can optionally be an array argument, denoted by putting an asterisk before the argument name. This argument absorbs any remaining values from the method call into an array. It's typical to give an array value the default value of an empty array:

```
def method(arg1, *arg2 = [])
method(1, 2, 3, 4)   ## arg1 = 1, arg2 = [2, 3, 4]
```

If you expect callers of the method to use the key/value feature to roll up arguments into a hash, it's customary to signal that by giving the last method the default value of an empty hash:

```
def method(arg1, arg2 = {})
method(1, :a => 3, :b => 4) ## arg1 = 1, arg2 = {:a => 3, :b => 4}
```

The final optional argument to a method is a block, which is the subject of the next section.

Blocks

A Ruby block is a sequence of executable code that can be defined in one place and executed later on. As mentioned earlier, a block can be defined after a method call using one of two possible syntaxes. In both cases, arguments to the block are placed between pipe characters. Block argument lists cannot have default values or array lists.

```
receiver.method(arg1, arg2) {|block_arg| ...}
receiver.method(arg1, arg2) do |block_arg| end
```

Within a block, you can place any arbitrary Ruby code. The block retains its context when it's called, and so any local variables that are visible from where the block is defined are still available when the block is called. This includes the values of self and super. Take the following example:

```
def outer_method
  alpha = 1
  beta = 2
  [:a, :b, :c].each {|e| p alpha * beta }
end
```

The values alpha and beta are defined outside the block, but can still be used inside the block even though the block is eventually executed inside the Array#each method.

Like other Ruby constructs, the value of the block when executed is the value of the last expression inside the block.

The block argument does not need to be specified in the argument list of the method being called. Instead, the block is just invoked using the keyword yield, which causes the block to be executed at that point. Any arguments that come after the yield are passed directly to the block.

```
def block_thingy
  block_value = yield(1, 2)
  p block_value
end
block_thingy {|a, b| a + b}

==> 3
```

In this example, the existence of the block is only important in the yield statement, which passes the values 1 and 2 to the block, which adds them.

To determine whether a block has been passed to a method, call block_given? at any point; it returns true if the current method is called with a block argument.

If the final argument of a method is preceded by an ampersand, then the method does check for a block argument in the argument call. The block is converted to an instance of the class Proc and can be invoked using the method Proc#call. The following example is functionally equivalent to the previous one.

```
def proc_thingy(&a_proc)
  proc_value = a_proc.call(1, 2)
  p proc_value
end
proc_thingy {|a, b| a + b}
```

The conversion works both ways; a `Proc` value can be passed inside an argument list with an ampersand preceding it and is treated like an ordinary block by the receiving method. In this example, the `block_thingy` method is called with an explicit `Proc` object, which it treats exactly as though a block has been declared:

```
def proc_thingy(&a_proc)
  block_thingy(&a_proc)
end
```

Internally, the method `to_proc` is called on the value after the ampersand, which leads to some interesting possibilities. For example, Rails ActiveSupport extends the class Symbol to override `to_proc`, such that the following two declarations are equivalent:

```
[1, 2, 3].map {|i| i.sqrt }
[1, 2, 3].map(&:sqrt)
```

In the first example, the normal syntax is used to declare a block. In the second example, the ampersand triggers a `to_proc` call on the symbol `:sqrt`, which converts the symbol into a one-argument block where the argument's method, named `:sqrt`, is called — identical to the first version. When used judiciously, the symbol-to-proc trick makes for some nicely readable code. This extension has been added to the core for Ruby 1.9.

Defining classes and modules

In Ruby, classes and modules are related concepts. A module has all the abilities of a class except for the ability to create instances. Instead, modules can be included inside classes to provide additional functionality.

Defining modules

A module is defined using the following syntax:

```
module <ModuleName>
  <all kinds of goodness>
    end
```

The module name is a constant, and must begin with a capital letter.

All expressions inside the module are executed when the module is loaded. Specifically, the module can include classes, other modules, instance methods defined with `def`, and module methods defined with `def self.`

Constants defined within the module, including nested modules and classes, are accessible through the `::` scope resolution operator, as in `Module::InnerModule::Class`. Module-level methods are available through normal method syntax — `Module.method`. Instance methods in the module are only accessible from an instance of a class that includes the module.

Defining classes

The class definition syntax starts similar to the module syntax:

```
class <ClassName>
   <class things>
end
```

Again, the code inside the class definition is actually executed. Constants and module-level methods are defined as in modules, instance methods are accessible to any instance of the class. In particular, many lines of code inside a class definition that look like declarations, such as attribute listings or scope descriptions, are actually method calls to either the class `Class` or `Module`.

The biggest difference between a class and a module is that a class can create instances of itself using the method `new`. Under normal circumstances, you would not override the `new` method. If you want your class to perform initialization when a `new` instance is created, override the instance method `initialize`.

```
class Animal
  def initialize(name)
    @name = name
  end
end
scooby = Animal.new("Scooby-Doo")
```

At the end of this code snippet, `scooby` is an instance of `Animal`, and its `name` attribute is set to `Scooby-Doo`. At this, point, the attribute is still private.

By default, the class is placed inside the current module at the location where the class is defined. However, you can explicitly place the class inside a specific module by including the module as part of the class name with the scope resolution operator:

```
class OuterModule::InnerModule::NewClass
```

To explicitly place the class at the top-level module, prefix the class name with just `::`.

An alternate syntax allows access to the singleton classes referred to earlier for binding methods to a specific instance. The form discussed previously,

```
def obj.method
  <method body>
end
```

is equivalent to the following:

```
class << obj
  def method
    <method body>
  end
end
```

Within the `class << obj` block, any code that is legal within a class can be placed. Methods defined within the block are bound to the specific object mentioned in the class declaration. This mechanism is frequently used with a class as the object:

```
class Animal
  class << self
    def this_is_a_class_method
      @count = @count + 1
    end
  end
end
```

The method defined in the inner class block is accessible as a class method `Animal.this_is_a_class_method`. The reason why this mechanism is sometimes used to define class methods is that, by using this method, each subclass of `Animal` gets its own copy of the instance variables, and can maintain separate values.

Superclasses and self

A class can have a special relationship with a class known as its *superclass*. The class inherits behavior from the superclass, meaning that instances of the subclass can access any methods defined in the superclass. To define this relationship, use the following form:

```
class Subclass < Superclass
```

The superclass is usually the constant name of the class in question, although it technically can be any expression that returns a class object. If no superclass is specified, the class is assumed to have `Object` as its superclass. `Object`'s superclass is `nil`.

The special variable `self` always refers to the current object whose code is being executed. Within an instance method, `self` is the receiver of that method call. Within the parts of a class definition that are outside instance methods, `self` is the class object itself.

The special method `super` is available inside any method definition and causes the same method name to be called in the superclass. If `super` is called with no arguments, then the original arguments to the subclass method are automatically passed to the superclass method. If explicit arguments are used for the `super` call, then those arguments are passed to the superclass method, allowing for the case where the superclass method may have a different argument signature than the subclass method.

Including and extending with modules

Previously, you saw that instance methods declared within a module can only be declared by an instance; however, modules cannot create instances of their own. In order for instance methods in a module to be accessible, the module needs to be mixed into a class.

The most common way to mix in a module is with the `include` method, if the following module is defined in `any_module.rb`:

```
module AnyModule

  def self.total_modulate
    p "calling the class method"
  end

  def modulate
    p "modulating"
  end
end
```

Then you can write the following in a different file:

```
require 'any_module'
class AnyClass
  include AnyModule
end

x = AnyClass.new
x.modulate
AnyModule.total_modulate     ### NOT AnyClass.total_modulate
```

By including the method, instances of the class can respond to instance methods in the module. The instance of `AnyClass` can call the `modulate` method, even though it is defined in `AnyModule`.

The `require` method takes the filename where the module is defined, minus the `.rb` extension. You only need to call `require` if the module's file has not already been loaded — if the module was loaded at startup, then `require` may not be needed.

Rails, for example, provides special functionality to look for unknown modules, such that modules on the Rails load path can be found and loaded without needing `require`.

However, while using `include` adds instance methods to the including class, it does not add class methods, and so the `total_modulate` method is still only accessible through the `AnyModule` module. In order to add a module's methods as class methods, use the `extend` method. If a module is extended into a class, then instance methods of the module become class methods of the class. Class methods of the module still do not become class methods of the class:

```
class AnyClass
  extend AnyModule
end

AnyClass.modulate
AnyModule.total_modulate     ### NOT AnyClass.total_modulate
```

Attributes

An instance variable can be declared for the current class at any time by prefixing the variable name with an @. This is usually done in the `initialize` method, but it can be done inside any method:

```
def doing_things
  @name = "fred"
end
```

The new instance variable is available wherever the object is used. Using an instance variable never raises an exception in Ruby; if the variable has not been explicitly created, its value is `nil`.

Ruby instance variables are never accessible outside the class they are a part of. In order for other classes to see the value, they must call a method that returns or changes the value. The standard getters and setters in Ruby look like this:

```
def name
  @name
end

def name=(val)
  @name = val
end
```

It's tedious to have to write all that for each instance variable, and so Ruby gives you a shortcut:

```
attr_accessor :name, :date, :score
```

The `attr_accessor` method takes one or more symbols as arguments, and creates standard getters and setters for each symbol for the instance variable of the same name. If you only want a getter, or only a setter, you can use the variants `attr_reader` and `attr_writer`.

Access control

Ruby objects have access control modifiers that can prevent outside objects from calling methods in the class. The default access is `public`, which means that any other object can call the method. The next level of strictness is `protected`, which means that the method can only be called inside the body of the class or one of its subclasses.

However, the protected method can be called on any instance of the class that happens to be available in the method body. A `private` method can only be called by implicit lookup where the method has no receiver, meaning that the private method can only be called on the `self` object in the current context.

The difference between `protected` and `private` may seem odd. Take a look at the following example of a comparison operator (assume that `outside` is a different instance of the same class):

```
def <=>(outside)
  key <=> outside.key
end
```

The comparison checks how the local value of the key attribute compares to the value of the outside object. The local value, key, is accessible no matter what the access of the key method is. If key is declared to be public, then outside.key is legal because all public access is legal. If key is protected, then outside.key is still legal, because it is being called inside the class, even though it is not the instance that is currently self.

However, if key is private, then outside.key is not legal, because a private call can only be made with an implicit self. The initial call to just key is still legal, because that call is an implicit self.

There are two ways to define access control. The most common way is to just include the method call public, protected, or private, with no arguments anywhere in the class. From that point, all methods have the newly declared access level, until the next no-argument access control method is called. If the access control method is called with arguments, then those arguments are the symbols of methods to be given the access. In the following example, protected_method is, well, protected because of its location, and thing is private because of the explicit call in the last line.

```
class Example
  def initialize
  end

  def thing
  end

  protected

  def protected_method
  end

  private :thing
end
```

Method lookup

The following is a complete list of the steps Ruby takes to find the definition of a method.

For an instance method, the receiving object is either the object explicitly designated as the recipient of the method, or implicitly, the current value of self. All method matches are on the name only, not the number or type of arguments. The search path is as follows for an instance method:

1. **The singleton class of the receiving object, if it exists.**
2. **The class of the receiving object, looking for an instance method.**
3. **Any module included in the class of the receiving object, looking for the instance method.** If more than one module is included, they are searched in order.
4. **The superclass of the receiving object, looking for an instance method.**

5. **Steps 3 and 4 are repeated for modules included in the superclass, and then the superclass of the superclass.** This continues until the lookup reaches the class `Object`.

6. **If the class `Object` doesn't have the method, the class `Kernel` is checked.**

7. **If the method doesn't exist there, then the special method `method_missing` is called, starting at the receiving object, and continuing along the same lookup mechanism until an implementation is found.** (`Object` is guaranteed to have one.) Inside `method_missing`, the program gets a last chance to do something, based on the method name and arguments rather than throwing an exception.

8. **If nothing is found, an exception is thrown.**

The lookup path for a class method is slightly different. In this case, the recipient class is the class being sent the message, as in `Employee.total_count`.

1. **The class is searched for a class method of the same name.**

2. **All superclasses are searched for a class method.** Notice that included modules are not searched in this path. An extended module technically adds its methods directly into the namespace of the extending class, and thus would be found just by walking up the regular class hierarchy.

3. **Eventually, the superclasses reach `Object`.** If `Object` does not define the class method, then the next step is to search for instance methods of the class `Class`. (Remember, classes are objects, too.)

4. **The path from there is instance methods of `Class`, instance methods of `Module`, instance methods of `Object`, and instance methods of `Kernel`, in that order.**

5. **If nothing is found, then a class version of `method_missing` is searched for, starting at the original recipient class.**

Module methods are similar to class methods, except that modules don't have superclasses, and so the search path is simply module method of the module, instance methods of `Module`, instance methods of `Object`, and instance methods of `Kernel`, then `method_missing`.

Appendix B

Ruby on Rails Guide

This appendix contains a reference for the most commonly used features and attributes of Rails. It is not exhaustive, but is intended to be a good first place to look for many frequently performed tasks. This guide is based on Rails 2.0.2. For exhaustive and up-to-the minute information, check out the official Rails documentation.

IN THIS APPENDIX

Getting started

Controllers and helpers

Views

Models

Database migrations

Plugins

Getting Started

In order to run Ruby on Rails, you need to install the following:

- **Ruby.** Version 1.8.6 is the officially recommended version for Rails 2.0.2. A binary installer is available for Windows XP and Vista. Most Linux distributions either include Ruby or have a binary package available. Mac OS X 10.5 ships with a suitable version of Ruby installed, but the version in Mac OS X 10.4.x needs to be modified slightly. See the Ruby on Rails download page (`www.rubyonrails.org/down`) for more details.

- **The RubyGems package manager.** This should be included with any binary distribution, but can also be downloaded from `http://docs.rubygems.org`.

- **Rails.** This is most easily installed through RubyGems and the command `gem install rails`. (On some systems, you may be required to run this command as `sudo`.)

- **A database.** Rails works with all of the most commonly available relational database systems. The Rails default for new programs as of version 2.0.2 is SQLite; however, MySQL is probably most common for typical deployments. You need to install the database, as

535

well as a Ruby gem that allows Ruby programs to interact with the database. As of Rails 2.0.2, commercial databases such as SQL Server and Oracle also require Rails adapters that are distributed as gems.

■ **A Web server.** Rails is distributed with WEBrick, which is slow, but enough to manage initial development. However, downloading Mongrel (`gem install mongrel`) is recommended for development.

Standard Rails application

Create your Rails application with the command, `rails <root directory>`.

The most common usage is to run the command from the parent directory of the intended root and use the name of the project as the directory, as in `rails twitter`.

The Rails command takes a few optional arguments; the most commonly used is `-d`, which specifies the database to configure Rails against. The default is `sqlite3`; other options are `mysql`, `oracle`, `postgresql`, and `sqlite2`. You can get a complete list of command line arguments with `rails --help:`.

The `rails` command creates the skeleton of a new Rails application. The top level contains a `README` file and a `Rakefile`. Table B.1 shows the directories and files created by the command, along with their standard usage:

TABLE B.1

Directories and Files Created by rails Command

Location	Description
app/controllers	All controllers go in this directory. The naming convention for the classes in this directory is of the form `UsersController` in a file named `users_controller.rb`. Initially, this file contains `application.rb`, which loads `ApplicationController`, the parent class to all controllers in the application (and yes, that does break the naming convention).
app/helpers	All helper files go in this directory. Typically, each controller has one helper in a filename of the form `users_helper.rb`, and that file loads a module named `UsersHelper`. Initially, the directory contains `application_helper.rb`, which is available to all controllers in the system.
app/models	All ActiveRecord model files go in this directory; filenames are of the form `user.rb`, loading a class called `User`. Model names tend to be singular; controller names tend to be plural. This directory starts off empty.
app/views	All view files go here, whether they are `erb`, `rjs`, or something else. Each controller gets a separate subdirectory, of the form `app/views/users`. To start, this directory contains one subdirectory, `app/views/layouts`, which contains background layout files for the application.

Location	Description
config	Contains a number of configuration files. The ones you deal with the most are database.yml (containing the database connection information), environment.rb (containing global configuration), and routes.rb (containing the rules for converting URL requests to controller calls). The subdirectory config/environments contains load requirements for individual environments. There are also a few other less frequently used configuration files in this directory.
db	Contains database files. This directory starts off empty. Eventually, this directory will contain schema.rb, with a definition of the current schema, as well as all migration files in the subdirectory db/migrate.
doc	Will contain any RDoc files you generate from this application. Initially, this directory contains a README file.
lib	Files you create that don't correspond to the subdirectories of app should go here. Initially, this directory contains lib/tasks, which is the place to put custom Rake files.
log	Contains log files, one for each environment type, plus one for the server.
public	Contains all static files. The main directory contains an index file and error files; subdirectories public/images, public/javascripts, and public/stylesheets are the expected location for static files of those various types. The JavaScript directory starts off with Prototype and script.aculo.us files.
script	Contains the basic scripts that you will use to control your application, including console (which starts an IRB session with the Rails environment loaded), generate (which triggers generation of standard files), plugin (which manages Rails plugins), and server (which starts the Web server).
test/fixtures	Fixture data for testing purposes, in YAML format. This directory has one file per model (more or less), named with the form users.yml.
test/functional	Functional test classes, in general one test class per controller, of the form users_controller_test.rb, with a class named UserControllerTest.
test/integration	Integration test classes, created explicitly by generating new tests using script/generator.
test/mocks	Mock classes that shadow actual user classes for all tests. Use only for large subsystems that you don't want to actually run during testing, for example, an external credit card payment system. More fine-grained mock objects should be defined in the individual tests.
test/unit	Unit test classes, typically one per module. Filenames are of the form user_test.rb, and class names are of the form UserTest.
tmp	Temporary files. Subdirectories are cache, pids, sessions, and sockets. Under normal circumstances, you don't need to deal with these files.
vendor/plugins	Storage for all installed plugins. Each plugin gets its own subdirectory.
vendor/rails	Not created by default, but an installation of Rails in this directory will override the system-wide gem version installed with Ruby. This allows each project on your computer to run its own version of Rails.

Generators

A generator is a special script provided by Rails that creates standard files for different kinds of Rails constructs. To invoke a generator, assuming that you are already in the root directory of your Rails application, the general form is as follows:

```
script/generate <generator name> <further arguments>
```

Rails provides the standard generators shown in Table B.2. In most cases, the name can be either camelCased or underscored, and Rails will switch between the two versions to create the appropriate file and class names.

TABLE B.2

Standard Generators

Generator	Description (first line is usage)
controller	controller <controller name> [<view1> <view2>…]
	Creates a controller package based on the given controller name. Assuming the controller name is users, the controller is placed at app/controllers/users_controller.rb. You also get a helper at app/helpers/users_helper.rb, a directory for view files, app/views/users, and a functional test class at test/functional/users_controller_test.rb. Each specified view after the controller name gets a file of the form app/views/users/view.html.erb.
	All files contain the appropriate class or module declaration — if views are specified, the controller gets an action for each view.
integration_test	integration_test <test name>
	Creates a skeleton integration test at test/integration/test_name.rb.
mailer	mailer <mailer name> [<email1> <email2>…]
	Creates a new ActionMailer structure. The mailer itself goes in app/models/mailer_name.rb. and a unit test goes at text/fixtures/mailer_name_test.rb. Each of the optional emails specified creates an entry in the mailer, a test case in the unit tests, a view in app/views/mailer_name/email_name, and a test fixture file at test/fixtures/mailer_name/email_name.yml.
migration	migration <migration_name> [<col>:<type>…]
	Creates a data migration in the file db/migrate/xxx_migration_name.rb, where xxx is the next available migration number. The optional col:type arguments are only used if the migration name is of the form add_<anything>_to_<model> or remove_<anything>_from_<model>, in which case, the attributes will be added appropriately to the migration.
	Note: in Rails 2.1 and higher the migration names are of the form db/migrate/yymmddhhss_migration_name.rb, where the name is prefixed by a timestamp instead of a single number.

538

Generator	Description (first line is usage)
model	model <model_name> [<col>:<type>…] [options]
	Creates an ActiveRecord model in app/models/model_name.rb. You also get a migration at db/migrate/xxx_add_model_names.rb, which creates the table for the model. Test files are created at test/fixtures/model_name.yml and test/unit/model_name_test.rb. Any column and type pairs that are included are incorporated into the migration and the fixture file.
	The option --skip_fixtures prevents generation of the fixture file, --skip_migration prevents generation of the migration file, and -skip_timestamps prevents timestamp attributes from being added to the fixture file.
observer	observer observer_name
	Creates a new ActiveRecord Observer at app/models/observer_name.rb and an associated test at test/unit/observer_name_test.rb.
plugin	plugin plugin_name [--with_generator]
	Creates the skeleton for a new plugin in vendor/plugins/plugin_name. This involves several files. If --with_generator is specified, then a generator skeleton is included in the plugin.
resource	resource resource_name [<col>:<type>…] [options]
	Creates a RESTful resource. This starts creating a model as though the same options had been passed to the model generator. Then a controller, helper, and functional test are created as though the controller generator were called with the plural form of resource_name. Finally, the routes.rb file is updated with a RESTful route declaration for resource_name.
scaffold	scaffold resource_name [<col>:<type>…] [options]
	Like using the resource generator; however, the generated controller is filled with skeleton implementations of the seven basic RESTful actions. The functional test contains nearly complete coverage of the generated controller, and view files are created for the edit, index, new, and show actions. A layout file is added at app/views/layouts/resource_names.html.erb, and a style sheet is added at public/stylesheets/scaffold.css.
session_migration	session_migration
	Creates the data migration necessary to store session data through ActiveRecordStore.

All generators take some standard options, as shown in Table B.3. Many of these have to do with how they behave when encountering files that already exist. The default behavior is to prompt for a decision from the user on any file that already exists.

539

TABLE B.3

Standard Generator Options

Option	Description
-c, --svn	Automatically add all new files to the subversion repository.
-f, --force	Automatically overwrite any files that already exist.
-p, --pretend	Show the list of changes, but don't make any.
-q, --quiet	Run without output.
-s, --skip	Automatically skip any file that already exists.
-t, --backtrace	Show a backtrace if the generator hits an error.

Controllers and Helpers

The controller is the first point of contact between the user request and your Rails application. (The Rails framework has already been at work behind the scenes converting the request into Ruby objects and method calls.)

Traditional routing

When the user makes a request to a Rails application, Rails converts the request to a controller and action through the rules in the `routes.rb` file. The blank project has two routes:

```
map.connect ':controller/:action/:id'
map.connect ':controller/:action/:id.:format'
```

The `map.connect` call takes two parameters: a string representing the path and a hash of options. The path segments are either strings, which much be matched literally by the incoming request, or symbols. A symbol segment takes the value in that part of the incoming path and converts it to a Ruby variable in the `params` hash. The special value `:controller` in the path is converted to the controller that should respond to the request, and the special value `:action` is converted to the action within that controller which should respond.

In the second line, a URL that has an extension (`users/show/3.xml`) will have the extension mapped to the parameter `:format`. In other words, the first line above converts a route such as `users/show/3` to the `users_controller` and the action `show`, and the `params` hash contains the pair `id => 3`.

The optional hash after the string is used to fill in any other parameters that are not set in the string. The `:controller` must be set, or alternately, a default can be set in the routing file using a rule of the form `map.root :controller => "users"`. The `:action` defaults to `'index'` if not set.

A common use of routing is to move parameters that would ordinarily be in a query string into a more elegant URL. For example, if you want to have a type parameter for users/show, you could create a route like one of these:

```
map.connect 'users/:action/:id/:type', :controller => "users"
map.connect ':controller/:action/:id/:type'
```

Both of these routes will map users/show/23/student with :type being set to student. The first route will only work for the users controller, and the second one will work for any controller. Another way to do this would be something like this:

```
map.connect 'students/:id', :controller => "users",
    :action => "show", :type => "student"
```

That route would map a URL of the form students/23 and set the controller, action, and type as specified in the options hash.

If you use a name other than connect as the method to map, a named route is created that gets its own helper methods that you can call to generate the URL.

```
map.students 'students/:id', :controller => "users",
    :action => "show", :type => "student"
```

This route could then be accessed in code with a call like students_url(:id => 23).

RESTful routing

The current trend in Rails programming is to structure controllers more consistently using the Representational State Transfer (REST) protocol. By using REST, a single line in the routes file generates several standard actions in the controller.

To add a RESTful resource to your application, add a line to your routes.rb file of the following form:

```
map.resources :users
```

This line is added automatically by Rails if you create the resource through the resource or scaffold generators.

Routes for a RESTful controller are different than standard routes. The controller action is not placed explicitly in the URL, but is inferred from the URL combined with the HTTP action of the request. You are probably familiar with GET requests being used for standard requests and POST used for form submissions. Rails with REST also uses the PUT and DELETE actions. (Where there is no direct browser support for these actions, Rails fakes it.)

For each of the seven basic REST actions, Rails creates a way to get to that action, and creates a path and URL method that calculates the route. Table B.4 shows the relationship between the URL and HTTP method, the controller action, and the Rails path and URL methods.

RESTful Action URLs and Methods

URL Called	HTTP Method	Controller Action	Path Method	URL Method
/users/1	GET	show	user_path(1)	user_url(1)
/users/1	PUT	update	user_path(1)	user_url(1)
/users/1	DELETE	destroy	user_path(1)	user_url(1)
/users	GET	index	users_path	users_url
/users	POST	create	users_path	users_path
/users/new	GET	new	new_user_path	new_user_url
/users/1/edit	GET	edit	edit_user_path(1)	edit_user_url(1)

In addition to the path and URL methods, you can also pass ActiveRecord objects to any method that expects a `url_for` style hash, such as `link_to` and `form_for`, and Rails will infer the URL from the combination of the object's class, the ID, and the HTTP method requested. So the following code,

```
link_to "User", @user
```

will generate a GET link to `users/1` (or whatever `@user.id` is), which will be the `show` action.

You can add your own actions to the resource by modifying the `resources` call in the `routes.rb`. Each of the available options adds a method for a particular kind of resource call, as described in Table B.5.

Methods for Resource Calls

Option	Description	URL Form
:collection	Adds actions that apply to a list of models in the resource, such as `index`.	users/<action>
:member	Adds actions that apply to a single saved instance of the resource, such as `show`.	users/<id>/<action>
:new	Adds actions that apply to an instance of the resource that has not yet been saved.	users/new/<action>

In each case, the value for each option is a hash of method names, with the values being the HTTP verbs to be used when calling that method. So, if you wanted to add a print action for your users, it would look like this:

```
map.resources :users, :method => {:print => :get }
```

This would generate new methods, `print_user_url` and `print_user_path`. If you are having trouble keeping track of the routes you have created, the command `rake routes` will print a list of all of them.

Controller variables

Within a controller action, there are several instance attribute methods that provide important information about the request. The most important are listed in Table B.6.

TABLE B.6

Instance Attribute Methods

Method	Description
`cookies`	Allows you to read and write browser cookies. The cookies are presented in your code as a hash where the keys are strings or symbols corresponding to specific cookies, `user = cookies[:user_id]`. The value of the cookie is always a string.
	When setting a value through the form `cookies[:user_id] = @current_user.id`, the right side of the assignment can be a string, in which case it is the value of the cookie, or a hash. In this case, the key `:value` is the value of the cookie, and other keys in the hash let you set the options `:domain` and `:path` to specify the extent of the cookie, `:expires` to set the expiration time, and `:secure`, which, if true, causes the cookie to only be sent if the request is through HTTPS.
`logger`	Always available logger object, which responds to the messages `fatal`, `error`, `info`, and `warn` (in decreasing severity). Log level is specified in the environment file for the running Rails environment (production, development, or test), and if the log message is severe enough, it is written to the log file for the running Rails environment.
`params`	Hash containing the parameters for the request, after Rails has done some processing. Items are placed into the params hash by being in the URL query string, in a form field, or converted from the URL through a symbol entry in a Rails route. Keys can be accessed either as strings or as symbols. The values are always strings.
`request`	An object representing the HTTP request (class `ActionController::AbstractRequest`). This has various useful attributes and methods, including `xhr?`, which returns true if the request has come through an Ajax request. It also allows access to the raw query string and URL data.
`session`	A session object stored by Rails and tied to the sender of the request. You can freely set and read objects to the session. Keys are typically strings or symbols. The values can be anything, but common practice is to limit them to simple Ruby types (meaning, store the ActiveRecord's ID rather than the actual ActiveRecord).
	There are several options for storing session information. The Rails 2.0 default is to store it in a cookie on the user's browser. Sessions can also be stored as ActiveRecords objects in your database.

Filters

You will often need to do the same repetitive task on multiple actions in a controller; a common example is the need to verify the current user's credentials before allowing access to a page. Typically, you would manage this by creating a common method to be called by each controller action. However, you can avoid the repetitive nature of including a common method call by using controller filters.

The most common usage of a filter takes a symbol as an argument, with the following form:

```
before_filter :authenticate_user
after_filter :log_results
around_filter :manage_resources
```

A `before_filter` specifies a method name to be run before the controller action is called, and an `after_filter` specifies a method name to be run after the controller method is complete. The most common alternate form specifies a block in place of the method name, with the same semantics. An `around_filter` specifies code that runs before and after the controller action. The method or block for an `around_filter` must contain a `yield` call in the method or block, which is where the actual controller action is invoked.

Multiple filters can be specified, in which case the filters are run in the order specified. (Both `before` and `after` have a `prepend_` version that puts that filter at the beginning of the list rather than the end.) A `before` or `around_filter` can end filter processing by explicitly rendering or redirecting the request; further filters are not processed. An `around_filter` can also end filter processing by bypassing the `yield` call to the actual action.

The scope of a filter can be managed by passing one of two optional key/value pairs to the filter call. The `:only` option takes one or more actions and means that the filter is only applied to those actions. The `:except` option takes one or more actions and means that the filter is applied to all actions except those actions.

```
before_filter :authenticate_user, :except => :index
after_filter :log_results, :only => [:create, :update]
```

Rendering and redirecting

A controller action can perform exactly one redirect or render. A redirect is managed through the method `redirect_to`. The first parameter to that method is anything that Rails can convert to a URL — it can be an ActiveRecord object converted to a RESTful action, the standard `:controller`, `:action` style hash, a string, or the special symbol `:back`, which redirects back to the referrer URL.

You can also specify a `:status` option (which must be last), if the default status code (302) is not what you want. The default response for a controller is formed by rendering the view in `app/views/<controller>/<action>.<format>.erb`. The format for most requests is `html`.

There are several ways to specify alternative behavior through the `render` method. The `render` method takes a series of key/value pairs as arguments, one of which specifies the type of rendering to be performed.

If the render contains a pair of the form `:action => "show"`, then the given action is rendered for the current controller; a `:controller` option can also be specified. The layout is assumed to be the layout matching the controller, unless otherwise specified with the key `:layout`. A value of `false` indicates no layout, and a value of `true` indicates the current layout.

Less commonly, a template render can be indicated by the keys `:template` or `:file`, both of which take a path string as a value. The `:template` version takes a path that is relative to the application root, does not include the file extension, and applies the current layout unless otherwise specified. The `:file` version takes an absolute path, with extension, and applies no layout unless otherwise specified.

A partial template can be rendered directly from the controller if the `render` command has a `:partial` key. If the key `:object` is set, then the value of that key is the main value of the partial template. The file name for a partial begins with an underscore character. In the following snippet, Rails will render the partial view at `app/views/<controller_name>/_user_ name_display.html.erb`.

```
render :partial => "user_name_display", :object => @current_user
```

If the key `:collection` is set, then the partial template is run once with its object set to each object in the collection in turn. If a `spacer_template` option is set, then that partial template is inserted between each object. The `:locals` option takes a hash value and sets values that are accessible locally inside the partial template. Unless otherwise specified, partial rendering does not include a layout.

Less commonly, small amounts of text can be rendered with the `:text` or `:inline` options. The `:text` option takes a string value (which can have double-quote interpolation), and renders it directly, without including a layout unless one is explicitly specified. The `:inline` option takes a string of ERb and renders it using the ERb parser. A `:locals` option can be used to assign values to variables referenced in the ERb string.

Other kinds of output can be specified with the `:json` or `:xml` options. The argument to those options is evaluated with the method `to_json` or `to_xml`, and the resulting text is output to the browser.

The `:update` option takes a block as an argument. Inside that block, RJS processing is used, which is described in more detail in the next section.

```
render :update do |page|
  page.visual_effect :puff, 'deleted_item'
end
```

Respond to

Rails allows you to easily adapt your RESTful controller actions to handle multiple types of output requests using the `respond_to` method. A sample usage is as follows:

```
def show
  @user = User.find(param[:id])
  respond_to do |format|
    format.html  # default
    format.xml { render :xml => @user )
  end
end
```

The `respond_to` method uses Ruby blocks and method calls in a slightly unusual way. The basic idea is that inside the `respond_to` block, the various formats that are expected outputs of the controller action are listed. Each format can have an optional block attached to it.

If the format is specified without a block, then the default behavior for that action is executed, which typically involves searching for a view matching the action name and selected format. If the format is specified with a block, then the block is executed.

In the previous example, if the controller action is called using the default URL of a GET request to `user/1`, which the RESTful route resolves as a `show` action, then the expected output format is HTML, and the `format.html` line is triggered. Although they look something like a `where` clause, technically each of those lines is a separate method call.

Because there is no block, the default HTML action is taken, which is the rendering of `app/views/show.html.erb`. If the action is called using the URL `user/1.xml`, then the XML line is the one that triggers, and the `render :xml` action is performed.

By default, there are eight formats that can be used inside a `respond_to` call, as shown in Table B.7.

You can add your own format for any MIME type. To do so, add a line of the following form to your `environment.rb` file:

```
Mime::Type.register "image/png", :png
```

The first argument is the actual mime type; the second is the symbol for how you want to refer to the type within the `respond_to` block.

TABLE B.7

Formats to Use Inside a respond_to Call

Format	Notes
atom	Used for syndication feeds in Atom format.
html	Ordinary HTML. This is the default if no extension is placed on the URL.
ics	Standard iCalendar format for calendar data.
js	JavaScript or Ajax. All Ajax calls from Rails helpers come in with this format. This can mean either that the call is a Web service or RJS call expecting JavaScript output, or that the call is from something like a `link_to_remote` and expects HTML output.
rss	Used for syndication feeds in RSS format.
text	Plain text, including, say, a CSV file.
xml	Used for generic XML output that is not a syndication feed.
yaml	Used for YAML syndication.

Helpers

Each controller has a helper module. Any method defined within that helper is available to be called from any view template of that controller (but not within the controller itself). The top-level helper `ApplicationHelper` is available in any template. If you would like to make a custom helper available inside a controller (this can be either another controller's helper, or a module of your own creation), then the method `helper` can be called inside the controller. If the helper module is within one of the Rails standard auto-load locations, then the method can be called with the module name:

```
helper OtherHelper, ThirdHelper
```

If the module is outside known Rails locations, then the method can be passed a string or symbol. The string `_helper` is appended to the name, the resulting filename is required, and the associated class name is included. The following line of code requires the file `common/common_helper.rb` and includes the module `CommonHelper`.

```
helper "common/common"
```

The special symbol `:all` causes all helper modules in the `app/helper` directory to be included.

Within a `helper` method, all instance variables defined in the template are available (although it's considered better practice not to rely on your own instance variables within a helper). The template itself is available as the instance variable `@template`.

A `helper` method can be called with a block of ERb text as an argument.

```
<% something_helpery do %>
  Text, can be plain text or with ERB markup
<% end %>
```

The `helper` method can use the normal `yield` syntax to trigger output of the ERb. This is typically used for conditional processing of the ERb text.

```
def something_helpery
  yield if is_logged_in?
end
```

The helper can also be declared with an explicit block argument.

```
def something_helpery(&block)
end
```

Within the method, the block can be run through the ERb parser and the value placed in a variable using the standard `helper` method capture.

```
output = capture(&block)
```

The text can then be placed in the template's output stream using the method concat:

```
concat(output, block.binding)
```

Views

Rails provides a couple of different mechanisms for template-bases output.

ERb

Embedded Ruby (ERb) predates Rails as the standard mechanism for merging text output with Ruby logic. Within Rails, any output file with an `.erb` extension is evaluated within Rails. The extension before the `.erb` file is intended to show what kind of file is the expected output of the template, as in `html.erb`. In addition to view files, all fixture files are also evaluated using the ERb parser, as are files used as part of a generator.

Processing in ERb is invoked by including the code inside a pair of delimiters starting with `<%`. Table B.8 gives a complete list of ERb's delimiter pairs.

In all cases, if the end delimiter is preceded with a minus sign, `-%>`, then the newline character after the closing delimiter is not included in the final output. This can be helpful if you'd like to keep a lot of spurious white space out of your HTML output.

ERb Delimiter Pairs

Delimiter Pair	Meaning
`<% %>`	Interpret the text inside the delimiters as Ruby code. This places no text in the output.
`<%= %>`	Interpret the text inside the delimiters as Ruby code and include the output of the expression in the template as a string.
`<%# %>`	Comment. Text inside this pair is ignored during processing.
`<%% %%>`	Insert a literal `<%` or `%>` in the output.

RJS

An RJS file is a Rails mechanism for generating simple JavaScript calls from your Ruby application. The RJS file can be the default response to an Ajax or JavaScript call. Also, RJS commands can be used within the block of a `render :update` call.

Inside the RJS block, a local variable called `page` is available. The `page` variable can receive several methods, which are used to generate JavaScript that is returned back to the client browser and executed there. Table B.9 describes methods available in RJS code.

Methods Available in RJS Code

Method Name	Description
`<<`	Takes a string argument, assumed to be JavaScript code, and inserts it directly into the output headed for the browser.
`alert`	Takes a string argument, and generates code for a JavaScript alert box.
`assign`	Takes two arguments, a string or symbol variable name and a value, and generates JavaScript to create a variable with that name and value.
`call`	Takes the name of a JavaScript function, assumed to be in scope in the client page, and the arguments to that function. This generates a JavaScript function call.
`delay`	Takes an amount of time in seconds and a block. This halts processing for the length of time, and then executes the block.
`draggable`	Takes a string DOM ID. This makes the browser element corresponding to that ID a `script.aculo.us` draggable element.
`drop-receiving`	Takes a string DOM ID. This makes the browser element corresponding to that ID a `script.aculo.us` drop-receiving element.
`hide`	Takes a DOM ID. This hides the browser element with that ID.

continued

TABLE B.9	*(continued)*
Method Name	**Description**
`insert_html`	Takes a DOM ID, a location argument, and text. The location argument can be `:before`, `:after`, `:top`, or `:bottom`. The text is placed in the element with that ID relative to the existing text. The `before` and `after` symbols indicate placement outside the existing tag, while the others place the new text inside the tag.
`remove`	Takes a DOM ID and removes that element from the DOM.
`replace`	Takes a DOM ID and some text and completely replaces the existing element with the new text.
`replace_html`	Takes a DOM ID and some text and replaces the text inside the element with the new text, leaving the outer tag intact.
`select`	Takes a selector with CCS-style syntax and a block. On the client side, the code executes the block for each DOM element that matches the selector.
`show`	Takes a DOM ID. This shows the browser element with that ID.
`toggle`	Takes a DOM ID. This toggles the visible status of the browser element with that ID.
`visual_effect`	Takes the name of a `script.aculo.us` visual effect, a DOM ID, and optional arguments. The visual effect is applied to the element. Any optional arguments are applied to the `script.aculo.us` effect object.

Any method that takes a DOM ID as its initial argument,

```
page.hide "user_1"
```

can also be accessed through the alternate form,

```
page["user_1"].hide
```

Models

Rails data models are instances of `ActiveRecord::Base`. By default, an ActiveRecord corresponds to an entry in a database table. The name of the table is plural, `users`, and the name of the ActiveRecord class is singular, `User`. Each column in the database is available in the record object through a standard Ruby getter and setter method of the same name, `user.name` or `user.name = "fred"`.

In addition, there is a test method for each attribute of the form `user.name?` that is equivalent to `user.name.blank?`. Every attribute also has a variant of the form `name_before_type_cast`, which access the database value as a string before Rails converts it to its Ruby type. To access an attribute directly without going through the getter or setter, use the form `user[:name]`.

> **NOTE**   ActiveRecord database attributes are not accessible as normal instance variables.

ActiveRecord provides support in Ruby for standard CRUD actions (create, read, update, and delete) as applied to database records.

Creating

Creating a new ActiveRecord object is done through the standard `new` method. Attributes of the object can be initialized by passing them as key/value pairs.

```
user.new(:name => "fred", :role => "writer")
```

ActiveRecord objects are sent to the database with the `save` method, which serializes the instance to the database, creating a new database record or updating an existing one, as needed. A record that has not yet been saved has an `id` of `nil`, and responds `true` to the `new_record?` method.

The `save` method returns `true` if the save is successful, and `false` if it is not (a variant, `save!` raises an exception on failure). The most common way for a save to fail is if it does not pass the ActiveRecord validations defined on the object, such as `validate_presence_of`. If the save is unsuccessful, then calling the `errors` method on the object shows which validations failed.

Table B.10 shows the existing validations that can be defined for your models. Each validation is a class method that is callable from your ActiveRecord. You can include as many as you want.

Most of these validations take an option called `:on`, which determines when the validation is triggered. It defaults to `:save`, but other values are `:create` and `:update`. (Save includes both create and update.) The option `:if` takes a method name or block; the validation is performed if the method or block returns `true`. Conversely, the `:unless` option takes the same arguments but only fires the validation if the method or block returns `:false`. The `:message` option specifies the error message to display if the validation fails.

The method `create` is equivalent to `new` followed by `save`, and takes the same options as `new`.

TABLE B.10	
Existing ActiveRecord Validations	
Method	**Description**
`validate`	Takes either a block or a list of method names to be called on save to perform arbitrary validation. Sibling methods `validate_on_update` and `validate_on_create` are only called in response to the associated event.
`validates_acceptance_of`	Primary argument is an attribute name, as from a form submission; the goal is to verify that the user has checked a check box or the like. By default, this assumes that the incoming value is supposed to be "1"; this can be changed with the `:accept` option.

continued

TABLE B.10 (continued)

Method	Description
validates_associated	Arguments are a list of one or more names of associations to this object. This asserts that the objects on the other end of the associations are valid.
validates_confirmation_of	Argument is an attribute name. This is designed to test the common pattern of a password or e-mail that must match a confirmation field. It validates that if there is a second attribute named <attribute>_confirmation, then the two attributes match. (If the confirmation attribute is blank, then the validation is not performed.)
validates_each	Similar to validate, but takes a list of attribute names and tests them against a block.
validates_exclusion_of	The main argument is a list of attribute names, and you also need to pass the argument :in, which takes any enumerable object. The validation verifies that the attribute is not a member of the enumerable. The options :allow_nil and :allow_blank can be set to true to allow those value sets.
validates_format_of	Takes a list of attribute names and the option :with, which is a regular expression. This validates that the attributes match the regular expression.
validates_inclusion_of	The opposite of validates_exclusion_of — this takes the same objects but validates that the value is in the enumerable.
validates_length_of validates_size_of	Two names, same method. This takes a list of attributes and one of several options, validating that the length of the attribute value matches the option. Options include :is for an exact value, :minimum and :maximum to set single boundaries, and :in to specify a range value. The :allow_nil and :allow_blank options can also be used.
validates_numericality_of	Takes a list of attributes and options. This validates that the attributes are numbers, by default Floats, but the option :only_integer can be set to true to limit the value to integers. The :allow_nil option can be used. The options :equal_to, :greater_than, :greater_than_and_equal_to, :less_than, and :less_than_and_equal_to can limit the available range, as can the options :odd and :even.
validates_presence_of	Validates that all options listed are not blank.
validates_uniqueness_of	Validates that every ActiveRecord in the database table has a unique value for the given attributes. The :allow_nil and :allow_blank options can also be used. The check is case-sensitive by default, but the :case_sensitive option can be set to false.

Reading

The workhorse method for retrieving records from the database is the `find` method, in its multi-faceted glory. The most basic form of the `find` method takes one or more integers, and returns the records in the database that have matching IDs. Multiple arguments can be presented as a list of arguments or as an array, but not as a range.

```
User.find(10)
User.find(10, 11, 12)
User.find([10, 11, 12])
```

If the first argument to find is the special symbol `:all`, then all records are returned (the `:conditions` option can be used to limit this). If the first argument is the symbol `:first`, then the first matching record is returned. In Rails 2.1 `User.all` is a shortcut for `User.find(:all)`, and `User.first` is a shortcut for `User.find(:first)`.

The `find` method takes multiple optional arguments that affect the underlying SQL query. Table B.11 contains a list of all the options that are recognized.

If those options are not enough, the method `find_by_sql` allows you to specify a raw SQL command as is.

For common cases where your search is based on the record being equal to one or more specific attributes, Rails allows you to build up dynamic method names, based on the attribute names. In other words, a `find` method of the form,

```
User.find(:all, :conditions => {:name => "fred"})
```

can also be written as

```
User.find_all_by_name("fred")
```

The dynamic method must start with `find_by` (which finds a single element), `find_all_by` (which finds all elements), or `find_or_create_by` (which finds a single element, creating it if it is not there). After that, any number of attributes can be strung together, separated by `and`, as in `find_all_by_last_name_and_home_state("Smith", "AZ")`. Each attribute has an associated argument in the argument list. After those arguments, any of the `find` optional arguments can be used.

Optional Arguments Affecting Underlying SQL Query

Option	Description
:conditions	A wrapper for the WHERE clause of the SQL statement in one of many different formats. If the value is a hash, then the condition is key = value for each entry in the hash. If the value is a list, the first element of the list is a valid SQL string with values represented by a question mark (?). Subsequent entries in the list are the values used to fill the placeholding question marks, in order. If the value is a string, it is inserted in the SQL statement as is. The string version is not recommended because it bypasses Rails security features on the clause.
:from	The table or view name to search in the database, in the event that you don't want to search the default table. (This could be used to search a specialized view in the database.)
:group	Wrapper around the SQL GROUP BY clause. If this clause is selected, then the result is a not a list, but rather a hash of ActiveRecords with the keys set to the group values.
:include	One or more of the ActiveRecord associations for this model. Those associations are automatically joined to the result set, and the subordinate ActiveRecord objects are created as part of this find call. (This uses a left outer join.) This could save a lot of database accesses in the case where you would find an ActiveRecord and then loop over all the associated objects.
:joins	An SQL string that is inserted into the find statement to provide an arbitrary join. This is used in cases where typical ActiveRecord associations are not flexible enough. Alternately, this can take a list of associations, as in :include, but performing a left inner join.
:limit	The maximum number of rows to return. This is useful for paginating.
:lock	A string of SQL specifying a non-standard lock that should be placed on the database table during the operation.
:offset	The row at which results should begin to be returned. Rows before this number are ignored. This is used with :limit for paginating.
:order	This string becomes the SQL ORDER BY clause.
:readonly	If true, then the resulting ActiveRecord objects are read-only.
:select	Becomes the SELECT clause of the SQL statement, in the case where the default (*) is not acceptable. This is often used to limit the returned columns for performance purposes.

Updating

A record can be updated directly with the class methods update and update_all. The update method takes an id and a hash of attributes, and applies the hash to the record with that ID.

```
User.update(12, {:home_state => "IL"})
```

The update_all method is a thin wrapper around an SQL UPDATE statement. The first argument is the SQL string corresponding to the values to be changed, and the second argument is the SQL string corresponding to the WHERE clause of the update.

Individual records can be updated with the method `update_attribute`, which takes two arguments, `name` and `value`. Alternately, the method `update_attributes` takes a hash and applies all the key/value pairs to the object and then saves the object.

Deleting

Deletion has a similar set of class and instance methods to update. The class methods `delete` and `destroy` take an ID and remove the associated object from the database. The `delete` method is just an SQL call, but `destroy` loads the ActiveRecord object first. They both have associated methods `delete_all` and `destroy_all`, which take a string argument to be sent to the `WHERE` clause of the SQL command.

Instances also respond to the `destroy` method to remove themselves from the database.

Relationships

Rails allows you to specify the relationships between various models in your application. These relationships assume specific foreign key or join table structures in your database. When the relationship is specified, a number of additional methods are added to your model to support working with related objects.

There are four class methods that Rails uses to specify a relationship, each of which takes several options and which generates a series of methods. These methods are `belongs_to`, `has_one`, `has_many`, and `has_and_belongs_to_many`. All of these methods take a single name, representing the other side of the relationship. Each method takes a hash of options. The options shown in Table B.12 are common to all four methods.

TABLE B.12

Options Common to All Four Class Methods

Method	Description
class_name	The name of the model class on the other side of the association, only needed if the name is not the Rails default.
conditions	A `conditions` structure, exactly as would be passed to `find`. This is used to limit the set of objects in the other class that are included in the association, for instance, to limit the associaton to only the most recently added objects.
foreign_key	Specifies the column name of the foreign key, if it is not the Rails default. This applies to the part of the model with the foreign key. If one-half of the relationship is a `belongs_to`, then both sides of the relationship need to specify the actual foreign key.
include	Lists any other associations of the related object that should be eagerly loaded when the related object is loaded.
order	An SQL string to specify the order that the associated objects are presented in.

belongs_to

The `belongs_to` relationship is one side of a one-to-one or one-to-many relationship. Specifically, it's the side of the relationship that has the foreign key in its table. The name used is the singular name of the other model. A call of the form

```
belongs_to :school
```

implies that the table in question has an integer column `school_id` and that there is another model `School` with a database table `schools`. The naming conventions can be changed through options to the method.

In addition to the common options, the `belongs_to` method takes the options shown in Table B.13.

TABLE B.13

Options for the belongs_to Method

Method	Description
counter_cache	If set to `true`, caches a count of the number of associated objects in the model; this cache is updated when associated objects are added to or deleted from the database. This assumes that there is another column in the database table named `<association>_count`. The name of a custom column for the `counter_cache` can be passed to the method instead of `true`.
polymorphic	If set to `true`, then the relationship is polymorphic, meaning that the associated object can be of more than one possible type. In this case, the name of the association does not reflect a specific class, but is instead a generic name for all associated objects, such as `taggable`. This assumes that the model has an additional string column named `<association>_type`.

A `belongs_to` relationship creates the following methods, based on the name of the association. If the declaration was `belongs_to :school`, then you get the options shown in Table B.14.

TABLE B.14

Options for belongs_to_:school Method

Method	Description
school	Getter method returns the associated object.
school=	Setter method. The assigned value must be of the correct type.
school.nil?	Returns `true` if there is no associated object.
build_school	Creates a new `School` object, and takes options equivalent to `School.new`.
create_school	Creates and saves a new School object, equivalent to `School.create`.

has_one

A has_one relationship is the half of a one-to-one relationship that does not contain the foreign key in its table. In other words, the declaration in the User class,

```
has_one :school
```

indicates that there is a School model, and that model contains a user_id column. (Compare that to the expectation of belongs_to.) The name in a has_one relationship is the singular form of the model name.

The has_one method takes all of the common options listed previously, even order. In the context of a relationship that expects only one method, the order option breaks ties, and so :order => "created_at DESC" creates a relationship with the most recently added model on the other side that associates with the given object. Table B. 15 lists the options that are specific to the has_one relationship declaration.

TABLE B.15

Options Specific to has_one

Option	Description
as	Used if the relationship is polymorphic, the :as argument takes the name of the association as specified on the belongs_to side, for example, :as => :taggable.
dependent	By default, the object with the foreign key is not changed if this object is deleted. If the dependent option is set to :delete, then the associated object is deleted when this object is deleted; if the option is set to :nullify, then the associated object has the foreign key ID column set to SQL null.

A has_one association gives its model the same set of methods as the belongs_to association.

has_many

A has_many relationship is similar to a has_one relationship, except that it assumes that there will be more than one object with the foreign key relationship. Like has_one, the declaration in the User class,

```
has_many :schools
```

indicates that there is a School model, and that model contains a user_id column. However, the methods added from has_many work as an array of School objects, not a single object. The model name in a has_many call is the plural form of the name.

In addition to the common arguments, has_many also takes the options shown in Table B.16.

TABLE B.16

Options for the has_many Method

Option	Description
as	Just like as in a has_one method call.
counter_sql	Specifies an entire custom SQL statement to use for getting the number of related objects. If finder_sql is specified, but counter_sql is not, then the counter statement is inferred from the find statement.
dependent	Exactly as the has_one option, except the valid values are :delete_all to delete all objects, :destroy to delete the objects through their own destroy method, and :nullify to change the foreign keys to SQL null.
extend	The argument is a module. Any method defined in the module is added to the association object, such that the method can be called as obj.association.method. Given the user/schools example, a sample method would be accessed as user.schools. <method>. The same functionality can be achieved by passing a block to the has_ many call; any method defined in the block is also added to the association object.
finder_sql	An entire SQL statement used to find the objects in the association.
group	Exactly as the group option for find. If specified, the association is hash-like, rather than array-like.
limit	Exactly as the limit option for find.
offset	Exactly as the offset option for find.
select	Exactly as the select option for find.
source	Used in a through association to specify a non-standard name for the association on the other side of the relationship.
source_type	Used in a through query where the other side of the relationship is polymorphic.
through	The option is an intermediate model for the relationship. The intermediate model is essentially a join table that has extra information about the relationship, but by using a has_many :through, this object can manipulate objects on the far end of the relationship through the intermediate object. So, for example, if the user/school relationship was on some kind of resume site, there might be a join table that would have to know what years the user attended the school. In this case, the relationship between user and schools would be has_many schools :through => :years_attended.
uniq	If true, then duplicate objects are not included in the relationship.

The has_many relationship creates an attribute in the ActiveRecord model that is an array-like container for the related objects. The object is Enumerable, and so all those methods work on the attribute.

In addition, the following methods are available on the ActiveRecord model itself, again using the User has_many :schools example. Because the use of has_many :through indicates an intermediate join table, some methods are not available. Table B.17 lists the methods that are available on the class that declares the association.

TABLE B.17

Methods Available for Classes that Declare Association

Method	Description
`schools`	Getter method returning the relationship object.
`schools=`	Setter method. This expects a list of records of the type of the associated object. The setter is not available in a `has_many :through` relationship.
`school_ids`	Returns a list of IDs, equivalent to `schools.map(&:id)`.
`school_ids=`	Sets the list of IDs, equivalent to `schools = School.find(id1, id2...)`. This method is not available in a `has_many :through` relationship.

The association object has some additional methods of interest, as shown in Table B.18.

TABLE B.18

Methods for the Association Object

Method	Description
`schools <<`	Adds a new element to the association (in other words, it changes its foreign key value).
`schools.build`	Creates a new member of the association, with the foreign key value set. This takes options as the `new` method would.
`schools.clear`	Removes all objects from the association by changing their foreign keys. This method is not available in a `has_many :through` relationship.
`schools.create`	Like `build`, but saves the new object to the database. This method is not available in a `has_many :through` relationship.
`schools.delete`	Removes objects from the association by deleting them from the database.
`schools.empty?`	Returns `true` if there are no associated objects.
`schools.find`	Specialized version of `find` that always includes a constraint on the foreign key. Takes all `find` options. In other words, `user.schools.find(:all)` is equal to `Schools.find(:all, :conditions => {:user_id = user.id})`, but is easier to read and more secure.
`schools.size`	Returns the number of associated objects.

has_and_belongs_to_many

A `has_and_belongs_to_many` (often abbreviated HABTM) relationship indicates a many-to-many relationship between two models. The implication of a HABTM relationship is that the other side of the relationship has a reciprocal HABTM relationship, and that there is a join table in the database linking the IDs of the tables. By default, the name of this table is the pluralized names of the two models in alphabetical order. So, the declaration in class User,

```
has_and_belongs_to_many :schools
```

implies that the School class has a HABTM relationship back to User. In the database, there will be a table named schools_users, which will have exactly two columns: school_id and user_id. If the join table has more data of its own, then the relationship should be managed with the has_many :through construct.

The has_and_belongs_to_many method takes almost the exact same set of options as has_many. It takes all options of has_many, except :as, :counter_sql, :dependent, :source, :source_type, and :through. It adds the options shown in Table B.19.

TABLE B.19

Options for the has_and_belongs_to_many Method

Option	Description
association_foreign_key	The foreign key used in the join table for the other half of the association.
delete_sql	A complete SQL statement used to customize the database call to remove elements from the join table.
insert_sql	A complete SQL statement used to customize the database call to add elements to the join table.
join_table	The name of the join table, if it does not match the expected default.

The set of methods added by a has_and_belongs_to_many call is exactly the same as that added by a has_many call.

Database Migrations

Rails allows you to modify your database schema using migrations. A migration is a subclass of the Rails class ActiveRecord::Migration, which is placed in the directory db/migrations. The name of each migration begins with a number, as in 001_create_users.rb for the migration named CreateUsers.

The number indicates a version number for the underlying database schema. Rails tracks the current version number of the running database and the rake task db:migrate brings the database in line with the most current migration. With an argument, as in db:migrate VERSION=12, the task moves the database backward or forward to the specified version. The task `db:migrate:redo` undoes the most current migration and reapplies it, and `db:migrate:reset` drops the database, then recreates it and resets the database from version 1.

A database migration defines two class methods. The method `self.up` is called when the migration is invoked to move the database version upward, as in normal usage. The method `self.down` is called when the migration is invoked to move the database version downward, as during a rollback. Typically the `down` method reverses the effect of the `up` method. If the migration is not reversible for some reason, then the `down` method should raise an `ActiveRecord::IrreversibleMigration` exception.

Within a migration, you can create, drop, or rename tables, add, remove, or change columns, and add and remove indexes. You can also execute an arbitrary SQL statement.

The syntax for creating tables is the method `create_table`. Normally this method takes a single argument: the name of the new table. It can also take an options hash of SQL fragments that are part of the SQL table declaration. The `create table` method takes a block that allows you to add columns to the table. The basic structure looks like this:

```
create_table :users do |t|
  t.integer school_id
  t.string :first_name
  t.integer :year_of_birth
end
```

Within a `create_table` block, you can use the `column` method or one of its derivatives (the derivatives are shown in the example). The `column` method takes two arguments: the first is a symbol representing the name of the new column, and the second is a symbol representing its type. Valid types are `binary`, `boolean`, `date`, `datetime`, `decimal`, `float`, `integer`, `string`, `text`, `time`, and `timestamp`.

Optional key/value pairs specify certain features of the column. The most commonly used are `:default`, which specifies a default value, and `:null` which is a Boolean that controls whether the column allows null values. Numerical types can also set `:limit`, `:precision`, and `:scale`.

There are a few methods that can be called inside `create_table` that are shortcuts to calling `column`. As shown in the previous code snippet, any type that can be a second argument to `column` can also be a method, with the name of the column as the first argument, as in `t.string :first_name`.

Any option that can be passed to `column` can also be passed to these methods. The special method `t.timestamps` creates the timestamp columns `created_at` and `updated_at`, which are automatically managed by Rails. The special method `references` (aliased as `belongs_to`) takes the name of one or more other tables and creates a foreign key `_id` column for that relationship, and so `t.references :school` would create the integer column `school_id`.

If the option `:polymorphic => true` is also passed, then a string `_type` column is also created.

If you add a column in the up method, you typically remove it in the down method, by calling `drop_table`, which simply takes the table name as an argument. You can also change a table name with `rename_table(old, new)`; again, the down method would typically reverse that.

Managing columns outside a `create_table` block starts with the `add_column` method. It is identical to the column method inside the `create_table` block, except that a table is now an additional first argument, as in `add_column :users, :last_name, :string`. The available options are identical between the two methods.

When a column is added in the up method, it is typically removed in the down method by calling `remove_column` with the table name and column name as arguments. A column can be renamed with `rename_column`; the arguments are the table name, the existing column name, and the new column name. The type of a column can be changed with `change_column`; the arguments are table name, column name, new type, and then any of the previously listed column options.

Database indexes can be added with `add_index`; the arguments are the table name, and either a single column name or an array of column names representing the set of columns to be indexed. Optional values are :name, which gives the index a non-standard name (by default, Rails creates a name, based on the columns involved) and :unique, which, if true, causes the database to validate that every row has a unique set of values for the associated columns.

Within a migration, you also have access to the entire Rails environment, including any ActiveRecord models, such as models whose database is defined or modified earlier in the same migration. (If the modification is done outside a `create_table` method, then you need to call the class method `reset_column_information` in order to work with the updated model. This makes migrations an excellent place to initialize data, move data into your database from another source, or otherwise manage data as well as schemas.

Plugins

Rails plugins are used to extend the functionality of a Rails application in many different ways, from just adding a rake task, to user authentication, to UI features, to internationalization. Plugins are typically installed using a command-line command of the form,

```
script/plugin install http://plugin.url.com
```

Under normal circumstances, the plugin URL is a Subversion or in Rails 2.1, a Git repository. Subversion installation is managed as a Subversion export, meaning the files need to be manually loaded and managed for your source control. If the repository is Subversion, augmenting this command with the -o option causes the download to be a Subversion checkout, meaning that repository information for the remote repository is included.

Using the -x command causes the plugin to be loaded as a Subversion external, meaning that a reference to the remote repository is all that is stored locally. Plugins added as externals are automatically updated when you update your Subversion working copy. Other plugins can be updated through the command `script/plugin update`. Without arguments, that command acts on all plugins. With a list of one or more plugin names, it only acts on those plugins. A plugin can be removed using `script/plugin remove <plugin_name>`. Rails handles any needed Subversion commands to remove the plugin cleanly.

If the plugin is in a known repository, the name of the plugin can be used instead of its URL location, and the known repositories are queried to find the plugin. The command `script/plugin sources` gives the current list of repositories, and `script/plugin discover` goes to a known page in the Rails Wiki server to get a more up-to-date list. Entering "script/plugin list" gives a list of all known plugins at the known repositories.

Index

F

JSON (JavaScript Object Notation)
    converting arrays, 390, 391
    data, sending to the browser, 162
    definition, 391
    objects, converting text to, 202
    Prototype library support, 391–392
`:json` option, 176
`:json` parameter, 162

K

keys
    composite primary, 111
    foreign, 111, 134–135
    functional tests, 356
    hashes, 49
    naming conventions, 111–112
    overriding primary, 111
    primary, 111
    table, 110–112
key-value pairs, hashes, 49

L

`-l` option, 24
`label` method, 190
labels, form fields, 190
languages. *See* programming languages
`last` method, 48, 50, 390
`:last` pseudo-class, 388
`lastIndexOf` method, 390
`last_login` field, 226
`last_name` field, 226
layout templates
    body content, 220
    body header, 219
    body sidebar, 219–220, 250–252
    code sample, 217–218
    contact manager, 96–98
    content insertion point, indicating, 97
    `<%=@content_for_layout%>` code, 97
    HTML head, 218
    index view template, 221
    page title, 218
    stylesheets, 97–98
layouts, ActionView, 182–185
legacy databases. *See* databases, legacy
`length` method, 39

less than, equal... (<=>)
    date comparison, 45
    time comparison, 44
`:less_than` key, 356
`lib` directory, 73, 431
libraries. *See also* Prototype library; script.aculo.us library
    Action Pack, 72
    ActiveRecord, 71–72
    architecture, 71–72
    ImageScience, 461
    Minimagick, 461
    required for plugins, 461
    RMagick, 461
    Ruby/AWS, 252, 254–255
Library Lookup Project, 330
`limit` attribute, 125
line mode, 24
links, Ajax, 394–395
`link_to` method, 193
`link_to_if` method, 189
`link_to_remote` method, 199, 306–307
`link_to_unless` method, 189
`link_to_unless_current` method, 189
Linux, Ruby on Rails, 6
literal expressions. *See* expressions, literal
`literal` method, 202
`:loaded` option, 395
`:loading` option, 395
`log` directory, 73
log files, 76, 130–131
`logger` method, 543
login, unit test, 367–368
`login` field, 226
login form, on signup page, 248
login function, 241–242
`login` method, 241–242
login partial form, 242–245
`login_count` field, 226
logout function, 242, 245–246
`logout` method, 242
loop keywords, 521
loops, 54, 519–521

M

MacDonald, Ian, 252
`mailer` generator, 538
mailer name, overriding, 490